David Williams:

The Anvil and the Hammer

Plate 1. DAVID WILLIAMS, by J. F. Rigaud, R.A.

DAVID WILLIAMS: THE ANVIL AND THE HAMMER

Whitney R. D. Jones M.A., Ph.D., B.Sc.(Econ)

THE UNIVERSITY OF ALABAMA PRESS

For sale only in the U.S.A. and Canada

Published by
The University of Alabama Press
P.O. Box 2877
Tuscaloosa, Alabama 35487

Library of Congress Cataloging-in-Publication Data

Jones, Whitney R. D. (Whitney Richard David), 1924–
David Williams: the Anvil and the Hammer.

Bibliography: p. 237
Includes index.
1. Williams, David, 1738—1816.   2. Intellectuals—
England—Biography.   I. Title.
CT 3990.W55J66 1986   320'.092'4 [B]   86-25011
ISBN 0–8173–0348–0

Printed in Great Britain at The Bath Press, Avon

In memory of my parents, E.E.J. and H.W.J.,
and of the Caerphilly in which we lived;
also of U. de la H.D., a Caerphilly Mountain boy.

Contents

Preface

I wish to express my sincere thanks to the British Academy, whose research award assisted the transition from a thesis to a book; to Professors Gwyn A. Williams, Gwynedd Pierce, Ursula Henriques, and Ieuan G. Jones for advice and encouragement at the thesis stage; and to the Reader of the University of Wales Press for useful comments.

For their generous assistance and permission to quote material in their copyright I am grateful to the librarians and trustees of the following: Archives Nationales, Paris; Bibliothèque Nationale, Paris; the Bodleian Library; British Library; Cardiff University College Library; County of South Glamorgan, Cardiff Public Library; Dr Williams's Library (whose Trustees have allowed access to manuscripts but are not responsible for the selections made, such extracts herein conferring no copyright which would debar other scholars from use of the same material); Glamorgan County Record Office; Greater London Record Office; Josiah Wedgwood and Sons, Barlaston, and Keele University Library (where the Wedgwood MSS are deposited); London University Library; National Library of Wales (and Mrs Hilarie Williams); National Museum of Wales; Public Record Office, Chancery Lane and Kew (transcripts of Crown-copyright records appear by permission of the Controller of H.M. Stationery Office); Royal Botanic Gardens Library, Kew; Royal Literary Fund; Victoria and Albert Museum; Archives Department, Westminster City Libraries.

I thank Mr John Rhys and Mr Iwan Williams of the University of Wales Press for their courteous assistance in preparing the book for the printer. All quotations are as in the source cited, both as to spelling and as to punctuation, save for occasional corrections of obvious slips of the pen or printer. My own interpolations, as distinct from those present in the source, are in square brackets.

As ever, I am greatly indebted to the encouragement and tolerance of my wife, Mona.

Abbreviations and Short-titles

B.L.	British Library
C.P.L.	Cardiff Public Library
C.R.O.	County Record Office
D.N.B.	*Dictionary of National Biography*
D.W.B.	*Dictionary of Welsh Biography down to 1940*
E.H.R.	*English Historical Review*
'Incidents'	'Incidents in my own Life which have been thought of some Importance' (Manuscript autobiography of David Williams)
N.L.W.	National Library of Wales
New C.M.H.	*New Cambridge Modern History*
P.R.O.	Public Record Office
R.H.S.	Royal Historical Society
R.L.F.	Royal Literary Fund
S.C.I.	Society for Constitutional Information
W.H.R.	*Welsh History Review*

Recurrence in the often somewhat lengthy titles of the works of David Williams of such terms as Letter(s), Liturgy, and Lectures makes any attempt at adoption of a general and uniformly consistent set of really short titles both difficult and potentially ambiguous. Recourse to abbreviated titles which exigencies of space have often entailed has therefore been upon an *ad hoc* basis which the immediate context, in text and in footnotes, should make clear.

List of Illustrations

Introduction

THE first biography of David Williams was published in 1792, almost a quarter-century before his death: arguably an indication of considerable significance in contemporary eyes. A sceptic might indeed contend that the continued absence, almost two centuries later, of any full-length treatment by a modern historian is equally indicative of some lack of import in longer term perspective.[1] Yet recurrent brief outlines, and numerous scholarly examinations of several aspects of his career and publications,[2] attest enduring recognition of his stature. The present writer is in no doubt that, judged by the criteria of his association with and positive contribution to the major currents of late-eighteenth-century British (indeed, Western European) thought – political and constitutional, religious, and educational – Williams is one of the most important Welshmen in modern history.

Considered by Mme Roland as superior to Thomas Paine in his potential *constructive* contribution to the French Revolution, and unquestionably a seminal influence in the drafting of the first albeit abortive Girondin version of a Republican Constitution; identified by the French historian, Alengry, as a neglected pioneer of the organic theory of society, anticipating much of the thought of Comte and of Herbert Spencer; a projector of a form of non-dogmatic social worship which won the commendation of Voltaire, of Rousseau, and of Frederick the Great, and which almost certainly contributed to the cult of Theophilanthrophy; proprietor of a school and author of a treatise on education which elicited admiration in Germany: all this, together with the translation of several of his works into French or German, may well suggest a prophet more honoured abroad than at home. Even within a purely British context, the achievement of the founder of what is now the Royal Literary Fund, the recognition by modern educationists of his anticipation of many of the most progressive aspects of twentieth-century teaching method and curriculum, and his detailed examination of several political and constitutional issues of enduring significance – should surely suggest a status which makes the omission of David Williams from a compendium of *Famous Welshmen*[3] barely credible.

Yet that omission is almost symbolic. An admirer of Williams might be excused the speculation that, of two mainstream currents of much of modern Welsh historiography – the 'radical nonconformist' in religion and the 'neo-Marxist' in politics, uneasy but determined bed-fellows beneath the blanket of a common commitment to political democracy and social progress – Williams has outraged the former by his explicit abandonment of even the most loosely doctrinal version of Christianity, and the latter by the political apostasy and retreat into an almost Burke-like conser-

vatism of his later years. Yet this, if true, is but part of any explanation; for in general
he has been accorded more space, and a higher estimate, in French or in trans-
Atlantic studies than in British works of history or of political thought.[4]

In truth, no clear-headed appraisal of David Williams can fail to note the flaws.
One is tempted to describe him as a 'nearly' man, in that the several impressive
aspects of his career and writings never quite cohere into a fully integrated and
successful whole. Sadly, in terms of public repute, he was sometimes his own worst
enemy. Contemporary allegations of an at best injudicious and at worst seamy edge
to some of his conduct were not disarmed by his overt contempt for much of public
opinion. The still-held view that he was not a very well-read man finds more support
in his own occasional expression of a Rousseau-like contempt for book-learning than
in any study of his writings and of the sources therein cited. Removal accounts for his
transfer from Brompton Row to Gerrard Street in 1805 include specific reference to a
large library.[5] His involvement in several volumes of translation of Voltaire, selection to write a continuation of a prestigious edition of Hume's history of England,
and successful production of a *History of Monmouthshire*, do not indicate any contemporary suspicion of lack of scholarship. Yet the variable quality of much of his
writing is undeniable and again is made the more exasperating by his explicit
assertions that he could not be bothered to revise.

Elijah Waring's unflattering characterization of Williams as 'one of those "odd
fishes"', that often turn up on the fluctuating surface of human affairs in times of
agitation, and swim with peculiar buoyancy in the surge and swell of public
opinion',[6] while a valuable pointer in any analysis of the nature and timing of many
of his published works, is unfair in any inference of shallowness of content. Yet a
contemporary assertion that David Williams might have been great, but chose to be
'singular', could have enlightened the world, but was willing only to dazzle it,[7]
sounds very near the mark. With all such reservations, his career and his work
remain of interest and of genuine significance not only as those of a colourful and
controversial personality, but also because the very range of his interests touched
most of the crucial issues of his age – issues, moreover, which are as relevant today as
when he wrote. In particular, though most of his political works were occasioned by
specific incidents or crises – ranging from those provoked by Wilkes, through the
American Revolution, the Association movement, and the Gordon Riots, to the
Regency Crisis and the French Revolution – they were all distinguished by discussion of the fundamental problems of civil and political liberty, the evolution of the
Constitution, the objectives and mechanism of the elective process (including
explicit consideration of such issues as the mandate and annual re-selection of
representatives), and the delicate balance between individual liberties and collective rights within existing social parameters.

His life was marked by paradox and by contrast – perhaps none greater than that
between the mountain hamlet near the small town of Caerphilly in which he grew
up and the Soho/Chelsea/Bloomsbury milieu in which he was to spend his time
from the age of thirty until his death. For he became and remained a London
Welshman. Again, amidst the ample printed and documentary bases for a study one
finds infuriating and sometimes crucial gaps in the evidence. The number of anony-

mous and pseudonymous articles devoted to Williams is appropriately symbolic, for many of his own publications were of this type, and it is unlikely that a completely definitive list of the books, pamphlets and articles which came from his pen can ever be produced[8] – indeed, one 'pirate' edition long considered lost has come to light in researches for the present work.[9] Surviving personal papers attest a magpie-like tendency to preserve not only fairly substantial manuscripts but also the veriest scraps of notes, alongside bills, accounts, and letters. It is thus supremely ironical that although the great bulk of those which he bequeathed are well-preserved, it is quite certain that a not inconsiderable number which were extant at the turn of the nineteenth century have now disappeared without trace.[10]

Yet the sheer quantity of extant material fully vindicates an allusion to Williams's prolific pen. The problems confronting the biographer are, in general, those of arrangement and interpretation. In this respect, the perennial problem of choice between a chronological and an analytical treatment is, fortunately, in part resolved by the kernel of truth contained in Waring's comment. For the difficulty in assigning Williams to a particular school of general or political philosophy, and the apparent shifts in his position against the background of changing circumstances, may both be considered in the light of an apposite phrase of J. M. Robertson. The career of David Williams, while certainly not devoid of the influence of personal ambitions and idiosyncrasies, may fruitfully be considered as a study in 'experiential rationalism',[11] and the evolution of his ideas as the development and testing of an enduring set of principles within the context of changing political, religious, national, and personal circumstances. The diversity of his interests, his determination, at times almost perverse, to resist association with any party or faction, the paradox of the thinker who cast himself as 'the Philosopher' and yet eschewed metaphysics as a journey into the irrational – in face of all this it is tempting to brand him a maverick. Yet it is fairer, and much more meaningful, to examine his career and his thought as epitomising the problems of a society in transition, as exemplifying the reality that relevant political and social philosophy does not evolve within a vacuum, and in particular as illustrating a complex pattern of interrelationship between a 'Commonwealth' tradition which goes back to Tudor times and the emergent threads of a utilitarian and of an idealist/collectivist approach to society.

Chapter One will essay an essentially biographical treatment of the background, family, and education of David Williams, leading to his early years as nonconformist minister and his first publications after the move to London. The next two chapters will consider, respectively, those religious innovations which evoked the soubriquet 'Orpheus, Priest of Nature', and his very real importance within the field of educational experiment. Just as these aspects of his career must be closely related to the development of his personal circumstances (at one point involving emotional crisis), so what may perhaps be designated as the first phase in the evolution and expression of his political philosophy must be set within the context of the Commonwealth or Real Whig, radical, and American dimensions in British political life in Chapter Four. The lengthy gap in his literary output after *Letters on Political Liberty*, 1782, was followed by such a spate of publications, educational and religious as well as political, during the years 1788 to 1791 as to suggest the title of 'high-water mark' for Chapter Five. Thereafter, we shall consider the significance, and irony, of his sole adventure in active political participation, as citizen of France, during a critical phase of the French Revolution. It is all too tempting, if one approaches David Williams with an *idée fixe* or makes a judgement by the values of a later age, to view the remainder of his career as one long anti-climax or, worse, as a process of erosion of principles in face of circumstance and self-interest. But this would be to over-simplify unjustly: Chapter Seven will trace, alongside the readjustment of his political conclusions, the widening of the social and economic aspects of his thought, as well as outlining the strange interlude of his return to France as an agent of the British ministry after the Treaty of Amiens. Chapter Eight, 'The Claims of Litera-ture', will examine his other writings during this last phase before tracing the accomplishment of a project first mooted during his early days in London: the Literary Fund. Finally, a concluding chapter will attempt to evaluate the achieve-ment and significance of a long and complex career.

Chapter One

A Philosopher's Apprenticeship

DAVID WILLIAMS'S own complaint, in his manuscript autobiography, that his birth, 'as if it could be of any importance, has been variously misrepresented',[1] was probably a reference to social origins, but a persistent error in later accounts was to locate his birth-place near Cardigan. Indeed, almost a century after his death, when Sir Marchant Williams unveiled a commemorative obelisk in the park at Caerphilly, he sought to enliven a rain-soaked crowd with the jocular remark that 'the people of Cardiganshire would grab any distinguished person'.[2] He was in fact born at Waunwaelod, on Caerphilly Mountain, some half-a-dozen miles north of Cardiff.[3] The Eglwysilan Parish Registers record his baptism on 9 December, 1738. His father, who came from near Cowbridge, was William David – persistence of the Welsh patronymic custom causing some indecision about the later family surname.[4]

Williams describes his father as having 'speculated all the Money & Credit he could command or obtain, in Mines of Iron Ore & Coals, in what the Americans call a Store or Shop for the supply of the Miners & even in Smith-Forges for their Tools'.[5] The mountain slopes near Waunwaelod and Craig-y-Allt were dotted with colliery 'levels', equipment for which was supplied by men whose names will recur in the records of David Williams and his family.[6] But the business ventures of his father failed, in circumstances which left the bitter recollection of the son that he had preserved the evidence of his educational expenses not only as a tribute to an excellent mother but in the abortive hope 'that one of my Father's Partners would lay open his books, & contribute something ...' Indeed, his autobiography explains how his promise at the age of fourteen that he would go to the Dissenting Academy at Carmarthen and become a Minister had been made to his father on his death-bed in ignorance of his 'Connections Partnerships or Circumstances which have been dishonorably concealed to this time'.[7]

The family was dogged by ill-health as well as financial misfortune, three brothers of David 'just entering into Life died of a Consumption the Malady of the Family'. Little wonder that his father turned to the consolations of religion, perhaps as a result of a visit to Watford (near Caerphilly) of the Methodist Howel Harris; hence, reputedly, the exaction of the pledge alluded to as he lay dying in May 1752. Certainly, David Williams himself is quite explicit as to the binding force of that promise – despite his declaration that a division of his time between the schools, respectively, of the parish clergyman and of a local dissenting minister, had turned him against the latter's calling.[8] 'But his Injunction & the State of his Circumstances left me no choice – For after remaining nearly two years, in the melancholy

Plate 2. The David Williams Memorial

contemplation of those Circumstances, at sixteen I took from my widowed Mother & two sisters, nearly their last shilling, to settle the Accompts of my Grammar School & the expences of being conveyed by its Master to the Dissenting Academy.'[9]

That Master was his namesake, the Rev. David Williams of Pwll-y-pant, himself a product of Carmarthen Academy, who had built Watford Independent Chapel in 1739 and taken up residence nearby at a large house in the Cwm, where he established a school.[10] Much less is known about the other school, directed by the Rev. Lewis Rogers, and emphasis has rightly been placed on the influence of Williams's namesake. The part played by Watford in the early days of Welsh Methodism has often been told. But relations between its leaders and the minister turned sour. One can still feel the Calvinistic outrage when the latter 'began to preach a most unevangelical doctrine, called Arminian, but in reality Arian' – arguably a prime cause of the secession and establishment of a specifically Calvinistic Methodist congregation at nearby Groeswen.[11] Indeed another pupil of the Cwm, Thomas Morgan (Henllan), who was also a student at Carmarthen, was at pains to attribute to the grounding received in childhood and youth the 'peculiar Doctrines of the Gospel' which impelled him to offer a free salvation to all sinners, being quite unable to believe that 'God made men *purposely to damn 'em* for ever'.[12] Such confirmation of the Pelagian drift of tuition at the Cwm may help to explain why the allegation that three of his sons 'went to the bad' was uncharitably seen by the minister's critics as a judgement on his doctrinal shortcomings.[13] Knowledge of this background may in turn have contributed to sharpen the edge of the pen which David Williams the younger was later to wield in attacking the Methodists.[14]

Meanwhile the heterodox theology of the institution to which he now proceeded was becoming notorious. The 'Great Arminian Controversy' which had commenced a couple of decades earlier had given way to Arianism and Unitarianism. Indeed, despite the undoubted scholarship of the instruction given, the heterodoxy of some Carmarthen tutors was to lead the Board of the Congregational Fund to discontinue its grant.[15] Predictably, a mere handful of the student output in the 1760s and 1770s were to become pastors of orthodox churches in Wales; the great majority abandoned the vocation or settled with Arian congregations in England, as did David Williams himself.[16] His acceptance at Carmarthen as a student is recorded in a Minute of the Presbyterian Fund for 3 December 1753, which grants him an allowance of £6 a year, to commence at Christmas. Fairly regular reports through the next four years from his tutor, Mr Evan Davies, attest his satisfactory behaviour and progress – reports which were no mere formality, for the dismissal of several of the relatively small number (ranging from eight to eleven) of his fellow-students is recorded. (Those fellow-students included one Benjamin Thomas, of Coety, later minister at Malmesbury, who was to cross swords with Williams on a wider stage.)[17] The only discordant note in the record is sounded in the Minute for 4 April 1757, which reports that 'as David Williams of Glamorgansh. has not returned to Carmarthen since Xmas last, it is agreed, that the Continuance of his Allowance be left to further Consideration'. No explanation for this absence is proffered – was it illness, family circumstances, or a reluctance to return for the completion of his training for a perhaps unwelcome vocation? At all events, a final report on 2 January

1758 records his departure from Carmarthen following a satisfactory termination of his four-year course of studies.[18] Some of the potential implications of that course and of the reading involved will concern us later. Meanwhile, his own rather brief retrospective allusions to his education include the coldly austere, even oppressive, impression of religion conveyed by a severely puritanical master. As for Carmarthen, at which he claims recognition of his considerable linguistic talent, he has scant praise for the absurdities of a purportedly liberal education, with its useless rote-learning of classical authors and comparative neglect of natural history and the physical sciences. Oddly enough, one finds no discussion of any possible influence of that academy upon the later most unorthodox course of his own religious philosophy.[19]

On leaving Carmarthen Williams found himself settled at Frome, in Somerset, at the age of twenty, with an annual salary of £45 and a mother and two sisters back in Caerphilly 'in great Embarrassment & Distress'. His sisters both married: one with Edward Hedges, whose descendants still live in Caerphilly, while the other, after the death of her first husband, became the bride of the Rev. Walter Thomas; but we shall see that both branches of the family required financial help.[20] It is hardly surprising that his contemporary biographer, Thomas Morris, relates how 'with filial reverence, he renounced his little patrimony in favour of a widowed parent, whose situation required that sacrifice'.[21] Oral tradition in his birthplace long attested the sacrifice, including physical labour in a small coal level, which that parent had made to pay for his education.[22] Williams himself declares, alluding to the poverty of the family, that 'it was that distress, which induced me to move to Exeter – for I was happy at Frome – & it was that Distress, which kept me from seeking an advantageous Marriage; though I spent nineteen parts in twenty of my time among Women'.[23]

A favourable account of his first ministry describes him as becoming a popular preacher, whose repute for zeal and piety was such that in two years he was invited to move to Exeter. But references in the same source to his being unsettled as to religious beliefs and to the perhaps more damaging insinuation of inability to subdue his passions raise complicating issues about the decade which he was to spend in the West Country.[24] He himself states plainly that spending so much time in female company 'seduced me into the Paths of Pleasure; which the Eye of Censure soon observed, & which soon led me, it does not signify how, out of the narrow Inclosures of my Profession'. He gives no detail, though at this point a whole line of manuscript is not only deleted but (uncharacteristically) rendered quite illegible.[25] But Benjamin Thomas, in a thinly disguised portrayal of romantic progress from Frome to Exeter and London, depicts a Buck pursued and caught by a member of his flock, '*one daughter of godliness*, and a fine piece of flesh and blood she was' – but alas, our hero paid superior attention to another lady, at which the first met another brother meditating in a lonely walk and found consolation. At this 'our buck was roused once more, and off he went at a tremendous rate . . . And London opens on his eyes! his ears! Here he found a safe harbour, and he herds now among buck of the first horn, enjoying a goodly pasture . . .'[26] Even the much more favourable notice in the *Cambrian Register* relates how, at Exeter, 'the eminent abilities and engaging manners of the young preacher opened to him the seductive path of pleasure, when the reproofs of some elder members of the society thought necessary, being administered in a manner to awaken resentment, rather than contrition; and the eagle eye of anger discovering in his accusers imperfections of a different character indeed, but of tendency little suited to public disclosure', the impending recrimination was avoided by departure to Highgate in London.[27]

Confirmation of a taste for female company and of behaviour which, in the context of his calling, was at best imprudent, surfaced in a group of anonymous letters to a newspaper or periodical at the time of the Margaret Street venture, of unusual provenance yet clearly based on personal knowledge and ringing true. Williams is reminded, by their female author, 'that there are many now in Town who were acquaintances of your very youthful Days, when you had not so much Philosophy as now to regulate certain warm and lively Passions, and when the Female Sex were to you instead of Religion and Philosophy, and determined every Event of your Life'. Though his present pretensions ill befit one who has spent the whole of his early life in pleasure, the writer casts no aspersions on Williams's morality (though many on his prudence) and concedes him to be ill-used by gossip by which 'Mole-Hills were swoln into Mountains'.[28] Sadly, two further (and independent) pieces of written comment ascribe the move from Exeter first, to the interception of a letter of Williams relating a 'jolly Scheme' which shocked its unintended readers,[29] and second, to mean and unworthy conduct which included 'writing anonymous letters to the disparagment of others, prevarication &c'.[30]

Alongside charges of romantic dalliance and imprudent conduct we find evidence of liturgical experiment. The record suggests a somewhat incongruent combination of a dislike for dissenting primness and precision (despite which his ministry was apparently successful)[31], of a taste for formality in ritual and in clerical dress, and of progression towards a Socinian theology. The move to Mint Lane, Exeter, entailed further formalities of ordination, for the congregation was Arian – the city having nurtured such tenets since the early eighteenth century.[32] But Benjamin Thomas describes a liaison with one of the congregation who persuaded him to wear a gown, then a sash, and to issue prayerbooks, as causing a need to reconcile Williams to his flock – a portrayal perhaps echoed in Sappho's allusion to 'a remarkably ecclesiastical dress'.[33] Wendeborn reports his acquaintance's own recollection that 'he was expected to be an Arian as well, but that did not suit him. Socinus' doctrine pleased him better and he soon brought his parish to the point that they became of his opinion and gladly allowed the introduction of a Socinian liturgy.'[34] This, closely modelled on that in use at the Octagon Chapel, Liverpool since 1763,[35] was indeed popular with his congregation; his successor allowed it to lapse, but in 1792 it was reintroduced at the members' request.[36] Whatever the relative weight of personal friction, doctrinal divergences, and romantic adventures, of personal ambition on the part of Williams and of a resolve to be rid of him on the part of some influential members of his flock, his record overall secured a cordial reception from his new charges.[37]

As to his own motivations, Wendeborn states bluntly that 'several love and marriage scandals' had brought Williams to the point where he was ready to abandon a Dissenting pastoral vocation (some acquaintances anticipating a 'transfer to the Episcopal Church to try his luck there'!) – a comment which reinforces Morris's cryptic assertion that he was finally induced to quit a vocation he had always disliked by the intrigues of a lady. Both concur that it was largely ambition which brought him to London and that it was solely the need to make a living which obliged him to take charge of a congregation.[38] But for as long as he remained at Highgate there would seem to be little doubt, once more, as to the success of his ministry. Indeed, a correspondent of *The Gentleman's Magazine*, while alluding to Williams as since dignified with the title 'High-priest of Nature' and as a long-term and avowed champion of Infidelity, is at pains to observe that during his years at Highgate the meeting was admirably well attended and even patronized on occasion by members of the Established Church.[39] David Williams himself claims to have been a stranger to religious and moral controversies when he resigned the ministry, 'without the slightest misunderstanding with my Congregation, which had considerably increased under my direction, & from which I had ever received, every possible testimony of respect'.[40] The circumstances of his resignation and of his religious publications therewith associated will concern us in Chapter Two. Meanwhile, before considering his first two books which appeared while he was still at Highgate, it may be pertinent to look briefly at the milieu within which he was to spend the rest of his life.

David Williams began and ended his residence in London in the most famous of its cosmopolitan quarters, Soho. The visitor today to the streets in which he lived – Frith Street, Meard Street, and Gerrard Street – cannot but be conscious of the uneasy and incongruous juxtaposition of tangible relics of the past with some of the seamier realities of the present. Williams himself left documentary evidence that he was no prude, with his fair share of the weaknesses and failings of humanity,[41] but one wonders what he would have made of some all-too-obtrusive aspects of modern Soho. Yet Soho Square itself remains a part of old London. Many of the buildings in the vicinity are still of eighteenth-century grey/red brick and, especially where cleaned, present something like their original appearance. Indeed, an authoritative survey describes the almost complete and little altered south side of Meard Street (including No. 7) as the best group of early Georgian houses surviving in the parish of St Anne.[42] Residents of Soho during these decades whose paths crossed that of Williams included the portrait painter, Rigaud, in Frith Street (where Romilly had been born), Thomas Bentley in Greek Street, and Edmund Burke in what was ultimately to be the home of the Literary Fund and of Williams himself in Gerrard Street.[43] French visitors who took up temporary domicile included Rousseau, Mirabeau, and Chateaubriand.[44] St Anne's Church, Dean Street, in which David Williams was buried, suffered a direct hit by bombing in 1941; the tower remains and restoration is taking place, while 'the Philosopher' would surely take comfort from a recent incumbent's attestation that the immediate incidence of violent crime is comparatively rare and from the evidence of healthy grass-roots community civic consciousness.[45]

The intellectual and social world which soon became much more attractive to Williams than the normal environment of a dissenting clergyman is contemporan-

Plate 3. SOHO SQUARE, *c.* 1755

eously described in Wraxall's depiction of 'a very numerous, powerful, compact Phalanx', the 'Gens de Lettres' or 'Blue Stocking Assemblies' which flourished during the era 1770–1785, their decline thereafter dating from the death of their giant with whom David Williams was to claim some acquaintance, Dr Johnson. The latter's coterie included one whose name will recur in the works of Williams, the young and beautiful Duchess of Devonshire.[46] This was the fashionable, literary, theatre-going world which increasingly demanded more time than the pastoral duties of Highgate. Williams confesses that he 'became as far as my scanty means, & the necessary decorum of my appearance would allow ... devoted to pleasure', cultivating a taste for literature and science far beyond his education. Significantly, he still 'delighted in occasionally producing compositions that pleased or affected' his hearers.[47] But his desire to be seen as a member of the literary set is made embarrassingly clear in the context of what can only be termed a pseudo-anonymous letter in which he describes himself (in the third-person) as 'intimate at Captain Pye's. Goldsmith knows him,[48] and I have seen him go into Johnson's, but perhaps it was for musick. Rice, the Instructor of English, was with him last night in the front Box of Drury lane; and they seemed very intimate.'[49]

This evident determination to thrust himself into the social scene, and his undoubted development of a keen interest in the theatre, form the context of the notorious quarrel with Garrick. Briefly, the minister's theatre-going had led to some acquaintance with the actor Mossop and to knowledge of his alleged grievances. The *Letter to David Garrick*, as published in 1772, is an odd amalgam of personal attack, on behalf of the supposedly injured Mossop; of barbed and effective, if overstated, criticism of Garrick's theatrical performances and influence; and of a strain of self-publicization. This last element is impossible to discount, especially in the light of the communication already alluded to, addressed to Garrick, on 2 October 1772: 'Sir, the following letter will convince you of my friendship. I am so circumstanced that I cannot appear, though it is in this case to do good. Among the many attacks which have been made lately on your character, none has so great effects as a Letter to you printed for Bladon. It is elegantly wrote; and the criticisms are plausible where they are not just. It is well spoken of by most people who read it; and to do you irreperable mischief, it only wants to be generally known. I believe it is wrote by a young man, who is making himself known as a first-rate Genius. My suspicion is grounded on the great Intimacy between such a person and Mossop ... I am more and more convinced that he is the author; and that he intends to pursue his blow.' There follows the name-dropping related above, and then the assertion that 'you may think I have some interest in this matter besides serving you. If I have, it is from a regard to the young man. He might be better employed, and his humanity better directed. I am persuaded he acts from the best principles and I have great obligations to him.' Then comes this audacious threat: 'If you show this letter, you will repent of it. If you act according to it, you will do wisely; and prevent a great deal of mischief to yourself, as well as vexation to your Well-wisher and admirer.'[50]

What is one to make of this? First, despite an admirer's assertion that Williams, as a man of honour, could not possible have written this letter,[51] he certainly did. Nor was this the first occasion on which he was suspect of such activity. In a letter dated 2

October 1769 a Rev. Mr Powell had endeavoured to exculpate him from the charge of writing anonymous letters, and we have already noted one other such allegation.[52] On this occasion Garrick himself was certain as to authorship. Of this there is the clearest evidence in a batch of letters preserved among his correspondence, entitled 'Curious letters written against me by one *Williams* a Presbyterian Parson a Great friend of Mossop's and a Great –––––'.[53] These include another letter in the same hand, forwarded, also on 2 October 1772, by the editor of a weekly paper, the *Westminster Journal* – an action which lends credence to the allegation that Garrick was sometimes not above using his ownership of shares to suppress any newspaper criticism.[54] This letter by 'Menander' takes up the cudgels for Mossop against the '*Great Roscius*', who cannot tolerate a rival, who speaks through his nose, has lost the power of enunciating many words, and who in any youthful character resembles 'an old doating shrivelled Bear'.[55]

A draft reply, endorsed 'A letter intended to be sent to one Williams, a dissenting parson upon his abuse of me', demonstrates both Garrick's very real concern and his aptitude for appropriate counter-attack. Williams is appealed to as a public writer and private teacher of ethics for his advice: 'there is a person of no small abilities has been lately discover'd, beyond a doubt discover'd, (for many proofs are in my hands,) to have been writing the most false, wicked & scandalous papers & pamphlets against a person with whom he has not the least acquaintance.' After a scathing denunciation of the author of this mixture of cajolery and threats comes the fittingly theatrical challenge: 'whether you think it would [be] best to publish the whole matter, with the Evidence to expose the monster', or to meet him 'and like a true Christian and a Philosopher forgive him ... The writer of this letter will see you whenever you please.'[56] The immediate sequel can only be surmised. Fitzgerald's biography describes Garrick as genuinely frightened and states that the letter was never sent.[57] For whatever reason, Williams did not carry out his threat (in his letter) that he would '*revise* you in the Winter'; indeed, one obituary notice states that the *Letter to David Garrick* was withdrawn, while the *Monthly Review* for July 1778 refers to its author's having 'candidly suppressed the first impression'.[58]

Meanwhile the sting in Garrick's use of the term 'Philosopher' in his proposed rejoinder is made clearer by another item in his clutch of Williams's correspondence. A letter addressed to the bookseller Becket in Pall Mall, dated from Frith Street on 25 September 1772, concerns the sales of *The Philosopher*. This further exemplification of Williams as a combative letter-writer (presumably, why Garrick acquired it) suggests that, despite favourable reviews, the sale of his first published work had proved rather disappointing. For this he blames the bookseller: 'Several persons have complained to me, that when they call at your house for the Philosopher, they are obliged to wait a great while to get one, & that it is always produced from some dark hole in the Ware-room', instead of being kept to hand and displayed in the window. 'You have some reason for this behaviour. I care not a farthing what it may be. I am not anxious about the advantages of a small publication; but no man shall impose upon me with impunity. I should wish to settle with you; to have half of the Copies which you have on hand; that I may throw them into the River or do what I please with them.'[59]

To revert to the centre-piece of what became a notorious squabble, the *Letter to David Garrick*, despite the justice of Boaden's contention that it concedes the splendid talents of its target,[60] contains barbs which must have sunk deep. Williams does indeed pay tribute to Garrick's career and his contribution to the theatre. But he goes on to allege that the actor-manager has, in public and in private, employed every device not only to stifle criticism but also to depreciate the merits and magnify the faults of his stage contemporaries in order to 'guard right well the fag-end of your reputation'. Yet despite Garrick's attempt to monopolize the reputation and the wealth of the stage, notably by the exclusion of any competing genius – with Mossop outstanding among those who have suffered from his ill-will – the ravages of time cannot be disguised. As Shylock he might yet gain immortal praise, 'but, for God's sake let love, and tenderness, and softness alone ... Your mouth has no sweetness; your voice is growing hoarse and hollow; your dimples are furrows; a coarse and disgustful dew-lap hangs from your chin.'[61] Among contemporary reviewers of this mixture of valid criticism and personal abuse, one conjectured that it was the work of some discarded player or disappointed author.[62]

The alleged suppression of the work, followed by a conciliatory exchange of letters on Mossop's death, did not quite mark the end of the story. For in 1778 appeared a second, 'pirate' edition. Williams's protestation, accepted by the *Monthly Review*,[63] that this was not of his doing can now be confirmed from the tone of the Preface of this second, quarto edition itself – a copy of which (for long presumed lost) was discovered, unbound but apparently complete, in the 'Garrick-Williams' material in the Forster Collection. For its editor[64] explains how the author's 'Evil Genius ... in the Form of a *Little Manager*,[65] blasted his Laurels; by tempting him, like the cruel Parent of a Natural Child, to smother his Offspring in the Birth; But Fate had otherwise decreed; the Bantling escaped' and is now made public.[66] Yet by now it was indeed a stale and unseasonable dish;[67] for Mossop's death had provided the occasion for explanation and reconciliation. In a letter dated from Chelsea on 7 January 1775 Williams explained to Garrick that 'the most unfortunate event that could have befallen me, the loss of an affectionate & excellent wife, has been the occasion of your not hearing from me immediately on Mr. Mossop's death.' Mossop's death-bed conversation, which made a dreadful impression on Williams, had included the confession of his false imputation to Garrick of unworthy motives and permission publicly or privately to use this admission at his discretion.[68] This *amende honorable* – reflecting as much credit on Williams, especially in the context of his personal tragedy, as his earlier brashness suggests reservations – evoked an immediate and equally conciliatory reply.[69] Certainly the whole affair lingered in the public mind. In 1781 the anonymous author of *Orpheus*, depicting the visitors to the Margaret Street Chapel, makes Garrick start with fright on seeing Williams:

> 'Not Shakespeare's feign'd but *Nature's* real fear
> He felt, and fled swift as a stricken Deer.'[70]

The real depth of the reconciliation may well be pondered.

There remains one other odd testimony to the at-first-sight incongruous interest of Williams in the theatre. A letter to Garrick from the Rev. H. Bate, dated 16 July

1778, includes the following: 'By the by, who do you think is prime minister to the Haymarket manager at this juncture? the atheistical parson Williams, who is shrewdly suspected of having belaboured Sheridan, &c. so unmercifully last year. Let little George alone for "making friends of the mammon of unrighteousness" in time of danger! And, to complete the rural scene, he is going to bring out a bawdy and blasphemous Welsh farce for him, which, it is conjectured, will entail d–––n on the irreligious priest and infidel manager at one stroke!'[71] One can only concur with a more recent verdict that this story is not as improbable as its earlier rejection by indignant defenders of Williams would imply.[72] A notebook which is undoubtedly in his hand includes a number of very *risqué* anecdotes. One of these, despite its earthiness, may fairly be excused as a supremely apposite illustration of contemporary politics; but the others are perhaps charitably described as after-dinner stories – and a long time after![73] One of them occurs again, in French and English versions, in another manuscript;[74] the real problem, surely, is why on earth Williams chose to record them? One can understand why, whatever its justice or injustice, the slur of injudicious or even near-licentious behaviour recurs in hostile contemporary comment.[75] Yet its equally frequent rebuttal must be given at least equal weight, and there can be little doubt as to the general esteem in which he was held.

Certainly his first major publication, on political and religious issues, *The Philosopher: in Three Conversations*, 1771, was well received.[76] Within a perhaps old-fashioned dialogue format[77] the book is provocatively and interestingly written. Lengthy tongue-in-cheek dedications address the first two sections (mainly political) to Lord Mansfield, and the third (religious) to the Bishop of Gloucester – as pillars of the establishment. Of the dialogue's participants, the Philosopher, a Courtier, a Whig, a Clergyman of the established church, and a Presbyterian minister, the first-named may clearly be identified with the author himself – indeed the soubriquet 'the Philosopher' was thereafter sometimes derisively applied to him. The publication and contents of the work must be set within the context not only of the events of the late 1760s but also of a number of works evoked by Burke's *Thoughts on the Cause of the Present Discontents*, 1770, ranging from Samuel Johnson's conservative rejoinder, *The False Alarm*, to the much more radical *Observations . . . on* Burke's work by Catharine Macaulay in the same year. Much of such writing was aimed at the political nation – so defined as to include those whose readiness to formulate and express opinions was hardening into an increasing discontent with the present machinery of parliamentary representation. For it has justly been observed that by the 1760s, while the political nation identified in the establishment, or indeed the electorate, had tended to shrink, the number of those who felt both qualified and entitled to exercise political influence and resented their exclusion therefrom – almost, a political nation *manqué* – was increasing: in brief, a conflict existed between the political establishment and the political nation in the wider sense.[78]

The element of immediate novelty in such writings must not be overstated;[79] neither must the circulation and impact of such works as *The Philosopher*. Despite broadly favourable reviews[80] and the accolade bestowed (albeit, specifically to the third, religious, 'Conversation') by the radical-minded John Jebb,[81] we have noted its author's apparent disappointment at the failure to publicize the book. Nonetheless, in several respects the work is of outstanding interest: first, as establishing the position of 'the Philosopher' himself; second, as an early example of a fair range of radical ideals; third, as an excellent though unintended exemplification of the relevance of 'Commonwealth' constitutional principles, and indeed of suggested procedures, to the Constitution which was to emerge in the U.S.A.; and finally, as delineating the principles of political thought which, with some (but surprisingly little) amendment, were to endure into the later more radical, and even into the ultimate neo-Burkeian conservative, phases of the writings of David Williams.

The author first defines his own position vis-a-vis the world of politics as that of a detached, though closely attentive, spectator, assuming the character of the Philosopher as his often unattained ideal.[82] Admittedly, in politics as in religion, a man who cannot unreservedly accept the tenets of any one party is liable to be condemned as unprincipled by all. But the Philosopher, impartial and disinterested, need not make the compromise *inevitable* for any *participant* in public affairs, or distinguish between a private and a public conscience, nor yet subordinate the general to any particular interest.[83] He is thus at pains to rebut association with what the Courtier dubs the seditious patriots[84] of the present agitations or with 'the supporters of the bill of rights'. Yet his distaste for the intemperance and fury of an opposition whose professed designs may be good is tempered by regret that the wisest and best in a community so often abandon the conduct of affairs to men whose insistence on meddling above their capacities succeeds only in producing a hubbub wherein the voice of reason is inaudible.[85] Indeed the stance adopted by Williams is reminiscent of Burke's assertion that 'it is the business of the speculative philosopher to mark the proper ends of government. It is the business of the politician, who is the philosopher in action, to find out proper means towards those ends, and to employ them with effect.'[86]

As we shall see, David Williams never made the implied transition, but his analysis and discussion of political issues in *The Philosopher* afford a fascinating insight into contemporary debate, especially when set alongside those of Burke and Macaulay in the previous year and Hulme's *Historical Essay on the English Constitution* which also appeared in 1771. Thus his starting-point, the assertion that a disorderly and unhappy people is a consequence of faulty government, and his portrayal of an empire riven by internal dissension, driven almost to despair by a wicked administration,[87] is very close to Burke's discernment of the reasons for a peculiar malignity in the present political distemper.[88] The Courtier's gibe that the recent endemic confusion and riot may be ascribed solely to the wish of a selfish opposition to change places with the ministry is scouted: discontent is not confined to a faction or a mob – the people in general have lost respect for their government.[89] Yet the assertion that the political talents of almost all the members of the present administration are subject to ridicule and contempt is balanced by a catalogue of the defects of the opposition. While Chatham's eloquence is now the greatest terror of a corrupt administration, his image has been ruined by venal ambition. His great talents have but served to exact a higher price: the champion of the Commons and scourge of corruption has been bought by 'a large pension; then a title of great honor;

and then an easy and lucrative place'. Likewise, Mansfield's earlier declarations of principle contrast with his present readiness to become obsequious to every administration 'as the creature of a Bute, the associate of a Sandwich'.[90]

The Philosopher shares the general contempt for those retainers of a faction or party who are 'always closing with that side, which bids the greatest price for their services', and even the belief that the very existence of faction is an indication of something amiss.[91] His approach affords an instructive contrast with that of Burke's definition that 'Party is a body of men united for promoting by their joint endeavors the national interest upon some particular principle in which they are all agreed.'[92] On this issue, indeed, the views of Williams were probably the more typical of the age.[93] Yet the Philosopher will not accept the Courtier's diatribe: 'D———n them; they are all rascals ... and as for those greasy thick-headed fellows, who speechify, and bellow, and belch at Guidhall; they are below contempt.'[94] For by now resolute action by honest men is essential to resist the threat to constitutional liberties from the administration in general, the Crown in particular, and even the House of Commons in compliant association. Surely we have not so far lost our virtue as to be deemed incapable of liberty? Yet a vile administration has most palpably infringed upon established and undoubted rights.[95]

Specific illustrations of this relate to the recurrent crises associated with the name of Wilkes and with the increasingly difficult relations with the American colonists. Allusions to such issues as general warrants and the invasion of rights of privacy and of property evoke the Courtier's sneer: 'Bravo! – Wilkes and liberty for ever!' But the Philosopher disclaims any attachment to Wilkes, though indeed he would wish 'to have his cause supported; his injuries redressed; and the opportunity taken, which he has afforded, to regulate the constitution'.[96] Indeed, David Williams's treatment of the aspects and implications of the notorious running battle between John Wilkes and successive administrations[97] (involving such questions as allegedly seditious libel and the limits of parliamentary privilege) is admirably balanced and perceptive. For in truth the Bute-baiter had by now provoked administration – and a majority of the Commons – into actions as dubious in constitutional principle and implication as they were ill-considered in practice. Thus this rather disreputable peg now served to sustain a complex of constitutional discontents and aspirations, symbolized in the emergence in 1769 of the Society of Supporters of the Bill of Rights, whose declared support of Wilkes marched side by side with a more creditable concern with derivative constitutional issues.[98]

The Philosopher himself re-iterates his rejection of 'Mr. Wilkes as a patron of liberty. He is not equal to such a character.' He concedes the justice of the Courtier's question: 'Has it not, in London, been dangerous to walk the streets, when the liberty-boys were out, bullying, and knocking down their fellow-citizens, unless they did homage to the idol of their choice, or joined in a riot, to save their country?' Yet surely the root of the trouble lies in the determination of the ministry 'to punish him, probably, beyond his demerit; without regard to law, or the established rules of the constitution'. Little wonder that 'as the ministry proceeded in their oppressions, the people increased their attachment; until the one became ridiculous in its revenge, and the other in its protection and generosity.'[99] The interesting suggestion that in the late Middlesex election 'the power then exerted was a dispensing power; it was in fact, that of the crown, but in the modern method of shewing its preroga-tives', is qualified by the assertion that administration was first to blame, in bringing down the King into a contest with a subject.[100] Nonetheless, the danger is real: 'Suppose the affair in St. George's Fields to be warranted by our constitution: and then, shew me the difference between our government and that of France, or Turkey.'[101]

A powerful if over-stated passage conveys the nub of his argument: 'In plain terms, administration is hated; and to preserve itself in being, it has recourse' to the devices of despotism. It both makes the law and executes it, while invasion of constitutional liberties is backed by a servile majority in both Houses of Parliament. In particular, as presently used, an allegedly inherent power of the Commons bids fair to render us slaves of the lowest kind. If indeed the powers of that House 'are words undefined: they may have been left so, to prevent the invasion of them by the crown; not to reserve a licence to stretch them to the destruction of the community.' What is particularly striking in his analysis is the extension of the normal appre-hension that ministerial abuse of power is the most likely source of danger to the constitution into a wider fear – always to persist in David Williams – that the arrogation of what was soon fashionably described as sovereignty, even by an elected and supposedly answerable body, was a much more insidious threat to individual liberties and fundamental rights.[102]

The recent persistent deprivation of a county's elective right is in itself clearly destructive of a basic constitutional principle. Yet not far behind there lurks the ever-present bugaboo of Commonwealth ideology: the spectre of a standing army which, as allegedly used of late, is not part of the Constitution. The Philosopher echoes the Clergyman's horror at any prospect of civil war; yet God forbid that dread of bullets should bring us into slavery. The Courtier's sarcastic cry 'To arms! to arms!' is answered 'Yes to arms! – Why not? . . . if we find arms employed against us?' Rejecting the spurious justification of an imaginary European balance of power, the Philosopher deems an army inconsistent with liberty, and settles on what was to be a favourite preoccupation of the author: a citizens' militia. Plainly put, 'the man who gives up his arms, gives up the best proof of his right to liberty', for in appointing a protector he creates a master. In this special sense, the man who will not be a soldier deserves to be a slave.[103] Significantly, this principle, basic in the Anglo–Saxon definition of a free-man, was to be written into the Constitution of the U.S.A.: 'A well-regulated militia, being necessary to the security of a free state, the right of the people to keep and bear arms shall not be infringed.'[104] Objections on grounds of practicability dwindle beside the danger to the rough and uncourtly spirit of liberty from the present trend towards arbitrary and military rule. For in phraseology in part anticipatory of Dunning's Motion (1780), 'the power of the crown is, daily though imperceptibly increasing. It commands not yet, in the voice of despotism; but it, gradually, enlarges a permanent influence, which may, in time, render it despotic.'[105]

In this context we meet what was, in many British as well as trans-Atlantic eyes, a test-case of civil and constitutional liberties: the position of the American colonists.

The dispute had long been rumbling. But by 1771 debate over taxation and the nature of American or indeed British liberties – for many professed to discern a concerted plot against the rights of British citizens at home and across the Atlantic – had sharpened to the point of attempts to coordinate resistance and to commission of overt acts of violence in defiance of authority, culminating, in the 'Boston Massacre' in March 1770 followed by a temporary lull.[106] The Philosopher's starting-point is unexceptionable. 'A mother-country, and colony, imply the ideas of parent and child; and, consequently, those of power, and protection; dependance and obedience.' Yet Britain may not ignore or revoke colonial charters, for her power is not arbitrary. Naturally, many Americans long for independence, while British politicians, apprised of the huge potential natural resources at stake, fear that rivalry and ultimate superiority may replace subordination. The Courtier urges that any establishment of an American (as indeed an Irish) militia can lead only to secession. But in reply a passage with overtones of Machiavellian-sounding realism poses the stark alternatives: in default of respecting their rights as natural subjects, military government must suppress all liberty, for a mixture of one and the other will not do.[107]

All free-born inhabitants of the British empire hold equal privileges. But, significantly, the mother-country must house a seat of government and a legislature enacting general laws, this latter to include provincial representatives for matters of imperial interest. Admittedly, the institution of an annual parliament,[108] and the distances involved, pose certain questions. Thus the colonists' subordinate legislatures must remain alongside their only effective form of domestic government: 'their *municipal laws* made at home; and appeal lying from them to the *supreme legislature* [my italics, in both cases]; their money raised by impositions of their own' for local purposes. 'Their militia should be on the plan of ours; every citizen being, in part, a soldier ... Trade ought to be a great object in the whole empire, and the regulations of it in the supreme legislature' – to the mutual advantage of imperial members and the exclusion of competing foreigners.[109]

This blend of the novel and the liberal with the traditional or even Mercantilist is typical of David Williams. Indeed his language in defining the nature and duties of government is reminiscent of Erasmus rather than anticipatory of the Chartists. The statement that 'the great offices of government are filled up by men, not in order to watch for any opportunities to distress; but to guard the interests, and to promote the happiness of the people', looks right back to the Tudor progenitors of the Commonwealth tradition.[110] His definition that 'the end of civil government, is to secure to the people of the community, the enjoyment of their most important natural rights', to which end other less important ones are given up, clearly reflects the Lockeian element in this body of thought.[111] Yet references to *historical* origins of government play no great role in *The Philosopher*. Indeed the first allusion to a topic which was later accorded so much space[112] is anything but complimentary. True, after butchering the Britons, the Saxons introduced a form of government which gave considerable participation to the people; but we do not find 'that perfect, glorious model, which the advocates of liberty call our antient constitution' – although indeed the position was not improved by Norman innovations, unfavourable to liberty.[113]

More recently, the impact of revolution under the Stuarts was crucial, for at that juncture 'the people were in a state to contend for their liberties, upon, almost, equal ground': yet their claim, since echoed by the advocates of liberty in every subsequent contest, to base them on the privileges of an ancient constitution, on principles apparently laid down by the Almighty, was erroneous. Indeed, while accepting Lockeian purposes, the Philosopher has found enquiry into the methods by which men have formed societies unrewarding – apart from the shrewd observation that any form of government will be adapted to the circumstances in which the people were brought together[114] so that its utility may wane as these change. More fundamentally, just as the rights of an individual are not determined by the accidents of birth, 'no more are those of a community, by any circumstances attending its formation ... Both may labor under disadvantages, from the peculiar circumstances attending those events; but their *natural unalienable rights* [my italics] cannot be set aside ... The state of society, should be considered as a state of progression, from smaller degrees of civil liberty and happiness to greater; and approaching to that perfection, of which we have an idea; but which we may never be capable of enjoying.'[115] Any attribution of originality in the history of ideas is hazardous; yet David Williams's assertion, at this relatively early date, of an ideal entitlement to inalienable natural rights combined with a perception that their recognition and expression are, like the political institutions of society itself, subject to progressive evolution, is surely near the mark.

While Williams would not lose a hair of his head, or pluck off one of another's, to restore any ancient constitution, he would forfeit his life 'to obtain that improvement, and perfection of civil liberty, which every society has a right to, and which is capable of producing the highest degree of human happiness'.[116] In such a progress, principles are more important than precedent which may be bad (as in the conduct of the Rump) as often as good (as in the Convention Parliament). Our rights are founded partly on precedents but principally on nature. Indeed, solutions to our current problems are impossible 'if our constitution were deemed a finished system; made up of invariable customs, and laws'. Its original structure supposed a state of things very different from the present. Certain powers thereby conferred proving subject to abuse, such abuse has in turn been subject to a remedy. Therefore, in a provision that anticipates the amendment powers in the Constitution of the United States, 'when we make institutions and laws for the purpose of government, and establish a plan or design, to the great principles of which we may recur; there should be ample room and power left, of changing the parts of it, as our circumstances change'.[117]

Williams rejects the imputation of yearning for a new constitution or Utopian schemes. Total and sudden change is generally impractical and sometimes fatal. Yet institutions of government, like all things human, are imperfect, while changing circumstances of themselves will necessitate amendment. In such change 'the power of the people, must generally, if not always, be the reformer: but, how to get that power properly directed, is, sometimes, a great difficulty'. For in general all common people 'appear to be so ignorant, that they can be said, only to feel when they are happy or miserable; and not to understand the causes of their being so'. Even so, such feelings are in themselves a valid test of the calibre of government.[118]

These crucial issues – the need for *gradual* constitutional evolution, and the perennial problem of the identification and implementation of the will and the interests of the people in determining the institutions and the policy of government – are destined to endure as constants in the political thought of David Williams.

Thus, specific programmes of reform are preceded by the caveat that '*the powers that be, are ordained of God*; this is true, in the same sense as, *whatever is, is right*'. The Philosopher submits to that set of laws which naturally arise from our present civil and religious circumstances. For all forms of government have derived, 'not from general, and well-digested systems of men; or any single and masterly exertions of the human understanding', but from a conjunction of determinants and expedients. An ideal form of government is admired in Plato's Republic, More's Utopia, or indeed in any millenium, but is not encountered in the actual affairs of men. Indeed Williams here qualifies his use of the very term 'constitution' which, as in describing the human body, may be taken to imply 'a compleat and perfect system; and includes the idea of permanence in the structure and disposition of all its parts'. His use, perforce, of the word (for 'institution' is no real alternative) does not imply immutability. The corporeal analogy here introduced, which was in fact to bulk ever larger in his treatment of political and social problems, goes right back of course through the works of the Commonwealth idealists of the mid-Tudor era to their own medieval inheritance.[119]

In David Williams's discussion of power and its exercise we meet a use of this analogy which is in fact strikingly evocative of John Ponet's *Treatise of politike power*, published in 1556 and speedily reprinted by opponents of the Crown in 1642. If any forcible assertion of men's rights proves fatal to the monarch, then better 'that he should be destroyed, than that they should perish; for, the whole is greater than a part'.[120] The rights and prerogatives of princes are either usurped powers or but held in trust for the community. 'A legal and constitutional magistrate ... is an officer of the community; his powers ... are to be continued or with held, according to its interest or pleasure.' His ridicule of any claim to hereditary succession of power itself, and assertion that, though no republican, he does not think of kings as gods, are not surprising. Much, much more striking is his declaration that when men come to understand their rights, 'there can be no restraints on them, from the claims of any magistracy. The rights of men, may be said to be enlarged, as their capacities are enlarged. To know them, is ever a sufficient title.'[121] The significance, and surely the genuine originality, of these last two sentences need hardly be laboured. The sentiment precedes by some two decades James Mackintosh's assertion in *Vindiciae Gallicae* that 'it is not because we *have been* free, but because we *have a right to be free* that we ought to demand freedom'.[122] Williams was concerned not with any 'metaphysical' (to use his own pejorative term) or even pseudo-historical exploration of the *origins* of men's rights, but with their establishment and exercise.

We have observed that the rights of the people are inalienable, indeed that 'the people are the best judges in many political questions: they feel all the effects of public measures; and, sometimes, they alone can tell whether they are proper or not. The government must be faulty, when the people are unhappy.'[123] But there remain the crucial problems of the definition of the people, a commonplace of radical

political discussion, and of the means and limitations of their active involvement in
the political process, to which David Williams devoted far more space and thought
than his contemporaries. The Courtier's sneer at 'the rabble; who know not what
they would have; catch at any pretence to be licentious; and are glad to throw off the
restraints of government', is reminiscent of the Tudor preacher's cry that 'even so
now (as ever) the most part seek liberty . . . but a carnal and fleshly liberty', a licence
to defy temporal magistrates – for anarchy is the natural aspiration of the
commons.[124] The Philosopher rejects this caricature of a rabble, canaille, or scum of
the earth, fit only to be ruled by their natural superiors. Yet while he speculates that
a democratic form of government is most agreeable to natural equity, he also
identifies the menace of the riotous mob, stirred up by the seditious demagogue. He
deems it necessary to explain that 'when I said, the people were to chuse delegates,
and representatives, I meant, the people in general, of a fixed property, to a small
amount'.[125] This codicil is in full accord with contemporary Commonwealth or
radical ideology. Thus a set of radical proposals in John Almon's *Political Register*,
1768, assert that 'the people (I do not mean the illiterate rabble, who have neither
capacity for judging the matters of government, nor property to be concerned for)
are the *fountain* of authority'.[126] The Courtier's gibe that there is no better method of
involving the people 'than distributing beer and gin among them; for they are never
patriotic till they are drunk' meets with the retort that this seldom gives concern to
administration. Yet the Philosopher concedes that the riotous mob may often be as
subversive of order and as pernicious to liberty as the intrigues of a bad administration. The perennial problem of politics is 'to get the will of the people freely and
properly expressed'.[127]

In the present circumstances, Williams deems 'the method of petitioning the
throne, on many occasions the best that can be' – but not always. The allusion is to a
veritable spate of such petitions between 1769 and 1770 consequent upon the affair
of the Middlesex elections and their aftermath. The right of a county or corporation
to address parliament was long established, but in some respects what was now
taking place foreshadowed by a decade or so the emergence of national extra-
parliamentary political organizations.[128] Williams describes the present
remonstrances as the measures of men with more zeal than knowledge, and is
sceptical of the impact and prospects of the Supporters of the Bill of Rights, other
than the mere adjustment of Mr Wilkes's affairs. Admittedly, the object of our
recent petitions was of infinitely greater importance, involving a principle of the
Constitution. But – alluding to a remonstrance submitted to the Crown by the Lord
Mayor of London in March 1770, at best barely civil, at worst gratuitously offensive
in its tone – the Philosopher 'was hurt at Beckford's behaviour; it was unjustifiable;
it was insolent'.[129] Yet equally to be deplored is the ludicrous concept of virtual
representation in the Commons. He derides the declaration of a 'frenchified
member' of that House that the people could have no opinion but as therein
expressed: 'I should have been glad to have asked him . . . whether he thought there
was a town or village in England, left to its own inclination, which would not duck
him in a horse-pond, rather than chuse him for a representative.'[130]

We thus reach the point of fundamental divergence of approach between David

Williams and Edmund Burke – despite the concurrence of so much of their diagnosis of contemporary ills. Catharine Macaulay identified the real intent of Burke's pernicious work as being 'to guard against the possible consequences of an effectual reformation in the vitiated parts of our constitution and government'.[131] To effect such a transformation was precisely the objective of the Philosopher – although indeed, in character, he prefaces his proposals with a reiterated warning that he thinks the people hardly ever capable of implementing the necessary remedies, especially in an empire so extensive, and with a commendation of Bacon's advice 'that men, in their innovations, would follow the example of time, which, indeed, innovateth greatly, but quietly; and by degrees scarce to be perceived'.[132] In respect both of general principles and of specific recommendations for reform, perhaps the closest contemporary parallel with *The Philosopher* is to be found (despite its very different format) in *An Historical Essay on the English Constitution*, by Obadiah Hulme, which also appeared in 1771.[133]

While disclaiming any impracticable and dangerous intent to change the form of government, the Philosopher is not surprised that neither King, administration, nor House of Commons itself will act to purge corruption. For 'a member who pays for his seat, conceives that he has a kind of private property in the house, purchased by his money'. Such will hardly welcome a dissolution with its consequence of renewed (and perhaps this time fruitless) expense.[134] His first proposal for amendment is a typical amalgam of the novel and the traditional: existing divisions such as counties, hundreds, and tithings, must continue; but their civil officers, while retaining their names and many of their powers, are 'to be all elective, by ballot'. Already, in 1767, *The Honest Elector's Proposal*, by 'C.W.' (John Almon?) had included details of the provision of as many boxes as candidates, each labelled and locked, with 'a round hole cut in the lid ... sufficient to admit a small ball', such boxes to be 'placed in a private room, with a curtain before the door on the inside'.[135] But Williams's advocacy that civil offices should be *all elective* is a striking anticipation of American procedure. Yet this radical innovation is expected to operate in a quite paternalist way; for those elected will naturally be 'of the best sense and character: whose residence among the people would enable them to know what was their best interest, and to express their general sentiments'. As to the form of legislature, while the monarchy and the House of Lords remain, with some provision against abuse of privilege, the deputies of the Commons must be chosen 'by the civil officers; or by the freeholders, and freemen themselves, by ballot, and once a year'.[136]

The Whig's objection that a secret ballot would produce the worst vices, falsehood, hypocrisy, and treachery, is met with pungent realism: what candidate would bribe a man who could then with impunity renege in secret? Yet would not annual elections exclude all candidates of modest means? Not if held at the expense of public funds! There follows a provision whose phraseology evokes a present-day debate: 'The members, being chosen, should be liable to receive instructions; to have their past conduct examined into at the end of the year; and to be dismissed or continued, as they were approved or disapproved of by the people; who, by assembling themselves, or by appointing their immediate delegates, would be able to judge and determine on their conduct.' The Philosopher's argument incorporates his critics' own cynical reservations – for 'the only security against corruption, where public virtue is wanting, is a duration of parliaments, the shortest possible'. Its effect upon our present parliamentary jockeys would be well-nigh infallible: for who would find it worth while, to procure a seat for a year, to corrupt a county or borough – unless it were a Cornish one?[137] Surely the Commons can be provided with men of integrity who, 'having sufficient fortunes for their ranks, would serve their country without a bribe?' The significant proviso is in the mainstream of Commonwealth assumptions. The declaration that 'in the regulations of government, the business of a legislator is to guard against all possible vices: he is never to give credit for the influence of any probable virtue', is in complete accord with the thinking which underlay the United States Constitution. To quote *The Federalist*, 'Why has government been instituted at all? Because the passions of men will not conform to the dictates of reason and justice, without restraint.'[138] But more immediate is Hulme's assertion that 'there is no chief magistrate, no political body of men ... but what will (if you once make them powerful, and fix them above your own control) most certainly degenerate into tyrants, and make you slaves'.[139]

Reverting to the means of representation and accountability, the Philosopher's observation that when the people assemble in parishes and hundreds 'there would generally be some men of knowledge, and temper, who might regulate their zeal, and inform them when they wanted information' is reminiscent of the role of the Saxon 'ealdorman'. The Courtier fears a kingdom swarming with politicians, whose meetings 'would frequently exhibit Hobbes's state of nature, where everything would be determined by club-law; and all would be confusion and anarchy', with problems of audibility compounding those of order. But of course David Williams, no lover of large assemblies, 'never meant that all the people of a county or a hundred should meet together on public business. I have expressly said, that the inhabitants of a tithing, should chuse their decennary who is to represent them in the hundred; where two or more may be chosen to represent the hundred in the county. In this manner, there could be no numerous assemblies; and no confusion; the sentiments of all the people in the kingdom might be easily and peacably taken, and laid before their representatives in parliament.'[140] The whole package provokes a predictable reaction from the Whig. But the modern student of political thought is struck not only by such radical suggestions as annual elections and a secret ballot but also by the implied limitation of the franchise, the leaning towards indirect representation, and indeed the endemic suspicion of all those endowed with power. Dislike of any form of direct democracy was to be an enduring feature of the thought of Williams, to be confirmed by the impact of the Gordon Riots and of his later experiences in France.[141]

Meanwhile, the assertion that when the King refuses to dissolve Parliament the people may exercise that function is immediately qualified by a prudent recognition that this is seldom expedient and certainly not at present. The suggestion that perhaps acceptance of the principle of annual parliaments may be required as a condition of future candidature, advanced by the Philosopher, was to be one of the articles in a programme set forth by the Supporters of the Bill of Rights in June 1771,[142] many of whose items had in fact been adopted by the Liverymen of the City, led by Beckford, as early as February 1769.[143] The Whig persists that any representative associations other than parliament itself may well be considered unlawful assemblies – indeed some already professed to discern the revolutionary possibility of the imposition of a new order by extra-parliamentary means.[144] But the Philosopher is equally insistent as to the complete legality of peaceful association.[145] To re-iterate, the effects are harmful only when innovations are great, sudden, and injudicious. 'In all cases, the rule of morality, and of policy, is to do what is right, and what appears to be best; and to leave the consequences to providence.'[146]

Despite their discursive presentation the political ideas of *The Philosopher* merit close examination not only because of their expression at such a relatively early date but also in their anticipation of the great majority of the ideas expressed in the author's later and better-known works. Ironically, in the light of the events of the next few years, this first publication of David Williams gives much more space to *political* than to *religious* innovation. Indeed, given his education and still-pursued profession, the scant attention accorded to any question of religious or even philosophical derivation, or even definition of the nature and purpose, of political liberty is quite surprising – inviting contrast with his fellow London-Welshman, Richard Price. As to the mechanics of the exercise of such liberty through a process of representation and accountability, the principles and methods here outlined will endure, with some elaboration and occasional amendment, throughout his subsequent writings. So, too, will his combination of idealism and realist scepticism and his highly individual amalgam of the traditional and the radical. In particular, the way in which the early-modern device of the corporeal analogy of society, ideally suited to the concept of organic evolution, is made the bearer of the advocacy of liberal-radical constitutional change (decked out in Anglo-Saxon historical antecedents) will become increasingly characteristic. The omission of David Williams from more than one authoritative explorations of the Commonwealth or Real Whig tradition has been remarked;[147] yet in truth he cannot with certainty be assigned to any one school of thought. For we shall find that in some respects his own opinions were subject to the process of evolutionary adjustment to circumstances which he commended for political constitutions as such.

The inscription on the memorial reads:

DAVID WILLIAMS
BORN AT WAEN WAELOD WATFORD
1738 DIED AT LONDON JUNE 29 1816
BURIED AT St. ANNE'S SOHO
THIS MEMORIAL
HAS BEEN RAISED BY A FEW ADMIRERS.
HE WAS ONE OF THE FOREMOST
WELSHMEN OF HIS AGE AND GENERATION
ENDOWED WITH RARE INTELLECTUAL GIFTS
HE DEVOTED THE GREATER PART OF HIS LIFE
TO THE HELPING OF THE POOR
THE EXPOUNDING OF THE PRINCIPLES OF
POPULAR EDUCATION,
AND THE FURTHERING OF THE CAUSE OF
LIBERTY.
BOTH IN SPEECH AND IN THOUGHT
HE WROTE MANY BOOKS HE DRAFTED
THE FIRST CONSTITUTION OF THE
FRENCH REVOLUTION,
HE SHIELDED BENJAMIN FRANKLIN
AND OTHER FRIENDS OF FREEDOM
FROM PERSECUTION AND HE
FOUNDED THE ROYAL LITERARY FUND
GWYN-EI-FYD.

Plate 4. PLINTH INSCRIPTION. DAVID WILLIAMS MEMORIAL

Chapter Two

'ORPHEUS, PRIEST OF NATURE'

BOTH the early career and the first publications of David Williams being closely concerned with religion, it is logical and convenient first to consider that aspect of the evolution of his thought which culminated in the Margaret Street Chapel venture and its aftermath. Yet any suggestion of a standard Dissenting progression from contention for religious liberties to an advocacy of their civil and political equivalent would be out of place. For Williams was no Richard Price. Indeed it may well be urged that any identity in approach to the religious and to the political aspects of human freedom derives as much from his rejection of his own inheritance in the first as from his criticism of the British Constitution in the second. In considering in its own right the development of his religious philosophy we shall first examine the highly individual creed enunciated in his writings after his formal breach with the Dissenting establishment. Then the nature and fortunes of the form of worship which he launched in Margaret Street – at once the culmination and the ruin of his hopes – will be studied. Finally, we shall trace the emergence of an ever more agnostic and humanist approach which increasingly coloured his attitude toward Dissenting efforts to secure a more explicit and formal recognition of religious toleration. It must be stressed, firstly, that the foregoing themes are interrelated and overlapping, and secondly, that we are concerned with an evolution of personal beliefs rather than with the emergence of an original, coherent and consistent religious philosophy.

Williams insisted that his relinquishing the ministry at Highgate betrayed neither dereliction of duty nor sudden change in beliefs. Yet an intensely personal disillusion is manifest in his later avowal that 'I was educated among the Saints; and I now live, thank God, among Sinners', and in his bitter allusion to such as 'maliciously attempted to seduce my friends, and to make unhappy the last years and days of those whom the tenderest affection and duty oblige me to attend and honor. All these people I must detest, and yet every one of them is a *Saint*; has told these falsehoods and attempted these mischiefs . . . with his lips wet from the sacramental cup.'[1] Such declarations ill accord with his profession of happiness in the friendship and kindness of his congregation. But if increasing distaste for his vocation was undoubtedly one influence, another is equally clear in his confession of habits of sociability the expense of which his clerical income could not support. Having no relish for tying himself to some disagreeable woman for the sake of her fortune, Williams had recourse to private tuition – and finding this accessory employment more lucrative and at least as meritorious, he renounced the ministry. Alongside this mundane explanation, which the establishment of a school at Chelsea would seem to confirm, he is eager to deny the charges that he had continued 'to preach a religion which I did not believe, till I had an opportunity of giving it this mortal stab' and that he left his profession because he had not for some time believed the Gospel.[2]

Yet religious as well as pecuniary factors were certainly involved. Both crystallisation and expression of a changed attitude towards Christianity emerged from events which followed the appearance of the third part of *The Philosopher*. A letter from John Jebb, dated at Cambridge on 26 October 1772, describing that work as 'much esteemed by the Liberal minded of this place', alludes to a proposal by Williams which clearly concerned his reformed Liturgy. This was based on the changes introduced while still with his Arian congregation in Exeter; indeed its Preface asserts that it had been drawn up for several years. But despite this earlier composition its appearance in print in 1774 was to be preceded by the publication of *Essays on Public Worship* in the previous year. These, so to speak, did the damage. Thomas Morris, no hostile critic, described them as so near to overt Deism in tone that their author was instantly deserted 'not only by the negociators for a reformed plan of worship, but by almost every friend and acquaintance he had in the world', so that the project 'could not have obtained five guineas from Edinburgh to the Land's End'.[3] Reviewers found the candour of the *Essays* equalled only by their impracticability, and one added speculation about the author's motives to reservations as to his prudence.[4]

The *Liturgy on the Principles of the Christian Religion*, although thus overtaken by events, adheres to that faith, declares this life 'a state of trial for immortality', and includes a Zwinglian-type Lord's Supper and a very adaptable Order of Baptism. There is indeed a tribute to a 'wise author of nature, who has planted in our minds the benevolent and social affections', but little other evidence of what was to follow.[5] As yet, the format was interdenominational, based 'on the rational principles of the Christian religion', albeit with heavy emphasis on its moral content and implications. Its author did well to pay tribute to the Liverpool 'Octagon Liturgy', for comparison reveals that, though somewhat shorter, his version is markedly similar in tone and phraseology.[6] Reviewers gave it a very mixed reception;[7] but Morris's assertion that the storm of illiberal bigotry which his publications encountered provoked Williams to a close examination of the evidence for Christianity which terminated in disbelief must almost certainly be related to the earlier impact of his *Essays*. For as early as 12 October 1773 the Minute Books of the Body of Protestant Dissenting Ministers in London and Westminister record that Williams has left Highgate. A later entry, for 4 April 1775, notes that he 'has declined the Ministry among the Protestant Dissenters' – which may mark a general or formal disavowal or simply a rejection of a call to another congregation.[8]

David Williams's own explanation of his decision to resign the constant charge of a congregation, though not as yet his character as a minister, relates it first to a wish for a higher income but secondly to a temperamental disinclination for his vocation. Indeed, 'I never approved of the common manner of public worship among them, and I thought their usages and manners were generally unpleasing and absurd. But

I thought liberty was harboured by them alone [my italics], and liberty was the object of my devotion. I soon found myself mistaken' – for perhaps even popery would be preferable to submission to the petifogging regulations of a Presbyterian Assembly or to the whims of an ignorant and insolent congregation. As for career prospects, compliance with the prudent counsel given on the means of popularity and advancement in their ranks would have made of him a thorough scoundrel.[9]

Significantly, his evocatively-titled two-volume edition of *Sermons, chiefly upon Religious Hypocrisy*, 1774, is concerned to rebut attacks upon the rectitude of his conduct as a minister. Yet he now avers that, regarding those principles of the Christian religion hitherto committed to memory and taken upon trust, 'I honestly confess, that from a fair and full investigation, I do not know whether they are true or false.' Moreover, he is at a loss to identify any doctrines of Christianity which differ from simple morality. Investigation of the tenets of the various Christian sects reveals peculiar creeds: 'Athanasius had one, Arius another, Socinus another, Calvin another: but not one of these peculiar doctrines could I ever find in christianity.'[10] It seems abundantly clear that while his apostasy derived primarily from financial and careerist considerations, the preaching of formal Christianity had for some time been irksome.

Yet he rejects any charge of being irreligious. The conviction expressed in *The Philosopher* that the truth of Christianity resides in its injunction of the plainest principles of pious and moral obligation was to endure, despite increasing reservations as to the immortality of the soul and the salvation offered by the Crucifixion. Williams continues to 'understand religion as implying every moral obligation, and animating the whole by the sublime principle of piety. This I conceive to be the religion of Christ'[11] – but not, as we shall see, of Christ alone. Williams was, in one sense, to deplore the lack of any evident and derivative relationship between faith and morality, and in another, to emphasize the reality and truth of the absence of any necessary relationship. While doctrine without morality is sterile, the latter stands in no need of dogma. Consider the present ludicrous contrast between doctrinal wrangling within a religious hierarchy which itself numbers bigots and blockheads alongside infidels, and increasingly widespread grass-roots irreligion – our nobility and gentry, if they are anything, being Freethinkers. Despairingly, he appeals to 'those western regions to which every thing excellent seems to be sojourning [to] take hints even from our little plan; and give to the world . . . *simple and pure religion*'.[12]

Before considering the outcome of the little plan, what were the characteristics of his simple and pure religion? The absence, in one who had received a formal education for the ministry, of any taste for doctrinal discussion is striking enough. Even more so is the presence of a clear expression of a concept of the *evolution* of religion itself as an aspect of Man's thinking: 'The first prayers of men, were certainly on the principle of Anthropomorphism. They conceived of God as in human shape, with human passions and human wants. They first of all dropped his wants; they are now relinquishing his passions; and it is possible the time may come, when they shall not conceive of him as a person, in any shape whatever. As people corrected their apprehensions of God, they altered their methods of seeing him.' Yet

Williams concedes that he himself can but seldom conceive of the Deity otherwise than as a person: 'When I endeavour to change my conception, it sometimes dwindles to a point, sometimes is dissipated into infinite space.'[13] As for Christianity, while it has improved our concept of God and enunciated *principles* which can give offence to no conscientious Deist, or indeed to any good and pious man, its *doctrines* are all subject to controversy. Now a genuinely comprehensive liturgy, whose objective is social devotion through public worship, must exclude all controverted doctrines.[14]

The essential features of his religious credo are fairly clear: the concentration upon the social and moral aspects of devotion; the progression towards a Deist concept of a first cause, which he never abandoned for atheism; the distaste for doctrinal controversy. Despite a later increasing reverence for Nature and ultimate scepticism as to any individual hereafter, these remained constants. Williams moves from a Dissenting tradition, in which he had never been entirely happy, to that which Enno van Gelder sees emerging in the mid-sixteenth century, by which 'religion is seen predominantly as an ethical value and determined philosophically, in which the miraculous in general and the mystery of salvation in particular recede in importance; the value of life on earth is placed in the centre of thought; . . . what is reasonable is accepted as true'.[15]

In stressing the sterility of religious dogma Williams suggests that tenets such as original sin or election reflect as much the temperament as the judgement of their champions – as in 'the man who will say that God has chosen him and a few of his friends for his companions in heaven, and doomed all the rest of the world to the devil'. Particularly repellent is any separation of faith (defined as dogmatic orthodoxy) from good works. One of his rare doctrinal expositions, a sketch of the evolution of the sacrament of the Lord's Supper, is typical in eschewing both those who had believed that 'the perfection of all religion is to feel the heart thrill and the head swim at eating and drinking *the real body and blood of their God*', and those who, despite the fact that at the Reformation this dreadful sacrament was altered so much for the better, would now make participation in a worthy manner the very summit of Christian perfection and the grand specific for the blotting out of sins – forgetting that our Saviour instituted the Supper when Judas Iscariot was present and partook of it in his company. Christ, whose whole gospel is packed with the moral duties of a good man, gave no room to imagine that it is anything more than a social remembrance, in which the elements are but bread and wine.[16] In essence, he assails the delusions of all mechanically ceremonious religion, as offering 'immortal happiness to mankind, without the beggarly elements of piety, charity, and goodness, for believing what they did not understand, and performing ridiculous and unmeaning ceremonies'.[17] Indeed, all doctrinal differences between Roman Catholics and Reformers are dwarfed by their joint agreement upon the prescription and enforcement of a set of truths. For if liberty of judgement be removed, no matter 'whether I were required to believe transubstantiation, or that two and two make four. The irreparable injury would be committed in degrading me from the rank of a man.'[18]

We shall see that distaste alike for authoritative dogma and for empty ceremonial does not preclude the need for a set form of worship or liturgy, nor is any assault on ethics and morality implied by freedom of thought. But his tolerance is more general than specific; his gorge rises as he contemplates each sect in turn: 'Put any of these denominations in power; and you will only exchange tyrants.' True, he commends more toleration of Romanists, whose former persecuting power has lapsed – but this may safely be extended only because their puerile ceremonies no longer pose a threat.[19] The Church of England has failed to evolve in response to the needs of society; yet with efforts to supply 'enthusiasm' Williams has no sympathy – the word itself is pejorative. Genuine piety and respect for the Deity have no place in 'the disgustful familiarity of our ignorant Enthusiasts' who speak of him and to him as a common acquaintance.[20] (Indeed, more than once, the modern field-preacher and the holy inquisitor on his dark tribunal are equated in his depiction of bigotry.)[21] Those rational and temperate virtues deriving from the contemplation of Nature, approved by reason and experience, contrast with the paroxysms of spurious passion called enthusiasm.[22]

The errors of the Dissenting interest include the adoption of a form of church discipline fit only for a democracy, the lack of good music in its services, the fetish of public free prayer which is absurd in hindering genuinely *social* worship, and the frequent dominance of 'the strongest lungs, the wildest imaginations, and sometimes the most shocking fanaticism'.[23] Yet even in proportion as this latter trait has declined, Dissenting worship has become cold and languid. As to doctrinal developments, whereas not long since Arianism was an object of detestation 'now a great part of them are become Arians themselves'. Modern research confirms the implied decline of Dissent, as also an almost commonplace progression from Presbyterianism through Arminian to Arian and even Socinian beliefs.[24] But Williams's analysis is shot through with charges in which a bitterly personal note is clear: of lugubrious demeanour, sectarian intolerance, and hypocritical personal attacks designed to blast a reputation – such worthless and wicked saints must surely merit a sojourn in a papist purgatory?[25]

Yet alongside this welter of sour disenchantment a pattern emerges which is neither atheist nor anti-religious. Freedom of thought must not be equated with scurrilous irreverence or with rejection of all morality. Free-thinking has no necessary affinity with vice, there being a certain ambivalence in the term itself. Yet all too often 'men have had recourse to infidelity, after they had become vicious', so that vice and free-thinking are often held to be synonymous. This point was fully and cogently developed in his *Sermon at the Opening of a Chapel in Margaret-Street*, 1776, where he stigmatizes such as 'sometimes go under the denomination of *Free-thinkers*; but they deserve not the appellation. They are distinguished by a certain libertinism both in principle and practice: they have thrown off the doctrines of religion, not because they were properly convinced of their falsehood, but because those doctrines were restraints on their vices. They first became profligates and then infidels.' We must not confuse real liberty of conscience and freedom of enquiry with a merely factious rejection of all creeds and all morality which would leave only the axe and the gibbet as motives for honest and virtuous conduct. Williams thus rejects what may properly be called infidelity: the belief that there is no God, 'that selfishness is the principle from which all human actions flow; and that there is no difference between virtue and vice, but what is created by the custom and policy of human societies.'[26]

In approaching the positive prescriptions of David Williams for his frequently declared goal of human happiness, one may discern the gradual emergence of two major themes: a Deism which was increasingly related to a much idealised picture of Nature; and a pleasure-and-pain based code of experiential morality which itself derived from Nature's precepts. These ideas owed nothing to theology or to metaphysics – the two conjoined in his aversion for 'the metaphysical and controvertible doctrines which run through the common forms' of worship.[27] Expressions of sympathy with Deism occur in his earliest work. The Philosopher deplores the fact that formal creeds exclude men of integrity for any slight deviation but admit any time-serving dissembler, while *Essays on Public Worship* commend both Bacon and More's *Utopia* (which is freely quoted) as having enunciated the admirable principle of purely moral and spiritual worship. The exclusion of disputed tenets should ensure that 'all *honest, pious* men, Calvinists, Arians, Socinians, Jews, Turks, and Infidels, might and *ought* to worship God together in spirit and in truth'. This perhaps too comprehensive definition of Deism must be understood in the light of the assertion that all sentiments and doctrines other than those of piety and morality must be kept out of an ideal liturgy. As yet, the near-adulation of Nature has not appeared, but later developments are presaged in an approving sketch of 'a Deist discharging the duties of life from a real principle of conscience . . . and rendering his whole life a happiness to himself, and a blessing to all about him, while he had given up all the common motives of religion, and *even the hopes of a future life* [my italics]'.[28]

One passage identifies the Rubicon in his own religious evolution: 'If christian charity will not suffer us to drop all controverted opinions in public worship, and to join with all honest men . . . in adoring the Deity [then] in that moment my infidelity may be dated.' He is now committed to the incomprehensible God, whom no man can discern to perfection, but whose existence all rational observation declares. He now believes Christianity 'to be a system of morality; agreeing in every article with the religion of nature; and deserving credit, for this only reason, that it no where contradicts the Deity; and never pretends to be more than publishing his will'. The Sermon preached at the opening of the chapel in Margaret Street goes further, in declaring that 'if I believed there was no Supreme Being distinct from *Nature*, I should adore Nature as I do God'. To repeat, 'all enquiries into the nature of that Being whose works we can see, are fruitless; *for none by searching can find him out*. Piety therefore consists in attention to the works of God.'[29]

Identification of these works with Nature becomes a major theme in the *Lectures on the Universal Principles of Religion and Morality*, purportedly as read at Margaret Street during 1776 and 1777. It is not material whether the atheist wishes to 'ascribe all we see to Nature, Necessity, or Chance: or whether the Deist [believes] that God is a spirit distinct from Nature . . . It is the moral character only, of Necessity, of Chance, or of God, or of the deified forms of human imagination, which can affect us'.[30] Man cannot hope to know more of the will of God than he sees in Nature's laws – which are wise and good indeed, but also permanent and immutable. Of all the metaphysical artifices first devised by priests, the worst is a pernicious attribution to the

Deity of something analogous to the will of man. An inescapable corollary identifies the folly of that type of prayer which resembles 'the desire of a fly, that the revolution of the earth may be stopped, and this universe desolated, that winter might not approach'. All prayer is reprehensible which cavils at the changeless laws of Nature; virtue and morality consist in a disposition to answer her purposes, as the only road to happiness. But finally, and of crucial import, that arrangement within Nature by which virtue necessarily produces happiness, and vice leads to misery, is the effect not of chance but of divine wisdom and beneficence.[31]

Before examining how this comes about, it must be emphasized that although the Margaret Street project in which it culminated was a genuinely pioneering effort, this line of thought in itself was not novel. A parody, 'The Unbeliever's Creed', in 1754, had included the article: 'I believe that there is no religion; that natural religion is the only religion; and that all religion is unnatural.'[32] Much more seriously, a full half-century before Williams, Wollaston's *The Religion of Nature delineated* had set down many identical views. Its recognition of a Supreme Being whose manner of existence transcends our comprehension, and acceptance that 'to be governed by reason is the general law imposed by the Author of nature upon them, whose uppermost faculty is reason', are strikingly reminiscent. So is the insistence upon a public worship of the Deity, who must not be depicted in terms of human emotion or motivation. But further, Wollaston had much to say on pleasure and pain and on a calculus derived therefrom: pain in itself is a real evil, and pleasure a real good; thus 'ultimate happiness is the sum of happiness, or true pleasure, at the foot of the account'. Yet in response to his own query, to which David Williams was at last to give a very different reply: 'And must [Man] *end here*? Is this the *period* of his being? Is this *all?*', Wollaston held fast to the belief that 'the soul of man subsists after the dissolution of his body: or, is immortal'.[33] Wollaston – whose book enjoyed a remarkable vogue over several decades, an eighth edition appearing in 1759 – must himself be placed within the tradition of Shaftesbury's insistence on the divine perfection of Nature, or indeed within a humanist trend emerging from the Renaissance.

Williams's early writings had often insisted on the need for *social* devotion: 'the people ought all to be engaged; and appear to each other to be so: it is then only that the religious principle is properly strengthened by the social'. Religion is equated with morality – for Christ himself was 'crucified between two thieves; for preaching morality to the Jewish nation.'[34] Yet the derivation of conscious principles and guides to moral conduct from the ever-present and constant laws of Nature does not receive explicit treatment until the *Lectures on the Universal Principles of Religion and Morality*. A remark in his *Sermons upon Religious Hypocrisy* that 'pain of every kind is always an evil, and always to be avoided and detested: and yet pain is evidently in the lot of mankind, and as evidently designed in the great plan of the Almighty, as pleasure',[35] is the precursor to enunciation in the *Lectures* of a full-blown pleasure/pain theory of experience-based, reflection-derived morality, in full accord with the natural scheme of things as instituted by the Deity. Thus, effectively, an experiential rationalist becomes an experiential moralist. The principles of morality derive from experience, much as, since Bacon, the truths of philosophy have been deduced largely from experiments. As to the criteria and objectives of morality, 'nothing can be of any possible use in this world, but as it has a tendency to make men happy'. Private and public happiness is produced only by virtue, virtue only by knowledge, and knowledge only by free enquiry. Crucially, the persuasion of an actual disposition 'to produce general order and happiness is grounded on the best of all possible foundations, experience, observation, and facts'.[36]

In this context, Williams reviews other philosophers on the emergence of the moral sense. Shaftesbury, in particular, has been misunderstood – for he never meant to make the moral sense a distinct and original part of the mind, brought into the world by every man. The moral sense is formed by time and experience, and is not in-born. Yet although *all* the senses develop with experience, the moral sense differs from simple feeling, and is subject to the conformation given by nature and by education. The mind is brought by experience to associate virtue with pleasure and vice with pain: therefrom morality derives. This optimistic and not over-precise empiricism, with its dismissal of any imaginary and everlasting rule of right, accompanies a couple of typical side-swipes at such as Berkeley and Hume – who question the reality of anything. Contention with the first-named is fruitless, for by his own reasoning he does not exist! More seriously, Williams has not time either for those modern philosophers who seem to regard governments as furnishing the only motives to virtue through their dispensation of rewards and punishments. The teaching of Mandeville, that private vices rightly handled may become public benefits is surely the ultimate in cynicism.[37]

Yet any attempt systematically to relate Williams to other philosophers is as exasperating as it is inconclusive. For it is doubtful whether he ever evolved a rigorous, logical, and fully integrated philosophy of his own.[38] His place within the tradition of Wollaston and of Shaftesbury (who taught that human virtue lies in following Nature and had produced a 'Scheme of Moral Arithmetick' which smacks of Williams's own yearning for mathematical certainty) seems clear. But insofar as concerns his derivation of a moral code, indeed a moral sense, from the pleasure-and-pain-based lessons of experience the significant influence is that of David Hartley. Hartley's position, necessitarian and yet still Christian, materialist yet still religious, was not precisely that of Williams – who was later to abandon beliefs to which Hartley clung, such as the immateriality and immortality of the soul, destined for an after-life. Yet his use of the principle of Association to demonstrate the necessary and mechanical generation of the moral sense is very reminiscent – as is his implication that we must so arrange Man's circumstances and education that the laws of Association will exert their maximum influence for good. Indeed, in his *Lectures on Education* Williams was to declare a specific preference for his opinions 'on the mode of forming the temper, directing or animating the understanding of my child'.[39]

When Williams himself goes on to assert that 'our character, our reason, our sensibility, or moral sense, depend greatly on the manner in which this experience is acquired', one wonders whether an experiential moralist is becoming a determinist or necessitarian. If so, it is as a necessitarian moralist – for we must remember that he sees the arrangement in Nature which renders virtue necessarily happy and vice miserable as divinely ordained. Yet the contention that if men would but act according to their God-given nature then universal happiness must follow is subject to the codicil that 'man is born with *capacities* [my italics], which, if not injured and perverted, in their growth, by a bad education, or a bad government, would answer the intention of God'.[40] Subject to the interaction of the experience of our senses and the reflective processes of our understanding, in the last analysis nothing strictly deserves the sacred name of truth but that which wins the assent of the individual. 'Truth, real and certain truth, can be found only in our own minds.' Likewise, conscience is acquired by experience and reason and is not an original gift of Nature.[41]

An optimistic assumption of an innate human tendency towards beneficence, subject to a properly ordered education, seems clear – and it is difficult, despite his protestations, to regard it as other than an innate principle, if only in the general context of the existence of a Deity which has implanted such a tendency within Nature itself. Yet any impression of optimistic *naiveté* is balanced by a shrewd rejection of the myth of an ideal 'state of nature'. Morality 'is not to be taught by lessons, principles, and doctrines; it grows like fruit on a tree, out of that kind of understanding and disposition which nature and education have given us'. Now if the first of these determinants comes near to postulating innate tendencies, the second is equally significant in its implication. For those philosophers who attempt to distinguish between a state of nature and a state of society envisage a situation in which no man ever existed: 'they have imagined children left on desert islands, where the prejudices and temptations of society could not mislead them; but they have always taken poetic licence, in furnishing them with understandings and affections which it must have been impossible they should have possessed.' Man is born in and for society, not as a solitary but as a social being.[42]

Within this context, his lengthy discussion of some principles of social justice is strikingly reminiscent of the Commonwealth idealism of the mid-Tudor era, rather than of the social reformist aspects of the Chartism of which he is sometimes held to be precursor. Equity, rather than equality, is the touchstone. Yet one passage in particular, in content and in phraseology, suggests a line of thought which reaches from More's *Utopia* through the anonymous mid-seventeenth century *Tyranipocrit* to some of the evidence submitted to the Parliamentary Committee of 1835 on the plight of the handloom weavers: 'This is the reason why the vices which infest society proceed originally from the rich and powerful; never from the poor. In all the communities of the world, the rich and powerful alone are in the condition of moral agents; they alone make laws and form customs; which are all in their favour; most of them injudicious, oppressive and cruel: the poor and common people are machines, acted upon by these laws and customs; and they are industrious, regular, decent, and tolerably happy; or they are idle, vicious, profligate, and miserable, according to the principles of that government which their superiors have formed for them.' There ensues a double standard: industry and honesty become obligatory duties of the poor, while any discharge of social obligations by the well-to-do is dubbed beneficence.[43] In particular, 'the frequency and severity of public execu-tions, and the number and cruelty of penal laws, are all of the same origin; a false idea of the general justice which should actuate the whole community'. Government, while not the primary is certainly the major secondary cause of the whole apparatus of vice and virtue.[44]

An immediate disclaimer of cherishing 'levelling principles, and wishing to introduce that equality among mankind, which visionaries have dreamed of' explains that a just government 'would make men start together from similar situations; but it would not, and could not, allot equal degrees of success, credit, and enjoyment, to unequal talents and industry'. Yet it must be reiterated that injustice originates in the interest and power of the rich; the profligacy and misconduct of the poor are effects, not causes. Thus his treatment of property rights and social obligations goes straight back to mid-Tudor Commonwealth, indeed to Erasmian, idealism. Property rights must be secure – yet such security 'is not the end for which rational beings associate; it is only one, among other means, conducive to that end; which is the greatest possible happiness'. Superior riches and wisdom must not be used capriciously, for vice and wretchedness derive as much from negligence among the higher as from dishonesty among the lower orders of society. The *duties* of beneficence are indeed just that, and as such are sacred. For the charitable potential of the rich itself derives from the industry of the poor. Though the well-to-do may disclaim ideas of natural justice and equity, their absolute obligations increase in conjunction with wisdom, power, and wealth. One simply cannot relate the social duties of the rich to moral and religious inducements whilst enforcing those of the poor by rigorous penal laws. Significantly, 'man is not made to be forced, even into happiness; and that society is ever ineffectual and miserable, in proportion to the number and severity of its legal restraints.'[45]

Significantly, because the ideas of David Williams on social justice receive their fullest expression within the context of his religious rather than in that of his political and constitutional works. He looked back at least as much to Erasmus as to Locke, and to duties and social obligations as moral norms within an hierarchical framework as much as to individual rights at any libertarian level. Moreover, within this setting we find some telling comments on liberty, or more correctly *moral* liberty. Compulsion is deplored: 'tell them they will be damned, if they do not perform certain rites – "Ay, that's a motive!" they'll say, – It is the ass's whip, and they'll move only while they tingle with the pain. It is time to be ashamed of these things ... Rewards and punishments are the expedients of ignorance and vice; and they will as soon produce day and night, and summer and winter, as they will true and genuine moral happiness.' The basic law of moral liberty, itself the only real foundation of all civil and religious liberty, is this: 'that our reflected pleasures, all degrees of moral satisfaction, depend on our conformity to the principles and laws of nature. *In this sense there is no liberty* [my italics]; there is no possibility of our deviating from the tendencies and directions given by God in the natural and moral world, without forfeiting our happiness ... The truth is, that the most perfect state of moral liberty; that in which we have the intire and free use of our faculties, and are never controuled or interrupted in the road to happiness, is that in which we most strictly and perfectly attend to and obey the absolute and invariable laws of nature; and is that which some philosophers have called a state of necessity.'[46]

This last allusion reflects a background of intense contemporary debate on the relationship between materialism and what Hartley had termed 'the Doctrine of Necessity'. While Hartley himself did not 'admit it at last without the greatest Reluctance' and had striven to preserve 'practical Free-will', Joseph Priestley, while paying tribute to his influence, did not shrink from enunciating 'the great and glorious, but unpopular doctrine of *Philosophical Necessity*'.[47] His book which bore this title, in 1777, was followed by a spate of publications on this theme and on the whole question of the relationship between matter and spirit.[48] Several referred to David Williams's contribution to the topic, one anonymous contribution alluding sarcastically to the Priest of Nature in Margaret Street as fit to be bracketed with John Bunckle, Esq.[49] More seriously, Manasseh Dawes, who was later to cite at length (and almost verbatim)[50] the passages from the *Lectures* quoted above, in his own *Free Enquiry into the Merits of a Controversy*, in 1780, applauded a long note of Williams's in his translation of Voltaire as to the folly of transporting the words of ordinary language into the depths of metaphysics and divinity. For 'we are but imperfectly acquainted with matter, and it is impossible we should have a distinct idea of what is not matter.'[51]

To conclude, one may well suggest the inclusion of David Williams alongside Hartley and Priestley in the suggested category of perfectibilist necessitarians.[52] For he contrasts his own ideal of conduct with any that is determined by false motives and irregular passions: 'The first is a submission to the direction of a beneficent, but absolute Power, leading to happiness; the other is submission to capricious tyranny, leading to wretchedness.'[53] The pattern of thought is familiar, endorsing the fact that his pleasure-and-pain determined basis of learning and of conduct is in no sense amoral. There remains, however ill defined, the concept of a benevolent Deity presiding over all. However, any attempt at comparative treatment of the philosophy of David Williams lies outside the compass of this book; it is time to move to a consideration of his impact on the public stage, in Margaret Street.

The Liturgy which was to be the centre-piece of that performance was not precisely a lineal descendant of that of 1774, nor were its origins derived solely from that abortive publication. Both must be seen in the context of attempts at Prayer Book reform for which Dr Samuel Clarke's version of 1724, in its deletion of much Trinitarian terminology, had set what is variously described as an Arian, Socinian, or Unitarian pattern.[54] When Theophilus Lindsey set up his Unitarian Church in Essex Street in April 1774, this reformed liturgy was adopted – though taking still further Clarke's distaste for 'the abstruse metaphysical doctrines of *election and original sin*'.[55] David Williams's version of 1774 (quite probably brought with him from Exeter) was closely modelled on the Octagon, Liverpool, ritual of 1763, but was still within this same tradition.[56] What was now to emerge marks a new departure in that it was non- (though not *anti-*)Christian. In this it reflects not only the by now declared apostasy of Williams himself but also the influence at least in part of Benjamin Franklin who had already essayed such a production in collaboration with Sir Francis Dashwood, a reformed rake turned Deist.[57] The subject was reopened, Williams explains, in the context of a 'Club of Thirteen' meeting for convivial discussion at the Old Slaughter Coffee House. Franklin's expression of regret at his inability to participate sincerely in any church service led to consideration of a projected *philosophical* liturgy by a group which included Thomas Bentley, Josiah Wedgwood, and Thomas Day.[58] Williams was asked to compose a specimen and, after repeated revision by the membership, a couple of thousand copies were printed. Normally, the involvement of Franklin might well have attracted a multitude of demi-philosophers, but the approach of the American troubles mutilated the scheme in embryo. It is in this context that Williams gives the fullest account of how Franklin, 'apprehensive that his Papers would be seized, took a Trunk under his arm, & unknown to the family where he lodged, conveyed it by a boat, from Hungerford Stairs to my house at Chelsea where he remained several Weeks, in perfect privacy ... until the Public Pulse was felt ... & himself in a condition to prepare for his departure.'[59] In August 1775 Williams wrote to Franklin informing him of the removal of the 'friendly Society ... from Slaughters T. to the Swan at Westminster Bridge' and of his own from Chelsea to Park Street, and also that the design of the Liturgy was revived, with a projected introduction the following winter.[60] Yet, while there is no doubt about Franklin's interest in its preliminary stages, out of the welter of later retrospective attributions of participation it is probably safe to indentify Williams himself (perhaps assisted by Bentley) as the principal author of the new Liturgy.[61]

Certainly there is no question as to the impact of the outbreak of hostilities. Williams was left with the publication and the hiring of the chapel on his hands; while some former enthusiasts still wished to subscribe or take pews, they were no longer ready to form a body to conduct the venture and bear the cost. Morris asserts that but one unnamed member of the society attended the opening service, while Williams himself declares that 'no Person gave me ostensible assistance.'[62] The Sermon preached at that opening, after public advertisement, on 7 April 1776, is effectively a formal avowal of objectives. Eschewing rivalry with existing denominations, and in direct pursuit of none 'but those who are out of *all* inclosures', designedly the form of worship will prove congenial to all honest men of any denomination or of none.[63] The Preface to *A Liturgy on the Universal Principles of Religion and Morality*, 1776, identifies acknowledgement of the power, wisdom, and goodness of the Supreme Intelligence (a term not often found in Williams but here used twice) as true religion.[64] In facilitating its public expression the author has always insisted on retention of a pious and rational liturgy. As to the claim that piety could be preserved without public worship: 'I will not say that this is impossible; but I never saw an instance of it.'[65] Hence this effort at 'a *Form of Social Worship*' open to all who acknowledge a Supreme Intelligence and the universal obligations of morality.[66]

The Liturgy itself, over a hundred pages long, bespeaks an Anglican format, including an Order for Morning and for Evening Prayer, a General Confession, Hymns and Psalms. The terms 'Lord' and 'Almighty God' are used, but deistic phraseology abounds: 'a being infinite and immense', 'the one glorious and active principle, directing every atom, animating every form'. The Deity has 'adorned our nature with reasoning powers and virtuous principles; made us capable of a moral temper, and all the happiness of a right and useful conduct.' We are placed in a

social state and endowed with social affections.[67] Benevolence, morality, and social
duties are enjoined throughout.[68] Certain of the hymns have a Wordsworthian note
– 'His praise, ye brooks, attune, ye trembling rills' – but are occasionally reminiscent of one of Charles Wesley's unhappier efforts.[69] There is a version of the Twenty-
third Psalm, while 'O God, our help in ages past' survives almost unscathed.[70]
When the congregation are enjoined to 'sing to the Lord Jehovah's name',[71] one
wonders how this reference to a tribal god slipped through. Humility and submission to Providence are commended, as is a resolve to adorn our several stations by
virtuous conduct:

> 'The patient soul, the lowly mind
>   Shall have a large reward;
> Let men in sorrow lie resign'd,
>   And trust a faithful Lord.'[72]

Before examining the reaction to this combination of novelty and morality[73] both
of the worshippers and of public opinion, it is appropriate to consider one aspect of
the personal background to these events which is of crucial importance. Between his
leaving of Highgate and the opening of the Margaret Street Chapel there took place
the marriage of David Williams, his establishment of a Boarding School in Lawrence Street, Chelsea, the birth of his daughter and the consequent death of his wife.
On these events (which will concern us in more detail in Chapter Three) his autobiography is starkly brief. Wendeborn describes him as marrying 'a person without
the slightest fortune, solely for love. She soon died and her death was sufficient cause
for him to ditch his educational scheme and betake himself to Derbyshire in order to
indulge his melancholy thoughts.'[74] The fullest treatment of this aftermath occurs in
a very hostile source. The anonymous author of *Orpheus, Priest of Nature, and Prophet
of Infidelity*[75] relates how, when this sad event upset his recent escape from Saints to
Education's more alluring schemes, 'the Hero of this work, instead of submitting to
Providence, like a Christian Philosopher, fled like a heathen one' from Chelsea to
Buxton,

> '*Enthusiast like,* free as the vagrant wind,
> Leaving Saints, Sinners, Pupils, all behind.'[76]

Curiously, although the picture of David Williams 'rambling like a person insane in
the wilds of Derbyshire, where he conceived the Plan of substituting Nature for
Revelation' is given some plausibility in near-contemporary sources it nowhere
occurs in his own writings.[77] Certainly there are several awkward questions. His wife
died on 20 December 1774 and we have noticed his letter to Garrick dated 7 January
1775, so that, though Morris confirms that he left Chelsea forthwith, clearly he did
not journey northward for some weeks.[78] Moreover, he left behind not only Saints,
Sinners, and Pupils but also his new-born child Emilia.[79]

Almost certainly the author of *Orpheus* has recourse to poetic licence in attributing
to the visit any formative influence – the climactic incident located in a cavern
underground:

'So hurried on *our Man*, but not, of God.
Snatching a flambeau, thro' the outer vent,
Into the bowels of Old Nick he went,
Without a Guide: awhile he look'd around,
Then dash'd, *Entranc'd*, the flambeau on the ground.'

Alone in the darkness, Williams ponders a thousand schemes:

'What shall he do, to break the *gen'ral bar*,
And rise o'er all, *supremely singular?*'

Amidst blue lightning flashes comes the answer: the female shape of Infidelity begot on Chance by Chaos, who charges her chosen instrument to 'Trample the *Cross*, like *Hollanders*,[80] in dust', and to revive the Eleusinian Mysteries (a phrase which provides the sub-title of *Orpheus*) whose votaries are delivered from fear of death by assurance that the soul is mortal.[81]

More prosaically, what was the real impact of the Margaret Street venture? Williams himself relates how, when it was evident that the service was highly approved, those who had privately encouraged now publicly avowed their attachment, and appointed a committee and officers with formal responsibility for the undertaking.[82] Several uncommitted visitors have left perceptive assessments. Thomas Somerville, accompanying General Melville,[83] found the spirit of the prayers devout and liberal, and their sentiments pure, rational, and practical. Select passages of Scripture were acknowledged as outstanding moral compositions. But the sparse and apparently indifferent congregation suggested motives of curiosity rather than of principle or zeal. Moreover, 'I did not count above half a dozen ladies;[84] and after the conclusion of the service I noticed this' as ominous. Indeed he now (writing in *c.* 1813–14) applauds the fair sex for withholding support from an institution subversive of the Christian faith. He also records, disquietingly, that his 'prediction was fulfilled; and the immorality of this moral teacher ... soon after becoming notorious, superseded the intervention of argument, and accelerated the disgrace and dispersion of his flock'.[85]

Thomas Holcroft's critique contains remarks on the contribution of certain participants, describing Banks[86] and Solander[87] as acting with great slyness, if not hypocrisy – they peeped into the chapel now and then and got away as fast as they decently could. Martin and Bentley were more open in their conduct, but the latter disagreed with Williams, 'because Bentley urged him *to insist on the immortality of the soul* [my italics], and W–– replied that he could and would teach no other doctrines than such as agreed with the original plan'.[88] Apparently Melville attributed ultimate failure to the defection of Banks, Solander, and Bentley, but Holcroft disagrees; his own diagnosis is inferred in his description of Williams's manner as 'much too dry and cold, and his reasoning too confused either to warm the passions, or sufficiently to interest the understanding'.[89] A similar point is made by John Taylor, another literary figure and acquaintance of Williams, to whom he would not have endeared himself by his conclusion that this new form of worship, in an obscure chapel in Soho, did not become popular chiefly because he did not imitate the enthusiasm of Whitefield and the Wesleys.[90]

Plate 5. DAVID WILLIAMS, engraving by J. F. Rigaud, R.A.

An unsigned manuscript in the possession of the Royal Literary Fund describes the service on 2 June 1776. Williams, 'a tall thin Genteel man with his own hair', read his Liturgy from the pulpit and the Clerk below announced the hymns. Of fewer than fifty people present, 'who seemed by their appearance to be middling Tradesmen & others about their rank', about a dozen were women. The unknown writer was sufficiently interested to preserve a number of cuttings of published correspondence in 1777 'from a Lady to a modern Moral Reformer, in Margaret-street', with rejoinders, all pseudonymous.[91] The coolly disparaging analysis of 'Sappho' suggests to Williams 'that your present System is principally owing to a former Opposition between your Temper and your Religion', originating in an inability to reconcile a taste for pleasure with the duties of his vocation and the expectations of the Saints. An able preacher, his ability and character are not in doubt, but the wisdom of his conduct is; in avoiding one extreme he has fled to the other.[92] It is probable that all this originated in ill-usage and disappointment, 'that *Love* and *Ambition* were your natural and ruling Passions; and that you exchanged these for the Project of introducing Deism, or for the Study of Religious Philosophy, not from Inclination or Choice, but from Disappointments in your favourite Passions'.[93] Worse follows; one hears that he takes liberties with religion when in company, especially in a song of his own composition (which he ascribes to Pope or Gay) replete with witty infidelity.[94] The edge of truth to much of this criticism (oddly reminiscent of his own admissions) seems unmistakable.[95]

As to the published reactions of the literary world, one reviewer deemed the venture the most extraordinary of all such projects, dryly alluding to its generous sentiments as far exceeding the too-contracted notions of Jesus Christ, and thought it unlikely to give offence to any free-thinker in the universe – were it not for the moral injunctions on confession and contrition.[96] Another could anticipate no benefit from this assembly of paltry and unthinking infidels, but pondered darkly as to possible effects on the minds of the vulgar.[97] Yet the first notice in the *Monthly Review*, by Andrew Kippis, a leading Dissenting clergyman, despite its fear of the misapprehensions of the ignorant and bigoted, believed that every liberal mind would applaud the venture and wish it success in the advancement of morality.[98] The tone of the review of the published Lectures, in 1780, was very different. No plan of worship, however equivocal, could comprehend such hostile extremes. The project was a mere curiosity or novelty, now attracting derision by attempting by a singular act of grace to embrace even the utmost extreme of infidelity.[99]

Already, by 1779, David Williams himself observed that the expectations of some and the apprehensions of others when the design was made public had been equally unfounded and extravagant.[100] His much later retrospective analysis of the course and fate of the venture is crucially illuminating: 'I conducted the Service & read the Lectures four years; but the Oeconomy of the Managers, not having been very attentive; & ~~the Society having often divided on speculative opinions~~ [deleted but legible] – the ballance was always on the side of the expence, & the Lecturer left without the smallest Compensation – The Undertaking was therefore relinquished'. Many causes contributed to its failure: 'those who associated, at the first preparation of the Liturgy were Shaftsburyists [sic], i.e. Deists, acknowledging a Supreme

Being, having moral attributes, & holding the Immortal Spirits of Men accountable in a future State. But these persons were soon superceded, by the disciples of Helvetius, & the Admirers of the *Systeme de la Nature*. Controversies therefore took place, & introduced in new forms, the spirit of Hostility and Intolerance, which the general Nature of the Public Service, was intended to remove.'[101] Such conflict may well explain why Bentley urged Williams to stand out against a drift toward an explicitly atheist position. While the latter later regretted the absence of Franklin's assistance in preserving the Society's first principle of universal toleration,[102] in the event a major influence in the conduct of the venture was almost certainly Thomas Bentley, an associate of Josiah Wedgwood, who had been closely involved in the introduction of the 'Octagon' Liturgy in Liverpool.[103] His regret at its failure was tempered by his enthusiasm for the new church in Margaret Street, his account of the delivery of the opening sermon by Williams 'in a very animated and striking manner'[104] suggesting that he may be the one member described by Morris as present.[105] While Bentley himself nowhere lays claim to the joint-composition of the new Liturgy sometimes ascribed to him, his biographers insist upon his formative influence and point to his death in 1780 as coinciding with the dropping of continued public worship.[106]

Certainly the correspondence of Wedgwood testifies to the significance of Bentley's participation, and indeed to the continued financial support of Wedgwood himself, as well as providing interesting side-lights on the fortunes not only of the Church but also of the Club. A letter from Banks relates how 'we attend the Club with tolerable regularity; Hodgson makes punch and talks of politics, Griffiths drinks it and makes jokes, but we all look out for your assistance'.[107] Indeed, from January 1775 onwards supper was usually eaten off a special service of cream ware supplied, possibly as a gift, by Wedgwood, who also made a present of a 'few pots' to Williams himself.[108] Wedgwood's reference to an acquaintance who 'sings an excellent song, much in the manner of our friend Mr Williams' reminds us of a charge made by Sappho – whose first letter evoked a dry postscript: 'So poor Mr Wms I find is attack'd by a Lady – What will become of him now?'[109] Indeed, a mention, in the context of a description of an impressive mine-working at Matlock (near Chatsworth, a seat of the Duke of Devonshire) and of stories 'of the *Old Man*' therewith associated, to a visit by 'a Mr Williams from Chelsea who is taking a young Gentleman he has had the care of, to Warrington Academy', while puzzlingly oblique, is the nearest confirmation I have found of the dramatic scenario in *Orpheus*.[110]

Early allusions to the projected Church in Margaret Street are followed, after its establishment, by a jocular account of how a friend of Wedgwood has schemes for its furtherance, to wit: by hiring parsons to abuse it in the papers, and by advising the government to burn preacher and worshippers together *in situ* or, less drastically, 'to lay the disturbances in America, & any other Public disasters which may happen at the Door'.[111] Later, more serious allusions include reminders that Wedgwood will remain a subscriber to a proposed second course of lectures and that he is 'a *perpetual subscriber* for four seats [but wishes] to do a little more by way of *freewill offering*' whenever needed.[112] But from April 1777 on one senses a feeling of anxiety, and on

11 April 1778 Wedgwood confesses that only the receipt of a reassuring report has allayed his growing fears that the Church '*was in real danger*' and pledges himself yet again to go hand in hand with Bentley in the necessary financial support.[113, 114]

We have already noted the impact of personal and doctrinal/philosophical differences, as well as monetary anxieties, upon the fortunes of the project,[115] and cannot discount the effect of Williams's often combative personality. In November 1774 Wedgwood had expressed himself as 'very sorry for the breach in your Clubb' – a quarrel between Williams and Griffiths (editor of the *Monthly Review*) – and in December couples his regret at the death of the former's 'lovely Emily' with a hope that friendship is restored.[116] Sadly, what happened in December 1778 was far more serious. An exchange of letters between Wedgwood and Bentley deplores a slanderous attack upon the latter. The first allusion is clearly to an anonymous attack and concludes with the hope that the author 'may prove to be a man of less genius & parts than W^s [for much] is mere Billinsgate', but that of 14 December fully explains the confident identification of Williams as the slanderer by Wedgwood's editors. 'The basest ingratitude in W^s' behaviour' can only indicate so 'vile & abandon'd a character. Is this the way he takes to shew his gratitude to his benefactor, & wipe off . . . the many & repeated obligations he owes you?' A few days later, in slightly more charitable vein, Wedgwood reflects that probably 'the poor man owed more than he was able to pay – Was too proud for his situation, & has made an effort with the sponge of ingratitude to obliterate the whole at once.' Advice to Bentley to keep clear of his malicious attacker evokes a rueful allusion to 'a Man who sets no Bounds to his Malignity when it is once excited'.[117] The evidence is not utterly conclusive as to either the identity of the attacker or a complete breach in relations, for a receipt in Williams's own hand dated 31 July of the following year, for £1-11-6, acknowledges completion by Bentley and Wedgwood of their subscriptions to two sets of Lectures[118] – although indeed this may well indicate the discharge of a debt of honour rather than a personal reconciliation. Regrettably, other evidence of a contentious character,[119] impatient reaction to any pressure, and even of a penchant for the writing of unpleasant anonymous letters, is all-too-indicative.

Predictably, *Orpheus* includes a caustic portrayal of dissension among the leadership at Margaret Street and of the reactions of fashionable society. Among the visitors depicted, the Artists learn with glee that there is no after-life with its attendant perils:

> 'They smile, they nod, they grin, they bless their fate,
> The joyful news at chop-houses relate;
> *Cellars*, and *Brothels*, hear their orgies glad,
> And conscience-freed, the *Knaves* and *Fools* run mad.'[120]

Some savage side-thrusts at public figures, including Garrick, Jebb, Mansfield, and Priestley,[121] are followed by a final, slightly scurrilous account of Orpheus' last desperate turn: the Priest of Nature turns the Priest of Love, applied to for death-bed consolation by the ladies of easy virtue:

> 'No *Priest* shall meet thee here with envious jostle,
> But Thou be fix'd the *Demirep's Apostle*.'[122]

In *Orpheus* Williams meets his end in an ambuscade by envious clergy;[123] his own more prosaic analysis of the failure of Margaret Street, confirming that personal ambition as well as principle was involved,[124] concludes somewhat lamely with the comment that 'after a fruitless Effort to render the public Service unobjectionable, the Society was dissolved'.[125] But an addendum (one of many in a rather untidy manuscript) reflects his mature assessment. He contrasts the local gods of sects and nations with the *probability* (a significant qualification, repeated) 'that all the systems of Nature, are governed & preserved by a relative Principle or Law; & that governing Principle is the *Universal God*... The God, even of Newton, was probably, the regulating Principle or *Good* of the Solar System.' It has been his purpose to direct the attention of the Society to this universal good, with which the general feelings of our nature must ever be in harmony – for 'this moral Sense, the principle of Universal Virtue, seems to *precede* [my italics] all those comparisons & calcula-tions by which afterwards the preference of Goodness may be demonstrated'. But several members of the Society itself thought such principles too refined, while the events of the American War affected public attitudes and 'the National God frowned on the Votaries of Universal Good & Universal Benevolence. Prayers & Thanks-givings, were offered around us to the Gods of Armies, for Rivers of Human Blood.' In face of this Williams had neither sufficient means nor power – nor even the prospect of support from a Society extremely disposed to internal contention on speculative propositions.[126]

His occasional allusions to the risks involved should not be dismissed too lightly. Not only had he put himself, in public declarations, beyond the pale of *de facto* tolerance extended to Unitarians, but also – and perhaps more dangerously – he may well have over-extended himself financially.[127] Indeed, Morris asserts that but for the receipts from the printed *Lectures*, which enabled him to discharge the debts incurred, he would have lost his liberty. He describes Williams as returning, disillu-sioned, to his private pupils, ever his reliable revenue, but as not ignoring public events – witness his *Letter to Sir George Savile* 'in which the expediency and policy of unlimited toleration were first stated'.[128] As we shall see, the Margaret Street Society underwent transmigration rather than abrupt abandonment, but Morris's claim directs us to a major concurrent preoccupation of Williams: the interaction of Dissent, politics, and the free expression of ideas. Effectively, the very title of the Toleration Act of 1689 encapsulates the realities of the position. Dissent was tolerated, but officially Dissenters were second-class citizens. At a strictly doctrinal level the criterion of acceptance of the Trinity applied; at a civil and political level, communicant membership of the Church of England was a normal – or perhaps nominal[129] – qualification; but at the level of practical enforcement a combination of prudent acquiescence on the one hand with prudent laxity on the other had by the mid-century produced a state of equilibrium.[130] The inroads of Unitarianism brought little actual persecution, as neither completely novel nor very shocking alongside the Deism which had already proved attractive to many educated minds; Priestley's version, from the 1770s onward, but breathed new fire into an old heresy.[131] By this time the leading contenders for religious toleration were the Rational Dissenters, identified by Ursula Henriques as those most affected by the current anti-Trinitarian doctrines.[132] It is at first tempting to locate David Williams within this tradition;[133] but we must recollect first, that he did not remain even an orthodox Arian; second, that the almost virulent animus which he harboured against old Dissent at least equalled that felt towards the Methodists; and third, that he contended not for toleration, which clearly implies excused departure from some authorised norm, but rather for utter liberty for all types of religious and non-religious thought and expression.

His first, moderate, discussion in *The Philosopher* couples an acceptance of a national religious establishment with a residual basic right of private judgement. The historical association of Dissent with democratic church government, and often with republicanism, does not please him, and he concedes a sporadic rather than a necessary connection between Dissent and the emergence of human liberty. Nonetheless, repeal of the effectively abandoned penal laws seems logical.[134] Yet by 1773/4, in his *Essays on Public Worship*, a change in tone is clear. Asserting that the real principle of Dissent is that of a true philosophical liberty, but that Dissenters themselves do not know it, he castigates the unwisdom of any attempt to tamper injudiciously with the reality of present toleration by venturing into the dangerous labyrinths of politics and petitioning parliament. Better the status quo within which a perfect liberty is enjoyed than an imperfect amendment which stops short of setting the human mind completely free. For the virtues of the times are candour and moderation; our rulers connive at toleration of much that they would not legally sanction.[135]

Before sketching the events alluded to one must reiterate that Williams's picture of *decay* amidst such toleration is endorsed by modern scholars. Overall numerically, Dissent was in decline: while Independency and Baptism about held their own, Presbyterianism has been described as dying of old age, heresy and disrepute. By 1770, apparently, only about half of Presbyterian congregations remained orthodox on the Trinity. In London and Middlesex in particular, near-disintegration of older Dissent persisted until the late 1790s.[136] Meanwhile, growing tensions found expression in 1772 in petitions for the abolition of compulsory subscription to the Thirty-Nine Articles. The Dissenting effort was preceded by an Anglican attempt which developed from a celebrated meeting of liberal-minded clergy at the Feathers Tavern in July 1771. Among the 250 or so present were Jebb, Wyvill, and apparently also David Williams – who is described as true to character in disapproving of everything: the matter, the manner, the people, the time and, above all, the *Confessional*.[137] Yet Williams, who frequently (if not always) attended meetings of the Protestant Dissenting Ministers between late 1771 and the spring of 1773, although not nominated to the committee to execute its presentation,[138] is clearly recorded in the list of 'such as concurred in the application to Parliament' compiled at the end of 1772.[139] That application proposed the following substitute declaration of faith: 'I A. B. declare, as in the presence of Almighty God, that I believe that the Holy Scriptures and the Old and New Testaments contain a revelation of the Mind and Will of God, and that I receive them as the rule of my faith and practice.'[140]

Williams's whole-hearted concurrence therein is very doubtful. Certainly the emergence, presentation, and ultimate rejection of the Petition evoked a welter of polemical tracts and broadsheets. Opposition thereto from within and without the Dissenting ranks was based, first, on suspicion that what underlay the movement was a wish to attack the Trinitarian and Calvinist content of the Articles. Kippis pointed to the common knowledge of how much the *Calvinistic* Methodists 'triumph in the Articles, as being decisive in their favour',[141] and in the event their opposition to the Application was both bitter and effective.[142] But the Body of Protestant Dissenting Ministers felt obliged to refute and censure an allegation that many of their own number '*disapproved* of the late Application to Parliament ... and *did not wish it success*'. Minutes of a later meeting, recounting how, having survived the Commons with some ease, the Bill was thrown out of the Lords by the Bishops, again refer to efforts made to obstruct its progress by 'a Set of Men calling them-selves Protestant Dissenters'.[143] Edward Hitchin, signatory of a broadsheet and author of a tract against the Application, identifies the current propagation of the tenets of Pelagius and Socinus and the notions of Deism and Fatalism as at once the undeclared objectives and his own real fears.[144] But his objection that 'the Petition substitutes one human *Test* in the Room of another',[145] raises a second issue, which is crucial for the position of David Williams.

For several of the tracts, commencing with Mauduit in 1772,[146] refer to 'one dissentient Voice' who, though attending all meetings, and not to be identified with the malcontent group which launched broadsheets and pamphlets against the Application, could not accede to the Petition 'because he objects to any Declaration of Faith, as a Term of Exemption from Penal Laws'.[147] While Williams is not named (and may well have held no monopoly of this position)[148] the coincidence of such a stand with the assertion in his *Essays* that *any* such declaration or test is wrong in principle seems clearly indicative.[149] Moreover, his contention that the author of the *Confessional* would not wish to open the church to Arians or Socinians[150] may well remind us that the position of such anti-Trinitarians could easily have become dangerous if the intolerant enthusiam of the Methodists had infected the establish-ment. For unlike such as Hitchin, his fear was not that too wide a door might be opened, but that a door now fairly wide ajar might be closed.

The debate continued in the years which led to the *qualified* Relief Act of 1779.[151] The next contribution of Williams himself was his *Letter to the Body of Protestant Dissenters* in 1777, combining specific advice with a general attack. For the history of Dissent exemplifies his charge that '*You have ever done good that evil might come*', oppos-ing arbitrary princes and persecuting priests only in order to introduce a yet more unrelenting oppression through a Presbyterian tyranny. Little wonder that nineteen in twenty meeting-houses are deserted: 'For your principle being Orthodoxy and not Liberty, and neither your authority or emoluments being sufficient to restrain and corrupt your ministers into an apparent uniformity' a scene of ridiculous con-fusion must ensue.[152] Acceptance of the *Donum Regis* (a Fund for poor ministers' widows set up by Walpole, which Williams considers but a bribe which demeans its recipients) is totally indicative.[153] It is thus in no way surprising that the Dissenters' Petition of 1773 was treated with such contemptuous duplicity – for a government which sincerely favoured such legislation would sooner have seen the Bishops thrown out of the windows than the Bill out of the House of Lords.[154] It is surely time to realise that the only refuge consistent with dignity and integrity is a recognition of *'Intellectual Liberty'*, a universal toleration of the right of unrestricted private judgement, as the only rational and tenable principle of Dissent. This would set free each congregation and its minister – though indeed a general council of Dissenters in London should continue to safeguard its members' interests.[155]

As for politics, 'your politicians and patriots will ever have their labour for their pains, when they attempt to reform the English state. Dr Price, an able and learned member of your body, is thus employed to no purpose.[156] He is arguing and reasoning on the principles of truth and justice ... where princes and ministers laugh at them.' To conclude, the Dissenters' only real bond of union, comprising both civil and religious freedom, must be an assertion of total intellectual liberty, for which, together with renunciation of the *Donum Regis*, he now appeals.[157] This publication evoked very mixed reviews[158] and one quite specific rejoinder by his former fellow-student Benjamin Thomas within the year: *Political and Religious Conduct of the Dissenters Vindicated*. Thomas follows a merciless caricature of Williams's early career[159] with a distinction between genuine *'intellectual liberty'* and an *'intellectual libertine'*. He discerns the evident effects of pride soured by disappointment. The sneer at the *Donum Regis* is particularly contemptible. What can be the real motive of such unjust and indiscriminate abuse of a community of Christians? 'I saw, from the beginning, you had some scheme of private advantage in view ... You want them to erect a *sanctuary* for every strange being who takes it into his head to run a muck.'[160]

This stinging rejoinder, with its obvious allusion to Margaret Street, did not deflect Williams from a sweeping advocacy of unrestricted intellectual freedom, reaching its most extreme expression in *The Nature and Extent of Intellectual Liberty*, addressed to Sir George Savile in 1779. The alleged error on a fundamental principle alluded to in its rather pompous sub-title consists solely in Savile's balking at any declaration of total freedom in expression of opinion, for in general the author admires his conduct in the debate on a new Dissenting Bill. Williams himself has, typically, regarded it as his duty to liberty 'to throw every obstacle I could in the way of the bill'[161] – as befits one who has abandoned all sectarian distinctions and introduced a public service on universally acknowledged principles. The nub of his case is that the proposal is not a genuine petition for liberty: adoption of its purportedly moderate test may well but serve to silence all ministers who cannot subscribe thereto. Existing laws, deemed over-severe, lie dormant; but a new test, because apparently just, could bring remaining penalties into real execution. 'The present bill, if passed into a law including *any test of opinions* will relieve no man (for all the religious world is at peace or asleep) it will revive malicious informations, disputes, persecutions.'[162] Williams parts company with Savile only in insisting that it is not enough to concede freedom of thought (whose inevitability a moment's reflection will demonstrate), but that freedom of *publication* should be equally unrestrained. Any coercive action of the state in this sphere should surely be directed against the intolerance of sects. Any test of opinion as such should be anathema to 'the parliament of Great Britain, *the school of political wisdom to mankind*'. (My italics – an uncharacteristically generous assessment!)[163]

This sweeping advocacy in effect now converged with the rump of the Margaret Street venture in a project alluded to in a curious and anonymous publication of 1780: '*A Petition* written With an intention that it should be presented To the House of Lords concerning *Freedom in Religion*'. Its Preface refers to the events of 1779, to Williams's *Intellectual Liberty*, and to a proposed petition signed by all Free Enquirers with 'the glorious name of the Rev. D. Williams, that great man' at its head.[164] But more immediately, a page of verbatim extracts sets forth the principles of the 'Constitutions of *The Philosophical Society*' lately established. The choice of name appropriate to a society open to all mankind has engendered debate – for whilst superstition has prejudiced opinion against philosophical denominations, philosophy itself may not employ the terms of superstition. 'Deist', though sometimes used of this Society, is 'too empty and sect-like for a moral philosopher, besides Atheists and Materialists of all denominations ... Naturalist, as being analogous to free-thinker or free-enquirer, who, in his pursuits embraces every object in nature, and not favouring of any sect, though never used in this sense before, was pitched upon; until the society agreed to take the appellation of *The Philosophical Society*.'[165]

Despite the fulsome personal eulogies therein, it is difficult not to discern the mind if not the hand of Williams himself in this unusual publication.[166] Fortunately, the 'Constitutions' are independently extant, undated and unsigned, but published as from 7 Meard Street, Soho, which seems conclusive as to authorship. An apologia for Margaret Street precedes a proposal, effectively, for its re-establishment upon a yet more liberal basis. Indeed Williams now protests that it was with a view of uniting all friends of free enquiry, and not of establishing any purported set of truths, that the chapel was opened. But, some members retaining a disposition to opinionated intolerance contracted in their religious education, it was with difficulty preserved from becoming a *philosophical* sect, as injurious as any religious one to real knowledge. The presently proposed regulations therefore formally eschew dogmatic or proselytising intentions, admitting all who would promote Intellectual Liberty. Their objective shall be '*To Shew The Utility Of Unlimited Enquiry, And Of The Decent Avowal Of All Opinions Relating To Moral Philosophy*'. Any difficulty in identifying this as an accurate statement of what had indeed been instituted in 1776 is met by Article V: 'Resolved, by the particular Requisition of the said David Williams – That the Form of Public Worship drawn up by him, the Lectures he has delivered or may deliver, however agreeable as Compositions, shall have no Authority in the Society; and may be discontinued, if any other Means of promoting its general Views' be preferred. Other rules deal with membership – including the somewhat illiberal condition that six black balls in balloting exclude new applicants. One is left with the impression of the hoisting of a yet larger ensign over a vessel long becalmed.[167]

This must surely be the '*retired* Society' depicted in *Orpheus*, withdrawn, defeated by the Methodists, from Margaret Street.[168] The more prosaic but equally uncomplimentary account of the *Annual Biography* explains how, the subscriptions and the number of auditors having become quite inadequate for anything more than a common sized room, Williams was at length persuaded to move to one. At the suggestion of General Melville the congregation, now dwindled to twelve or fourteen, adjourned to an apartment in the British Coffee-House, Charing Cross, for a considerable period. 'The wits of that day were accustomed to remark that the dinner, accompanied by excellent Madeira, and no small share both of good humour and hospitality given by the above-named patron of the institution, in Brewer-street, after the lecture, operated as no small inducement to attendance.'[169] Ironically, but not altogether inappropriately, in regard both to numbers and to ambience, the venture had come full circle. Sadly, one cannot quite leave it there, on a convivial note. A letter of Williams to Melville, on 24 February 1786, confirms the duration of this phase, suggests yet another change of name, but also indicates a breakdown in personal relationships. Opening with the truly remarkable claim that 'it is with great reluctance I ever enter on Controversy', it charges Melville with reneging on the quite explicit terms of agreement for re-imbursement of Williams as 'Lecturer to the Liberal Society'. Williams is not prepared 'to degrade myself in my own Estimation, & that of the Public by reading Lectures, at a lower Price than a Dramatic Candle-Snuffer would recite fragments of Plays; and to submit that miserable Pittance to your Disposal, or that of a Committee'. He disdains an 'offer of *Contribution*', requiring only payment in return for value given; those who think this inappropriate are not welcome at his lectures.[170] This uncongenial missive may remind us that the protracted venture as lecturer in moral and religious philosophy was not solely an adventure in ideas, but involved an element of financial risk.

It may not now be inapposite, with the long-drawn-out demise of this his most ambitious project, to essay a tentative assessment of this aspect of a colourful career.[171] It is not easy to decide whether the evidence should be related primarily to a personal career or to the emergence of a distinctive (if limited) philosophy. In regard to the first, some have pointed to the main-springs of ambition (if only frustrated), vanity, self-publicisation, and even perversity, as furnishing an adequate explanation of his actions and writings. Yet amid all the sometimes caustic criticisms known to the present writer, that of conscious insincerity or charlatanism is seldom encountered; if any deception was involved, Williams himself was its first victim. As to the second – the evolution of a coherent philosophy – the inconsistencies and lack of precision (self-evident even to the non-specialist mind) make it clear that too much should not be claimed. Yet that there was an evolution, even if only as the reflection of experience, and that the most striking insights were often felicitously expressed, can hardly be denied him.[172] As to any element of genuine innovation in the realm of moral and religious philosophy, perusal of Stromberg's *Religious Liberalism in Eighteenth-Century England* and Robertson's *History of Freethought* will moderate any hasty claims. Ironically, Robertson indeed concludes that it is as Founder of the Literary Fund that David Williams has his best claim to remembrance; yet it may well be urged that his career exemplifies the trend of thought identified by Robertson as 'experiential rationalism'.[173]

Margaret Street itself had been at least in part anticipated in 1774 by Theophilus Lindsey's opening of a Unitarian Chapel in Essex Street, described as the first church built in England for Unitarian worship.[174] The *Critical Review* in 1776 could not resist comparing 'the respectable Mr Lindsey' with 'the speculative Mr Williams'.[175] Yet the immediate impact of the latter's venture, and the extent of the influence of the ideas which he expressed, should not too readily be underrated. In describing the opening of a 'Temple of Reason' in 1796, William Hamilton Reid pays a back-handed compliment to such influence in relating how 'the lectures there delivered were generally compiled from the writings of Voltaire, David Williams, and other authors, distinguished for their rancour or prejudices against Christianity'. Yet he also concedes, with reference to Margaret Street itself, that 'neither the gentleman, then known by the appellation of the *Priest of Nature*, and who delivered Deistical lectures in his chapel ... nor his congregation, should, by any means, be ranked with those pestiferous clubbists of late date; although it unfortunately happened that his renewal of a dangerous profession of false philosophy continued the concatenation of Infidelity nearer to the aera of the French Revolution'.[176] In 1801 David Bogue referred back to the venture as the solitary exception, to his knowledge, of a *worshipping* society of deists in England, and made comments oddly reminiscent of those of Williams himself.[177]

The very phrase 'Temple of Reason' recalls the European context within which the immediate éclat and the enduring repute of Williams's experiment may well have been greater than they were at home. His autobiography, supplemented by Bentley's 'Journal of a Visit to Paris', conveys an entertaining account of Rousseau's reception of both the visit and the Liturgy. Bentley's first arrival at the Paris garret was greeted by Madame Rousseau, who said that he saw no company; the explanation that the visitor was an Englishman, bearing books evoked the rejoinder: 'So much the worse, for he never reads Books'. But a return on the following day was met with a much more enthusiastic reaction from Rousseau himself:

'"He worships the God of the Universe, in the open Air, I hope Sir – he does not coop him in a House or a Church" –

B——— Our Climate will not admit of Assembling in the open Air.

R——— Very well – Tell W——— it is a consolation to my heart, that he has realized one of my highest Wishes – & that I am one of his most devoted Disciples.'[178]

Meanwhile, foreign visitors looked in at Margaret Street. Williams's reference to 'many of the German Literati & some Illuminees', including Bahrdt and Raspe,[179] reminds us that the European repute of the chapel was not confined to France. The reaction of Frederick the Great afforded the author of *Orpheus* a glorious opportunity for lampoon: 'Immortal Frederic' writes to Williams and dubs him Knight (the *Annual Biography* suggests confusion with the diplomat Sir Charles Hanbury Williams!),[180] but sends no money and is therefore warned, in a clever play on words:

> 'But now beware of thy *Knight-errant's* curse!
> What *bitter thoughts* spring from an empty purse!'

Voltaire and Rousseau learn of the project but are both jealous of all rival worth and of each other – 'Two *Madmen*, like two *Taylors*, ne'er agree.'

> 'Yet Orpheus' principles and fame fly wide,
> Through *Europe* borne on rumours' ceaseless tide.'[181]

David Williams himself states frankly that when his Liturgy had been printed he sent copies 'to those persons, of whom I entertained the highest opinion'.

Fortunately, although the originals seem irretrievably lost,[182] the replies received from Frederick and from Voltaire were among those printed in the *Lectures on Education* in 1789. That of Frederick, in French and addressed to 'Mr le Chevalier Williams', dated at Potsdam 10 August 1776, is brief but complimentary. It was accompanied by a letter from his private secretary, de Catt, who replied to another communication, in June 1777, at greater length – requesting copies of all further writings of this fine thinker. A letter from Teller, an eminent Berlin divine, is of particular interest, apart from applauding the establishment of a belief in one Supreme Being and in universal benevolence, first in its quite explicit enquiry as to the public reception of the form of worship attempted, and second in its enclosure of a similar specimen 'proposed by Mr. Basedow, at Dessau, in the Principality of Anhalt'. Voltaire's acknowledgement describes his perusal of the precious book received 'with the pleasure that a Rosucrucian[183] would enjoy in reading the work of an adept. It is a great comfort to me, at the age of eighty-two years, to see the tolerance openly teach'd in your country, and the God of all mankind no more pent up in a narrow tract of land ... I am with all my heart one of your followers ...'[184] But the assessment of learned periodicals in contemporary France[185] was far more sceptical. Granted the novelty of the spectacle of Deism preached publicly, with a liturgy designed for Deist worship, the conclusion is proffered that 'M. Williams est un peu singulier'! In seeking to enlighten men he will succeed but in leading them astray; for universal beneficence, the sole duty imposed upon his proselytes, will not long suffice to hold them in the paths of virtue. Sadly, few men are more dangerous than the perennial preachers of beneficence.[186]

A retrospective account by a German observer, von Archenholz, *Picture of England* (translated from the French, 1789), devotes a couple of pages to Williams's new sect. Its impact is engagingly translated as 'this hardy attempt made much noise' and its projector is credited with combining real talents with knowledge of the world. But a clear-headed analysis observes that, despite the attractive simplicity of the service, 'its sameness was not sufficiently fascinating to mankind in general' while to the Deist, doubtful of the efficacy of any form of worship, it remained too ceremonious. Thus, although the Liturgy, in itself an excellent composition, is still read with pleasure, the scheme has failed.[187] A rather later French assessment is that of the Abbé Grégoire (formerly Bishop of Blois, but sympathetic to the cause of the Revolution) who knew Williams during his sojourn in France.[188] After a sketch of the period during which affluence, admiration, and curiosity combined to excite interest in the chapel, the most pertinent part of his critique cites Williams himself on the reasons for ultimate failure of his society: 'such as the debts contracted, for which he was made responsible, although he officiated without recompense: moreover his health and preoccupations would not permit him to preside with regularity at the gatherings'. In his *Lectures on Education* Williams indeed declares that 'the operations of a disease, frequently pronounced mortal, gave the appearance of indecision or caprice to my undertakings for many years'.[189] But Grégoire believes that the real reason for failure lies deeper: as many of the sectaries of the new cult moved gradually from deism to atheism they naturally abandoned an increasingly purposeless institution. This he bases on the personal testimony of Williams himself, following which 'I hastened to remind him of Bossuet's prediction, based upon experience: the wanderings of the spirit freed to itself lead it to abandon all the principles which console humanity, and which are the basis of morality. Of this David Williams himself provides the proof.'[190]

Nonetheless, cogent testimony as to the direct and formative influence of his teachings in France, and in particular upon the cult of Theophilanthropy, is found in two major historians of the Revolution, Mathiez and Aulard – in this uncharacteristically at one! Mathiez describes the Margaret Street enterprise as having assumed the proportions of a European event. A direct link with France is suggested in his identification of La Rochefoucalt as having assisted in 'the theist society' of David Williams which professed almost the same principles as one formed in Paris. Certainly, later efforts in France to endow Deism with the form of a cult emulated the work of Williams and of Basedow. In general, 'the cult of the Supreme Being, the *culte décadaire* [my italics, see note[191]] were no more than a reconsidered and amended successor to the cult of reason. Theophilanthropy came only after several other attempted or projected deistic cults.'[192] Aulard defines Theophilanthropy itself as the natural religion which Voltaire imported from England (*not* Rousseau's 'still mystical christianity'). After Voltaire's popularising of the concept it was once more taken up by the English, notably by David Williams. His project had indeed no more than the temporary success of a curiosity; 'but it was celebrated in France, it perhaps inspired in part the sectaries of Reason and of the Supreme Being, in 1793 and 1794, and it, or something like it, was taken up once more under the Directory, by the theophilanthropists'.[193]

John Walker's translation, in 1797, of the *Manual of the Theophilanthropes, or Adorers of God, and Friends of Men* adopted by their societies established in Paris, contains many precepts reminiscent of the teachings of David Williams at Margaret Street.[194] Thus 'the Theophilanthropes believe in the existence of God, and the immortality of the soul. The spectacle of the universe attests the existence of the First Being', defined also as the Supreme Being and as Father of Nature. They also 'are convinced that there is too great a distance between God and the creature, that it should attempt to comprehend him ... Their morality is founded on one single precept. *Worship God, cherish your kind, render yourselves useful to the country*', but is expanded into a long and familiar list of social and moral injunctions.[195] Most significantly, the far-from-sympathetic contemporary, David Bogue, concedes that 'that portion of the French deists who call themselves Theophilanthropists appears a very superior class of men to both the old French and English deists'.[196]

Modern British historians have pointed to the strong resemblances between the object, form, and even content of the Margaret Street services and, successively, Hébert's worship of Reason, the adoration of the Supreme Being, and finally Theophilanthropy.[197] Also, in a different direction, they have identified the influence of Williams upon Iolo Morganwg as one factor in the emergence of the Gorsedd.[198] Certainly the number and duration of the French contacts of Williams, as well as the considerable popularity and publicity achieved by his works, makes some line of descent of ideas very probable,[199] while insofar as the Gorsedd link is substantive then it is not completely true that in this sphere as in that of political philosophy the prophet has received more honour abroad than at home. As always, in any investigation of the history of ideas, in the absence of avowed acknowledgement or direct quotation it is difficult to decide between their attribution either to a specific source or to some generally held contemporary body of opinion. Quite certainly, more detailed enquiry lies outside the scope of the present work. Yet equally surely, the evidence in contemporary sources[200] both of some element of genuine innovation – if only in practice as distinct from theory – and also of a recognition of real, acknowledged, and extensive influence, is sufficient to suggest the justice of granting David Williams a higher estimate than he is sometimes accorded by historians of ideas.

Chapter Three

'A Practicable Education'

THE qualification, by the author of *Orpheus*, of his abhorrence of the record of David Williams 'as a daring and mischievous Innovator' by a handsome tribute to his integrity as a teacher of youth[1] is not without irony. For it is precisely as an innovator – in objectives, method, and curriculum – that Williams is esteemed by modern educationists. Although he published but two works devoted to education – his *Treatise* in 1774 and the much longer *Lectures* in 1789 – his activities as teacher and tutor became and remained a major source of income. It is difficult to apportion the elements of push and of pull in the metamorphosis from dissenting minister to schoolmaster.[2] The account in his autobiography is infuriatingly brief: 'I then took a House at Chelsea & was married, with a view to a Plan of Education which I had long considered; & in which I should have greatly succeeded, if I had not suddenly, lost my Wife, & had not been left to the depredation of Servants.'[3] Fortunately, the addendum to his *Treatise on Education*, entitled 'History of Philo and Amelia', contains a full and transparently autobiographical apologia. A frank review of his own character – independent, pleasure-loving, impatient of patronage and unfit for intrigue, not over-industrious or financially prudent – leads to a specific rebuttal of the charge of libertinism which his admitted sensibility to female charms had unjustly provoked. He had been some-time acquainted with his Amelia, who had been warned against him; but matters came to a head with the implications of the move to Chelsea. (Indeed, less romantically, the *Annual Biography* identifies the imperative need of a female to preside over his new household as at least a partial determinant of his marriage.)[4] Of his partner we know only that she shared both his tastes and his lack of any fortune; but with her support 'he took up the scheme with spirit, and pursued it with honor and success'.[5]

That scheme's location, Lawrence Street, Chelsea, resembles the Soho which Williams now left in that enough remains today to suggest the ambience of 1773. Just off Cheyne Walk, a stone's throw from the river, its choice as the site of a select educational establishment seems perceptive.[6] Numbers 23 and 24 are particularly impressive in what appears to be their near-original condition. The school established, apparently in the house at one time occupied by Catharine Macaulay, the radical historian, was impressively successful. For once, business acumen accompanied a taste for innovation and experiment. Fees which reached £100 per annum for each boy restricted the intake to children of opulent parents, yet the impact of the school was such that it was soon filled; for perhaps the only time in his life Williams contemplated a prosperous future. No copy of its prospectus has come to light, but no fewer than three contemporary sources attribute to Comenius a particular influence on the approach adopted.[7] In his *Treatise on Education*, enterprisingly published in conjunction with the venture, Williams himself refers specifically to the ideas of Milton, Locke, Rousseau and Helvetius.[8] Questions of pedagogic content will concern us later; more immediately, the happiness of 'Philo and Amelia' in this new, successful milieu was soon shattered. The unmistakably personal declaration that it was 'almost two years before Amelia gave him hopes of being a father. The joy he expressed was excessive; for he had almost despaired of it', is made poignant by his reader's knowledge of what was to come.[9]

For the birth of his daughter was swiftly followed by the death of her mother, the abandonment of Chelsea, and the undated and far from satisfactorily explained visit to Derbyshire. A record in his own hand of 'Events relating to my dear little Emily' relates how 'Emelia daughter of David Williams & Mary Emel[ia] his wife, was born in Laurence Street Chelsea on Friday the 9th of December 1774 about ten [in] the evening – On the 20th she lost a most [ten]der & affectionate mother'. It would seem, from Wedgwood's allusion in a letter to Bentley to Williams's loss of 'his lovely Emily' that it was by this name that his wife was known. On 28 December the baby went to a Nurse (a Mrs Mackuller) at Highgate. Then comes the entry: 'Feb 12 Baptized by Revd Mr James Thomas at Mr Rigaud,[10] of 8 Dean Steet Soho by the name of Emelia, & registered at the Church of St. Anne's Soho on the 21st of March; Mr Thomas having neglected to do it on the day she was baptized.'[11] This belated entry in the Register for St Anne's confusingly puts the date of birth at 20 December.[12] Meanwhile, the Burial Records of St Luke's, Chelsea, include that of 'Mary Amelia Williams' on 22 December.[13] These scanty records raise obvious problems for the story of an abrupt departure and lengthy sojourn in Derbyshire – although indeed a doctor's bill acknowledges receipt as late as 22 May 1775 of 'the sum of seventeen Shillings & six Pence, for Medicines for the late Mrs Williams, in full of every demand'.[14] For was David Williams not present at the baptism of his child? A meticulously listed record in his hand, of sums paid to the nurse at, on average, six-weekly intervals, ends on 6 December, 1775.[15] No further record of Emelia has been found; her fate remains one of several enigmas in the life of Williams. No further record; but not, perhaps, no further allusion: in his *Lectures on Education* he quotes in full a speech from *King John*:

> 'Grief, fills the room up, of my absent child;
> Lies in his bed; walks up and down with me;
> Puts on his pretty looks; repeats his words;
> Remembers me of all his gracious parts;
> Stuffs out, his vacant garments, with his form;
> Thus, have I reason to be fond of grief.'[16]

There would seem to be little doubt that it was the double impact – emotional and practical – of his wife's death which ended the short lived but very successful school at Chelsea, despite the puzzling (and isolated) inference in a letter of Wedgwood as early as August, 1774, expressing no surprise that 'our Friend Mr. Williams's School does not answer his wishes'.[17]

Certainly his interest in educational activities persisted, and with the gradual falling-away of the Margaret Street enterprise the individual tuition of adults seems to have been a major source of income. In 1789 he was to define such instruction as having been 'applied to the assistance of mature age, or of persons approaching maturity, but of defective education'.[18] A surviving example of the type of tuition involved is an exercise in translation of a letter from 'Count Algarotti to Abate Franchini Envoy of the Grand Duke of Tuscany of Paris' which is fairly spattered with corrections in Williams's hand.[19] Several allusions support the contention that such tuition was frequently to improve 'qualifications for the senate, diplomacy, and the learned professions'.[20] In addition to individual instruction, Williams concerned himself with a 'Society for Promoting Reasonable and Humane Improvements in the Discipline and Instruction of Youth' and with formal courses of lectures on political principles. After leaving Chelsea he lived in Park Street, Grosvenor Square, then at 7 Meard Street, Soho, before moving in 1786 to 28 Great Russell Street, Bloomsbury. It seems probable that it was at this last address that his lectures attained their greatest éclat – he himself writes of the need to seek a larger room – although his friend Brissot alludes to their popularity as necessitating a larger venue as early as 1784.[21]

While the *Lectures on Political Principles* were almost certainly delivered to a relatively specialized group, his *Lectures on Education* (also published in 1789) were addressed to the educational 'Society' rather than to students. The three-volume edition was accorded a very mixed reception by contemporary reviews. The lectures are indeed rambling and repetitious, comparison with the *Treatise* exemplifying the case of an early sketch being fresher and more effective than a later development. Yet, taken together, these books set forth the principles of the approach to education of David Williams – an approach which bespoke the practitioner as well as the theorist. Indeed, the mixed reviews of the *Treatise* in 1774 (which had nonetheless descried, amidst inflated claims, a healthy tendency to inculcate respect for Nature)[22] had evoked a correspondent's defence of Williams as having had 'desperate cases from the universities, and the greatest schools in the kingdom under his care ... and been the means of restoring several young gentlemen to the favour of their disgusted friends'.[23] As for the *Lectures*, while the *Critical Review* was almost unrelievedly scathing, the contributor to the *Monthly*, who had spent fifteen years on the staff of Warrington's Dissenting Academy, found the sketch of contemporary education, though overstated, grounded on reality. Yet he also confessed himself unable to form a clear picture of the day-to-day practicalities of Williams's scheme; his assessment is that of the professional and the strictures are accurate.[24]

A pointer to Williams's own approach emerges from his critique of contemporary education, whose 'superstition, mere mechanic order, and poor unwholesome diet, check the vigor of the body and mind; or break the spirit into a disposition to be ever insincere, hypocritical, and servile ... Learning is everything; and the use of learning – is to be learned.'[25] His own schooling under the severest maxims of established methods had inspired an early revulsion against 'the custom of learning what I did not understand, or had no use for'.[26] More surprisingly, he himself has assisted 'in the education of youth on the same plan [whose] obvious and invariable error, is to *force out purposes prematurely*' (my italics).[27] Present-day schools resemble not families but prisons, wherein all is sacrificed to silence, order, and affectation; even the best are strong on ambition but weak on morality – their inculcation of competition converted into envy producing indeed fit candidates for the present legislature, with the dispositions of prize-fighters ready to contend with acrimony on every topic considered. Little wonder that in the public estimation 'a school-master is something analogous to a viper-catcher, or any unfortunate being, whose lot it is to be conversant with venomous or incorrigible animals'. Hence the present predilection in favour of domestic education. Yet children who escape the schools are often left to the devices of nurses and servants. Nurses indeed 'have ever been sought among the lower classes of the people, because they disobey nature the least', but nothing good can be said for consigning children to servants, who promptly take dreadful revenge on the minds in their care. For 'servants are at this time, a distinct class, cherishing a tacit spirit of opposition or enmity; as all the subjects of arbitrary governments secretly abhor their masters'. What hope for those whose habits are formed by such vicious models?[28] A near-obsession with the servant problem will recur,[29] meanwhile, what are the *positive* desiderata of a well-conducted education?

In the first chapter of his *Treatise* David Williams defines the objective: 'Education is the art of forming children into happy and useful men . . . the art of forming a man on natural principles; and yet making him capable of entering into the community, and becoming a useful and good citizen.'[30] The significance of this apprenticeship for the employments of life is such that the *Lectures* pose the question whether the art of education transcends that of government. Indeed the two are entwined in that while ignorance and vice may serve to intimidate slaves, only knowledge and virtue can govern free and enlightened subjects. Predictably, the guidelines will be found in Nature which, having first produced the child, furnishes its ideas and forms its mind by certain and effectual laws which constitute the fundamental principles of education. In particular, habits are formed by laws of Nature, and in the educational process, most significantly, 'the first, and simple principles of habit may be discerned *and influenced*' (my italics).[31]

The bases of his educational prescriptions are stated with clarity in his *Treatise*: 'I apprehend the doctrine of innate ideas to be nonsense, and that all ideas are derived from education. I think however that nature has not given all men the same capacity of intellectual and moral improvement. The mind is certainly as blank paper; and the capacities of mankind not so various as by some they are supposed to be.' But already, in terms which bespeak the exasperated teacher rather than the educational philosopher, he repudiates the contention that 'on Helvetius's principle there could be no blockhead but from the negligence of his instructors. I believe there are blockheads whom no management, no education would ever raise into men of sense.'[32] The absence of innate ideas does not infer equality of natural endowments or indeed of innate *potentialities*. A surprisingly modern-sounding passage anticipates no resolution of the problem of such inequality 'till we are able not only to raise men in artificial matrixes, as we can raise a sallad out of season; but till we can scrutinize and prepare the very seed out of which they spring, and make men altogether'.[33]

As to the moral sense, Williams rebuts Helvetius's contention that we are born indifferent to good and evil as contrary to his whole experience; for if a man is happy only when he is good, then he may be said to be good by nature. The moral faculty, like that of feeling or hearing, is inborn – although indeed developed by experience. It is true that in very early life we have no *ideas* of moral distinctions; yet there are 'certain *permanent, natural ideas*, which have ever, and ever will create a difference of good and evil. A child has no knowledge, in the science of morality, without experience. He has no knowledge, in the art of seeing, without experience. There is an actual provision in nature, for the one, as well as the other. And a man, by education, might as well be taught to see without eyes, as to be virtuous without what may be called a moral sense. The whole science of morality is, to be good, in order to be happy.'[34] The nub of what is, for David Williams, an unusually long and coherent *credo*, is that man, though born without innate ideas or moral code, possesses an innate tendency towards, and capacity for, the pursuit of what is morally good, because only thus can he be happy. Since all capacities develop with experience, one can hardly overstate the significance of the educative process – whose importance is reinforced by an apparent shift in position in the later *Lectures* when Williams declares that 'experience produces the *faculty* [my italics] of reason'.[35]

The crucial importance of educational *method* derives from his contention that the moral character evolves naturally together with the intellectual, subject to the nature and direction of the management received.[36] Whilst at pains to stress that his own prescriptions are the fruit of experience, Williams reviews those of other educationists. Oddly enough, Comenius is not mentioned in the *Treatise*, but a chapter on Milton questions his views on governmental action in education and on the order in which subjects should be introduced to children.[37] Locke is admired not only for his emphasis on the formation and the power of habits (in which he resembles Hartley), but also for his decision in favour of private education. As for Helvetius, Williams rejects his basic premise and cannot accept all his criticisms of the philosopher on whom he himself has most to say – Rousseau.[38] His own critique of Rousseau is intelligent and balanced; he was certainly no slavish imitator, and anticipated the modern view that Rousseau had no monopoly of original ideas in the actual management of children.[39] Indeed Rousseau, despite his gibes, is often merely tracing the footsteps of Locke (whom Williams finds more reliable) in seeking to establish a natural and reasoned educational process. *Émile* itself depicts a scheme derived neither from Nature nor from any real society (to be fair, Rousseau himself did not purport to have written a realistic treatise on education).[40] Though Rousseau is more truly a disciple of Nature than Helvetius, it is unfortunate that he goes to extreme, rails against all academic learning, and discounts the merits of his predecessors while adopting many of their maxims.[41]

Williams asserts that 'Rousseau's essential "meaning" might have been expressed in a few sentences. That memory and curiosity are the first faculties, susceptible of management or direction in the minds of children. That simple ideas, the materials of knowledge, are the objects of curiosity to be treasured in the memory; and converted by the mind, when it has obtained the capacity, into propositions, maxims, rules, and principles. That the order of nature is inverted, when attempts are made to impress propositions or principles by their signs, on memories susceptible only of the images of objects.' Surely the teacher should now look around for suitable material on which the memory and curiosity should be employed? But 'No' says Rousseau: 'he is wrong; the child is to seek his own amusement; and not to be employed at all.'[42] Thus a natural Education becomes a phrase without meaning.[43] Granted the real ingenuity of Rousseau and the fact that many recent improvements in the management of children and in the discipline of schools reflect his influence. Yet many of his injunctions are in reality so remote from nature as to evoke incredulity or, where too literally applied, to produce disaster. Thus Williams relates his encounter with a youth whose father had attempted to comply with Rousseau's principles: 'With the usual folly of those who seek assistance in education, I had been announced as something more dreadful than the surgeon . . . The father opened the moral consultation, with producing his son, at thirteen, as a child of nature; who had never been contradicted or taught; was nearly ignorant of the alphabet; spoke a jargon he had formed out of the several dialects of the family: and was a meer animal, on the supposed plan of Rousseau.'[44]

The omission of 'Filial Affection' is yet another indication that Rousseau's *Émile* is not founded on experience; Locke's *Essay* has more utility in regard to domestic affections.[45] On *utility* itself, Williams urges that the concept (dismissed by Rousseau) is the perhaps unconscious determinant of the earliest voluntary actions of children and remains through life a universal principle. In short, Rousseau, in rejecting contemporary errors, leaps to the other extreme and reduces the pupil to total self-dependence: the decision that Émile was to possess no watch is a typical piece of pseudo-scientific pedantry.[46] Rousseau combines excessive criticism of his predecessors with excessive *naïveté* in his own prescriptions: specifically, his concept of periodicity is crude and unrealistic, his assessment of the child's own power for self-education is too high and that of the beneficent influence of a correctly-ordered curriculum and a correctly-orientated teaching method far too low. Williams may fairly be considered not only as a pioneer in the *practice* of many progressive modern teaching methods, but also as an early example of one who derived from such experience a balanced and sceptical reservation as to any tendency to envisage an uncontrolled and undirected interaction between child and environment as producing, automatically, an endlessly successful quest for understanding.

As to other educationists, Williams pays tribute to the originality of Bacon, especially in his advocacy of a natural approach to the curriculum, and recognizes the striking similarity of approach of the contemporary Basedow's school in Germany. But the most unstinted admiration in his *Lectures* is reserved for Comenius – whose plan, in turn, derived from Bacon's precepts and influenced Basedow.[47] John Amos Comenius, a Bohemian, had come to England in 1641 and remained for almost a year. His method is quite literally symbolised in his *Orbis Pictus* or 'A World of Things obvious to the Senses drawn in Pictures' (the sub-title to the English translation, of which a twelfth edition appeared in 1777). This, one of the most popular school-books ever written, illustrated the principle that 'there is nothing in the understanding which was not before in the sense. And therefore to exercise the senses well . . . will be to lay the grounds for all wisdom.'[48] As far as possible, everything should be placed before the senses and taught through examples – the original image (or, in default, an illustration) leading in turn to active response and verbal interpretation.[49] In regard to purpose, as distinct from method, the fundamental aim of universal education was to make every human being good. There were major issues on which the views of Comenius would not prove congenial to David Williams – his belief in well regulated competition and honest rivalry as teaching incentives, and advocacy of censorship of evil books and scandalous pictures.[50] But in general, though Williams wrote as much about Rousseau as he did about all other educationists together, his contemporaries would seem to be correct in identifying his major debt to Comenius. One comment perhaps encapsulates his own assessment: 'The truths rendered practical by Comenius, and dispassionately stated by Mr. Locke, occurred to Rousseau, as oil falls on fire; and they blazed more to the terror, than the conviction of Europe.'[51]

The suggestion that the Comenian method which, with its assimilation of the processes of nature and its attention to observation, anticipates much of modern educational psychology, influenced the Dissenting Academies,[52] may indeed be extended to the line of descent of ideas on method from Bacon via Milton, Comenius, and Hartlib, to John Locke, as a whole.[53] This in turn suggests that, despite his less than complimentary references to his old College,[54] David Williams's own experiments and precepts were based upon firmly established trends. His educational inheritance from Carmarthen may not have been very different from that of Joseph Priestley (with whose ideas in this sphere he had much in common) at Warrington. Quite certainly, the student of the writings and thought of Williams will encounter many old friends in perusing the still extant 'Catalogue of Books, Presbyterian College, Carmarthen.'[55]

Williams himself professed, on the basis of work with students and pupils ranging from five to forty-five years of age, to present 'the result of experience; not only in the management and instruction of youth; but in directing the improvement, accompanying the assiduity, and correcting the errors of the middle and later years of life'.[56] His plea that, having fought through the errors of predecessors to discover the right path he is now too weary to pursue or to describe it,[57] anticipates his critics' disappointment at the absence of an orderly, coherent exposition.[58] Yet a pattern of approach is fairly clear, including: the supreme significance of a family atmosphere; the utter abhorrence of rote-learning with its associated use of competitive emulation and corporal punishment as the carrot and stick; the emphasis upon an activity- and experiment-based teaching method, closely related to children's natural aptitudes and enforced solely by a voluntary and consent-based code of discipline; the assessment of the validity and the limitations of the concept of periodicity in education, with special reference to infancy; and finally his suggested curriculum.

Everything is geared to his assessment of the natural instincts, interests, and abilities of children and of derivative implications in terms of practical and desirable teaching opportunities; above all, education is a *social* process, not the mere acquisition of knowledge. With uncharacteristic modesty he confesses his inability to produce a complete plan of education, which will indeed be one of the last and most perfect productions of the human mind. But in general, education should consist not of precepts but of exercises. Since 'the general occupation of infancy is to enquire; the business of instructors is to *direct* curiosity to *proper* objects [my italics] . . . This is the apprenticeship of wisdom.' The art of the teacher is to harness a disposition to knowledge which is as natural to the mind as is the desire for food to the body in such a way as to lead to virtue and happiness. Instruction must consist, for the mind as for the body, of actual exercises. But significantly, in Education, all generalization is suspect: 'maxims should be brought to the test of experiment; and experiments should be conducted with judgement'.[59]

Williams challenges the premature use of books and injunctions by authority to inculcate (admittedly desirable) order, quiet, and industry. Now if, 'instead of being forced, children were led into employments and pursuits adapted to their capacities; the various interests engaging them would fill up their time, and divide it into portions, having no intervals of that weary and mischievous idleness to be observed in pupils of common schools . . . Every pursuit in which we would interest young people, is susceptible of an impulse similar to that which engages the boy to drive his hoop. The Education by impulse directing the choice, must therefore be more effectual than that which violently forces the mind; and *converts it into a resisting mass.*' (My italics – again, the voice of experience!) Utility, broadly defined, is the key: the child's repeated question is 'What is this for?', and this single principle is sufficient.[60] Thus the 'present method should be inverted; and children be led from facts, to sentiments, maxims, or principles', not vice versa, lest they become as hot-house plants and wilt at the first breath of fresh air. His own pupils, therefore, were furnished with facts and encouraged to compare them before initiation in the art of reasoning on ideas or principles.[61] Williams pays specific tribute to the opinions of Hartley and of Hume 'on the mode of forming the temper, directing or animating the understanding'.[62]

His great aversion is to the use of a combination of competitive emulation and punishment to inculcate what would now be called inert ideas. How ludicrous to contemplate 'little girls lisping *Angels and Ministers of Grace defend us*, when the highest object of their knowledge and attention is a sweet-meat or a cake'; young people must be brought to the Deity by his works, not through unintelligible and useless jargon. Too often, the memory is misemployed, and the reasoning capacity never formed, by parrot-like[63] repetition of what is not understood in a fallacious effort to anticipate nature, or to force on children the principles of men.[64] Sadly, 'almost every species of learning has had the same fate with religion, and on the same account; because they have not been taught at the proper season, and have been imposed by mere authority.'[65] Ill-chosen methods entail hurtful sanctions: 'every solemn and pedantic brute may terrify feeble and helpless infancy into compulsive efforts'. True wisdom seldom punishes because it can adjust, correcting errors by removal of their causes. Corporal punishment is never necessary with children unless they have been injudiciously managed – an important qualification, for upon occasion Williams himself felt impelled to use force![66] Above all, there is a fundamental difference between the processes of reason and the discipline of mere authority; intellectual and moral regulations must coincide. 'It was a law in my little institution, that no punishment should be a motive to learning. I was therefore obliged to be attentive to the disposition and character of the pupils; and to touch, sometimes to rectify, the springs of action in their minds.' All disagreeable notions of authority were eliminated in a common quest of teacher and of pupil for instruction.[67]

The *ideal* educator is the properly qualified parent; in default of this, schools should be '*as much like well-regulated families*' as is possible – his own is frequently referred to as 'our family'.[68] Parental influence is a crucial determinant of the character of a child. If affections derive from causes which may be traced and influenced, our duty transcends obedience to impulse: 'we have the power of reflecting on the springs that actuate us; of correcting their irregularities; and sometimes *changing their nature*'. (My italics – a rather sweeping claim!) Regrettably, most parents look for their children's affection as they do for rain or sunshine. Worse, the first condition of many families is that of contest and war, in which the short-sighted expedients of weak and injudicious parents (or their substitutes) do positive harm: 'In acts of kindness, they sought their own gratification; and in compliances, consulted their own peace and quiet.'[69] One or two splendid passages depict such misguided parents. A mother of six 'has been wholly occupied by attention to brutes; while two of her depraved sons were destined for my torment'. His visit finds her deeply distressed at the indisposition of a lap-dog (at first mistaken for a muff) which has refused a morsel of chicken. Her rebuff of Williams's observation that a hundred poor people would eagerly devour it, as mere vulgar humanity, provokes revenge: 'Perhaps, said I, the dog is bitten.'[70] Uproar follows, but the subsequent death of the pet brings Williams enhanced respect and the offer of promotion to superintendence of the dogs! Such were the families, he states, from which his pupils were generally drawn.[71]

Not surprisingly, corporal punishment *was* sometimes deemed appropriate. One pupil, of a wealthy family yet still just beyond the line of idiocy, sought assurance on this issue soon after his arrival. 'I answered, it was our desire to proceed without violence; but that occasions might arise which would oblige us to depart from that rule ...' They did indeed: one parent reported his son's complaint that 'he is constantly punished at your house; and more miserable than he ever was at school', while another, after Williams's infliction of a box on the ear on one astounded youth, proposed that the affair be terminated, by himself or his son, according to the laws of honour. At one stage public knowledge that extraordinary measures were sometimes taken, combined with the rumour that Williams had sunk a dungeon beneath the house where chastisements were inflicted unobserved, yielded an ironic and unlooked-for bonus. For 'the story of the cavern brought me a great number of moral patients; and if a fatal event in my family had not intervened, I should soon have had a hospital of incurables ...'[72] But corporal punishment was unusual in what is described as 'decision of domestic differences by equal laws, enacted by general consent, and executed with general approbation', by a pupils' court – of which Williams was sometimes a member but never a judge. Yet he sometimes employed 'collateral contrivances', as when he borrowed from a nearby workhouse a lad whose dishonesty and deceit were such as to evoke from the pupil-magistrate of the week the observation that there was no hope of stemming his misdeeds without punishment. The warning that precedents thus established must apply thereafter to the gentlemen pupils produced profound silence, followed by reluctant recognition of its justice. Williams adduces the device as exemplifying his objective of rendering children the instruments of their own improvement while they appear to be correcting the faults of others.[73]

Against this family background with its collective and voluntary discipline, the emphasis in teaching method is on activity and involvement. Williams scorns the device of saving the poor child the trouble and effort of intermediate steps. As far as possible, children must learn by experiment, in which they are subject to error. Indeed, ambitiously, he 'ventured to deliver the oeconomy of the house into their hands, and they managed it some months. The first tendency of the measure was to render me poor', and despite subsequent improvement the arrangement lapsed! Again, the proximity of the capital facilitated investigation of its arts and manufactures.[74] But before tracing the implications of this principle for the curriculum, we must define his position concerning a concept so much emphasized by Rousseau: the existence in child development of identifiable and educationally significant periods.

Certainly Williams recognizes a process of development, and never tires of relating the results of neglect or of inappropriate treatment. A disposition and character formed at random by ignorance or accident in the early years is permanent. Alternatively, the common method, in endeavouring to anticipate may defeat its own end, by attempting in infancy an approach appropriate to a later stage. Yet 'Nature does not accurately define the boundaries of youth, manhood, or age, and the qualities or virtues which may distinguish are not confined to them'. His own approach was firmly based upon Comenius and Locke, rejecting Rousseau's dogmatism.[75] This latter would forbid attention to moral dispositions during infancy, whereas Williams is quite sure that once vices are suffered to shoot up and harden unchecked, like growth in the wilderness, 'it may then be too late. It has generally been too late, in the instances that have occurred to me.' Attempts at belated correction are often as harmful as the earlier neglect. Development toward virtue or vice commences with the child's reactions to the first impressions received. The parents' power and responsibility alike are crucial, when we may conjecture that the pretension of a bigot to appropriate the possession of eternal bliss while consigning opponents to hell, may be 'founded on the disposition of a child, to the exclusive enjoyment of a rattle'![76]

Yet although (or perhaps because) Williams has sometimes known a character to be completely fixed by the age of nine or ten, with that of twelve as the top-most limit, his wider educational conclusion regarding that period 'which Rouseau denominated the first, which should be conceived as the period of impressions, and from which sentiments, opinions, or principles should be excluded' is to reject the definition. For within this period which Rousseau assigns to idleness or simple ideas the children Williams has encountered had made considerable advances in the art of reasoning,[77] while the memory has acquired maxims and prejudices and various passions are emerging. To obviate such developments a child would have to be taken at birth and brought up protected from all possible influence upon its passions, habits, or principles of parents, nurses, and servants. This would require a greater invention to contrive than that of Rousseau![78]

Thus Williams rejects the dictum that 'Infancy is the sleep of reason', with Rousseau's derivative caveat against the cultivation of reasoning powers, development of the passions, or establishment of moral or religious principles therein.[79] While some customs satirised by him may well be absurd, 'yet his general conclusion may be unfounded, that infancy is the season of idle or active ignorance; and that we should wait the moment when reason unfolds, as the sun rises, at a given period. No opinion, in common life, can be more visionary, or more pernicious. Infancy is the period of information, principally from impressions; where reason receives its birth, and has all the characters of a child, when attempting the first use of its limbs. A system of education, neglecting it in these circumstances, on the supposition of a future miraculous birth, in full stature, maturity, or strength, would deviate from common error, into an extreme as unfavourable to knowledge and happiness ... The common method of confining children to formal lessons to be committed to memory, I will allow to be injurious to the understanding, as it is to health. But it does not follow, that children are to be left to their own devices, or to obtain information by accident. There is a mode of instruction, suitable to the restless activity and curiosity of infancy; as philosophy or policy may be to mature reason or inactive age. The first desire incident to children, is that of food; the second, that of an acquaintance with outward objects. The art of education, in the period under consideration, is to direct the latter, without force or violence, to a sufficient number of objects, to fill up the child's time, employ its activity, and improve its strength or constitution. No province will admit of this employment but that of natural history and philosophy', unencumbered by any barbarous jargon.[80]

In fairness, Williams might be accused of combining 'Infancy' and 'Boyhood'; yet Rousseau's general emphasis upon 'negative education' up to the age of twelve, his injunction against the inculcation of *any* habits and against all verbal instruction, and his assertion (against Locke) that 'if children appreciated reason they would not need to be educated' could not but be as uncongenial to Williams as his advice to follow nature, and to teach through experience, were appropriate.[81] To move on to what he characterizes as the equally fanciful definition of a period commencing at twelve and terminating at puberty, Williams remarks that Rousseau has, perhaps unconsciously, crammed in far too much – perhaps to make up for the years already lost! Williams, who can claim more teaching experience for these years than for those of infancy, has gone so far as to enquire of Rousseau, through an intermediary,[82] for the evidence of the claimed 'superfluous faculties, or any peculiar season of application and industry, previous to the dominion of love'. The rather peevish response, that the questioner was conversant with artificial rather than natural children, has but confirmed the belief that here, as elsewhere, lack of real experience has led Rousseau to replace one dogmatic and over-simplified approach by another.[83]

In sketching a desirable curriculum, Williams identifies the teaching of languages as the first business of a practicable education – but echoes Locke, concurs with Priestley, and anticipates modern progressives in deploring any concentration upon grammar. In general, his method 'would have been to make words the names of *things*, and not the names of *ideas*'.[84] After recommending drawing as an aid to observation, he discusses individual languages – Greek, Latin, French, and English (enriched by other tongues and now the great repository of learning). A general grasp of Mathematics is obligatory for every gentleman, as is that of the civil history, laws, and constitution of his country. Later comes oratory and the art of written composition. The teaching of science, so essential, is made more difficult by the absence of guidance in easy methods and also of many good but elementary books.[85] Finally, a long discussion of the syllabus in his *Treatise* is followed by the significant observation that pupils should receive a type of education suited to their prospects and employment,[86] that preferred for the children of 'Philo and Amelia' to be imitated only by those with appropriate talent.[87]

In his nuts-and-bolts discussion of the teaching of individual subjects, Williams finds particularly regrettable the lack of suitable teaching materials for children under the age of ten. Embarking on one particular course of instruction was a common odyssey for pupil and for teacher, for Williams 'was nearly ignorant of natural history: the first pursuit of the human mind; because it furnishes the materials of all convenience and all science'.[88] Clearly, he feels the effort was successful for a later chapter on Sciences contrasts Rousseau's emphasis on the importance of Chemistry with his ignorance of its content! This chapter contains much of interest on the teaching of Geography and of magnetism, and it is also within this context that he describes how Franklin, at that time taking refuge in the family at Chelsea, was 'particularly pleased with the early application of arithmetical dexterity, to questions of obvious or important use. All those calculations, on the power of compound interest in annihilating debts, or accumulating property, were made as amusements, which have since raised political writers into high degrees of reputation.'[89] (The allusion is impossible to miss!) Still in the sphere of science, he praises the essays on Chemistry by the Bishop of Llandaff (a tribute not without irony, for Watson had been appointed as Professor of the subject while almost totally ignorant therein!)[90] and commends the scientific emphasis of Basedow in Anhalt Dessau.[91] A chapter on the 'Utility of Books' contains the oft-cited reference to the absence of that quality from many of the effusions of the Royal Society – whose pedantry is ridiculed in a mock Questionnaire drawn up by his pupils.[92] A treatment of Jurisprudence lays claim to having rendered Blackstone's Commentaries perfectly intelligible to very early youth (in contrast with the spectacle of a British Senator dozing over Montesquieu) by relating all the concepts to the house and its environs.[93]

A chapter on Pity relates his introduction of what would now be called Economics – or perhaps Sociology. Williams alludes to his previous account (alas, untraced) of 'several fruitless trials, by my direction, to relieve apparent poverty and misery in the neighbourhood of this town. The young men were so frequently the dupes of artifice, that I became apprehensive, their minds would be rendered inaccessible to any sentiments of pity.' He therefore instituted an inquiry into the general revenue of the land and industry of the kingdom and as to the number of people among whom such revenue must be divided. 'My candid little family was astonished at the result; that, on the most favourable estimate of the income of this country, it will not furnish eight-pence a day to each of its inhabitants', while all payments 'from the king to the various orders which verge on indigent labour, are encroachments on this allotment of eight-pence; and that these encroachments, the interventions of Sundays, holidays, and sickness, generally reduce the actual income of the lowest, most numerous or laborious classes, below two-pence. How to manage this two-pence, to furnish any kind of subsistence for the day, became the subject of experiment ... until malice sent out the rumour, that I had reduced the young men to a scanty allowance for my own emolument.' The impact of such inquiries upon his pupils had barely sufficed to direct them into humanitarian paths when the closure of his school supervened, but Williams points with pride to the evidence of its enduring effect upon one of their number of terms of beneficent management of his estate. In the study of History, he enunciates the same type of general rule: 'to attach the pupil, not to professed historians, but to state papers, treaties, or the fluctuations of industry in trade, manufactures, and commerce'.[94]

David Williams does not eschew religious instruction – or perhaps more properly *enquiry* – but we have already noted his comments on meaningless rote-learning in a futile effort to inculcate piety to God.[95] The fundamental error has been that men have begun where they should have ended, in the premature infliction on young children of religious doctrines and concepts which are far beyond their grasp. Thereby is religion indelibly marked as a painful and unpleasant task, imposed by mere authority. In 'Philo and Amelia', it is only after the boy has been taught to reason and to comprehend good and evil that contemplation of His works brings him at last to the Deity.[96] Despite some deviations from the advice of his mentor, Locke, in this aspect of education, some striking similarities remain.[97] The long chapters on Religion, Devotion, and Intellectual Reformation in the *Lectures* reiterate that morality might either be 'blended with the dogmas of superstition and enjoined as a matter of faith, or separated and taught on distinct and rational principles'. As yet, Williams remains convinced that 'the impertinence of vulgar atheism, is similar to a worm contemning the system of Newton. The being of God may be incomprehensible; but it cannot be denied, because it cannot be pronounced impossible.' But as a teacher he is content 'with opening the instructions of universal history to my pupils; and tracing the pretensions of all sacred systems to their origin'. He proudly relates how, on Sunday, the children of his educational family went off to worship as on the different radii of a circle, according to their religious persuasions, returning in the evening to a common centre.[98] It is clear that, at this level, David Williams has pretensions to having been a pioneer in the teaching of comparative religion.

This indeed epitomizes his general educational philosophy, in particular his distaste for an approach which had all too often rendered the whole of education a mere exercise of memory, designed to engender passive credulity.[99] Yet experience has taught him that the way of the innovator is hard: in Education men are governed mainly by habits, and change may require wise action over very many years. Further, and most significantly, those convinced of the errors of current methods 'should check their passion for improvement or reform, by attending to *the possibility that the evils they complain of may be heightened by substituting principles for prejudices in the processes of ignorant and unskilful persons.* [My italics, this reflection of Williams's educational experience and acumen is also an interesting pointer to the ultimate evolution of his constitutional and political approach.] The progress of truth is slow; but, in the ordinary course of things, it is certain and effectual ... And if the wise and virtuous were content with accelerating, instead of being impetuous to accomplish; their efforts would seldom be lost in contentions with those they would benefit ... All revolutions in prepossessions and customs have exemplified these observations: and we are not to expect, Education should be excepted ... Projectors, who would reform general plans by introducing reasonable principles, where habits only can have effect; are indebted to inexperience and folly for their disappointment and mortification. Habits are blunt instruments, suited to unskilful hands: reasonable and philosophical principles are edged tools; and they might destroy instead of serving those who are not instructed in their uses.'[100]

In life, as in literature, it is much easier to demolish institutions than to replace them with others as useful and convenient. Thus in education the difference between Locke and Rousseau is as that between wisdom and enthusiasm. For above all, a balance is essential. It is supremely important that children should acquire industrious habits as soon as possible. Granted indeed that by employing pupils on subjects beyond their capacities we are in danger of breaking their hearts before they should be conscious of having any! But the business of education has been plagued by yet more errors since authority has been superseded by caprice, passion, and sentiment in the course of injudicious or fanciful experiments. A similar note of realism is sounded in his allusion to 'the conduct of young men, whose dissipated and inattentive habits I bestowed some pains upon, with very little effect ... They are now full-grown harpies: and those parents or friends, who would not concur in their suppression, must endure the consequences.'[101] Despite their many defects the *Lectures* often display the balanced judgement of an experienced and innovative teacher, prepared to learn from his own mistakes as well as to pontificate upon the errors and follies of others.

Since his *Lectures on Education* constitutes the last publication of Williams devoted to that subject it may not now be inappropriate to assess his standing in that field – although indeed we shall encounter lengthy treatment of one particular aspect of education at a later stage. Among contemporaries, save for an occasional disgruntled parent, that standing was uniformly high, as in general has been the estimate of history – whenever it has periodically rediscovered him. The inference is not unjustified. The Oxford *Information Gazette* for February, 1899, describes him as 'one of our English Educationalists, whose name was in his lifetime widely known even beyond this country, but which is now almost forgotten'.[102] Half a century later Nicholas Hans was to credit Williams with employing scientific methods of experiment in building up an original theory of education. More recent treatments concur as to his anticipation of many nineteenth and even twentieth century trends in regard to psychological approach, teaching methods, and the curriculum.[103]

Such recognition is well merited. Yet a cautionary note must be sounded. First, as Williams himself observed, many of his ideas and practices were not new. A reading of their works confirms his own estimate of his debt to Comenius and Locke among seventeenth-century educationists – to whom the slogan 'study things, not words' was commonplace. Above all, the need to concentrate on the relationship between individual character-traits and educational possibilities and its significance for teaching methods had been fully stated by Locke.[104] Again, his general philosophy of education, and in particular his concept of the inter-relationship between education, society, and government, is quite traditional. Given his belief in the absence of innate ideas but also in the supremely beneficial impact of correctly nurtured and directed natural forces and instincts, his concern with the social and indeed political implications of the educative process is not unexpected. But nowhere is there any advocacy of a duty of government to direct, or even to assist, the conduct of education; in this Williams concurs with Priestley rather than with Bentham. Further, government itself reflects and embodies the moral standards of the people: it may indeed be judged according to its efforts to safeguard those standards, but to look to government for the removal of moral evil is like looking to a College of Physicians to eliminate disease.[105]

Similarly, his innovative experiments in educational method were attempted against a limited and *accepted* social background. A school where an increase in numbers to about twenty necessitated the employment of several assistants and where annual fees were about £100 per pupil was only for the well-to-do. The introduction of the incorrigibly mendacious workhouse boy[106] was indicative in more ways than one. His behaviour and the moral and disciplinary deductions drawn therefrom were designed as object-lessons for the regular pupils; he was the subject, not the purpose, of the experiment. Williams prefaces his account of another such device by explaining that, in borrowing children for such purposes from such charitable institutions (significantly described as nurseries of vice supported by piety and virtue), he is careful to inflict no injury – and may perhaps mitigate suffering and check propensity to villainy. On this occasion, involving two brothers from an institution,[107] he explained 'to all the family, except the poor boys themselves, my purpose of trying on them the different effects of emulation and brotherly love'. Thus, by means of competition for plentiful, well-seasoned meals in the first stage of the exercise, the slight degree of attachment attributable to kinship was soon dissolved and the boys were brought to hate each other. Thereafter, in a switch of tactics, all incitements to emulation were dropped in favour of mutual assistance and brotherly love.[108] While in no way reprehensible by the standards of the time in which he lived (or indeed derogatory from the general educational achievements of David Williams), these instances remind us of the extent to which he remained a prisoner of his age. Equally certainly, the contrast with certain seventeenth-century appeals for an extension of education to embrace all children, rich and poor, and with several contemporaries – notably a pioneer of popular education, Morgan John Rhys, who was born but a couple of miles away from Williams's own birth-place and attended the same school[109] – can hardly be avoided. For when he wrote at any length about the education of the poorer sections of society as a subject in itself it was, as we shall see,[110] in a very different context, with much emphasis upon the harmful effects of their *over*-education.

Finally, it is worth reiterating the genuine significance of certain aspects of his educational ideas, methods, and conclusions within the context of the general evolution of his religious, social, and political philosophy: the faith in nature supported by correct educational direction; the emphasis upon the potentialities of human reason combined with natural instinct, nurtured within beneficent channels; the constant emphasis upon the moral lessons to be derived from any experiments or developments and the consequent inculcation (by example and deduction rather than by precept and authority) of a desirable moral code; and, most notably, the caveat as to the unwisdom of reckless innovation, based on unsubstantiated generalisation, and the stress on gradual, integrated, tested change as the means of progress which we shall find becoming ever stronger in the emergence of his concept of the organic nature of society.

Chapter Four

Political Thought; The First Phase

WHILE those issues considered in the last two chapters were not without political implications, it was not until 1776 that David Williams published his next avowedly political work. But the dominant theme of his writings thereafter was unmistakably political, and the development of that aspect of this thought will lie at the heart of the next four chapters. That development took place against a complex but fascinating interplay of British and overseas constitutional and political events. Already, in *The Philosopher*, he had explored the relationship between internal constitutional problems (the nature of civil and political liberties; the Crown, political parties, and the balance of the Constitution; the nature of parliamentary representation) and the impact of events in America – seen by many as leading to civil war within a transatlantic British community.[1] A mere handful of years after treaty recognition of American independence there occurred, contemporaneously, the Regency Crisis in England and the genesis in France of what was seen (according to taste) at first as an unlooked-for imitation of either the Glorious Revolution or the movement for reform of Parliament or the American example, and later as a classic case of democracy triumphant, democracy unmasked, or democracy gone wrong. The group of works published between 1776 and 1782 developed, in rather different ways, those political and constitutional ideas examined in Chapter One. While all four appeared during the War of American Independence the first two only were directly related to the issues raised thereby; the next was written as a fairly rapid response to the Gordon Riots, against the background of the Association movement; the last, *Letters on Political Liberty*, the author's first attempt at fairly methodical treatment of such problems as a whole, was wider in scope and probably his most notable book.

In 1776, coincidentally with the outbreak of American hostilities, appeared an anonymous 28-page tract: *The Morality of a Citizen; in a Visitation Sermon*. Williams's later avowal of authorship appended a new sub-title: 'an ironical Injunction to Passive Obedience',[2] – perhaps indicative not only of satirical intent but also of the fact that reviewers had been puzzled and many readers baffled![3] A study of the pamphlet reinforces this impression. For the parody is interwoven with perceptive analysis and it is not always easy to distinguish where one begins and the other ends.[4] An introductory discussion of religion and politics declares the clergy a division of government for the public benefit and identifies all dissent as a political disease which threatens our boasted constitution. For civil constitutions are not the product of reason: 'They are combinations of customs, and habits, and laws, and expedients, reduced by necessity into some kind of form: broken in upon by accidents; and restored again, and settled, in tumults and convulsions.' Thus freedom of conscience is an unexceptionable principle – so long as no one expects to act upon it! For 'a rope might as easily be made of sand, as a society formed of men whom it is impossible to unite.' No form of association is compatible with an unrestricted right of private judgement; men must either flee society or submit to it.[5] While such ideas are reminiscent of *The Philosopher* the next two pages reflect bitter personal experience, thinly disguised in a familiar third-person device. A friend, despairing of projected reform of the Church of England, found on joining the Dissenters that he was subject to the whim of every subscriber of his flock. But upon attempting to set up for himself 'he found himself involved in considerations and expedients, before he could advance one material step. Every man in his association was singular in his opinion . . .' In short, after distressing his friends and ruining his own health and fortune, he was driven to concede that, with the firmest moral principles, he could promote the public happiness by compliance with established customs with less danger to his integrity and less mental anguish 'than he could keep together, and conduct the smallest community, formed nearly on his own principles'.[6]

This obvious allusion to Margaret Street brings us halfway through the pamphlet before its author turns to his avowedly principal concern: the political situation in America. He relates how the first settlers fled this country because they disliked its constitution and could no longer submit to its laws; thereafter they were granted charters and left to formulate their own laws – provided they were not inconsistent with the fundamental laws of England. The ambiguity is already apparent, but is perhaps no greater than that inherent in the actualities of the position! Later realization of the need for a power to regulate their interests and decide their disputes led to the assumption of such power (particularly regarding commerce) by the British legislature and to its acceptance by the Americans. The assertion that this development has also been accepted by the Crown has the ingenious corollary (supporting the governmental case) that if it were established that powerful states might continue as chartered governments solely by the will of the King, then Britain itself would run the risk of becoming an absolute monarchy! Against this some standard American objections are rehearsed: that the Stamp Act is but an expedient of administration to extend royal influence through idle droves of placemen and pensioners, and that in England itself the constitution is endangered by bribery and by a standing army.[7] Yet as to the essential nature of that constitution, the writings of Montesquieu, Sidney, Locke, and Blackstone are dismissed as descriptions of what has never been. In reality, every seven years[8] takes place a pretended election in which it has been an established Whig principle, ever since the Revolution, that administration should secure a majority to facilitate its business and legislation. Yet even if it be contended that if the term monarch be taken to include the King, his ministers, and their dependents then English Government is 'as simple a monarchy as can be conceived', its peculiar distinction consists in that it rules not by fear but by influence, by an army not of soldiers but of placemen, pensioners, dependants and expectants. This, then, the note of parody now clearly heard, is the established government of our country for which the colonists so earnestly contend. Our proposals offer them indeed 'all the rights and privileges of Englishmen [as] fellow-citizens'. They may demur that the constitution has been altered – but where? In the writings of political philosophers and in their own constitutions grounded thereon which they refuse to adjust to accord with ours. This is what lies at the heart of the dispute.[9]

Meanwhile, in practical terms, it seems clear that both sides have abandoned arguments for arms. 'In that case all speculation on the general interests of a vast empire gives way to the *morality of a citizen* and the *duty of an Englishman*. The first law of nature is that of self-preservation; and that law extends to societies, as well as individuals ... The Americans pleading for their constitutions, and the rights arising from them; and the Americans in arms, are two very different objects.'[10] By now, one is no longer certain that the tongue is in the cheek. Nor are one's doubts resolved by the appearance of a favourite device of the Tudor moralist: the folly of the members of the body in revolt against the belly, who 'perceived not, till too late, that it was owing to the belly, that they had power to starve him, or spirit to rebel against his authority'.[11] Well may one sympathize with the puzzled contemporary reviews. Yet, arguably, the very ambivalence of tone is in itself an accurate reflection of the dilemma of liberal-minded Britons. While sympathetic to the Americans' case, and critical of the high-handed blunders of British administration, they wished neither to see the ruin of the first by aggressive overstatement and a needless appeal to violence, nor to witness the second made the occasion of the disruption of what was still potentially the greatest vehicle of political freedom: the British commonwealth.[12]

The ideal to which this should conform, the element of patriotism which is ever-present in David Williams, and the urgent appeal for political reform, are all combined in the slightly longer pamphlet of 1778: *Unanimity in all parts of the British Commonwealth*.[13] While deploring alike English unwisdom and American intemperance, he launches a scathing attack upon the systematic deceit and perfidy of France, whose entry into the war presumably occasioned the pamphlet's publication. His quarrel is not with the French nation but with its government, whose record of treatment accorded to its colonies will bear no comparison with that of the British. Indeed, the spectacle of American recourse to France 'is like a child threatened by its parent, and flying for protection to a *crocodile*'.[14] Significantly, 'whatever were the rights of the Americans by nature',[15] by all contemporary European standards they are subjects of Britain, while nothing could be more bizarre than their attempted liaison with France – distinguished by an oppressive nobility, the intrigues of licentious women and abandoned priests, and the absence of all civil and religious liberty. Even if the first fruit of this alliance should be a total independence from Britain 'the states of America would disunite; for hardly any plan of union which can be imagined for them will long hold together *nations* [my italics] so totally dissimilar as those of Massachusetts-Bay and Pennsylvania, or those of New-York and Carolina'.[16] The prognosis should not be dismissed too readily, especially in the light of the later assertion by John Quincy Adams that, when it came, the Constitution of the United States 'was extorted from the grinding necessity of a reluctant people'.

Urging that every hostile step on either side has been taken with great reluctance,

Williams believes Britain to be guilty of unsuccessful brinkmanship. Had the end been foreseen the attempt to subdue America by force would never have been begun, nor would the colonists have conducted themselves in the same manner. Our despatch of mercenary German troops is especially deplorable.[17] In short, the present melancholy position derives not from permanent principles but from passions and their consequences; for subjugation is not in the British nor separation in the American interest.[18] His case for conciliation is bolstered by an interesting and perceptive interpretation of what he terms the moral constitution (or character and disposition) of the British nation, in which plain sense and humanity are more important than speculative legislation, so that potentially cruel laws lie dormant. (This coincides with the opinion of his contemporary De Lolme,[19] and also with some modern analysis of the at-first-sight draconian criminal law of Hanoverian England.[20]) Just as an English government is now effectively incapable of exercising its legal power to victimize religious heterodoxy, so even an America totally subdued would not long have to suffer arbitrary regulations. The French threat might yet serve to resolve a ruinous quarrel if only administration would combine realism with imaginative generosity. The British commonwealth still consists of branches of one family, and it is imperative that its two great divisions reunite, for 'the welfare of millions for many ages depends on it; – and it can never offer itself again'.[21] A thought-provoking prophecy indeed!

Such views exemplify the verdict not only that the main line of English radicalism during the age of the American Revolution derived from the Commonwealth tradition but also that its representatives continued to hope for reconciliation long after an impartial observer would have deemed the quest useless.[22] Equally typical was Williams's wishful thinking in regard to public opinion; his later retrospective commendation of the English people's abhorrence of governmental efforts to abase the Americans beneath the level of British subjects[23] was utterly self-deluding. His friend Franklin had remarked on English assumption of *sovereignty* over America. Chatham might have urged that the colonists were the sons not the bastards of England, but in proposing his Conciliation Bill used the filial metaphor to insist that 'this is the mother country, they are the children; they must obey, and we prescribe'.[24] Certainly within the Commons itself the majorities in support of governmental measures, by eighteenth-century standards, were very large.[25] Indeed, nowhere in the pamphlets just considered does Williams himself condone armed rebellion. Yet his approach is of particular interest not only as exemplifying pro-American sympathies in what one might term a political nation *manqué* (feeling deeply concerned involvement, but bereft of power), but also in that the outbreak of hostilities presented the radicals with a dilemma by posing a choice between the constituents of their usually combined appeal to radicalism and to patriotism.[26] *Unanimity in . . . the British Commonwealth* sought to resolve that dilemma with the aid of a providential *deus ex machina*: France.[27] Surely those who had felt impelled to take up arms against their mother-country in defence of those very liberties which had been nurtured within her bosom could not now make common cause with a state whose whole political ethos was a negation of those values? In the event, continued American acceptance of French help was to pose nice problems of conduct for radical sympathizers. There is clear evidence of correspondence between members of the Club of Thirteen, including Williams, and Franklin during the war. As late as March 1780, a member, William Hodgson, still 'believes that American and English liberty must stand or fall together'.[28] Williams himself, in February 1783, was to congratulate Franklin on his part in 'an Event of such astonishing magnitude, as the Emancipation of your Country',[29] though he later insisted that his friend had sincerely wished to prevent armed conflict.[30]

Before leaving *Unanimity* (which was well received in contemporary reviews)[31] it may briefly be related to the context of the long-term impact of the American debate on such basic issues as natural rights, fundamental law, and sovereignty. It has been argued that much of the concern expressed was in reality about the condition of England,[32] and even that the Americans 'acted as an ideological midwife, bringing into the political world a qualitatively different sort of reform' by changing the parameters of debate about electoral changes.[33] Yet it may equally well be urged that participants in the debate – and those on the *progressive* side – looked back to the lessons of the *seventeenth* century rather than forward to the evolution of parliamentary democracy.[34] The common Anglo-American appeal to a tradition of opposition to arbitrary government, inherited from Stuart times, was becoming the basis of divergent interpretations – in England, a drift toward a theory of parliamentary sovereignty; in America, an enduring belief in the concept of limited government. But as yet many Englishmen would support Lord Camden's repudiation of parliamentary sovereignty and enunciation of a right of 'resistance to tyranny; whether it be tyranny assumed by a monarch, or power arbitrarily unjust, attempted by a legislature'.[35]

The almost inevitable effect of the tensions created by internal colonial constitutional arrangements (rightly described as analogous with mid-Stuart rather than with Hanoverian England) in the context of deteriorating relations with the mother-country, was to deepen suspicion of executive government itself – especially when in collusion with an elective body allegedly prepared to set aside natural rights. Little wonder at the American attempt to crystallize the concept of fundamental law as a permanent guarantee of political liberty, within a formal and written Constitution which restricted the power of both legislature and executive.[36] It is totally symbolic that it was Harrington's influence which underlay John Adams's draft of the Massachusetts Constitution in its inclusion of the separation of legislative, executive, and judicial powers so that 'it might be a government of laws and not of men'.[37] Thus, if indeed the 'Honest Whigs' were the true ideological kinsmen of American revolutionaries,[38] it was as the custodians of an old rather than as purveyors of a new concept of liberty. Without opening the Pandora's box of debate as to whether or not, within the colonies themselves, the American Revolution was 'double-barrelled', it may be suggested that on the British side of the Atlantic as yet any appeal to the people was far more often addressed to a presumed trustee of last resort of individual rights than to a putative partner in governance. The views of David Williams were firmly grounded upon this Commonwealth tradition, and we shall find throughout their later development that his grasp of the inevitable problems in maintaining solid guarantees of individual liberties against all arbitrary power (executive or legislative) whilst extending the active participation of the people (however defined) in the political process, was almost certainly more perceptive than that of any contemporary.

He next published in response to an event which touched on several favourite preoccupations: freedom of worship; abhorrence of mob rule; protection of individual, including property, rights; and implementation of civic consciousness. Early in 1780 John Wilkes, at a meeting of 4,000 inhabitants of Westminster 'to agree on a Petition to Parliament, to control the shameful Waste of the publick Money, &c ...', expressed his Happiness at that Spirit of Association, which, at this Period, pervades the Kingdom'.[39] But the Gordon Riots, in June, afforded a splendid example of Association gone wrong. David Williams's *Plan of Association on Constitutional Principles*, 'for the parishes, tithings, hundreds, and counties of Great Britain; by which the outrages of mobs, and the necessity of a Military Government will be prevented, and the English Constitution in a great measure restored', seized the opportunity. After preliminary strictures on an administration which has lost a vast empire just after its acquisition, he concedes humanitarian motives in its support of some measure of leniency to Roman Catholics – for wisdom must tolerate error.[40] A well timed word of judicious explanation would have allayed the anxieties of over-sensitive Protestants, for the anti-Catholic outrages in Edinburgh in 1779 had served notice of what fanaticism might breed.[41]

The absence of such precautions opened a door through which Lord George Gordon – of impetuous temper, of understanding rather wild than weak, tinctured with religious enthusiasm via the breasts of a presbyterian nurse – perceived his road to glory. Contact with Scottish Presbyterians and English Methodists of the same intolerant complexion[42] has led him to the Presidency of the Protestant Association and to the device of a petition to Parliament, where the derision evoked by his uncouth and extravagant manner produced a vindictive wish for revenge. Indeed, Williams has no doubt of 'the intention the people should break into the Houses of Parliament, and either compel them into some humiliating and ridiculous action, or drive the members out'. His account of events, commencing with a gathering of 20–30,000 in St George's Fields incited to intimidate all opposition, is largely eye-witness, although the mob prevented his access to the Commons gallery to witness the celebrated and effective threat to run their leader through.[43] Thereafter the 'Associated Mob' destroyed Catholic chapels and houses before returning on June 6 to the Houses of Parliament where they would probably have killed many members but for the intervention of the soldiery. Receiving minimal opposition they ventured to dabble in State affairs and sent a deputation for the release of all those in the Fleet and King's Bench prisons. 'It was not perceived they had blended *politics* with their principles of religious cruelty and depredation, until they had destroyed Lord Mansfield's house, and declared in the public streets, their intention of paying off the National Debt, and being revenged on the Dutch by totally destroying the Bank of England.'[44]

Ultimately, despite a cautious and reluctant start, the casualties inflicted by the military, especially at the Bank, dispersed the rioters. But every man had now seen that 'in a country which boasts of its civil Constitution; where personal liberty and security are said to be provided for in a better manner than in any other part of the world, that the first links and ties of the Constitution were broken; that every family was almost detached and unsupported; and that the slightest combination of villainy, might lay waste a neighbourhood, a town, or a district; or *might over-throw the state* [my italics], unless prevented by a power, whose protection must be purchased at a price to which nothing on earth is an equivalent ... Timid wretches, called Englishmen ... bless providence for the *quiet* and safety they experience under military regulations, as sheep bleat their satisfaction in the inclosures of butchers, where they may escape the depredations of wolves.'[45] Thus emerges, with some element of hyperbole, the twin-spectre of the moderate reformer; mob-rule on the one hand, and arbitrary power backed by a standing army on the other. These then are the 'Discoveries' alluded to on the pamphlet's title-page. While probably not what the average reader expected, Williams sees them as crucial for constitutional development: for his concern is not with the alleged involvement of French or American agents in any plan to destroy London (which would have needed naval and military help), but with the riots' implications for governance. They have most cruelly exposed something soon noticed by any visitor to England, the total absence of police.[46]

Letter II of the pamphlet now presents the author's own Plan of Association, his familiar plea for constructive reform on first principles rather than on speculative plans now acquiring an extra dimension by appeal to an historical base. For despite the damage inflicted by the Norman Conquest, the bloody contests of Lancaster and York, Tudor tyranny and Stuart folly, all but partly repaired by the Revolution, there still exists in name and form, and in every English heart, the essential parts of a structure first created by the genius of Alfred. This involved division into counties, hundreds, and tithings within which 'ten families were associated, their names entered, their occupations defined: the males in them from eighteen to fifty, or sixty years of age ... to obey the summons of the decennary or tithingman, on the least apprehension of danger', appropriately armed. Mutual knowledge, concern, and obligation thus subdued all violations of peace and order or corrected them at their source. Most significantly, 'all the decennaries or tithingmen were *chosen by the people* once a-year, and this is an *essential* circumstance in the institution'.[47] A pyramidal system of representation and consultation, with ten tithingmen per hundred and so on upward, answerable to the earl of the county, ensured the security and freedom of the people.[48]

Restoration of such a system would not set the people against the government nor interfere with royal prerogatives. Significantly, 'this is the *moment of time* in which these institutions may be restored'. Indeed, there is evidence that the people, apprehensive both of their danger and of the undesirable consequences of relying on troops for their protection, are endeavouring to combine in several parts of the metropolis. They are right to reject a military police, but, embarrassed by the shoals and quicksands of the law, seem totally at a loss as to how to construct the necessary Associations. The implied need for guidance is important: for it is within this context that we find a rare piece of evidence of any readiness of David Williams to involve himself in political action, as distinct from speculation. An undated draft among his papers, in his own hand, is addressed to 'the Author of a Pamphlet entitled a Plan of Association on constitutional Principles'. It takes 'the liberty of requesting, that you will adapt your Plan to the Parish of St Anne Westminster, & permit us to lay your Letter before the Inhabitants at the Vestry on Monday next. We are ———' The gaps in the computation of the present state of the parish in terms of Houses, Magistrates, Constables, Beadles, Watchmen, etc., remained unfilled and the document, alas, unsigned.[49]

The third and last Letter refutes the charges of illegality and of impracticability levelled at any idea of armed Associations, and rejects the contention that the army is a necessary part of our Civil Constitution.[50] In a lengthy discussion of constitutional background and public attitudes he scorns the pretence that such proposed Associations will produce riots and commotions instead of preventing them. Williams accepts the comment of Cardinal de Retz, that all numerous assemblies are mobs, adding his own opinion that all mobs are mischievous. But his proposed Associations are designed 'to prevent large and tumultuous assemblies, and to destroy all ideas of *appeals to them*'. These crucial statements are soon taken further in an exposition of fundamental and enduring import in the development of his political philosophy: 'A whole nation, like the human body, in order to act with harmony and pleasure, must be divided into small parts, each having its local power, subject to the direction and controul of the general will.'[51] This sentence, evocative at once both of the organic analogy of society so popular with the mid-Tudor Commonwealth idealists[52] and of a concept closely identified with Rousseau, touches the heart of the problem of political organization within a free society – a problem to which David Williams was always to return and to which, in the end, he despaired of providing a definitive solution.

Meanwhile, he believes that the system envisaged would have pre-empted or at least controlled that tumultuous assembly called the Protestant Association, which was in truth unconstitutional, without recourse to the military. Armies indeed as such have been tolerated only by means of annual bills and under repeated pretences. Williams is at pains to counter any attempt to portray the military power as a necessary and beneficent custodian by his own most unflattering sketch of what was still the standing bogey of political liberty.[53] He goes so far as to urge that nothing can properly constitute a soldier – 'bought from the refuse of our gaols, unprincipled, ignorant, and savage; impelled to do any thing by the command of his leader; and subject to death on disobeying it' – a citizen of England.[54] The present fear is that troops may be used, during General Elections, to disperse those peaceable and orderly assemblies who are in several counties petitioning Parliament for redress of the most oppressive grievances. Hence his seemingly ambiguous conclusion that 'the interposition of the army in the late outrages, was an *act of prerogative, unconstitutional* and *illegal*, though perfectly seasonable and beneficial'. Hovering between Scylla and Charybdis, with the threat of descent into anarchy weighed against submission to arbitrary power, we must beware lest an increase in numbers should produce a military police for the nation.[55] Providentially, recent events have at least shattered our complacency and indolence and pointed to the paramount need 'of resuming the parts of *men* and *citizens*; of associating for reciprocal defence'.[56]

Certainly the imprint made by the Gordon Riots upon the political nation (particularly in London) was deep and indelible. Horace Walpole recorded threats to members of Parliament, peers 'torn out of their chariots', and one escape by a bishop across the leads of the House. The Duchess of Devonshire (to whom Williams was to dedicate one of his volumes on Education and whose reaction typified that of the milieu in which, increasingly, he was to move) described herself as 'very much frightened'.[57] Sir Nathaniel Wraxall was to contrast the resolution shown by George III himself in the ultimate use of the troops with the behaviour of Louis XVI on 10 August 1792, and to suggest that similarly bold action by the soldiery would have suppressed the French Revolution at birth.[58] As to David Williams himself, recollection of these scenes must surely have coloured his reaction to those witnessed from the galleries of the Convention late in 1792. It has indeed been contended that the fear engendered by the Gordon Riots never quite disappeared, that it cast its shadow over Wyvill's very different Association movement, and that it is from 1780 rather than a decade later that a ground-swell in English opinion back toward conservatism should be dated.[59] Of the several tracts[60] evoked by the riots that by (the later Sir) William Jones is of special interest. For *An Inquiry into the Legal Mode of Suppressing Riots with a Constitutional Plan of Future Defence* is strikingly similar in its views on military intervention, historical precedents, and the formation of self-armed county-based companies entirely as part of the *civil* state. Ironically, the second edition in 1782 alludes to an unknown person who has also written on the topic and warned against standing armies.[61] The biography of Williams by Thomas Morris, a decade later, regrets the disappointing impact of the *Plan of Association*, for its 'ideas were so new, and so remote from the common prejudices concerning parliaments, and parliamentary laws, that it obtained little attention but as an ingenious speculation; while a technical pamphlet by Mr now Sir William Jones, on the *Legality* of Associations, was much extolled'. Indeed Williams still 'frequently laments the loss of this moment; for if the householders had taken the police into their own hands, every necessary *reformation of government* would have ensued'. Despite this lingering might-have-been in its author's mind, contemporary reviews confirm the lukewarm reception accorded to the pamphlet itself.[62]

Very different in public impact was the publication, less than two years later, in March 1782, again anonymously, of what was probably his most important work: *Letters on Political Liberty*, 'Addressed to A Member of the English House of Commons, On his being chosen into the committee of an associating county'. James Martin of Tewkesbury, their recipient, had taken some interest in Margaret Street, evinced an apparently genuine concern for parliamentary reform, and expressed to Williams some doubts as to the procedure and prospects of County Associations and City Remonstrances.[63] While in fact reiterating many ideas already expressed, this is the most sweeping and methodical as well as most daring exposition of Williams's political beliefs. Wishing to see politics assume the status of a science,[64] he counsels philosophers to leave the barren labyrinths of metaphysics to investigate its principles. Granted that government as an *art* may best be understood by its practitioners, yet the comprehension and synthesis of its underlying principles is an arduous *science*, worthy of the greatest intellects. Without wishing to incur an imputation of vanity by seeming to place himself within their ranks, he can perhaps throw new light on the subject and help secure recognition of its importance – for over many years he has envisaged no political problem which he could not solve. The often made distinction between theory and practice 'has ever been the expedient of knaves and blockheads. If in geometry, all clear and accurate demonstrations are reducible to practice, why not in politics?' Because unlike the science of geometry that of politics is not understood by its practitioners, legislators and magistrates alike[65] – a dismissive contempt which was shared by many contemporaries.[66] Ideally, to perfect the Constitution, a body of men of the profoundest and coolest speculation should be denominated 'guardians of the state, without having the slightest interest in its official departments'.[67] Whether or not this was the role for which he yearned, Williams saw himself as a pioneer in this task. For if in all the sciences men are still young, in that of politics they are but newly born. Precursors receive short shrift: Englishmen have learnt their political creeds from romances converted into political breviaries, such as 'Blackstone's Introduction copied from Montesquieu; and De Lolme's Constitution of England copied from both'.[68]

His own excursions into constitutional history seek for the emergence and definition of civil and political liberties rather than for any purportedly ideal form of government. Despite his admiration of Saxon representative methods, political liberty was not then accompanied by civil liberty or equality, while from the Norman Conquest to the Revolution the contest was between a would-be despotic monarchy and a powerful aristocracy – with the House of Commons, then as now, a pawn between them. The Glorious Revolution itself, while brought about by popular support, was led by those who were as disinclined to any constitutional exercise of democratic power as the adherents of the ruler they expelled. This then is its real meaning: a compact between an aristocracy which virtually controls the House of Commons, and the Crown, to establish a constitution with an apparent, but not real, tendency to political liberty. Thereafter, the pitiful efforts of a venal court and intriguing aristocracy have but built a house on sand, in formulating a supposedly free constitution without its essential foundation of political liberty. For the House of Commons is not 'what it pretends to be, a delegated power from the People ... and the History of England, from the revolution to this day, will exhibit a history of contending factions for the government and direction of the king, in the exercise of an enormous and mischievous power; while the great, industrious, and valuable part of the people is destitute of proper means of relief, because it is destitute of political liberty.'[69]

This scathing critique was not novel. Catharine Macaulay had seen the Revolution as enabling cabals to share the plunder of a credulous people.[70] Obadiah Hulme did not hesitate to date the *decline* of our constitution from that event, identifying as the great father of corruption Sir Robert Walpole in his creation of 'a power that might become ten-thousand times more dangerous to the elective rights of the people, than the crown could ever possibly be', with such rights tethered 'like a dog to a manger ... suffered to go abroad, Once in Seven Years, for an airing'.[71] Bishop Watson had envisaged erosion of the great fabric of civil liberty by venal representation and political prostitution.[72] All this stands in marked contrast with De Lolme's panegyric which designated 1689 as introducing the third grand era of the English Constitution.[73] David Williams was in no doubt that constitutional progress was incomplete. 'The Saxons enjoyed political liberty, by reserving the supreme power in the people: but they held labor, industry, and the arts, in a state of slavery; and the administration of justice was at the pleasure of individuals. The community therefore was destitute of civil liberty. At the Revolution in 1688, provisions and arrangements were made, which introduced a high degree of civil, while they have almost totally suppressed political liberty.' Sadly, we have preferred the lesser to the greater blessing, so that the English Constitution 'now presents to the world, one of the most aukward and unmanageable fabrics which has ever been produced by human folly'.[74]

Clearly, his definition of civil and of political liberty now becomes a crucially important yardstick for specific criticisms and proposals of reform. 'Civil Liberty is the result of laws or regulations, which define the boundaries of men's actions as citizens of the same community, and leave them free within those boundaries. Political Liberty has a reference merely to the grand divisions of the state; the popular, the executive, and the legislative [a new and interesting constitutional trinity]; and consists in *their freedom from the incroachments of each other* [my italics]. Thus a community has no political liberty, whose executive power influences or commands the legislature; or where the people have no regular or practicable method of checking and controuling all the branches of government, when they transgress their proper boundaries. A society therefore may enjoy civil liberty; i.e. all interference of individuals with each other may be regulated by laws; while no method may be ascertained to regulate the interference of the several branches of government, or the encroachments of any or all of them on the happiness of the whole people.'[75]

His definition of political liberty is so closely entwined with an evident belief in the separation and balance of powers that a word on this crucial issue can hardly be avoided. The significance of the concepts (sometimes almost inextricably intermingled) of the separation of powers, mixed government, a balanced constitution, and fundamental law, in mid-eighteenth-century thought has long been emphasised.[76] But of special interest in some recent treatments is the tendency to look back beyond De Lolme and Montesquieu to Bolingbroke – notwithstanding varying estimates of the clarity of his position.[77] Particularly relevant is his insistence that it is the existence of division of power and distinct privileges which constitutes a limited monarchy. Thus if any one of the three constituent elements of government usurps unlawful power, the others may combine to correct it – the safety of the whole depending on the balance of the parts. The mutual control which ensues is in a sense a constitutional dependency; but this is only truly *mutual* so long as each part remains essentially independent and does not become subordinate to another.[78] Bolingbroke's trinity of King/Executive, Judicature/Lords, and Commons, was not that of David Williams; but the stress on balance and the suspicion of all untrammelled power typify the tradition within which the latter was to find himself. (Indeed, if we append the mutual hatred of corruption, suspicion of politicians, and the ultimately derivative appeal to a patriot king, we might venture the paradox that the radical Williams looked back to Bolingbroke as much as forward to the Chartists.) Certainly he shared the bluntly cynical view recently enunciated by Hulme: 'There is no chief magistrate, no political body of men ... but what will (if you once make them powerful, and fix them above your own control) most certainly degenerate into tyrants, and make you slaves.'[79]

To look ahead, given his obdurate belief in individual rights, suspicion of power *per se*, and belief in a separation and balance of powers and/or functions as an essential guarantee of freedom, then the problem for David Williams, as the ultimate sovereignty of the people (however defined) replaces the *spurious* balance advanced as an untenable justification for the present ostensibly mixed constitution, will be to devise a balance within and between the institutions and functions of government (rather than an attempted balance between classes) which will obviate all fear of tyranny – even from an elected body itself. Meanwhile, dismissing the inadequacy of previous attempts at definition of civil and political liberty,[80] his own analysis reiterates an instructive order of priorities. The power reserved by the people (its political liberty) to insist on the limitations of all offices and to resist all 'oppressive encroachments of government, is of much superior importance to the private security arising from the administration of justice to individuals' – which indeed may not long subsist without the former.[81]

His further exposition of this theme presents a fascinating amalgam of the old and the new: the corporeal analogy is combined with the principle of a balanced constitution including a residual power inherent in the people as an active and if need be corrective factor.[82] Thus, 'all bodies, whether natural or political, have a principle of self-preservation resulting from their formation; from the union and harmony of their parts; and without which they cease to exist. The offices of all the members are distinct; and they cannot encroach on each other ... The legislative power deliberates and ordains; the executive puts the laws in force *for the whole body*; which [must] provide against the erroneous and mischievous exertions of its own members. *Power, without a resisting and balancing power, is like a muscle without a balancing muscle, called the antagonist* [my italics][83] ... A legislature and magistracy, without an actual power in the people to preserve their political and civil liberty, are absurdities; or they are masques for the features of despotism.'[84] The present mischiefs of English government are attributable to a fallacious independence (and effective irresponsibility) of several parts, whereas ideally, as in the human body 'so in a political state the deliberative and executive parts are free and independent in their particular exertions, while annexed to the general body; and tied to it, by such ligaments as render them subservient to its collective force'. Above all, every constitution with any pretension to the preservation of liberty must hold fast to one fundamental truth, the two faces of which are of equal significance: 'All delegated powers have assumed the tone of tyranny, when the people could not readily and easily balance them: and the people become capricious, violent, and despotic, where they could assemble in multitudes; and annihilate the authority of their deputies.'[85]

Williams's resolution of the implied dilemma will form the climactic consideration of his book. Meanwhile the abuse of delegated power and the fraudulence of existing representative institutions are major targets in Letter IV which reviews administration under George III. This traces the impact of a doctrine at first insinuated and then established 'that the king can do no wrong; and is not in any respect accountable: that the responsibility should be in the king's advisers, who might be his visir or prime minister, his cabinet council, his favorite, or his mistress'. This device indeed pre-empts all fear of any recurrence of the fate of Charles I – but does so by subjecting the Crown not to a genuinely constitutional limitation but to a species of perpetual tutelage under the hereditary guardianship of those families who had brought the House of Hanover to the throne. To consolidate the position it was so contrived that any impact of parliamentary deliberation should be negated by providing a settled majority in favour of the administration and by casting an odium on all opposition to its measures.[86] George III had not been long enthroned before his favourite, Bute (lacking the talents of Pitt), was driven out by public pressure – but not before a new pattern had been firmly set: 'to emancipate the throne from a state of tutelage; to apply the produce of finance, which seemed inexhaustible, to establish a decided majority in Parliament for the Crown; and to make a king his own minister, who had been solemnly declared incapable of wrong, and accountable to no power on earth'.[87] Thus could it bechance that a delegated executive power could impel one major part of the empire to oppress the other and thereby desolate the whole, in declaring the American colonists the *subjects* of a nation which had forgotten its own political liberty and lost control of its own government. This partial but increasingly popular interpretation of events is followed by the question-begging assertion that 'the great body of the people of this country abhorred the attempt at reducing the Americans beneath the rank of British subjects'. Had it succeeded then such as were 'amused with the promises of being lords of America, would have seen the chains which had bound down their fellow-subjects, rivetted on themselves, and despotism . . . would have enthroned itself in horrid majesty on the ruins of the commonwealth'.[88]

The change in tone from his earlier *Unanimity in . . . the British Commonwealth*, 1778, and the almost unqualified adoption of the argument that the Americans have been fighting the cause of British liberty, are quite striking. Yet he next subjects the conduct of the opposition to an equally scathing analysis. Put bluntly, the Whigs' exasperation and anger derive from being hoist with their own petard. Government has long been the object of contending factions; it is indeed possessed by a faction; but whenever it may be regained by the Whigs, by means of parliamentary influence, it will still be held by a faction – responsive not to the people but to a handful of powerful leaders.[89] Indeed the very recent majority for a Commons motion condemning the measures which had caused the war exemplifies 'the principle that success and disappointment are the tests of right and wrong'.[90] Accordingly, Williams foresees no salvation in any administration formed by the leaders of the late opposition. For the expedients of patronage and family influence are as fatal to liberty as the influence of the Crown. Further, if the Whigs who effected the Revolution of 1688 had not thereafter been suffered to arrogate unconstitutional powers then the late administration could not have provoked an absurd and cruel civil war.[91] Nor is he deceived by the present Whig flirtation with demands for reform. Repeated disappointment and accumulated insult have turned their leaders' eyes to the people, ignored for a thousand years but now perceived to be the basis of all legitimate political authority. But the people have long become an inert and unwieldy body, and know not how to conduct themselves in face of a parliament which has colluded with executive power to extinguish every spark of real political freedom.[92]

Thus, regretfully, he must speak against contemporary plans for Associations as hastily and crudely formed, as exciting false hopes in the people while often calculated to serve sectional interests. Called on a county basis by the sheriff or a nobleman, such associations are quite inadequate. Nothing less than a nation-wide plan for consultation 'can give rise to the constitutional and permanent power of the people to prevent and correct *the perpetual disposition of the executive and legislative powers to oppress them*' (my italics).[93] The associations, which constitute not a thousandth part of the nation, are also in error in their acceptance of opinions imposed from above rather than arising spontaneously from the people.[94] Regarded by administration with contempt, and by the country with a mixture of hope and pity, characterized by indecision and timidity, frightened by the horrid spectre of the outcome of the Protestant Association, they will crumble silently into oblivion.[95] Perhaps not all commentators would endorse this ultra-pessimistic analysis – yet in 1780 William Jones had expressed regret that the well intended efforts of the petitioning and associated counties were not over well directed, excess of zeal causing departures from the original plan.[96] In October of that year Walpole had attributed a falling away of Associations first to 'the panic on the riots', and second to the fact that 'the greater number of those who had joined . . . had only concurred for fear of their elections, of which they were now secure'.[97] David Williams concedes that the intervention of the City of London, which possesses real power, is a different matter. Yet attempts at alliance have but revealed a fundamental discord: 'The Association petitioned for one thing; the City of London for another – the party of one great lord objected to all such petitions and measures which would remedy the whole of our diseases at one time . . . In short, this region of the political world became a chaos of discordant views.'[98] Modern research has confirmed the perceptive accuracy of this critique.[99]

Yet none of this is to derogate from the case for reform and for an immediate need to correct a situation in which 'the people, or rather the populace (for there is a material distinction between them) became of consequence in their clamours and tumults' – which foreign theorists wrongly ascribe to certain inherent defects in all free government. What has happened is that a people who saw themselves shut out from all real influence in a Constitution which amused them with the forms of freedom have conceived a hatred of government which in turn is erroneously deemed essential to a spirit of liberty.[100] Letter VI, 'The Method of introducing, establishing, or recovering a State of Political Liberty' bears at its head the quotation that 'revolutions which are formed by liberty are only confirmations of that liberty', while the next, 'Plan of an equal Representation of the People of England' is described as not in the author's first design but drawn up in haste in response to Martin's request and goes much further in its proposals.[101] Their contents may conveniently be related to two major issues: the objectives and qualitative nature of political liberty, defined to include participation by the people in the political process; and the operation and mechanism of such participation, notably (but not solely) through a representative system.

Williams contends that it is a sense of political exclusion deriving from the perfidy of its pretended representatives and the ambitions of the Crown, which gives the English people an air of perpetual discontent, impatience of authority, and insolence toward their superiors. For no species of despotism is more resented than that of a free Constitution half formed, whose very abuses assume the authority of establishments. Yet how may one counter the common belief that although smaller states may enjoy political liberty its introduction in populous nations by direct action of the people will but incur perpetual anarchy? His own most revealing explanation is that 'if a multitude were collected at random, and every man of it were moderate and wise as a Newton;[102] the whole would act with folly and violence: because the lowest and most violent passions only can be instantly diffused, and made effectually to agitate large assemblies'. Now just as an animal derives vitality from its orderly composition rather than determinate size, so a body of people is capable of sensibility and judgement depending on correct arrangement. A small number, permitting the free and intimate exchange of thoughts, is capable of rational decision; a larger obeys only the impulse of strong and common emotions. Williams never tires of pointing the difference between his ideal of political liberty deriving from the participation of the people as individuals, and the threat from 'the populace; the dregs of vicious governments, who usually assemble in mobs'.[103]

Yet, crucially important, 'any number of men may be arranged, so as to form a general judgment or will: without forcing them out of their situations and employments; or producing any of those tumults and dangers which attend the assemblies even of the smallest democracies'.[104] Granted the definition of free political organization as the art of governing all by all,[105] the difficulty has been to arrange large nations into regular bodies which might, for this purpose, act without disorder. The solution is found by a daring and surprising combination of the corporeal analogy with that of the army – the significant characteristics being those of sub-division, communication and discipline. For the divisions of the army are connected by ranks of officers, who thus form the nerves, arteries, and ligaments of this artificial body. Indeed, if 'the organs of military sensibility and judgement, were inverted, the army would exhibit the model of a people in a state to assert and to enjoy the highest degree of political liberty: . . . a people in a state to form judgments; to have a will; to delegate legislative and executive powers, which would be free and uncontrouled, within certain limits'. A great merit of Saxon arrangements, probably made for policing purposes, had been to give the people as a whole a universal and instantaneous sensibility.[106'] The existing advantages of the creatures of the Crown consist in arrangement and discipline; our purpose is to give similar advantages to the people.[107] The arrangements proposed will also ensure that 'the degrading and levelling principles of common democracies could not be introduced; the utmost variety of characters and distinctions would take place: and yet all orders would be impressed by a political necessity of obeying and executing the public will'. Adoption of the scheme which he had advocated after the Gordon Riots would have introduced that universal sensibility which is the sure foundation of political liberty.[108]

Williams rebuts the charge that so much power in the people would be subject to abuse, but is careful to explain that he does not advocate the exercise of legislative or executive powers by large assemblies (as in some ancient democracies) but merely that such powers, clearly defined and delegated, should operate without abuse within their limits. If discipline and scientific principles may be bestowed upon a rabble in order to form it into an army, then surely they may serve to organize a people in the exercise of that political power on which their civil liberty depends! In Letter VI he still insists that his purpose 'is not to specify the necessary regulations for an adequate representation in parliament: but to give the whole community a security against that breach of trust, and that collusion with the executive power by which *parliaments* have often reduced the whole nation to the utmost distress. All powers, in a free country, should be checked and limited by the power of the people regularly and fairly obtained.'[109] He is equally careful to explain that the precise boundaries of those powers lie outside his present design; he is laying, or rather restoring the foundations – all the necessary structures may easily be erected.[110]

Rebutting any charge of innovation (of which the Crown itself is guilty in the introduction of a standing army), Williams returns to an earlier preoccupation: if the people 'were to arm themselves slightly, they would also have a police on the best footing; and be perfectly secured against the collusions of thieves and thief-takers, watchmen, constables, church-wardens, overseers, trading justices, and the whole train of expensive appendages to the science of robbery'. This compendious but not too inaccurate indictment is reinforced by an allusion to June, 1780, when the violence of desperadoes exposed the feeble basis of our governance and demonstrated the imperative need for self-reliance. A disposition to associate almost universally prevailed but was not welcomed by administration which discouraged all local efforts. Yet it is still within the competence of any public-spirited man 'who can induce a single parish to institute and regulate its own police, on the principles already pointed out'. Once begun, we may project a snowball effect, with healthily draconian social implications, such as 'clearing that parish of vagrants, beggars, and all those useless and pernicious wretches who daily heighten the enormity of poor rates. These, passing into other parishes, would put them under a kind of necessity of having recourse to the same measures. And when the people were arranged for one purpose, they would be, *for all the purposes of political liberty.*' Hopefully, 'there is no part of the kingdom where this plan of police might be introduced so easily, as in Westminster' – where its effects would be far more beneficial than those of haranguing an idle and profligate populace.[111]

Discussion of the nature of the representative process includes important, sometimes novel, proposals. Existing divisions are unequal, not so much in respect of geographical extent as in regard to electors. Real significance in the community derives not merely from the possession of land but rather from the productive application of talent and industry; men, not possessions, should be the constituents. Within the equal electoral divisions thus implied participants should include 'free-holders, tenants, householders, or lodgers, who live on their fortune, industry, or talents'. Based upon the tything system, election of representatives by representatives may proceed in pyramidal fashion until every million of the inhabitants or citizens is represented by one, so that the 'business of the universal representation would be done in London by two persons; who would on all occasions accurately ascertain the general *inclination* and *judgement* of the nation'. Skipping the awkward questions of practicability involved in what sounds like a device for plebiscite or referendum via personal (if indirect) consultation, some further conditions are crucial in their implication: all representatives are to have their expenses liberally defrayed by their constituents; to obviate any attempts at corruption by the Crown, elections shall be annual; and 'all the deputies should be *representatives*: whose election should be void, if they departed in the slightest degree from the judgement of their constituents. For the design of this arrangement being to attain the sense of a whole people, whatever it be, and not the opinions of their deputies; the slightest latitude should not be given to representatives.' This advocacy of closely mandated delegation is followed by the proviso that the minority must acquiesce in enforcement of the public inclination.[112]

Letter VII, which probably marks the farthest reach of the radical tide in the political thought of David Williams, goes on to deride the ludicrous idea of *virtual* representation (especially of overseas possessions), together with an M.P.'s assumption of independence once elected. A House of Commons which was a genuine delegation from the people would not be able to vote itself independent and continue its sessions at pleasure, in collusion with other branches of government – an expedient which renders the English Parliament one of the most absurd institutions in the world.[113] Williams declares his immediate object to be 'not a representation for the purposes of legislature; but to form a political power in the whole body of the people, to balance; to give stability and effect to the legislative and executive powers; and to answer all the purposes of defensive and internal police'. Yet he also outlines certain changes in the *parliamentary* system, starting with equal electoral districts and a radical definition of the electorate which goes further than anything yet proposed. 'All men, at the age of eighteen, who are not vagabonds or in the hands of justice, have a right to vote; because they contribute by their industry to the support of the state. I have had doubts concerning menial servants; on account [of] their dependence on their masters: but the injustice of excluding them, would bring greater inconveniences, than the trouble of preventing the ill effects of that dependance.'[114] His suppression of his doubts is surprising not only in the light of his earlier (and later) comments on servants[115] but also in that this is an innovation in *radical* tradition. The suffrage envisaged by such representatives of that tradition as the Levellers, Rainsborough, and Harrington in the previous century, or Burgh and William Jones among contemporaries, excluded servants and paupers.[116]

To obviate all clamour and tumult in the electoral process, the system of tithings and hundreds must be used, with all expenses of representation paid for by constituents and with the significant addition of election by ballot, until the member for each district is chosen. 'The very essence of the plan is, that the judgement of the people be expressed by the delegate; and that the parliament be a *representation*, in the strict and most severe sense of the word ... because there is no general principle of government which can be substituted for the *judgment* and *will* of the people.' Strict delegation and accountability will eliminate any fear of corruption or of self-authorized long parliaments. As to procedures within Parliament itself, not surprisingly, 'the deliberative business should always originate in small committees. I should wish them not to consist of more than ten or twelve persons; because in all my life, I have not known a larger assembly, capable of forming wise and good determinations.' But the deliberations of such committees should be made public – and not only to the House, on the principle that the press must be perfectly free.[117] The revealing concession that wherever reform extinguishes a property right then the proprietors, of even the most infamous boroughs, must receive full compensation,[118] is justified by suggesting that the sum involved is probably less than that at present wasted in diffusing perjury and immorality at every election. But despite his regard for the near-sacred rights of property the author's fears that his plan 'simple and practicable as it is, will be ranked among those speculative visions which are stored for better and more enlightened times',[119] were indeed justified.

Nonetheless, while the element of novelty must not be overstressed, it is probably through this work (whose expanded second edition contained an impassioned address 'to the People' tracing their exploitation through the ages by political impostors and charlatans)[120] that David Williams made his greatest impact upon serious political thought. Certainly, any attribution of originality in this field must be made with considerable caution: for his biographer concedes that even Cartwright satisfied this criterion solely in his advocacy of unalloyed universal manhood suffrage,[121] while in spite of his criticism of the Association movement there is a fair amount of overlap between Williams's proposals and those which had been drawn up by a committee of Westminster electors, Fox presiding, in 1780.[122] It is also true that, despite presentation of a copy of *Letters on Political Liberty* to the Society for Constitutional Information by its newly elected President, James Martin, in April 1782, that body never gave it the endorsement of printing and distribution accorded to so many other selections.[123] (It is perhaps further testimony that he was a constitutional 'non-joiner' that the list of members numbering Cartwright, Day, Hollis, Jebb, Price, and Sharp does not include David Williams – perhaps because membership fees were high.) The *Critical Review* was unimpressed by its constitutional analysis and appalled by its alleged appeal to popular prejudice.[124] But the enthusiastic reception accorded by the *Monthly Review* (whose contributor, Alexander Jardine, as an artillery officer was understandably delighted with the analogy between Williams's proposals and the army!) is far more typical of the public impact. Not recognizing the author, Jardine believed him destined 'to go beyond most of his contemporaries as a theorist' but also (in partial prophecy) to be among the unsuccessful benefactors of mankind whose visionary and impracticable ideas might win the reverence of the future.[125] The pamphlet evoked one direct rebuttal, again from Manasseh Dawes, which roundly declared that 'a government of all by all is imaginary'.[126]

The book's extensive circulation and very considerable éclat, in England and in France, were certainly major factors in its author's invitation to Paris, a decade later, to assist in revision of the French Constitution. The review, in the *Journal*

Encyclopédique ou Universel in November, 1782, of the *English* edition, welcomed the pamphlet's exposure of the self-deception of those who still admired an English Constitution vitiated by corruption, where political liberty had been lost and civil liberties were at risk. Forecasting brilliant success for an author new to the political field, who writes with wit and elegance, it claims that his fellow-countrymen are already comparing Williams with Montesquieu. Yet, perceptively, despite recognizing his originality, the review regrets the failure of the author to develop his ideas sufficiently.[127] Williams himself suggests that 'the year 1782 should be distinguished in History, as having in England given birth & organization to the spirit of Jacobinism, which afterwards displayed itself, in the French Revolution'. This at first puzzling allusion is explained by his sketch of the way in which the Whigs, determined to recover their power, advertised and organized meetings of their partisans, denominated county associations, and then 'affiliated the whole to a maternal Society at the Thatched House in the Metropolis, which had all the Character & Disposition of the original Jacobin Club'. He then depicts the reaction to this ingeniously interpreted scenario of Brissot – having first observed that, despite the calumnies with which both Burke in England and Robespierre in France were to load his memory, 'there has never existed, a Man of greater Integrity than Brissot; but he had neither Genius nor Knowledge, for the Post destined for him in the Revolution of France: to prepare him for which I was in some degree an instrument'. This not overmodest assertion is explained in that, although at first greatly impressed by the Whig proceedings, 'on seeing a Pamphlet which I published *against them* [my italics], Brissot's opinions fluctuated as usual; he translated the Pamphlet, in conjunction with a Marquis de P who had quitted France for some offences against the Queen; & who annexed Notes repeating those Offences – I know not, whether the Translation was printed here or at Boulogne; where Brissot had connections with a Printing Office; both the Translators, however, were taken up at Boulogne, & conveyed to the Bastille.'[128]

Much of this is confirmed by Brissot himself in his *Journal du Licée de Londres*, his memoirs, and his correspondence – but with one puzzling omission. Brissot lived in London (in Newman Street, off Oxford Street) between 1782 and 1784, attempting to establish an international literary society (with the *Journal* as its periodical). Always short of money, he even considered an offer of Williams to share premises for meetings. To Williams himself his writings accord a glowing tribute for his efforts in philosophy, religion, and education, but above all in politics – where he is rated superior to both De Lolme and Priestley.[129] Impressed by his beneficent approach to politics and morality as sister-sciences, Brissot was to own himself surprised that Williams had since published two very successful satires – the 'Voyage to Cheltenham'[130] and the as-yet undiscovered 'Dream of the Prince of Wales'. Significantly, he considers English savants as unlikely to concur in his eulogy of Williams: 'It seemed to me that they did not rate him highly, some because he took no notice of the charlatanism of literary and philosophical societies, others because they thought him an infidel. Williams belonged to no sect and gloried in the fact.'[131] He has of late devoted all his time 'to perfecting political science, in which he instructed pupils who would one day remove the blots with which the English constitution is tarnished. He conducted a course closely studied by all the members of the Constitutional Society, and even by the most enlightened members of parliament', attendance at which has forced him to seek a larger venue.[132] Alas, his hope that Williams would one day publish a major study of the British Constitution was not to be fulfilled.[133]

Yet amidst all this we find at best oblique confirmation of Brissot's translation of *Letters on Political Liberty* and of its responsibility for his subsequent arrest. A letter from Newman Street to Williams towards the end of 1783, using the third-person device of which its recipient was so fond, states that Brissot now 'hears that the translator is preparing a new edition'.[134] The *first* edition of *Lettres sur la Liberté Politique*, of which there is now a copy in the Bibliothèque Nationale, is dated as from Liège in 1783. His *Journal* for February of the following year contains an extensive treatment of Williams, including a full digest and perceptive discussion of his ideas on civil and political liberty which was later to be quoted verbatim by Jérôme Pétion in a publication of 1789,[135] the year in which, perhaps significantly, the *second* edition of *Lettres sur la Liberté Politique* appeared.[136] Yet despite the full citation of the *Letters*, including a translated extract from the address 'Au Peuple' which as Brissot points out did not appear until its second edition, there is no mention of his involvement in publishing the translation.[137] Brissot's *Mémoires* ascribe his subsequent misfortune to the charge of having composed libels against the French Queen while in England, in complicity with the 'Sieur de Pelleport', thus tending to confirm Williams's own recollections and suggesting that it was indeed the additional notes to the book which outraged the French establishment.[138] Perusal of these notes, in both editions, purportedly by 'l'Abbé Pacot', accompanying the text by 'R. P. de Roze-Croix' as translator, speedily explains the reaction of French ministers.[139] Yet Brissot elsewhere conveys his own impression of the real and underlying reason for his imprisonment (which lasted from July till September 1784), as communicated to him while in the Bastille, as being the hatred felt by the Minister Vergennes for all admirers of English constitutional liberties 'and the *contagion* which they diffused'.[140] Williams himself, in a source written and published nearer to the time of these events than his manuscript autobiography, refers to the translator's committal to the Bastille in phraseology which implies that he was himself in Paris at some time in 1784.[141]

Perhaps one must beware of a temptation to set this book and its translation against the background of the French Revolution rather than against that of the closing year of the war against the Americans (and their French allies). In the context of the development of David Williams's own political philosophy it must be emphasised that the fairly radical nature of some of his proposals in regard both to the *right* and to the *manner* of participating in the political process emerged against a background of traditional British reformist thinking – given particular urgency by impending defeat in the American conflict, changes in the ministry, and the widespread Association movement. Significantly, in some respects (the extension of the franchise) *Letters on Political Liberty* embodies his most radical ideas on constitutional reform; in others (the development of detailed proposals as to the institutions and processes of representation and of government, and a certain change of emphasis in his approach to the nature of the balance and separation of powers) some later works go further – although not always in a more radical direction. Ironically, the impact of the French Revolution, and in particular of his own involvement therein in 1792–3, will be not only to confirm certain aspects of his *ideal* desiderata for a constitution but also to deepen his conviction of the need for gradual and organic change and to produce a more pessimistic assessment of its feasibility. Most notably, the deep-rooted suspicion of governmental power *per se* in any hands which was so strong in David Williams was to remain a permanent feature of American thought[142] and become crystallized in certain aspects of the Constitution of the United States, whereas the trend towards 'gouvernement d'assemblée' during the course of the French Revolution will be one of the reasons for his ultimate disenchantment with its fruits.

Chapter Five

'High-Water Mark'

THE publication of *Letters on Political Liberty* in 1782 was followed by a gap of some six years before the appearance of a spate of works so striking in number, range and impact as perhaps to justify the application of the term 'high-water mark' to the years 1788–91. This gap is itself initially surprising in the case of a prolific writer who was now, presumably, at the height of his powers. Insofar as one accepts the contention that many of the publications of David Williams were written in response to (or indeed to take advantage of) a surge of public interest in a particular issue, then the general agreement as to some falling away of enthusiasm for the cause of political reform during the mid-1780s may well account in part for the lull in his output. But this may also derive from his personal circumstances. The demands on his services as lecturer and tutor seem to have reached their peak during these years; indeed his longest publications in 1789 were avowedly based on lectures actually delivered. In May 1787 Brissot wrote to dissuade him from a projected course of lectures in politics in France, urging that, besides encountering language problems, he would not find six people who understood him, while 'if your teaching were grasped, the Government would immediately oppose it'.[1]

The fullest pen-picture of Williams at about this time is that by a German pastor resident in London, Wendeborn, writing *circa* 1784–85. He claims a fairly close personal knowledge of his subject, dating from the time when 'a few years ago, he frequented the identical cold bath in my neighbourhood into which I used to plunge myself at the same time, seven o'clock in the morning'. He describes Williams, at time of writing, as being about forty-two years old (a kindly estimate, by several years!), and as tall of stature but adopting a languid gait.[2] There is nothing very striking in his rather impassive countenance but 'in his costume and dress Williams is on his own. He bears carefully coiffeured and powdered hair, and from his clothing one could almost conclude that he belonged to that type of smooth clerical gentleman the like of which I have seen running around in the faubourg St Germain in Paris.' The full-length portrait by Rigaud (now with the Society of Authors) confirms much of this. Its subject, depicted pen in hand at an elaborate escritoire (with, perhaps symbolically, a couple of books apparently tossed aside) is tall in stature, with dark eyes and an aquiline countenance. He wears a long blue gown over a darkish suit, with a white frilled shirt, and his shoes have large and presumably silver buckles.[3] Wendeborn goes on to confide that Williams 'is reproached for being too much a man of pleasure and this may well be true – Perhaps he himself recognizes this failing'. Nonetheless, he is a man of sound character and good heart, with something pleasing in his dealings with his fellow-men. While endowed with many natural gifts and talents, it is unfortunate that, perhaps because of insufficient perseverance, his command of languages and of what would be termed academic learning leaves something to be desired. As to his occupation, since relinquishing his public deistic office he has been giving private lectures on both his system of belief and affairs of state, though Wendeborn can scarcely believe that this provides him with an adequate income.[4]

Williams's own comments, in his lectures on education and on political principles published in 1789, confirm the source of his livelihood but are rather more sanguine as to its sufficiency. Indeed, pressure of work upon a mind checked by precarious health is such as to threaten a return of illness. Yet he is reluctant to relinquish 'private engagements, which, by giving me a species of independence, were important to my happiness'. Most revealing is a long apologia in which he refers to 'a supposed unpopularity, or a disposition to obstruct my utility. But the unpopularity, I suspect to be imaginary. Though the operations of a disease, frequently pronounced mortal, gave the appearance of indecision or caprice to my undertakings for many years ... I have never returned to business without considerable encouragement; I have had liberal offers to engage in literary plans, the most successful of the time;[5] and have not been unnoticed by the instruments of political power. The employment I have chosen, principally for the independence it procures, has been, and probably will be, attended with sufficient emolument ...'[6]

Success in his chosen *métier* may well in part have been related to yet another change of residence. The ten years following his departure from Chelsea had been spent in Park Street, Meard Street (Soho), then Park Street again.[7] But he now moved, perhaps in search of more commodious premises, to 28 Great Russell Street, where he was to spend some eight years – but not alone. For significantly, the earliest document extant addressed to him there, dated 22 September 1786, concerns the lady who joined him, became the subject of many respectful references in subsequent correspondence, went with him to Paris in 1802, and was accorded a splendid funeral ten years later.[8] Yet the fullest published reference to Williams's attachment to Mrs Frances Martyn (appearing in a Supplement to the *Town and Country Magazine* as early as 1778) leaves little doubt that this had commenced within a few years of the death of his wife. Its sketch of Williams, described as the son of a Welsh collier, and of a reputed visit to France during which he met Rousseau but also pursued a 'career of exotic pleasures' cut short only by financial problems, is of particular interest and in full accord with his aura of indiscreet behaviour. But his friends would have looked askance at the assertion that Margaret Street's revenue produced such affluence that 'he now made an elegant figure in dress'! More immediately relevant, her frequent visits to his chapel produced an acquaintance with Mrs Martyn, whose own background is accurately if anonymously described, and whose 'fortune was sufficient to support her within the line she moved, as a gentlewoman'.

With 'that natural affection for the fair sex, which sometimes too forcibly activated him, [and] as the Priest of Nature, in the prime of life, [Williams] did not consider it reproachful to have a female connexion ... He imperceptibly found his heart too deeply engaged to recede.' In fairness, the sketch concedes that he did not yet know that the lady had a husband living, and prefaces its slightly scurrilous account of her earlier romantic dalliances with the observation that her spouse's affections had long since 'roamed at large'. After skirmishing with a certain captain of the guards and then, allegedly, with his colonel, 'the discourses of the Priest of Nature afforded her great relief ... [Yet] fearful of incurring his displeasure, and interrupting his fond career, in which her happiness was now deeply concerned, she concealed her marriage for some time ...' When Williams ultimately learned of her married status, and listened to her story, his sympathies were but confirmed by his own discovery of her husband's current liaison 'with a certain lady of easy virtue, who was said to encourage at the same time the addresses of Dr H———. The world at that period ascribed a satirical print ... exhibiting this complicated amour, to our hero.' This print of Martyn, 'himself in the clerical line ... not far from Soho-Square', and his rector Dr Hind, is quite certainly that described below (Appendix III) – though its provenance remains doubtful. To conclude, Williams 'having now perfectly reconciled himself to his alliance with Mrs M———, they form one of the most agreeable Têtes-à-Têtes within the bills of mortality.'[9]

In view of the relatively early date at which it appeared, illustrated with cameo-type prints of 'The Artful Mistress' and 'The Priest of Nature' (reproduced on page 91), the almost complaisant tone of this exposé is significant in seeming to confirm a recognition, which was fully borne out by subsequent events, that this was no fleeting affair but the commencement of a permanent devotion. Frances Martyn was the daughter of Edward Beadon of Devon and niece of Richard Beadon, Archdeacon of London from 1775 to 1789 and later Bishop of Bath and Wells.[10] In 1759 she had married Thomas Martyn, who became curate of St Anne's, Soho, and proceeded to exercise a contentious character in acrimonious dispute until his departure in 1778.[11] What happened to her husband thereafter is not clear; but the documentary evidence of her family's concern with the financial and personal difficulties of her marriage, and indeed of her father's resignation to its breakdown, is unequivocal,[12] as is that of ever-closer links with David Williams. In September 1786 a Mr Wood of Tiverton sent him ten pounds 'for the purpose of Conveying Mrs Martyn towards her mother – and when they are together in Somerset I will come and meet Them ... I now only add my best compliments to Mrs Martyn'.[13] Some two years later the Sun Fire Office recorded an agreement whereby Frances, still described as 'Wife of the Revd Thomas Martyn' undertook to pay four shillings per annum 'for Insurance from Loss or Damage by Fire, on her Wearing Apparel in the now Dwelling House Brick of The Revd. David Williams No. 28 in Great Russell Street, Bloomsbury'. Through all subsequent moves, as insurance endorsements and correspondence alike confirm, Mrs Martyn was to remain a permanent and highly esteemed companion.[14]

Against the background of this settled ménage Williams wrote once more for publication. The seven works which are extant for the period 1788 to 1791 include the lectures on education already considered, the *Constitutions of a Society to Support Men of Genius and Learning in Distress*, 1788, which will later illustrate the genesis of the Literary Fund, four assorted politico-constitutional publications, and a final

N.° XXXVIII.   *The Artful Mistress.*   N.° XXXVIII.   *The Priest of Nature.*

Plate 6. 'THE ARTFUL MISTRESS' AND 'THE PRIEST OF NATURE'

and most advanced declaration of his religious philosophy, which included an avowedly Theist Liturgy. This last, his *Apology for professing the Religion of Nature*, 1788–9, is so striking in its further development of those trends in his thinking examined earlier[15] as to demand fairly detailed treatment. It ran to at least four editions and may most meaningfully be considered in conjunction with several lengthy and very revealing passages in the near-contemporaneous *Lectures on Education*. These now assert, retrospectively, that 'in opening the chapel in Margaret-street, it was my object to claim for moral philosophy, the toleration allowed the extravagancies of gloomy enthusiasm, or the dogmas of ferocious sedition'. Commending the Hebraic idea of the unity of an invisible and ineffable God, he urges that 'Theists are amply justified in rejecting all grosser and more improbable pretensions of participating the Divine nature'. In defining adoration of the Deity as his first duty he identifies nature or the God of nature as its object. He now confesses that 'when I introduced a Liturgy on the general principles of religion and morality, I had not divested myself of the error concerning the personification, and social attributes of the universal cause; and on relinquishing it, some of my hearers charged me with Atheism ... But when I affirm the attributes of Deity cannot be similar or even analogous to those of men, I do not adopt the language of Atheism concerning necessity or chance.' Yet he concedes that in seeking to avoid worship of a phantom endowed with human attributes men generally sink into atheism: this was the dilemma he had sought to resolve.[16]

His venture had suffered from ill-health and the consequent 'difficulty of frequently assembling new congregations on my returns to town from journies or excursions to save my life; from the habit of disputation which many of the society had contracted in their religious education; and the accumulation of debts'. Having himself but lately relinquished the habits of professional superstition it is hardly surprising that in preparing a public service he should retain complimentary epithets, appropriate to human qualities, and annex them to the Deity. Despite this failure he remains convinced that enumeration of the principles of Nature in a public service, devoid of adulatory absurdity, is practicable, and indeed necessary for those who have habitually associated morality with the forms of religious observance. Therefore, incorrigible to reproach, he will essay one last composition in this field – though his health will not allow the contest of a public introduction! Admittedly, curiosity had led some to attend his first attempt and even to remain for the later lectures; it had not been in his power to perpetuate the novelty which attracted them. But his assertion of a right to separate morality from any specific religious dogmas had breached the dyke of intolerance: 'I point it out as the very circumstance which may honourably distinguish my life, and make me lie down in my grave with the consciousness of some effort for the interest of society.'[17]

As indicators of the position he has now reached, his discussions of sin and of the traditional religious palliatives of repentance or absolution are crucially important. For 'Nature knows no such doctrine as forgiveness. Men may and ought to forgive. God is immutable. Every crime has its punishment, without the possibility of interposition: and there is nothing in nature analogous to our idea of atonement.'[18] This idea is more fully developed in the *Apology for professing the Religion of Nature*, of which one may say that if, together with its associated Liturgy, it represents the culmination of the evolution of the religious philosophy of David Williams, it also marks the nadir therein of any residual element of religious faith. Though loosely constructed it signals the conjunction of an abandonment not only of Christianity but also of any concept of revealed religion (together with any associated vision of an after-life) with an equally explicit identification of such concepts with political tyranny – all leavened with bitter personal allusions. Addressing Watson, Bishop of Llandaff, whom he regards as the most decent defender of Christianity,[19] he nonetheless asserts that 'a spirit of enquiry, which in you, has been held by the reins of interest; in me, has burst the boundaries of prudence; – and it has laid waste my expectations and hopes'. Avowing disbelief in the doctrines and articles of the English church, and in the authenticity of the revelation on which they are allegedly founded, Williams has chosen to forego both the beliefs and the *advantages* of Christianity, to decline powerful patronage, and to prefer anxious and laborious effort to affluence procured by insincerity. He suspects that Watson himself, in common with a majority of the episcopal bench, is Arminian – yet a scrupulous Arminian cannot possibly subscribe to the thirty-nine articles! Indeed, doctrinally, he can discern 'no asylum for integrity, from the confines of Calvinism, to those of licentious and unprincipled Atheism'.[20]

In proceeding to deplore what he terms the execrable impiety of bringing the Deity into questions of civil obligation, he puts the question whether 'the motives of social and public spirit, or the desire of social and public happiness [are] sufficient to hold men in society; to produce the useful virtues of the mind and heart: – or is it necessary to have recourse to the hopes of future rewards and the fear of future punishments?' His conclusions are: that virtuous conduct does not spring from fear of punishment, in this life or the next; that such fears cannot honestly be related to a God who will inflict chastisement in an afterlife; that, indeed, the whole nature of the first cause in the universe can never be descried; that reason alone is capable of comprehending (and is capable *only* of comprehending) the immutable laws of Nature which govern our existence; that adherence to these laws and attention to the fruits of experience and experiment within their compass offer the sole hope of happiness in this life; that such happiness, the fruit of a rational and social application of a pleasure-and-pain based calculus, is the only proper object of human hopes and endeavours; and that immortality of the soul is a delusion, a chimera – worse, a myth deliberately converted by despotic rulers into a bugaboo to bring to obedient compliance 'the common people, who are the sheep of religious establishments, and whose fleeces are the objects of concern'.[21]

Since we are incapable of crime or of merit before God, the threat of punishment hereafter can only be a device of despots, for surely the immortality of the soul is no clear and general principle in Nature.[22] As to the soul itself, materialists, having established that the child is born without a soul, treat as absurd all attempts thereafter to insert it. For 'if we enquire, what is a soul? and define it to be an intelligent and virtuous principle; it is certain, man is born with no such principle. All the philosophers who have supposed knowledge arises from sensation, have, in fact, argued in favor of materialism; and rendered the distinction between soul and body unnecessary.'[23] The issue of immortality is related to a favourite theme – that the character and attributes of the Deity are but poetic fabrications of the human imagination, perhaps of human vanity, ever seeking to reduce the Universal Principle to a level with man. But the assertion that it is absurd to say, God is merciful, or even just, presages development of this line of thought into something which verges on determinism when Williams urges that in the *moral* as in the *material* world all things 'are circumstances in the general processes of nature; of the good or evil of which we have often no comprehension'.[24]

His own more immediate concern is to consider the inducements needed to secure the observance of the standards and canons of society. In the first stages of emergence of communities, a mutual desire for freedom from violence was followed by a gradual recognition of the goal of finding happiness in the happiness of others.[25] But sadly, 'on the establishment of the magistracy, the principle of selfishness separated the magistrate from the public' and brought him to regard society, of which he was in truth but the instrument or servant, as an opportunity of private power and advantage. In pursuance of such motives, politicians have sought for sanctions extraneous to society to compel observance of the regulations imposed, and among these '*the last, the utmost effort of human villainy, is discoverable in the doctrine of eternal damnation*'. Thereby, men have been induced gradually to relinquish their civil rights ostensibly to obtain the rewards or avoid the punishments of another world.[26] Setting aside any gaps in logic or the simplistic historical interpretation, the argument itself is far from novel: the deliberate fusion, by opponents of all reform, of the taint of doctrinal heresy, involving eternal damnation, with the charge of political and social subversion, was a commonplace complaint among radical or liberal socio-political pamphleteers in the mid-sixteenth and mid-seventeenth centuries.[27] But it is here of particular interest as evincing David Williams's identification of his philosophical and political *bêtes noires* as but two sides of the same coin.

Seeking for a *true* calculus of socially desirable behaviour, he finds the only foundation furnished by Nature – a sensibility to pleasure and pain. 'By ascertaining the quantity of pleasure and pain, in the effects of various principles, institutions, customs, or opinions; we may determine their comparative value.' Everything, including forms of government, is to be evaluated by the happiness or misery produced.[28] Within this calculus, which again is in no way new,[29] how are we to appraise the concept of immortality? Enunciation of the purported benefits for virtuous behaviour of the doctrine that this world is but a state of trial for futurity evokes his contemptuous dismissal of the concept as 'the ignis fatuus, which draws off man's attention from his immediate path'. For Nature has formed and fixed us on this earth; here, therefore, and here only, are we to employ our talents and enjoy our happiness. The doctrine of a hereafter 'confuses or perverts our ideas on the purposes of human society. It teaches mankind to rank governments, magistrates, kings, and other occasions of their sufferings, as they do storms, earthquakes, or pestilences; among the ordinances of Providence, to which they are to submit in a state of trial, to obtain better conditions, or better situations in a future world. Who does not see, that all wretched constitutions of government owe their support and continuance to this doctrine?'[30]

Its pretended utility, to keep the common people in order beneath oppressive government,[31] thus exposed, has the concept of immortality any *intrinsic* justification? In one of the few passages of his works in which a note of very personal emotion obtrudes, David Williams puts the question: 'Will it be said, because the violet has drooped unobserved in the wilderness, or has been crushed by the foot of a brute – that it is entitled to a resurrection, in order to answer the purposes of its creation? The blooming infant, snatched away by death, is like that violet nipped in the bud: each having equally obeyed the laws of the Deity, in just entering life, and disappearing; each equally destitute of all claims to immortality. That we should wish the child we love never to die; nay, that affection should hold before us the image of a beloved friend; and make it difficult to credit, that so much excellence can be no more – all these are amiable delusions, which I have often and deeply felt: but they prove nothing to rest our hopes upon in the cool hours of reflection.' Such considerations but obscure the truth: that *'the efforts of the world should be exerted to break this great chain, which bends the neck of its inhabitants to slavery and wretchedness'*.[32]

The Liturgy 'on The Principles of Theism' which accompanies the *Apology* is so far removed in tone from Williams's earlier compositions as almost to resemble a parody. Some passages sound like Calvinism without Christ, conveying a note of sombre resignation rather than of any joyous intellectual liberation. Disclaiming any intention to form a sect for his own emolument, the author pays homage to the impenetrable methods and purposes of the Universal Principle of all existence, which enables us to choose that which is agreeable and avoid that which is painful; which *'conducts us to our dissolution* [my italics]; and subjects us to that law, from which nothing can be exempted'.[33] It is folly to question the existence of such a uniform and universal cause, the evidence for which is as certain and inexplicable as that of our own. We do well, therefore, 'neither to adore, or to arraign, the equity of Divine Providence'; for wisdom, justice, mercy, and patience are human virtues and their 'application to Thee is absurd. In thus retailing Thy excellencies, we destroy every idea of Thy infinity.' For our efforts must ever be vain to penetrate the sanctuary of Nature and seek out the Deity.[34] This ironically neo-Calvinist insistence upon the complete incomprehensibility of a transcendent first cause is followed by a similarly reminiscent rejection of any quietist attitude *within* this world. Since we cannot by searching find out God it is to man, to society, to our country, that our talents and virtues should be related.[35] Mankind must have recourse to bold and laborious experiments which alone can force out Nature's secrets.[36] Since it is impossible we should resist the will of God, or that the Author of all beings should have enemies of his own creation, 'the homage of man should be on the altar of virtue'.[37]

Any participants in this strange Liturgy would have found themselves declaring that, Nature having furnished the means of augmenting the sum of human happiness, 'we will not offer up to Heaven, vows, sacrifices, or oblations, to escape misfortunes, which are the consequences of our own negligence and ignorance; the folly of our institutions, customs, or opinions'. To do so would be to envisage and bow before an arbitrary tyrant – equally reprehensible in heaven or on earth. Indeed, 'we are ashamed of that frenzy, which, to prevent the smallest evil to

ourselves, has tempted us to ask, that the eternal chain of things may be broken . . .
or to imagine our cries and vows can interrupt an universal force acting by universal laws. We submit to our lot: we seek, in Nature, remedies provided for the
ills she occasions.'[38] One has encountered this distaste for ill-directed prayer
before, and indeed not all of this is new; yet the change between this and his earlier
liturgies is unmistakable. If it is fair to characterise their credo as suggesting that
'True *God* is Nature to advantage dressed' it might now be urged that Nature is
stripped. His position is near to that of the Grecian sage whom he cites in his
Lectures on Education: 'What the deity is, I know not; what he is not I know.'[39] Yet
the contrast with his fellow-Welshman Richard Price is neither simple nor without
its irony: for while Price concurs that human characteristics must not be attributed
to the Deity, he also contends (understandably, in his revulsion against Calvinism) that God himself is subject to the moral law, His power thus limited by His
rectitude.[40]

   As an avowal – or more accurately disavowal – of religious faith, the *Apology* is of
great interest as illustrating, if not the logical clarity of his position, then at least
the far reaches to which the former student even of heterodox Carmarthen had
now removed. But in regard to the Liturgy one must sympathise with the reviewer's suggestion that it was surely intended not as a serious form of devotion
but rather as a burlesque on liturgies. Another equally hostile notice confessed
that a suspicion that the author intended to serve the cause of religion by opposing
it was checked only by the calculated misrepresentation of some passages.[41] Their
recognition of its erudition was shared by the anonymous author of *Letters addressed
to the Apologist for the Religion of Nature*, 1790, a specific rebuttal, who deplored the
alloy of such brilliancy of talents and charm of style with lurking and indignant
malevolence, and the combination of denial of all divine revelation with the appal-
lingly gloomy 'doctrine of annihilation'.[42] Such reactions may well have been
typical – yet the book was several times reprinted and it has indeed been suggested[43] that it was books such as this which were used in the infidel societies of the
1790s, though no direct evidence of its influence has been found.

   Even greater success, in terms of sales and popularity, was achieved by a very
different publication: *Royal Recollections on A Tour to Cheltenham, Gloucester, Worcester,
and Places Adjacent, in the year 1788*. Although anonymous this was undoubtedly by
David Williams.[44] Based on an actual royal progress, it ran to some fourteen editions. There seems to be no direct evidence for the assertion that the book was
inspired, indeed almost authorised, by the party of the Prince of Wales as part of a
campaign against the King and his friends.[45] It may well be that the prospect of lucrative sales was a sufficient inducement – though it is true that Williams was an
admirer of the Duchess of Devonshire, to whom he pays a glowing tribute as a
supporter of Fox's cause. There is a partial resemblance to *The Morality of a Citizen*
in that serious points are interwoven (this time far more successfully) with satire
and caricature.[46] Despite its condemnation in the serious reviews, by contemporary standards of personal and political satire the composition was restrained.[47]
Within the framework of a purported royal diary, certain themes recur: George
III's own idiosyncrasies; his relations with the Prince of Wales; the position of the

Crown; corruption in church and state; fear of all projects of reform; and, as focal point of many political allusions, the recent Westminster Election.

The pages are studded with often caustically witty cameos of public figures. George himself is made to relate his determination to excel in the arts of familiarity (the people 'shall laugh heartily whenever I appear'), particularly at Windsor where 'if I had continued my familiarities, I should have depopulated the neighbourhood. The doors were shut up and barricaded the instant I appeared [for] I have hunted families out of closets, cellars, and coal-holes, when they were not disposed to a little chat with me in the morning.' The business of the mouse-trap, which had seized upon an exploring royal finger, occasioned some uneasiness, as did an encounter with a tobacco-chewing operative at a china-manufactory. The effects on the royal bowels of changes in the water, and the parsimony imposed by the problems of clothing and feeding Queen Charlotte's numerous brood, are good for several gibes.[48] Remarks about the Prince of Wales convey mingled regret and recrimination. In general, the King has no fancy for heirs apparent, while speculation as to what son George would do with five and twenty millions evokes the fantasy that he would build and furnish an harem. Yet alongside such badinage we encounter the suggestion that the Prince would 'expend ten millions a year, and every farthing should go to the encouragement of industry and talents', together with a tribute to his conciliating grace which, combined with prudence, will render him the most popular king in the world – for after all, the infirmities of love have ever been those of great minds. Whether or not they bespeak the provenance of the book, such touches seem to indicate the hope of patronage which was reflected in a couple of later works.[49] If this is the case, then the King's protestation that 'Velnos' Vegetable Syrup shall not approach our family' was dangerously near the mark – for extant caricatures depicted the Prince with a bottle of this 'venereal nostrum' at his bedside![50]

The royal diarist's political pronouncements combine candid confessions with resolute assertions of purpose. Born a Briton, he concedes that the enthusiasm of the friends of liberty for his dynasty has diminished in response to familiarity with its blessings. Yet he insists that although the real power of the Crown was never so great as at present, that power is not blatantly tyrannical: 'it always moves in a masque, and saps the rights of the people unperceived'. Consigned by his mother to a priest and a borough monger, he was ever fated to be leader of a *party*. Yet though now disenchanted with the party system he has 'waded so far in the waters of corruption, that I must not think of tracing back my steps; – and I will shew myself in the country for the benefit of the general election'.[51] This is an interesting, if at first sight puzzling comment; the next general election was in 1790, but preparations therefor (on the Opposition as well as the Governmental side) apparently commenced in 1788.[52] Yet there is little doubt that the royal journey was in fact taken for medical reasons. George answers his own question as to the object of these parties? '*To be brought to market*; and I am the purchaser.' Little wonder that Parliament is a bottomless gulf; the puzzle is that people do not realise the futility of such a body, where majorities are secured through lavish corruption. But then, 'who is the people? or where is the people? It is a bugbear, no where to be found.'[53] Yet it inspired a dread of all free discussion of possible reform. In unconscious and ironic accuracy of prophecy he goes on to declare that 'the state of France is critical; – I was pleased to see it harassed; but I like not the language of its remonstrances. This d–d philosophy, with its rights of nature, humanity, and reason, is the mortal and irreconcileable enemy of power; and princes have a common interest in suppressing it.' Indeed 'if a reformation take place in France, it will be *on a plan of greater liberty than that of England; we must then follow, instead of giving the example* [my italics: in this, David Williams showed more percipience than many others]. Scotland, Ireland, and even India, will require emancipation; and I shall be reduced to be only "first among my equals".'[54]

In contemplating the surge of seditious and heretical ideas, George is astonished the clergy cannot silence them. How ludicrous to pay two million a year to a mercenary band, then find them hesitate to tackle a deist whose hands are tied by penal laws. But then, though laymen may be influenced by various motives only one will move a churchman! There are exceptions: 'Watson is not as he should be. He is restless and ambitious, and would have an opinion of his own ... Immediately on ascending the bench, he recommended a mode of equalising the portions of the church revenues.[55] One step further, in allowing the parishes to chuse their ministers,[56] and the clergy would have been of no utility to administration, or to patrons in its interest – in short, the *alliance of church and state* would have been totally dissolved.' Thus, in appointment of bishops, more regard should be paid to their principles, for such as Watson and Shipley are dissenters at heart, advocates of toleration and reform. It is not the King's custom to think over-much of religion, after discharge of its public duties, but when he does he cannot much relish the prospect of heaven – with no distinction of rank or family and none but levelling principles. Would that the clergy would review the concept and establish it on more monarchical lines![57]

In contrast with the kindly treatment accorded Watson, Williams did not hesitate to lampoon erstwhile friends or acquaintances such as Jebb (of discontented and seditious memory, lately sunk into the grave in poverty and vexation)[58] and James Martin. The member for Tewkesbury is portrayed as 'the *chattering starling*'[59] who, though vain of his apparent honesty, may easily be handled if allowance be made for his oddities. 'Jenkinson says, he affords a good *test of practicability* in the house ... When an artifice reaches *his* understanding, it is too gross to pass; and it is high time to withdraw it; but the political constitution may be frittered into a thousand atoms before such understandings perceive the danger. I wish we had more such *honest men!*'[60] Whatever the reasons which underlay such a change in attitude, the picture is not attractive. Many others feel the lash, sometimes in a barbed flick, as with Sackville (Lord George Germain) who fought bravely on a map, or Shelburne who would use his right hand to deceive his left, rather than *not* deceive,[61] and sometimes at length. Thus Priestley typifies sectarian Birmingham, which counterfeits religions as readily as coins. In reviving socinianism, and passing for novelties the rags and tatters of a forgotten heresy, 'he goes to the very shore of fidelity; but he prudently stops, where his interest will allow no further license'.[62] Predictably, Pitt is often mentioned, as when George protests that the term of this boy's insolence shall not be long, for he slyly steals much more than Fox would openly purloin (not unexpectedly, for 'Charlotte justly observes, the Chatham family will ever be *on the parish*'), or observes that he is at heart a Tory.[63] Other personal and topical allusions range from the cyder-tax to Howard and prison reform and to an issue which will recur: the education of the poor.[64]

Yet pride of place is given to the Westminster Election. The references are presumably to the by-election of 1788 – but this has been described as a virtual repetition of the contest of 1784 which left a legacy of political legend and personal notoriety.[65] The royal diarist is mortified that the residence of both Court and Parliament should favour his enemies – for Pitt declares that Hood himself (chief governmental candidate on both occasions) is in danger. A lengthy discussion of tactics and canvassing includes a fulsome tribute to the Duchess of Devonshire: 'Animated with intelligence and goodness; the friend of merit in every form, I regret the politics that withholds her from court ... How firmly attached to Fox! Indeed how justly!'[66] Discounting any all too possible double-entendre, this seems a clear indication of the direction of the author's political sympathies at this time. But there remains the puzzle that it was during the election of 1784 that the Duchess had achieved notoriety by behaviour in support of Fox which a not-unsympathetic biographer has described as incredibly reckless and foolish – indeed in later life she was to declare that 'I never canvas, and have never done so since the great election'.[67] Even so, modern research confirms that many of the references to electoral skullduggery are true of *both* occasions.[68] The King complains that 'the manner of assembling the sailors[69] was too bungling: – artful occasions should have been created for the *guards*. – They are only *armed citizens*; and with a little address in their introduction, they may terrify, maim, and murder ... whenever the views of administration are endangered.'[70] Sailors were used, battling against Irish chairmen and coal-heavers, in both elections; in 1784 the King had a detachment of the Guards marched to the hustings to vote; and a print in 1788 depicted 'Election-Troops' collecting pay.[71] All sources agree, first, as to the impact of Georgiana in 1784, and second, as to the closeness (if not as to the degree of propriety) of her relations both with Fox and with the Prince of Wales during the mid-1780s.[72] One would like to know more, but the inference of some sympathy with this grouping on the part of David Williams seems plausible – though any such attachment did not endure.

Finally, Williams contrives a brief reference to himself, making the monarch toy with a wish to commit him to Newgate, and a longer puff for his newly emerging project: 'A hint has been given of a literary fund; and the committee of the privy council are enquiring its destination. Care must be taken to prevent the independence of men of letters; and, if the plan be introduced, it must be regulated to *our* views *by the clergy*. Prettyman advises the idea of provision for poor curates to be tacked to it; which would frighten away subscribers, or secure the management in our interest. – Mem. to be very attentive to this business, as it is of great importance.'[73] Naturally enough, the book fell foul of the serious reviews. These discerned both party prejudice and personal injustice, and even their reluctant admiration of touches of humour and pointed satire was muted by distaste at the ridicule of a monarch 'whose virtues will be remembered and revered when all the squibs that have been directed at him by the *wits* of the age will be extinguished . . .'[74] Yet there is no doubt that the book's cutting humour and witty – if often cruel and near-scurrilous – anecdotes secured a large and eager readership. There is some irony in the probability that one of Williams's least serious and more ephemeral pieces may well have been financially the most successful.

The remark of one reviewer that he 'could have heartily smiled at the pleasantry of this publication, did the present situation of the person who is the principal object of it, admit of a smile',[75] points to the poignant developments which were the background of the *next*, and much more serious, composition of David Williams. *Constitutional Doubts, humbly submitted to his Royal Highness The Prince of Wales*, a 34-page pamphlet, was an obviously quickly written comment on the great Regency Crisis, dated at 12 December 1788 – in the very middle of the crucial House of Commons debates. The circumstances of the two works were not unrelated. For it now seems probable that the indisposition which had led to the royal departure to the healing waters of Cheltenham spa was a precursor of a later attack, commencing in October. This, although still physical in origin, undoubtedly led to mental derangement, to the common assertion of royal madness, and to eager Whig acceptance of a chance of getting rid of Pitt.[76] The crisis evoked a spate of publications (John Derry lists twenty-one) on what at least one appropriately termed the 'National Embarrassment'.[77]

One recent assessment of *Constitutional Doubts* finds its point not entirely clear,[78] and the overlapping themes, together with some element of reservation in its author's own position, make for occasional lack of precision in its argument. But the hatred of Pitt, the deference toward the Prince of Wales, and the reiteration of the need for constitutional reform, are all clear enough. The Constitutional Doubts (now openly avowed as those of the author of *Letters on Political Liberty*) concern 'the pretensions of the Two Houses of Parliament to appoint a Third Estate'. This is made clearer by direct reference to a speech of Fox 'on the competency of an imperfect Parliament,[79] to dictate the present melancholy duty of your Royal Highness; or to determine [i.e., decide] for the whole body of the people of Great Britain'.[80] Yet any temptation to classify the pamphlet as a straightforward pro-Fox contribution to the Regency debate is checked by its later warning that any suggested change of ministry at such a delicate time should be effected with the greatest prudence, indeed that there is much to commend continuance of the present Ministry, despite Pitt's personal insolence.[81] Indeed Fox's conduct of his case won the admiration neither of his friends nor of later historians.[82]

An early and lengthy reference back to *Letters on Political Liberty*[83] is followed by Williams's declaration that 'I have not since, sullied my fingers with English politics. But I cannot see your Royal Highness approaching a precipice, without obtruding myself among those who would suggest your danger.' This concern for a Prince who was later to become a generous patron of the Literary Fund is joined with a determination to defend the rights of the British nation. But what exactly was this danger? Briefly, that both the essential balance of the constitution and the liberties of the nation on the one hand, and the position of the heir to the throne on the other, would be undermined by the suggestion that this present Parliament usurp the role of '*paramount Sovereign*', and act as absolute disposer of Kings and Regents at the behest of an 'undefinable, unconstitutional monster, the *Prime Minister*'.[84] With considerable if often contrived ingenuity, a professed concern for the interests of an admired Prince of Wales, a wary and guarded support of Fox, and an inveterate hatred of Pitt, are combined with some favourite generalisations about the Constitution. Its only paramount sovereign is the nation as a whole; its dangers have arisen from the usurpations of *delegated* powers upon each others' spheres or upon national rights – as by the present administration which he credits with the most impudent and atrocious violation of the Constitution since Charles I.[85] In the immediate crisis the author voices his agreement with Fox: 'that, on the civil as well as natural demise of the King,[86] the Heir Apparent in England, being of full age and unexceptionable capacity, should exercise the royal power, is a proposition susceptible of demonstration; and I know of no man so capable of stating it as Mr Fox'. He condemns outright the contention that Parliament should arrogate the power of appointing a Regent.[87]

Yet his own most pressing concern is to expose the calculated imposture which he descries in Pitt's assumption of 'the indecent assurance to adopt a principle, to which his public conduct has been uniformly hostile – "That the origin of political power is in the people".' The Prince must not be deceived by any such pretended appeal to popular power in making or declaring decisions. For in sad reality, from the Conquest to the present day the English people have never once expressed a will, pronounced a judgement, or performed an action for the realm. When Pitt had assumed office the throne had been depicted as assaulted by an enormous giant with two heads (the Coalition) and the Interior managers[88] 'produced a young and virgin[89] Knight to assault that dreadful monster . . . Not a syllable was uttered on that occasion, by the miraculous youth, concerning the paramount privileges of the Houses of Parliament, or even the ideal authority of the people.' Are we now to acquiesce that the public will is or is not expressed in Parliament according to what minister holds power?[90]

Reverting to historical analysis, Williams traces how, after liberty was discredited by mid-seventeenth-century excesses, the Revolution had introduced a new form of government (under old constitutional forms) which became as dangerous to the rights of the Crown as insulting to the common sense of the people. 'It has been the fixed object of every Administration to give vigor and stability to *an intermediate power, founded on corruption; which might set equally at defiance the King and the People* [my italics] . . . It is from this power you can have any thing to apprehend.' The peculiar genius of Sir Robert Walpole having fully introduced this system it now remains only to secure guarantees of permanence, consistent with the apparent observance of certain forms.[91] The Heir Apparent must therefore beware of the present *finesse* of substituting the House of Commons for the people, thereby assuming paramount sovereignty, suspending the legislature, and appointing the Regent. Thus the spectre of inordinate and illegitimate power of a subject as in the person of Warwick the Kingmaker is evoked; the Prince is warned that 'if you receive the Regency by *appointment* . . . you will actually receive it from *the Walpole of the day*' and thereby sanction the claims of a new and undefined power, superior to the whole legislature.

In effect, he will be Ram Rajah, confined to his palace amusements while the English Constitution gives way to that of the Mahrattas![92]

The overstatement is palpable, though similar comments on Pitt's ambition and on the threat of excessive arrogation of power by the House occur elsewhere.[93] Yet when, protesting that he has no connection or acquaintance with the leaders of any party and no ambition for their notice or favour, he entreats the Prince 'to be extremely scrupulous *in the use of words*', for precedents are made of words, Williams was wiser than Fox. The suggestion that 'if the great council of the throne had respectfully requested your Royal Highness to exercise the prerogatives of the executive power in trust for an afflicted Parent' then the present spectacle of the people being made the stalking horse of the minister and of an interested faction would have been avoided,[94] evinces a moderate and balanced assessment of realities, confirmed by the advice on retention of the present ministers of the Crown. Several aspects of his analysis coincide with the more methodical treatment by De Lolme, notably his strictures on the constitutional errors of either side, while one review grasped and commended his basic aim: to warn the Prince against accepting Regency by appointment.[95] Paine's retrospective comments in 1791 reached conclusions very similar to those of Williams.[96] Indeed the pamphlet typifies a strong impression that constitutional issues bulked as large as factional rivalry. Much longer after the event, we may observe the elements of unity in the two very different compositions of Williams evoked by political reflection on the personal circumstances of the King: a virulent dislike of Pitt, some cautious sympathy for the Foxite Whigs, and a fairly clear attempt to attract the not unfavourable notice of the Heir-Apparent. Yet the basic principles of David Williams's interpretation of the constitutional past and present needs of the nation also remain in evidence, soon to be developed in two much longer publications.

The first of these, *Lectures on Political Principles*[97] appeared in 1789. Its dedication to the Prince of Wales alludes to the 'late suspension of the executive power – which exhibited to me nothing so truly great and affecting, as the tender and dutiful moderation of your Royal Highness'.[98] Despite one's obvious reservations on the accuracy of this comment, the juxtaposition (in the Preface) of the recent Regency Crisis with developments in France is significant – for it must be remembered that while the course of events south of the Channel could not accurately be foreseen, neither could contemporaries take for granted the semi-permanent recovery of the King's faculties. Williams himself is in no doubt that France is poised upon the brink of developments for which England must be ready, not in any hostile sense 'but on the ground of political competition'. In preparation for this challenge the Prince, whose manners attract general applause and who demonstrates consummate prudence, should consult with Adam Smith in fitting himself for a task which approaching revolutions on the Continent render of peculiar importance.[99] In what seems, prima facie, an unlikely piece of casting, Williams appears to urge upon this future British monarch what the French ruler was so disastrously to shirk: the seizure and manipulation of a powerful ground-swell of constitutional reform.

The Lectures themselves are geared to discussion of Montesquieu's *Spirit of Laws*, in a critique which is sometimes most impressive. It does not endorse contemporary panegyrics of what is not so much a systematic political analysis as an elaborate description of forms of government. Montesquieu's brilliant maxims are sometimes as fallacious as they are entertaining, as are his assertions on the effects of climate or the relationship between size of states and feasible forms of government.[100] But his greatest disservice, says Williams, is to have cast an air of enchantment over a fabric which has as many weaknesses as merits, thereby condoning the perpetuation of abuses in order to avoid any change of form in the British Constitution.[101] Among other political philosophers, Hobbes, despite the odium of his atheism, emerges as the general fountain-head of principles and systems (used, unacknowledged, by Locke), but while boldly smashing the chains of religious was guilty of riveting those of political tyranny.[102] Harrington's *Oceana* depicts a nobler design than that of the *Spirit of Laws*: it derives from bold and inventive genius, while Montesquieu but delineates what is already done. Perceptively, Williams claims that 'when the remote and full effects of American institutions take place, it will not be a question who has been the greater benefactor of mankind'.[103] But his basic criticism of the generality of political theorists (among whom, as yet, Rousseau is not mentioned) concerns their erroneous concept of a state of nature.[104]

Discarding both myths of origins and metaphysical speculation, David Williams commences with his own conviction that human institutions are regulated by final causes whose principles, like those of all the sciences, are deduced from experience, observation, and reflection. Since a political state, though an artificial body, is constructed on principles similar to those of the natural, it follows that 'constitutions of government are never stationary, but in some of their trifling forms'. Yet underlying the evolution so clearly implied, civil policy has principles as fixed as the general nature of man.[105] One such principle is the wish for preservation, security, and happiness. Indeed, since the general end of government is not the preservation of any specific Constitution but the happiness of society, then their respective interests should never be dissociated. Thus, logically, 'the feeling or judgement of the community on its own happiness is the first principle in political science.'[106] In the achievement of that happiness, some limitation of government activity is essential. In particular, Montesquieu's association of the laws of education with the principles of government is erroneous. For whilst education, life's first duty as the general instrument of knowledge and virtue, is directed by no *certain* laws, it *is* the natural guardian of that sacred wish for happiness and liberty which is rooted in every human heart. A state resolved at all costs to preserve its existing constitution might well subordinate education to its authority; but *all* public institutions are susceptible of improvement, and the principal means of such improvement lie in education. Had education been subject to control, would Harrington, Sidney, Locke and Montesquieu have written as they did? For the very idea 'of permanence, or of perpetuity, incident to the invention of political institutions, is hostile to the constant agitation, or the innovatory spirit which may arise from domestic education.'[107]

What then are the problems in construction of the state? That the people who compose it cannot collectively perform its particular offices and functions 'is too evident to admit of disquisition: as it is, that the whole of the human body cannot perform the offices adapted to the finger or the hand. But that political or civil power should be so connected with this general mass, as to be influenced by the general sympathy of the political constitution – is as evident, as that the head or the arms should be connected with the body, and have their motions and actions controlled by its general sympathy. How to animate the mass of the people; how to furnish it with limbs and members, which shall have particular portions of activity and power; how to connect those members with the body; and to subject them to a control, not impeding their action and utility? – these are the great problems in the science of government.'[108] This is one of the clearest statements of what is perhaps the most distinctive contribution of David Williams to political thought: the attempt to combine the wholly traditional corporeal analogy of society with a belief in limited forms of government held rigorously accountable to an established and regulated power in the people as the only foundation of political liberty. For harmony of powers in political constitutions derives not from mere regulation of their respective operations, but from their attachment to the community as members to a body, responsive to its general sensibility, judgement, or will, and confined to their appropriate functions by its general force.[109]

The issues touched upon – the organic analogy; civil and political liberty; the balance and separation of governmental powers; the expression of the general will of the people; the mechanism of representation, delegation, and accountability; and the relationship between political equality and social equity – while not altogether new, will receive full treatment later. But first a few of the myths in Montesquieu's encomium of the English Constitution are exposed. With its injurious immunities become prerogatives, and former trusts converted into arbitrary rights, any real difference in government derives solely from this fact: 'the power of Oppression in France is confined to the king and nobles. In England it is extended into several inferior ranks.' The British monarch, endowed with superstitious sanctity and supposedly born with correlative talents, chooses ministers who relieve him of both the trouble and the blame of real business, but leave him free for the irresponsible indulgence of his whims even in important political issues. 'There are young men in this room', remarks Williams, in a slightly confused parallel, 'who may furnish the Tartars with as many reasons for adoring the Dalai Lama; as can be alleged in a free nation, for the support of such royalty.'[110] Nor is he reassured by the division of illegitimate power between royalty and nobility or by the factional quarrels which have wracked the state ever since the Revolution – indeed he reproaches his students that their display of 'an inveterate spirit of party, often impedes my endeavors to assist your studies'.[111]

In regard to the *principle* of separation and balance of powers, naturally Williams commends the assertion 'that every man invested with power, is disposed to abuse it'.[112] But Montesquieu's picture of the reciprocal influence of King, Lords and Commons is as plausible but delusive as his idea of the need for rivalry between the several divisions of a free government. For a community once adequately represented in a legislative assembly would never permit any executive magistrate or privileged body of nobles to reject its resolutions. But the English Commons has ever been an appendage of Crown and aristocracy, and this is what determines their decisions, 'not any scientific idea in those who formed the Constitution to poise or balance its parts'. Accepting Montesquieu's tripartite division of political powers, his whole idea of balance or counter-balance deriving therefrom is vitiated by prerogative, influence and corruption. No balance of powers surreptitiously contrived gives real security: 'either a general collusion or one iniquitous power will extinguish the appearance of liberty'.[113]

A *spurious* balance or separation of powers thus offers no safeguard to liberty. But how is liberty itself to be defined? His relatively complex answer derives not only from the classical eighteenth-century version of humanity's individual rights but also from a more corporate concept which relates historically to the organic interpretation of society and contemporaneously to the idea of the 'general will'. Nor does he forget the constitutional mechanics needed to implement liberty, which is susceptible of order and discipline. The supreme blessing which society can bestow is political and civil liberty, but there is a significant distinction (which Montesquieu has not grasped) between its constituents.[114] Political liberty rests on the existence in the body of the people of constitutional power 'analogous to that of a Lord Paramount, when he has delegated offices for the administration of its affairs. This power does not act by interference in the business of delegated departments; but by requiring an account, or correcting abuses.' This renders a people 'secure from danger, or apprehension, in its *collective* [my italics] relation to the government it has appointed ... This, not any division, or melioration of uncontrollable power, is political liberty in regard to the constitution!'[115]

For a citizen's *individual* liberties should be called civil, not political, 'Government is to the collective body of the people, as the citizen is to government. If the people, collectively, were at the caprice of the administration; or if the business of the administration were continually interrupted by the interference of the people – there would be no political liberty: if the individual or private citizen were at the caprice of the magistrate superintending him – there would be no civil liberty.' Montesquieu's accurate definition of a citizen's liberty to be a power of acting as he pleases, within the limit of the laws, should have been denominated civil, not political, although a better definition would be the right of doing whatever is not expressly forbidden by the law – thus avoiding any inference that liberty derives from the permission of the state. For government was created to confirm an antecedent and existing liberty; it is not within its gift.[116]

The concept of collective political or constitutional liberty (as distinct from individual liberties or privileges) is closely integrated within an exposition of the traditional corporeal analogy of society which places novel emphasis upon a logical corollary: the expression of the general will of the body politic. The combination is supremely important in its reconciliation of the realities both of differentiation of function and of social inequality with a resolute belief in *political* equality. The early modern Commonwealth assumption that the ordinary man had a right, not to participate in government, but to be governed well, is now qualified through a process of consultation, representation, and delegation.[117] The parts or members of political as of natural bodies have their quite specific functions, but are not independent of the body as a whole. Thus the people, although incapable of the ordinary business of government, must have an organized means of forming judgements and exerting power to correct abuses and to punish violations of any public trust: without this capacity there is no political liberty. But, and of crucial import for electoral arrangements, that liberty 'must arise principally from gradual subdivisions to the utmost degree of minuteness. In the constitution of the human body, nature is as attentive to a capillary nerve, as to sinews and bones. By subdivisions sufficiently minute . . . and all elections made by representations, or by representations of representations – the general will would be the law.'[118] In the proper exercise of the powers conferred by and answerable to this general will, the principle of delegation in trust is crucial: the instruments or servants of the public being answerable not to some meaningless interaccountability but to the whole community. For in default of recognition of some reserved and superior power delegation becomes in reality a mere *transfusion* of power.[119] Yet Williams is again at pains to stress that this reserved and supreme power in the people does not mean 'any faculty warranting the interposition of the whole community, or any part of it at pleasure, in the executive, legislative, or judiciary offices of government. That species of intervention was called liberty in ancient republics. I consider it, among the most pernicious species of usurpation, or tyranny.'[120]

This apparently striking anticipation of his reaction to scenes in the French Convention late in 1792 may perhaps more correctly be designated the wisdom of hindsight (after the Gordon Riots) than of foresight. Meanwhile, in what seems a partial reconsideration of his assertions in 1782, Williams goes on to insist that, though we must eliminate the present ludicrous freedom of a member totally to betray his trust, the functions of a representative should not normally be merely mechanical, or those of a minutely mandated delegate. Given a properly conducted electoral system, constituents will appoint a representative who will attempt to deliberate and to act as they would do if present. It is indeed possible that 'things may appear to him in a light of which he had no conception on undertaking the charge; that a difference in opinion may arise between him and his constituents. In that case, he is to act from his own judgement; and submit to the consequence. But as his judgement may be wrong, and that of his constituents right; as it is possible he may have been influenced, or corrupted, the constituents should have a speedy or easy mode of discharging him.' Unfortunately, he does not explain exactly how or how often this may be done; but his reluctance to abandon the right of individual judgement is underlined by his description of a Dutch practice of referring every proposition to one's constituents as 'sinking the representative into a post-boy'.[121]

As for those constituents themselves, he spurns the notion that the suffrage should be related to possession of property – which is of itself a sufficient advantage without the unjust addition of political privilege at the expense of industry, labour, and talent. Only crime or civil offence should disenfranchise. As for the political sophistry of excluding the lower orders for alleged defective intelligence,[122] David Williams's experience nationwide (despite occasional difficulty with dialect) leads him to prefer the farmer and the labourer to the ignorance and folly of their so-called superiors.[123] In the process of election and consultation, disruption of any sort may be avoided by a 'mode of *imitating nature* [my italics] in the construction of societies' which, as he points out, was fully explained by him in 1782 – though with much more emphasis on strict mandation of delegates.[124] His dread of large and unruly assemblies is reiterated: 'Democracies have generally exhibited only the caprices of a rabble.' To establish a government resting upon the systematically ascertained judgement of a people requires a degree of scientific skill greater than that which disciplines an army. For democracies 'where the people are the immediate legislators and executive magistrates, may be as despotic as the governments of single tyrants.' Thus the fundamental problem in the construction of a free state is that of *organizing* the expression of the considered political will of the people.[125]

Its resolution would appear to lie not in any definition of status which would confer, and hence by implication also deny, a right to vote, but rather in attitudes and procedures. In ancient republics their assemblies were composed of an idle and tumultuous throng, a small and irresponsible part of the state, the partisans of particular demagogues. The pejorative phrases exemplify his *bêtes noires*. In contemporary England Williams understands but cannot condone any interference by the populace, albeit driven desperate by bad government, and deprecates those who 'crowd to the harangues of modern orators, and *dishonor the cause of the people, by assuming the appellation*' (my italics).[126] In passages which anticipate not only his immediate evaluation of events in Paris in 1792–3 but also his later writings, he describes how, in ancient Rome, 'when the senate had engrossed the power of the community, the populace, who had the same object, broke in forcibly on that iniquitous body; and participated the authority by which they had been oppressed. The right of that participation, seems to have been the idea of liberty entertained by the Roman populace.' The modern custom of assembling such promiscuous multitudes – while the sober and useful members of society remain in their proper pursuits – presents a similar danger. If power be seized by such assemblies then 'the dregs of the community would be its tyrants; and the capital being the asylum of profligacy, and furnishing perpetual successions of tumultuary assemblies, the populace of the capital must govern the state; and a species of tyranny take place, as capricious, oppressive, or ruinous, as that of monarchy or aristocracy.'[127]

If Williams is anxious to dissociate the legitimate political rights of the people from such 'mobocracy', he is equally clear that *political* neither implies nor derives from *social* equality. In the previous century, Winstanley had developed in earnest, and to its logical conclusion, Rainsborough's gibe in answer to Ireton in the Putney Debates: 'Sir, I see that it is impossible to have liberty but all property must be taken away'.[128] David Williams was typical of his age in adhering to an older line of thought: the sixteenth-century Commonwealth idealists' acceptance of social inequality combined with the demand for social *equity*, with the addition now of political equality as a necessary guarantor of *all* rights. Plainly put, 'equality cannot take place, in a pure and rational government comprehending the interests and consulting the happiness of all the inhabitants'. For in nature both beauty and utility derive from inequality. A proposal to render men of equal height or weight would be about as rational and useful as any attempt to impose equality of fortune or power. 'It was probably a design to correct such imaginary errors of nature, that gave rise to the fable of the bed of Procrustes ... or the Agrarian laws, with which wild imaginations have disturbed the public peace.'[129] For the moment talent or industry is exerted then notions of equality must disappear. The task of civil and political institutions is to extend equal justice and encouragement to equal effort and talents, not to persons or to plots of land. Any successful attempt to fix property and power would produce universal torpor.[130]

Political equality has naught to do with fortune or talent but grants protection from injury and security in the exercise of ability. 'If a state were to be formed, all men should start from equal situations and with equal advantages; as horses do on the turf: afterwards every thing is to depend on agility and merit. The only idea of equality remaining, is a right to the same justice.' But this in turn implies electoral equality lest the inequalities of civil will be transferred unjustly into political life – although indeed such political equality ceases once the votes are cast. Though a warm and devoted admirer of liberty, Williams insists that it emerges from in-equality not uniformity. For men are not equal by nature; neither are they equal in civil or political society, save for that purely temporary but quite essential equality at the moment of casting of votes which reconciles all differences through a safeguard of private and public justice.[131]

Yet if private property and social inequality are perfectly consistent with political equality and social equity, David Williams is equally clear that the pur-suit of wealth *ad libitum* is reprehensible. In this, again, he is within the idealist Commonwealth tradition; but the point is made in terms which indicate some recognition of the implications of modern industrialisation. Mercantile wealth cannot atone for the degradation of the greater part of society into unthinking machine-like functions. 'When the people are reduced to slavery, civil or commer-cial, by mechanic and habitual dependence on taskmasters' the wealth of the com-munity is of little consequence to its members. The ancients prized liberty above all, but some moderns would obtain wealth at any cost, even by those divisions of labour which reduce the mass of the community below the condition of brutes.[132] If this resembles an industrial version of Goldsmith's *Deserted Village*, another brief excursion into social and economic problems smacks of Malthus: 'It seems demon-strable, that the utmost industry in the most favourable situations, would not pro-vide for the utmost effects of the generative faculty'; if the present 'vicious procreation' goes unchecked, many must perish.[133] As for taxation, another topic which recurs in his later writings,[134] in general it is an oppressive burden imposed on poverty and industry by ignorance and profligacy.[135] Yet his overwhelming pre-occupation was with political and constitutional issues in what was, as yet, his longest publication in this field.

It met with a tepid reception.[136] If the modern reader, searching vainly for a co-herent exposition of political thought, shares the exasperation of contemporary re-viewers, it must in fairness be recalled that these were lectures avowedly related to Montesquieu. Much of their content is repetitious, developing themes encountered earlier. But the coincidence is not absolute: in particular, the *social* dimension of his political thinking here receives its first considerable airing, and in that respect the work, while not attaining the éclat of *Letters on Political Liberty* or even *Lessons to a Young Prince* (1790), has its own importance. Indeed, its rather greater attention to this aspect may well remind us of the economic and social dynamism of the period spanned by his long career as a writer.[137]

Near the end of these Lectures a few most interesting paragraphs are devoted to the American and the French experience, which gave an extra dimension to British political thought. While commending the attempt of American legislators to disprove Montesquieu's contention that freedom is possible only in small states, Williams fears the outcome. 'Their constitutions are judicious in the general form of the confederacy: but they have been inattentive to the organization of the extremities, with which the heart should have rapid and intimate sympathies.' In fact, just as they owe their country's independence more to the folly of its oppressors than to their own efforts, 'they may owe political tranquillity for ages, more to situation, than to any peculiar wisdom in the construction of their constitution'. Unfortunately, his promise of a critical study of the recently established American Constitution was to be fulfilled only in a brief treatment in his next publication.[138] Finally, he invites the reader to 'look over into France, where a scene is just opening, that should excite your noblest emulation. The king of France, instead of forcing on the nation the minister of his choice, has submitted to the public opinion[139] . . . France, under such direction, will spring suddenly into a condition of vigor and prosperous activity, that may astonish Europe.'[140]

Such comments, like much of the content of his *Lessons to a Young Prince*, published in September, 1790, which essay a detailed assessment of the events and impact of the early stages of the French Revolution, look ahead to what was to be the climactic experience of David Williams's political evolution. Indeed the full title presents the Lessons as written 'by an Old Statesman, on the Present Disposition in Europe to a General Revolution'.[141] But the first chapters are still preoccupied with English constitutional problems, and although the Introduction describes the author as concealing his name even from printer and publisher the dedication and early pages continue to pay court to the Prince of Wales – though once again it is impossible to avoid the suspicion that the tongue is in the cheek. He seeks 'to rouse some latent principles in a mind I think excellent, which has been neglected, or misled with design'.[142] Yet if the Prince's frivolity is but a natural reaction against his parents' disposition, it has unfortunately generated an opposition of which the great factions of the day have availed themselves and to which alone it can be beneficial. The change of attitude toward Fox's group, foreshadowed in *Constitutional Doubts*, is now very clear; 'for the great evil of the opposition that boasts your Royal Highness's sanction is, that by an odium which time and talents have not abated, it shadows an administration incapable, ignorant, and at enmity with the essential principles of a free constitution'. The nation stands aghast at the realization that the insidious chicanery of the present extraordinary administration, which uses the pretence of paying off the national debt to increase taxes and multiply the expense of private establishments,[143] may be replaced '*merely by the universal dread of the depredations of a needy and profligate cabal!*' It is essential to convince the people that this is *not* the case.[144]

Fox himself, the leader of the group, is remarkably defective in political wisdom: his errors include the Coalition, the India Bill, the assertion of inherent right to the

Regency, and the trial of Warren Hastings – 'events which mark the public life of Mr Fox with national odium'.[145] Thus Pitt, with abilities which are inferior but with the art of profiting by Fox's errors, has won the prizes. As for Burke's superficial and ostentatious talents: '*Satis eloquentiae sapientiae parum*'. Sheridan is a mere artificer of scenes, contriving chameleon-like to be all things to all men, and yet without a friend. What was it that had 'sanctioned resolutions of Parliament the most absurd, the most unconstitutional, the most inimical to Liberty ... directed the public wishes to the royal coach with a fervor little short of idolatry; and hailed the King's recovery as a national salvation?' Simply the dread of seeing the nation's government degraded by its entrustment to a cabal.[146] The intensity of feeling is not overstated. The managers of one theatre, during the crisis of the royal illness, had been forced to cease production of a play 'lest the People should pull their House down'; its content was in no way contemporary, but its title, *The Regent*, was quite sufficient![147]

Hence this appeal to the Prince, couched in mind-boggling terms: 'Henry V, to whom your Royal Highness is frequently compared, indulged his eccentricities at eighteen: your Royal Highness is approaching the age of thirty.' It is surely time to divest oneself at once of an interested and sordid set and of a name for incurable frivolity. For although the nation has escaped that precipice to which the American War had brought it, England now faces the challenge of a general disposition in Europe for which philosophy has long prepared and which must soon reach this island. It is now imperative that the Prince should comply with the earnest wishes of his parents and his country by contracting a marriage and establishing a household alike consistent with his dignity. The nature of the challenge has been identified by George III: '*What! what! if they go on at this rate, in thirty years they will not leave a King in Europe.*' If arbitrary monarchy is meant, then Williams will endorse the forecast, but fortunately it is not the purpose of political philosophy to degrade *constitutional* kings.[148]

For Williams now identifies as the great object of philosophical enquiry not the nature of God or the mechanism of the universe, but the principles of society. How may we produce a model 'which may protect and defend with its whole force the persons and property of every one of its members, and in which *each individual, by uniting himself to the whole, shall nevertheless be obedient only to himself*?'[149] (My italics: the phrase, while completely consistent with David Williams's own organic or collective interpretation, is irresistibly reminiscent of Rousseau.) Granted that the repository of supreme power is the body of the people, which is not disposed to injure its own members. 'But how is the general will to be obtained? Individuals may have private wills regarding private interest; but the general will is directed only to the general good.' History is of little help: in a few states the appointment of representatives has been agreed, '*but the supreme power or the actual sovereignty of a state cannot be represented or deputed*'. For the act which constitutes government is not even a contract; it is the arbitrary decision of an absolute sovereign. The depositaries of delegated power, whether princes or parliaments, are subject to the people by an eternal law of nature which subordinates a part to the whole.[150]

Application of such criteria to the English Constitution exposes the legislature –

despite the romances of Montesquieu or Blackstone and the fashionable myth of a balanced constitution – as a fraudulent deception. The grand secret of monarchical management of political bodies is that of dividing them, then passing off the prostituted parts for the whole. Allusions to puppets at the helm and to variegated herds of ecclesiastical and political hirelings are par for the course as Williams presents a parody of the royal case. But allusions to finance and to the press are of particular interest. 'By the present system of finance, the interests of the treasury are so entwined with the general property, that it requires the most delicate hand to lay the axe at any of the roots of corruption.' Thus speculators in funds, contractors, and brokers abound. 'Enlighten the soul of our *heaven-born* minister with the strongest rays of invention [and] confirm him in the exquisite hypocrisy by which fallacious hopes are held out, that the public burdens will be removed ... We thank thee, that by his assiduity, the arms of the customs and excise nearly embrace the land.'[151] As for the liberty of the press, enlistment of a band of mercenary scribblers has converted our bitterest enemy into a friend.[152] Above all, 'thou knowest *we can do no wrong*; the blame is on bad councellors. Let the evils of a detestable and disgraceful war be on Lord –––; *we* have changed *our* administration.'[153]

Lesson V, which credits Alfred with the first correct attempt to secure the concurrence of the general will, proposes to assist the Prince's understanding with a diagram, the first of some half-dozen. By the concentric constitution delineated, with the freemen's representative power exerted via tythings, hundreds and counties to the Myclegemot and Witenagemot at the centre, 'the head and the extremities are united; not by occasional elections, or by pretended delegations of national power. The whole surface of the body, by minute subdivision, is formed to receive and transmit instantaneous impressions, external and internal.'[154] Text and diagrams thereafter depict the subsequent development of the form of government – for in truth England has no formal political constitution.[155] English Government at the Revolution, again concentric, shows the Aristocracy at the centre unequally divided, the major part holding the Crown in tutelage and appointing a Legislature in its name, while a dotted line at the periphery indicates the body of the People, variously exploited and amused by forms. By 1790, significantly, an emancipated Crown exerts considerable influence upon the larger part of a more equally divided Aristocracy.[156] In conclusion, the Prince is reminded that all discretionary power is tyranny, just as 'the force and will of the body would be inconvenient and destructive, if wholly confined to the feet, the hands, or the head'.[157] All parts of governance, like members of the natural body, should be directed by the same animating principle: the general interest or will. By these standards the English nation is not yet a political body. Those householders who have even nominal votes are controlled by their alleged superiors. In short, a factious body within society has arrogated the denomination of the state.[158]

The book made considerable impact. Two anonymously published works in defence of the English Constitution in 1791 gave it considerable if unfavourable notice. The one brackets its author with 'the American Spy', Thomas Paine, as the most formidable and mischievous of the designing apostles of sedition. It concedes the brilliant and elegant presentation of a writer whose 'genius, or learning, or knowledge' appears superior to that of Paine, recognizes the justice of his critique of Burke, and suggests that had he but confined himself to theory his talents would be much admired. Yet his book's real purpose, to expose both government and religion to ridicule and contempt, vitiates it all. Sadly, however, 'the wonder of fools has been excited; the book hath rapidly sold ...'[159] Another anonymous work cites extracts purporting to prove that certain passages in Paine are obviously derived from *Lessons to a Young Prince*. But the pretensions of its author to be considered 'an old statesman' are derided; 'His anxiety about what the news-paper critics have said of his performance, indicates that he is nothing but some ordinary person ... who has need of all the profits of his seditious labours ...'[160]

The reception accorded by the major reviews was indeed very mixed.[161] Yet the book (whose remaining Lessons, devoted to France, will appropriately be considered in the next chapter) is of outstanding interest in that – as reflected in its own internal changes of mood and approach – it comes nearest to a conjunction of all those political and constitutional issues which engaged the attention of David Williams: his country's own internal crises; the contingency of the successful American and emergent French Revolutions; and the search for a body of political and governmental norms of general applicability, in which respect it rivals *Letters on Political Liberty* as the high-water mark of his radical political philosophy. The attribution of this term as a general description of this most prolific phase of his authorship has been mooted. Most of his best-sellers, covering the full range of his varied interests, were now published and his best-remembered project, the Literary Fund, was formally established.

Thereafter, no known publication of Williams devoted to religious philosophy or to education is extant; but in regard to his political and constitutional thought a new phase was to commence. As yet, from *The Philosopher* onwards, his political principles had been expounded from the standpoint of a keenly interested but avowedly detached observer, with minimal evidence of any readiness for actual personal involvement. But in the near future he was to measure and test his constitutional theories within the arena not of British but of French political realities. He who would neither espouse nor find himself taken up by any political party in his own country was to play a short-lived and tentative role as a constitutional *éminence grise* of the Girondist grouping (if party is too strong a word) at the heart of the French Revolution. Ironically, it was as a 'Citizen of France' that David Williams came nearest to playing an active part in political life or at least in the making of constitutional decisions.

Chapter Six

'CITIZEN OF FRANCE'

THE contribution of David Williams is seldom accorded a substantial place in modern treatments of the relationship between the French Revolution and British radical thought. Yet, in terms both of his writings and of personal participation, his case is surely the embodiment of that pattern of transition from euphoric approval to disillusioned discomfiture which typified so much of British reaction to events in France. As ever, he was not inclined in retrospect to understate his contribution; yet any scepticism as to its real significance is checked by a wealth of contemporary evidence in independent, notably French, sources. We noted earlier[1] his friendship with Brissot, whose involvement in the translation of *Letters on Political Liberty* increased their impact in France. Now more fully, in his manuscript autobiography, in *Lessons to a Young Prince*, and in a published article not hitherto attributed to his pen,[2] we may examine his claim to have had some influence in the ideological genesis of the French Revolution as well as his contemporary reactions to its outbreak and early course.

Williams relates how Brissot, returning in 1788 via England from a visit to America (the only land of liberty, in which he contemplated the establishment of a colony of republican Frenchmen), consulted his personal oracle.[3] A prediction that the establishment in France of Provincial Assemblies was the clearest portent of the onset of revolutionary trends[4] in which he could play a part changed his mind. After lengthy discussion of Williams's published ideas Brissot 'departed for France – where he was useful in suggesting to Mirabeau and Sieyes those divisions of the Country which they called its organisation; & where he was instrumental in establishing the Jacobin Club. – Such are the Contradictions to which Men are liable, who take their Measures principally from Books.'[5] This last rather cryptic remark typifies Williams's assessment of Brissot: indeed in general his claim to have influenced the ideas of those who produced the first French Constitution (of 1791) is always qualified by the observation that events have proved 'that Brissot and his successors, in the formation of several French constitutions, have never thoroughly comprehended the ideas of Alfred, or the theory derived from them by his English interpreter'! Whether or not we believe the assertion that Brissot 'first carried into France the idea of *organizing* a community, by forming deputations, and deputations of deputations, to produce a general will', whose novelty endowed him with a lustre which his own abilities were not afterward able to support,[6] it is clear that Brissot retained some contact with his mentor during the elections to the States General.[7] Moreover, the enduring impact of the ideas of David Williams elsewhere among what now became effectively the French political nation is attested in Jérome Pétion's *Avis aux François sur le salut de la Patrie*, 1789, which cites approvingly long passages from *Lettres sur la Liberté Politique*.[8]

Williams's first *contemporary* discussion of revolutionary events in France is in his *Lessons to a Young Prince*, 'by an Old Statesman, on the Present Disposition in Europe to a General Revolution',[9] first published in 1790. Indeed this and similar discussions may serve as a salutary reminder that we are so used to the perspective of hindsight that it is difficult to look at France through English, or at England through French, eyes in the first year or so of the Revolution. In 1789, while some Englishmen looked back to 1689, others looked only to the Gordon Riots of 1780. Again, in a cross-Channel context it is suggested that the Regency Crisis underlined a potentially crucial weakness of the British Constitution just when the French were debating its emulation. Yet again, in an age far more conscious of an essential interconnection between political and religious liberty, the impact upon English Dissent of the early and sweeping victory of religious tolerance in French revolutionary theory can hardly be over-emphasised.[10] Significantly, Sir James Mackintosh's *Vindiciae Gallicae* or 'Defence of the French Revolution and its English Admirers, against the accusations of the Right Hon. Edmund Burke', 1791, suggests that those attacks have polarised national opinions which could not previously have been defined with any precision. Sir Samuel Romilly's earlier *Thoughts on the Probable Influence of the French Revolution on Great-Britain*, 1790, conceded a reception which stopped well short of universal and enthusiastic admiration, and anticipated Mackintosh's caveat against identifying legislative programmes with popular excess, and permanent achievement with personal outrages at which humanity revolts.[11] In her *Vindication of the Rights of Men*, 1790, yet another reply to Burke, Mary Wollstonecraft depicts the sufferings of the poor and asks: 'What were the outrages of a day [identified as 6 October] to these continual miseries?'[12]

David Williams, customarily, produced his own highly individual assessment: 'Burke may declaim,[13] "that a bloody and ferocious democracy is demolishing ancient and venerable institutions" ... Stanhope may rummage conventicles for saints to hail an approaching millenium, *on the principles of the English Revolution!* when *Priestley* with the zeal and verbosity of a *Baxter*, and *Price*, with the *meek* and *holy* ambition of a *Praise-God Barebones* may trample on the *Lauds*, the *Bonners* ... of the time.' This combination of personal gibes with an implied attack on a misplaced seventeenth-century radical-dissenting interpretation of events is later repeated in a caricature of how, employing those rites of pious magic which are presumed to involve the Deity in even the most sordid of human affairs, 'a club, calling itself the Revolution Society, employed a nonconformist clergyman as its magician: and he solemnly invoked his God, on a festival destined to another purpose, in behalf of those "levelling furies" in France, who, in demolishing the ancient and "sacred" temple of absolute monarchy, nearly buried the king, the queen, the nobility, and the clergy, in the ruin.' A derisive codicil that the magician's doctrinal unorthodoxy, as a professed Arian, must surely nullify the resolutions of the Society of which he professes to be Pontiff, suggests that Williams has as little respect for Price as for Burke (who used a similar term).[14] But his basic purpose is to expose 'the artifices of

elf-interested empirics; who, like the fly in the fable, place themselves on the
wheel of human events, and buz to the ideots around them, that they influence and
egulate its rotations'.[15] Above all, contrary to current English misinterpretations,
while the objective of the French National Assembly is not to introduce a democ-
acy (at least, in any pejorative sense), neither is it to imitate the measures of the
English Revolution.[16]

His own assessment is preceded by a full appraisal of other political philosophers, from Locke to Adam Smith: all have failed to grasp the crucial issue in
politics, the art 'of governing All by All'.[17] But Rousseau at last receives a lengthy
and quite friendly examination. Indeed, though his idea of a social compact is
fanciful, 'for the idea of a political constitution is produced like that of a wheelbar-
ow,[18] it is wonderful how frequently he approaches the truth'. In particular,
Williams seizes upon a sentence which was to engross many later commentators:
The general will is always in the right, but the judgement by which it is directed,
is not always sufficiently informed.' Yet in face of this dilemma, whose resolution
would be of inestimable benefit to society, Rousseau's genius deserts him. For
despite his recognition of the need for '"working a total change in human nature"
- He does not bear in mind, that *government is the principal instrument of that change*
[my italics]; and that the public will, being expressed by a permanent Constitution, would form that public judgement and public reason, by the necessity of re-
lection on the events it produced: effects would become causes, and errors
instructions.'[19] This concept of participation in self-government as in itself a part of
the process of social education will be repeated'.[20]

Turning briefly to comparative treatment of Constitutions, while acknowledging
the skilful formulation of the American federative version he contrasts it unfavourably with the French determination 'to level all provincial distinctions, and to
organize the whole nation into one body'.[21] (Reflection on the durability of
American Constitution-making as against the prodigal career of the French, may
tempt one to dismiss this criticism; but, in recollection, Williams's U.S.A.
approximated to the Atlantic seaboard,[22] while pre-revolutionary France, with its
internal customs barriers and diverse systems of law and weights and measures,
was not then in any modern sense united.) Williams asserts that this federative
attempt to combine thirteen separate entities 'is the defect of the American State;
and not as Mr. Adams has asserted; the want of that balance by the counteraction
of three powers, on which Montesquieu has taught him to imagine the liberties of
Englishmen depend.'[23] His question-begging congratulation of the Americans on
having 'wisely avoided the Mystery of the three powers' underlines his distrust of
any mechanism of balance along traditional lines. He deplores the absence of that
'capacity of common judgment and general will, which would have resulted from a
general organization of the republic into one body'. The Public Will and the
Public Force arising from such organization would guarantee both liberty and
security without any need for imaginary balances. As it is, Williams ventures a
forecast which the Civil War was almost to validate – that, given existing arrangements, in time the disparate interests and characteristics of the American States
will alienate and disunite them. Despite such reservations, undoubtedly the return

of the French auxiliaries from America brought the spark of Liberty which fell on touchwood.[24]

Lesson VIII, on the Constitution of France, assesses the achievement thus far of the National Assembly – an appraisal of particular interest alongside that produced for his Girondin friends in December 1792. Williams reiterates his identification of its positive aim as neither the wrong type of democracy nor an imitation of the despised principles of 1688–9. Its purpose is not to impose a *machine* (a word which will recur), whether denominated Monarchic, Aristocratic, or Democratic, but rather 'to organize the community itself; to form it into an actual body; to diffuse a lively and poignant sensibility' which will ensure the welfare of all its parts. Not surprisingly, he discerns the influence (partly through translation) of such ideas as presented in *Letters on Political Liberty*, *A Plan of Association*, and *Lectures on Political Principles* whose author little thought that 'the National Assembly of France would immediately publish so glorious a Commentary on his work'.[25]

Yet he now hopes to induce these philosophic politicians to reconsider some fundamental laws in the emergent Constitution, notably relating to electoral procedure. Thus the definition of citizens lacks justice in forgetting that 'the first and general purpose of society is to guard the weak against the strong, and the poor against the rich. The first division of all the people of France is into cantons; but in voting for the next rank of citizens called Electors, those who do not pay a certain sum towards the public expense are excluded: i.e. they are enslaved.' The social overtone continues. Such unjust deprivation, of those whose poverty is in itself a sufficient evil, of their only stimulus to acceptance of their lot – the choice of their masters – will be a constitutional disease which no palliative can remove.[26] A second, familiar criticism is that the Cantonal Assemblies are too large. Williams has never seen an assembly exceeding twenty, regardless of its members' abilities, which was not more disposed to tumult and passion than to reason and judgement. Indeed, the National Assembly itself would function more effectively if it were smaller, with business entrusted more to open committees and printed proposition than to oratory.[27] Having established basic voting assemblies not of Alfred's ten householders but of six or seven hundred incapable of reasoned judgement, the French Assembly has next endeavoured to rectify one error by another: the device of Electors. Admittedly, 'when a few incidents[28] had shaken to the dust the remains of ancient despotism, the Assembly gradually changed its tone'. But its prudence verges on timidity, and sometimes becomes equivocation.[29] In fact, the concession of making *all* 'active' citizens eligible as deputies was offset by raising the qualification for election to an electoral College, while in any case the new Legislative Assembly was elected under the original proposals.[30]

While Williams does not attempt an overall analysis of the new Constitution (as yet, unratified) and has little to say on certain aspects which concerned later critics – unicameralism and the extreme emphasis on the separation of power[31] – one comment is strikingly prophetic: 'The members of the National Assembly often insinuate that future legislatures will not have their powers; but will they not, like the English Parliament, assume them? ... To prevent this evil, the National Assembly should separate its constitutional from its legislative acts.' Indeed it may well be necessary to hold annual meetings in a purely *constitutional* capacity. This wisdom *before* the event, reminiscent of that of Adams,[32] presages his comments on the Convention in his 'Observations on the late Constitution' and points towards the enduring tensions within his own political philosophy. At a *social* level, the emphasis upon organic unity is pre-eminent; but once the mechanics of the constitution are involved then the resolve to guarantee individual rights and to entrench constitutional procedures against any over-hasty revision, indeed something near to a residual belief in fundamental law, are never far below the surface.

Nonetheless, the French and English nations, respectively, will henceforth be an organized and active body as against a passive mass. Thus French reforms imply 'a perfect police; for the magistrates are *chosen* in all the neighbourhoods, and their offices are annual',[33] while the grant of perfect liberty of opinion must impress all conscientious Dissenters. By contrast, the English Government remains a machine which manages the people at the will of sectional interests.[34] The long additional lesson, answering Burke, restates his ideal: the nation, organized as sovereign, expresses the general will, 'that every citizen, without distinction of birth, possessions, or talents, enjoy the great objects of society – liberty, property, and security'. Liberty is the power of every citizen to seek his own happiness, without injuring others; all beyond this is licence. The right of property includes 'the necessary justice, that men of every condition should enjoy the advantages of their honest industry, and not be obliged to sacrifice them to the pride and pleasure of others: And social security, arises from the engagement of the whole community to preserve the person, property, and liberty of every individual, untouched while unoffending.'[35]

This sounds like a Rousseau-like concept of the General Will dedicated to the preservation of basically Lockeian individual rights – with Commonwealth/paternalist social overtones. Equality before the law, equality under the law, are clearly envisaged – but not equality in any social or economic sense, by the law. Reverting to constitutional procedures, Williams insists that the general will may be expressed without need of large assemblies or of investing the people with executive power – the vulgar idea of democracy. He goes on to explain, and illustrate, that in Alfred's Constitution the Mycle-gemot was not a standing part of government; 'it enacted no laws, but such as were constitutional; it performed no office of the executive power, but adjudged it'.[36] Setting aside idiosyncrasies of historical interpretation, we seem at this point to be near to a concept of the General Will as exercising a power of judicial review on constitutional issues. Certainly, Williams hopes that the example of the National Assembly, using powers analogous to those of the Mycle-gemot to organize society into a vitally integrated political body, will be emulated by England.[37]

A lengthy rebuttal of Burke's misinterpretation of events in France (and indeed in British history) combines savage personal attack with political explanation,[38] while the seventh English edition of 1791 has an Appendix which couples another furious assault with a very revealing apologia for its author's own position: 'It is alledged, the author acts in politics the part of a knight errant ... and that he might produce greater effect, by associating with others, who have views similar to his own. In every attempt of the kind, he has hitherto been unsuccessful. All the parties with which he has had any communication, have been actuated principally by their peculiar interests. And the author is so much an humourist, that he would not submit to be the instrument, and it would not gratify him to be the idol of any club, sect, or faction ... That the Author's satire is the offspring of disappointment, is an opinion industriously circulated. The paths of ambition, civil and ecclesiastical, have been sometimes opened, and the hand of power held out to him; but his mind has been intractable to the political discipline of the present reign, and he could never command the servile patience to be cursed and damned, by avowed and profligate impiety, even into the the flattering and profitable privilege of dispensing the gifts of the holy spirit. To administer the affairs of the smallest village, by the fair election and consent of its inhabitants, would highly gratify the Author: to be appointed to the government of a kingdom, by the caprice of arbitrary power in a prince or patron, would humble and mortify him. The nature of all possible disappointments to him may therefore be accurately ascertained.'[39]

Whatever the accuracy of such allusions to negotiations with parties in England, it is supremely ironic that David Williams was to come closest to practical political participation on the other side of the Channel – the impact of his writings and his personal acquaintance with a few leading French politicians providing the entrée. The fifth edition of the *Lessons to a Young Prince* contains a notice of a new edition of *Letters on Political Liberty* which asserts that (despite a burning of its translation by the Executioner) its opinions 'had some Effect in the Appointment of Provincial Assemblies, and in the Efforts of the present Revolution; and its Principles *must* soon be adopted in England'.[40] Allowance for an utter absence of mock modesty should not perhaps lead to a complete discounting of the claim to influence. For the translator of *Leçons a Un Jeune Prince* itself (Paris, 1790, 'Baudoin, Imprimeur de l'Assemblée Nationale') urges that the intelligence of a new edition with a full refutation of Burke 'must not prevent me from spreading with haste the principles of philosophy and of liberty which have created our Constitution'.[41]

Yet for a year or two personal contact became tenuous. Williams himself relates how his correspondence with Brissot '& through him with the Party of which he was the English Agent' petered out '& when the Leaders of that Party became, in effect, Sovereigns of France it was dropped'.[42] This recollection coincides with his version, written nearer to events, in his article on Brissot in *Biographical Anecdotes*: 'Warned from England of obvious dangers from the power of that club [the Jacobins] and its affiliations, he renounced his first and best acquaintance, by a long silence.'[43] Nonetheless, a letter from Bancal, in London, to Brissot toward the end of 1790, numbers the author of '*Leçons au prince de Galles*' among several excellent English writers who have refuted Burke, and writes in glowing terms of David Williams, 'a true philosopher'.[44] Williams goes on to describe how Brissot, seeking guidance on English legal administration 'procured some hints on that subject from *Mr. Jeremiah Bentham*. But, not being fully satisfied, he endeavoured to recover the friendship of his former counsellor, and sent *Pethion* to be instructed ...'[45]

Jérôme Pétion (who had accompanied the royal return from the Flight to Varennes and who was to become Mayor of Paris) has left his own account of his visit to London in October-November 1791. Amidst much sightseeing he met Romilly, Priestley, Stanhope, Stone,[46] and David Williams. His brief account of his visit to Williams's home confesses that 'our conversation lacked the vivacity and interest which it could have had if we could have spoken the same language'. The need for an interpreter suggests that, despite his literary translations, there were limits to the French conversational powers of his host. In spite of his earlier allusion[47] to Williams's political writings the only topic of discussion which Pétion mentions is that of excessive religious controversy in England. The visitor accepted an invitation to return for dinner, but gives no further detail.[48] His host was to describe him as thinking himself above the need to trouble overmuch and as spending much time at meetings of the Revolution Society.[49] After Pétion's return to France some correspondence ensued which suggested a meeting with Talleyrand when he came to London in February of 1792.[50] But when the Emperor Leopold died in March Williams wrote to Pétion complaining that Talleyrand 'did not send me a message, or do me the honor of calling at my house'.[51] More significantly, his letter goes on to allude to 'the impeachment of the King & Ministers. Let them be punished legally but exemplarily: – & if the King be a Traitor, notwithstanding his numerous Perjuries, now is the Moment to decide on his Fate, by a truly national judgment'.[52]

The traumatic events, including the downfall of the Bourbon monarchy, of the summer and autumn of 1792 were followed by Williams's acceptance of French citizenship and sojourn in Paris itself at a crucial stage of the Revolution. His autobiography explains that, when the now triumphant French leaders of his acquaintance 'determined to bestow the privilege of Citizens, on foreigners, friendly to their Liberties; they could not with decency, pass over my Name; so numerous had been their applications; & so much had been the trouble they had given me, by the Visits of Petion, & of several other of their Missionaries'.[53] An English fair-copy of his letter of acceptance, dated 26 October 1792, addressed to Roland, expresses his sense of the honour paid him. As to the French Constitution (that of 1791) 'it is not wonderful the first attempt should not have fully succeeded'. But its principles have frightened despots throughout the world, and the eyes of all who believe in political justice are now firmly fixed on the National Convention. The conspiracy of European tyrants is defeated, the obstacle of hereditary royalty and aristocracy removed, and France has the first opportunity afforded to Philosophy of constructing a Constitution on the principles of reason and virtue.[54] Several aspects of this missive, whose receipt was recorded in the session of 13 November of the Convention,[55] merit comment: the acceptance of the at least partial failure of the first Constitution, the unflattering absence of any recognition of the American experiment, and the anti-royalist tone.

Meanwhile, both the grant and acceptance of citizenship[56] evoked some interesting contemporary comment. One John Hurford Stone (erstwhile member of Richard Price's congregation, the Revolution Society, the Friends of the People, and the London Corresponding Society, who was to remain in France and live as husband and wife with Helen Maria Williams)[57] wrote from Paris on 27 August 1792 that 'the assembly did a very silly and contemptible thing yesterday, in admitting

Mr Wilberforce, David Williams, and Clarkson, to the rank of citizenship. They are wretchedly informed respecting characters in England; and from this sample they will get themselves laughed at . . .' In a subsequent characterisation of those named it is impossible to mistake the dismissal of Williams as 'a man of no character but a bad one, in a very low rank, either as to political or literary fame, and avowed by no one'. Was this mere sour grapes? Some three months later Stone was still so convinced that citizenship had been thereby devalued that he purports to have prevented all other grants of citizenship – whether Fox's, Sheridan's, or his own![58] Disapproval for different reasons came from a former dabbler in the Margaret Street project, Joseph Banks. On 20 November, replying to a letter concerning a projected prestigious edition of Hume's *History of England* with an added section by Williams, Banks sought 'information from Mr Bowyer whether the Mr D. Williams who the newspaper of this day informs us has accepted the Citizenship of France is the Mr D. Williams who is engaged in his history of England'. Bowyer's embarrassed reply protests that 'if the Revd D. Williams has accepted the Citizenship of France' it is without his knowledge. A call at Mr Williams's has met with the information that he has gone to Bath to recruit his health, which has of late been much impaired. In any case it will be at least five years before his contribution is required![59]

Certainly it had by now become clear to Williams himself that the citizenship granted by his Brissotin friends was not intended to be merely honorary. He recalls how, 'when their private Agent here, applied to those who were destined to the Convention, previous to their nomination in the Newspapers to the Departments, he held several Conversations with me, on the consequences of my being nominated & elected (which was wholly in their power) if I *checked the rapidity of the Revolution* [my italics] or commenced Hostilities in the Jacobin Club'. Williams declined, explaining that to attempt to change the fundamental laws of a nation of which he had little knowledge would expose him to the ridicule of Europe.[60] Suspicion here of retrospective self-importance must not be pushed too far.[61] The idea of internationalising the benefits of and participation in the Revolution was characteristic of Girondin thinking at this time (and partly explains their disastrous miscalculation in hurling France into war). Equally certainly, Williams was offered a seat (as was Paine, who accepted) in the forthcoming Convention. Most significant of all, French sources leave no doubt that his help was indeed sought for the purpose above italicised, which was in turn perceived and condemned by the Jacobins, Montagnards, or Maratistes.

As to the Convention itself, the assertion that this assembly was perverted from Brissot's imported English concept of a Constitution-making body into 'a despot, a legislature, a court of justice, a magistrate of police, – a many-headed monster, which nearly desolated the country that produced it',[62] became even more sweeping in Williams's autobiography in his allusion to the dreadful career of a body 'collected principally from the Dregs of France, by the extension of the right of Suffrage, in violation of a Constitutional Law'.[63] This is a far cry from the commendation of something approaching manhood suffrage in his contemporary writings, though the implication that the Constituent Assembly had established fundamental constitutional law (though retrospective) is less surprising. Nonetheless, whatever his con-

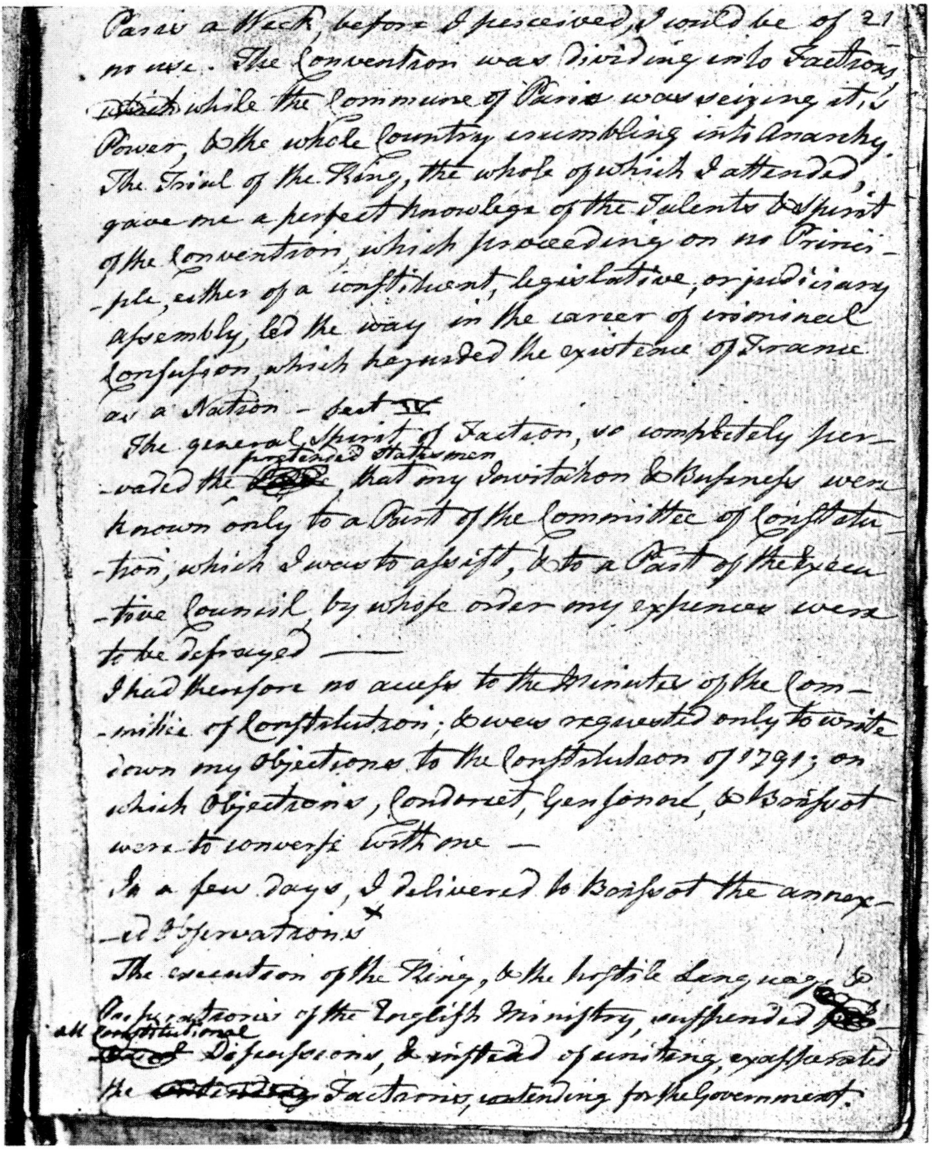

Paris a Week, before I perceived, I would be of no use. The Convention was dividing into Factions, while the Commune of Paris was seizing it's Power, & the whole Country crumbling into Anarchy. The Trial of the King, the whole of which I attended, gave me a perfect knowledge of the Talents & Spirit of the Convention; which proceeding on no Principle, either of a constituent, legislative, or judiciary Assembly, led the way in the career of criminal Confusion, which hazarded the existence of France as a Nation — Sect XI

The general Spirit of Faction, so completely pervaded the parties & Statesmen, that my Invitation & Business were known only to a Part of the Committee of Constitution, which I was to assist, & to a Part of the Executive Council, by whose order my expences were to be defrayed ——

I had therefore no access to the Minutes of the Committee of Constitution; & was requested only to write down my objections to the Constitution of 1791; on which objections, Condorcet, Gensonné, & Brissot were to converse with me —

In a few days, I delivered to Brissot the annexed Observations +

The execution of the King, & the hostile language & Conspirations of the English Ministry, suspended all constitutional Discussions, & instead of uniting, exasperated the Factions, contending for the Government.

Plate 7. PARIS IN 1792–93

temporary as distinct from retrospective reservations, Williams responded to an appeal from Brissot and Roland which he relates to the difficult task of the Convention's Committee of Constitution.[64]

A letter from Brissot, dated 11 November 1792, supporting an official communication from Roland, Minister of the Interior, invites Williams to Paris for about a month. This request, agreed to also by Le Brun, pledges all assistance including full payment of expenses. Its declared purpose is the wish of the 'patriot ministers' to enlist all sources of wisdom or guidance to advance the cause of liberty. But also, 'we have many things to say to you which cannot be entrusted to paper'. Williams is begged to lose no time in coming, whatever the weather, for he will have no better opportunity to serve humanity – indeed there is no mistaking the impression of an urgent plea.[65] Its recipient complied with the request, but explains that he had not been in Paris for a week before perceiving that he could be of no use. 'The Convention was dividing into Factions, while the Commune of Paris was seizing its Power, & the whole Country crumbling into Anarchy. The Trial of the King, the whole of which I attended, gave me a perfect knowledge of the Talents & Spirit of the Convention, which proceeding on no Principle, either of a constituent, legislative, or judiciary assembly, led the way in the career of criminal Confusion, which hazarded the existence of France as a Nation ... The general Spirit of Faction, so completely pervaded the pretended Statesmen, that my Invitation & Business were known only to a Part of the Executive Council, by whose order my expences were to be defrayed – I had therefore no access to the Minutes of the Committee of Constitution; & was requested only to write down my Objections to the Constitution of 1791; on which Objections, Condorcet, Gensonne, & Brissot were to converse with me. In a few days, I delivered to Brissot the annexed "Observations".[66]

A letter in mid-December establishes his Paris address as at 'ru d' richelieu, (Hotel?) des Princes, pres le Boulvard' – a near-contemporary street-plan identifies the building still standing at the junction of Rue de Richelieu and what is now the Boulevard des Italiens.[67] The Rue Neuve des Petits Champs, in which Roland's *ménage* was installed,[68] was conveniently near. For despite the assertion in French sources that Williams had visited the salon of Madame Condorcet at some time in the late 1780s his focal point of consultation seems now to have been that of Madame Roland.[69] Her letters contain but a few brief, though complimentary, references to David Williams. But the lengthy pen-picture in her *Appeal to Impartial Posterity* compares him favourably with Thomas Paine, whom she deems better fitted to sow the seeds of popular commotion than to formulate a constitution: 'For cool discussion in a committee, or the regular labours of a legislator, I conceive *David Williams* infinitely more proper than he. Williams ... was not chosen a member of the Convention, in which he would have been of more use; but he was invited by the government to repair to Paris, where he passed several months, and frequently conferred with the most active representatives of the nation. A deep thinker, and a real friend to mankind, he appeared to me to combine their means of happiness, as well as Paine feels and describes the abuses which constitute their misery. I saw him, from the very first time he was present at the sittings of the assembly, uneasy at the disorder of the debates, afflicted at the influence exercised by the galleries, and in doubt whether it were possible for such men, in such circumstances, ever to decree a rational constitution. I think that the knowledge which he then acquired of what we were already, attached him more strongly to his country, to which he was impatient to return. How is it possible, said he, for men to debate a question who are incapable of listening to each other? . . . A giddy manner, carelessness, and a slovenly person,[70] are no recommendations to a legislator . . . Good Heaven! what would he say now, if he were to see our senators drest, since the 31st of May,[71] like water-men, in long trowsers, a jacket and a cap, with the bosoms of their shirts open, and swearing and gesticulating like drunken *sans-culottes*? He would think it perfectly natural for the people to treat them like their lackeys, and for the whole nation, debased by its excesses, to crouch beneath the rod of the first despot who shall find means to reduce it to subjection. – Williams is equally fit to fill a place in the parliament, or the senate, and will carry with him dignity wherever he goes.'[72]

Surprisingly, in view of her avowal that abandoning the illusions of an empty faith has left her still desirous of congregational worship of the Supreme Being,[73] this perceptive encomium makes no reference to the religious experiment of its subject. But Mme Roland's allusion to the almost total dominance of the Paris Commune by Danton and Robespierre,[74] and to a 'notorious harangue' by the latter in favour of Marat against Priestley,[75] points not only to a change in the balance of the faction-fighting background against which Williams was to attempt to make a contribution, but also to an increasing emergence of some anti-British feeling. By this time, also, there may well have been some divergences of attitude within the ranks of English sympathisers with the revolutionary cause. Thus J. G. Alger (alas, citing no sources, but writing at the turn of the century and much nearer to oral tradition) in recounting a British dinner held at White's Hotel on 18 November to celebrate French military victories, states that although Williams, the friend of Condorcet and Madame Roland, was in Paris at the time, he apparently kept away from the event as being too Jacobinical in tone. Alger also repeats the story that Williams warned the Girondins that unless they put down the Jacobins, whose club had denounced him as a Royalist because he sought to excuse Louis XVI, they would be destroyed.[76]

Contemporary evidence substantiates this picture. The Debates of the Jacobin Society for November–December 1792 record repeated efforts to smear an alleged Cabal comprised of Brissot, Roland, Pétion, and even Paine by association, with the charge of counter-revolution, with plots to delay the trial of the King, and even with contemplation of a military coup. On 14 December Chabot claimed to have exposed the purpose of the Brissotin faction, which he linked with British influence: '*elle veut faire retrograder la révolution*' (my italics).[77] Vague assertions on 8 December that Chabot held documentary evidence of a great conspiracy had been followed next day by a bizarre scenario in the Convention itself in which David Williams himself was named. This centred on the reading of a letter which purportedly informed the president of the assembly that 'the citizens Narbonne, Malouet, John Waris and Williams, demand of the Convention that they act as official defenders of Louis XVI; you have decreed that he will appear at the bar; we will accompany him there with a guard which we have assembled, consisting of twelve thousand men, good republicans, who do not desire the death of Louis XVI'. Amid scenes of mingled derision, denunciation, and counter-accusation, examination of the letter left no doubt that all the signatures were forged; discussion of its provenance left many members (and the present reader) with a very strong impression that any plot involved was one designed to discredit Roland and that Marat was deeply implicated.[78]

A letter written to Williams requesting his intercession on behalf of an emigré family of St Omer would, if known, having done nothing to appease Jacobin rage by its conjoint appeal regarding Louis – 'spare his Life – and let this be the policy of an English man' – or by its reflection 'how glorious will it be for an Englishman to teach them that their constitution may be as glorious and enviable as that of England'.[79] The attribution of such attitudes as English constitutionalism or a wish for clemency toward the King damned Williams in the eyes of Marat[80] and Robespierre, whose comprehensive Anglophobia burst forth in the claim that: 'All our miseries are the work of Pitt and his associates . . . Do you know Thomas Paine and David Williams? . . . They are both traitors and hypocrites.'[81] An Englishman contemporarily resident in Paris, Dr John Moore, recorded the current Jacobin-inspired rumour that the Brissotin/Girondist grouping had actually been bribed by the Foreign Powers at war with France to attempt to save Louis.[82]

The atmosphere within and around the Convention itself is vividly conveyed by Brissot's depiction of groups of cut-throats placed outside to outrage and menace the deputies, among them female bacchanals who speak of nothing but cutting off heads, and to the Galleries where the sovereign masses dominate, or by Barère's description of petitioners arriving at the bar to demand the death of Louis, 'women and children holding and waving in their hands torn garments and strips of shirts and cloth covered with blood' – behaviour which, ironically, despite its menace, he found more suited to the English stage.[83] Brissot, in common with Mme Roland, always insisted on the distinction between 'the immortal revolution of 10 August' and the September Massacres, allegedly the work of brigands, abhorred alike by France and by English and American friends of revolutionary principles;[84] but the great divide had been passed. Williams might indeed have helped imbue his French political allies with a hatred of anarchy and horror of the demagogue.[85] But his spectre of 'the People', pejoratively interpreted, with its proclivity toward tumultuous assemblages whether 'at Westminster-Hall or in Saint George's Fields to choose a senator or watch a bear dance',[86] now stalked the streets of Paris. Quite simply, as he himself was later to recall, faced with 'the howl of *Marat* and his ragged myrmidons . . . the Girondins held the sceptre they had wrested from Louis, with trembling hands'.[87]

This was the far from promising background against which David Williams composed and presented his 'Observations' on the previous French Constitution, embodying suggestions for substantive change. The extent to which those ideas were reflected in the 'Girondine' Constitution must be more a subject of inference than of proof – in the total absence of the Minutes of the Committee of Constitution. Certainly its membership was overwhelmingly Girondin, though Condorcet was not as yet so classified and Brissot himself withdrew.[88] Predictably, Aulard and

Mathiez proffer somewhat different interpretations of its motivations and procedures,[89] while indeed the impressive treatment of *The Girondins* by M. J. Sydenham and the full analysis of the thought of *Condorcet* by K. M. Baker are alike in making no reference to Williams.[90] Yet the present writer sees no reason to question Aulard's assertion that the susceptibility of the Brissotin/Girondist circle to Anglo-American ideas was crystallised in the personal influence of Williams and of Paine.[91] Above all, Franck Alengry's *Condorcet, Guide de la Révolution Française*, 1904, stands out in its appraisal of the significance of David Williams. It was for Condorcet's *Chronique du Mois* that Thomas Morris wrote his friend's biography in 1792, while the sub-title of Alengry's monograph, 'Théoricien du Droit constitutionnel et Précurseur de la Science sociale', points to an obvious empathy with Williams, described as a neglected fore-runner of the organic theory of society.[92] There seems to be agreement[93] that in the formulation of the first republican and democratic Constitution to be written and presented in France the leader in Committee was Condorcet, followed by Paine (whom Alengry rates more highly than did Mme Roland), but Alengry states plainly that Williams was consulted and indeed called to meetings where he expounded several important ideas.[94]

One would like more contemporary testimony, but for direct evidence of the *potential* contribution of Williams to the 'Girondine' we must turn to his *Observations Sur La Dernière Constitution de la France. Avec des vues pour la formation de la nouvelle constitution*, translated by Citoyen Maudru in 1793. A manuscript copy of the original English version is extant, its brief preamble dated at 'Paris 7th of Janry. 1793 – & the second year of the Republic'. This explains that his supposition that the Committee has already made considerable progress and his own lack of preparation for the task assigned have led him to introduce ideas about a new structure alongside his comments on the foundations of the old.[95] The impression conveyed by the manuscript that another section, itself incomplete, has been added thereto is confirmed by its absence from the translated and printed version.[96]

Its content and presentation bear out his introductory note. Sceptical remarks on the utility of a doctrinaire Declaration of Rights precede a typical[97] comment on Article I's inaccurate assertion that Man is born and remains free and equal: for 'Man is born, under the dominion of his parents, which is in general capricious & cruel'. The references to equality therein beg far too many questions – causing fear and suspicion in England, while in France herself a dreadful misinterpretation has given rise to the contention that people should be equal in fact as well as in words.[98] In regard to Article II he observes that 'the ends of all political associations are justice; the liberty of employing our faculties without injuring others & of resisting oppression, & the security & enjoyment of our property'[99] – a list indicative of his own civil liberties and suggesting an instructive contrast with the Jacobins' self-description of 'Amis de l'Égalité et de la Liberté'.[100] Articles III, IV, and V he considers good, but the sixth would better define the law by making it 'conformable to' rather than 'the expression of the general will'. Indeed one is not surprised to read that the problem of organizing society into a body susceptible to the exercise of judgement and will has been an occasional preoccupation of his mind for twenty years.[101]

Declaration of Rights

As Declarations are not Instructions — & can only
be committed to memory, & as they cannot be rendered
unequivocal until a new & republican language be
formed, I doubt their utility — Truths offered in the
form of simple & clear arguments, accustom the
mind to exercise & the convictions they leave are
removeable by better arguments & more improvement;
those fixed by declarations are prejudices, & like all
matters of belief indispose the mind to action &
improvement.—

If the declaration of Rights be continued, I object
to the first article — which declares men to be born & to
remain free & equal in rights. This is disproved by
fact; & is susceptible of controversy; which is a sufficient
objection — If the word equality must be used it should
be as in art. VI.

Man is born, under the dominion of his parents,
which is in general capricious & cruel; he ought to
feel no other dominion, but as domestic customs are
subject to the laws; which, if just & reasonable, regard
comen, on their entrance into society, as equal, and
which provide against the general consequences of
their actual inequalities, in the powers latent & acquired

In turning to consider the first principles of civil society the authorities cited are now extended to include Francois Hotman's *Francogallia*[102], and with equal diplomacy Williams proceeds to associate the Franks with the Germans and Saxons as precursors in the evolution of a just political Constitution as attempted by the late Constituent Assembly. In more recent experience, Pennsylvania has led the way in settling her Constitution by a Convention – though Williams follows this common-place tribute of all progressive thought with his usual rather ungenerous assertion that the Americans have done little to enlarge the boundaries of political science, their prosperity depending on purely fortuitous circumstances and their security on their situation.[103] In assessing the experiment of the 1791 Constitution, Williams concedes that although the first analogy of the constitutional organization of society must have been that of Man himself, 'the constructor of the political machine [hitherto, in this context, a pejorative term] must soon take leave of his model ... For the mode of Nature we substitute what we call Representation. What has hitherto been effected should rather be called deputation or delegation; [regardless of the terms employed, Williams's real problem, and that of many since, was whether what was delegated was a power to make decisions or a strictly-mandated authority to express decisions already made] & it is on the construction of this power, that the properties & faculties of a political constitution must depend' – until some Newton discovers a method nearer to Nature.[104]

Sadly, in this basic task the Constituent Assembly committed a fundamental error, but partly corrected by its Legislative successor.[105] For a just Constitution, Williams urges, must surely recognize as *full* citizens all reasonable inhabitants, subject only to certain basic qualifications. In regard to age, attaining that of twenty will suffice, while as to sex, 'where women remain single, or become widows, they are unquestionably intitled to vote' (the implication is normal to eighteenth-century minds though perhaps infuriating to some in the twentieth century), for education should fit them for the functions of citizens.[106] Touching employment, while Williams is disquieted by the exclusion hitherto of servants from the ranks of citizens, his ambivalent approach to this uneasy issue persists. Recognizing the evil side-effects of an obvious injustice he concedes that 'in their present equivocal circumstances, between freedom & slavery,[107] they retain the vices of the one condition without acquiring the virtues of the other'. Yet his inability to abandon all reservations is very clear: for 'if we make servants citizens at a certain age, & *after certain evidences of good conduct* we insure their being what they ought to be, *our humble friends* [my italics, in both phrases: Williams has retreated from his position in 1782]; instead of being as they now are our latent enemies & perpetual tormentors'.[108]

Moving to a wider, and fundamentally important issue, a nation which has achieved a state of political liberty has the choice of its mode of self-government but, that choice once made, *individuals* resign that liberty of which society as a whole becomes the custodian. The people should be very carefully instructed in this distinction lest 'they become exasperated & licentious, & wish to exert, each for himself, the power which resides only in society'. This utterance of an endemic early-modern fear of anarchy as the natural aspiration of the commons is followed by a neo-Benthamite definition of the purpose of socio-political organization as not only to liberate the talents of its members but also to produce the greatest possible quantity of happiness. Yet in pursuit of this objective Society cannot act as a mass; like matter itself, it can only acquire faculties, judgement, and will by means of appropriate organization. The fundamental problem is to evolve 'an organ, analogous to the economy of the human frame [which can] concentrate, compare, reconcile and form into one all the crude & various opinions & views of all the members of the society'. For the individual opinions of people who often lack both time for reflective consideration and freedom from the influence of local or personal interests are frequently different. 'Hence the necessity of a species of commission or delegation, the offices of which participate of the nature of representation or arbitration & the members of which are the elements of the public reason.'[109]

This necessity is more significantly illuminated by the experience of our forefathers than by the fanciful systems of dogmatic pamphlets of modern times. Predictably, such experience suggests adoption of a basic unit of ten families for purposes both of police and of representation until, by a now-familiar mechanism, the whole society is ultimately reflected in a general assembly. Unfortunately, the primary divisions as established by the Constituent Assembly are such that people are frequently obliged to leave their work and mingle in distant and tumultuous assemblies, swayed by prevailing passions. This is a fundamental error. For 'reason, judgement, & the public virtues require a minute & capillary organization, by which they can regularly & silently influence the whole community.' It is essential that the industrious householders who may truly be designated the people should be so organized as to facilitate reciprocal communication, formation of opinion, and expression of a will, without disruption of normal employment. Yet is this now possible in France? 'The people have been accustomed to larger assemblies, the love of talking & the ambition of oratory has been excited in those who can afford to attend, & numerous little employments & offices are created, which favour the intrigues of the cunning & enterprising.' These tendencies may be checked only by new arrangements which subdivide the people and avoid disorderly assemblies.[110]

As to electoral procedure, Williams then goes on to urge, surprisingly, that choices should be expressed freely and openly, not by complicated and secret contrivances. For 'the various machinery of ballotting is to public virtue, like the art of fortification to public courage, it diminishes & corrupts, instead of guarding & encouraging it'. At first it is not readily apparent how or why his experiences in France, which had clearly confirmed his aversion to large assemblies and the arts of the demagogue, should also have persuaded him to abandon his previously consistent and fervent advocacy of a secret ballot.[111] But he explains that such a device, apart from concealing a species of venality and corruption which could not be practised openly,[112] may vitiate the supreme objective of making the primary assemblies 'the real & most effective schools of the people', in which they 'should comprehend, & from their hearts assent or dissent on every proposition made to them. The influence of property & talents may occasionally prevail; but the people will gradually rise above them, & acquire a character of virtuous independence, which is the only security of political liberty.'[113] Presumably his uncharacteristic rejection of the secret ballot must be seen within this optimistic context of his ideal of a citizenry participating in small electoral units; but in the light of such aspirations his complete lack of interest in organized universal education is again surprising. To revert to procedure, each primary division should despatch a delegate with the names of potential deputies to a meeting which then compiles a departmental list. This in turn, marked with a distinctive seal to obviate counterfeiting, must then be carried back and submitted to a process of election by a majority of votes – the delegates being merely messengers, corruption will be quite impossible. Two or at most three deputies thus elected for each of the 84 departments should then meet in annual sessions. Such provisions would preclude the emergence of pernicious intrigues and cabals within a large and unmanageable assembly.

Additionally, every fourth year the departments should elect a convention, empowered to revise the constitution, confirm or annul acts of the legislature, and express approval or censure of the other branches of government. This sounds rather like a convention *per se*, a constitutional court of appeal (in general terms, the enduring wish for checks and balances to allay distrust of governmental power as such, and more specifically certain American parallels, spring to mind), and a second chamber – all rolled into one. Williams disclaims any novelty: French history attests 'that the ordinary legislature or council of the king, was a different assembly from the Etats Generaux, which were conventional like the Folkmote of the Saxons', with an overseeing power.[114]

Next, a Constitutional Council, its twenty-one members (aged over forty) annually-elected by normal procedures, shall report to the primary divisions on all governmental transactions, such publications to be at the public expense.[115] This body, empowered to receive complaints, shall be wholly destitute of any patronage and responsible to the people, who may call it to account before a special commission if need be. Endowed with authority to summon an extraordinary convention in case of a national emergency, this Council shall also constitute a court of appeal in any inter-departmental or electoral disputes. Finally, it shall be the channel of communication with foreign states and shall receive their ambassadors – though not itself possessing the right of ambassadorial appointment.[116] Institutionally, one is at a loss to characterise this body, endowed with some of the attributes of the Senate of the U.S.A., of a Ministry of Information, Court of administrative appeal, Committee for Foreign Affairs, or even of an Ombudsman; but nothing could be clearer than an almost obsessively neurotic search for safeguarding checks and counterchecks.

Nor is Williams yet done. Although the people shall assiduously be taught to regard each other as brethren, disputes which remain unresolved at the level of the primary divisions will necessitate a judicial system extending through the departments to a national appeal court. While the English jury system shall function in all courts, all judges and other arbitrators must be subject to election, including the Minister of Justice himself. This system of election, 'by delegations bearing the *absolute choice* & *express commands*[117] of the primary divisions', shall extend to the selection of officers of the militia, 'where every citizen from 18 to 55 should be a soldier, & every man, in person, discharge duties of the police'. Indeed it must embrace finance (ranging from collectors to the Minister) as well as the Minister and ambassadors for foreign affairs. All elections, together with both the military exercises of the citizens and their necessary instruction in public affairs, might generally take place during Sunday leisure hours and not encroach on normal patterns of work.[118]

Rigid adherence to the elective principle, presumably to maximise participation *and* accountability, thus extends to judicial and administrative as well as representative functions. Indeed the executive power as such seems to emerge piecemeal as a correlative of such functions, rather than as a coherent and decision-making entity in itself. In this, as in so much else, we shall find a striking similarity in the Girondine Constitution. Since each office will be destitute of patronage, beyond its immediate servants, and each department answerable both to an appeal court and to the people, the executive function will become a duty, not a power which is 'perpetually struggling & intriguing against its constituents'. The device of strictly mandated delegation will ensure expression of 'the will of the majority *of all the people*'[119] in contradistinction to the English spectacle of large assemblies where the rich intrigue and dominate and 'a vicious profligate oligarchy prevails'. With all decisions reconveyed to the people by the Constitutional Council, and a Press absolutely free,[120] 'the public reason ... will gradually & perpetually correct & improve the public will'.[121]

The optimistic ideal of a participating democracy, self-educating in its civic and political functions through the very experience of that participation, is manifest. But now comes a breath-taking statement of an idea not yet encountered in David Williams but which is reminiscent at once of his contemporary Godwin and of Spencer (or even Marx) in the next century: 'By constructing & perfecting a wise government, *we gradually diminish the occasion & necessity of any government* [my italics]; & we prepare men for that condition, which I believe to be practicable, but which I will not pretend to describe, lest I should be charged with improperly blending poetry, with the lucubrations of politics.' The clause italicised, despite its apologetically-phrased addendum, is of a piece not only with contemporary suspicion of government *per se* but also with his own particular credo of the educated individual's ability fully to act in harmony with others within the body of society: the striking feature is the vision of the educative process as occurring in and through the political and governmental functions of society. The hope goes further, embracing the prospect of international peace, achieved at the expense of despots whose sophisms, significantly, and even whose armies, 'will be more rapidly dissipated by the *example*, than by the *conquests of Liberty*'.[122]

This abortive aspiration was at first the final peroration, as it remained in Maudru's printed translation. But an added section follows an allusion to the difficulties caused by the hurry of a short visit, while not yet recovered from an indisposition,[123] with a discussion of the problem of the clergy. While approving an intention to abolish *established* religion and to leave the people free to choose their religion as well as their clergy, Williams makes the perceptive comment that the old order has the prepossessions of the people so strongly in its favour that any remedy will produce convulsions if not prudently administered. His discussion of the nonjuring clergy includes a fascinating though not really surprising cross-current: for 'in all my experience, the priests most submissive & obedient to the requisition of oaths, are not better men than those who refuse them: & in the late schism of the French church, the republic may not have preserved the most valuable division'. Thus the resolutely non-compliant priests, defenders of an order which to Williams embodies perhaps the most abhorrent aspects of organized religion, now stand forth as men of integrity and principle, resisting state coercion, and evoke his reluctant admiration. His own solution to the problem (for unemployed clergy may well turn to activities that are politically pernicious) would be to extend to each parish the right to choose its own form of religion and its own minister. 'The continuation of the priest should be during good behaviour in the opinion of the majority of the parishioners; their appointment should be his ordination, without further mystery or conjuration.' Such a congregational proposal, he concedes, would stand little chance of papal sanction, and the manuscript concludes with the more limited suggestion that Sunday instruction of the parishioners in civic affairs might usefully employ and perhaps evoke the loyalty of refractory clergy.[124]

While of obvious interest in the context of the evolution of the political thought of David Williams, what impact did the 'Observations' (or their author) have upon the emergent Girondine? The fullest French analysis, that of Alengry, attaches great significance to the way in which they base all powers and functions upon election, delegation, and the principle of national sovereignty, and also to certain duties of the 'Committee of 21' which are analogous to the Girondine's Referendum.[125] While going so far as to suggest that the influence of the two British advisers, Paine and above all Williams, was so great that at first sight the production might appear to be their work, Alengry finally concludes that the Girondine was essentially Condorcet's Constitution, integrating their contribution with his own.[126] While the sheer length of the Girondine (made up of over 400 articles, not counting its Declaration of Rights) precludes clause by clause analysis, both the general orientation and specific features of this abortive Constitution at least attest to a major conjunction of minds.

In regard to the sociological dimension of his work, his interest in comparative constitutional analysis,[127] and above all in his preoccupation with the search for an objective mathematical calculus which would fairly enable voting procedures to reflect an *enlightened* public will,[128] much of Condorcet's thought runs parallel with that of David Williams – albeit at a more scholarly level, for a modern monograph on the mathematics of voting theory rates Condorcet highly not only in his appreciation of the problems and complexities involved but also in his attempts to *resolve* them.[129] On the not unreasonable assumption that some face to face discussion took place[130] it is as well to envisage a two-way traffic of ideas: Condorcet may be reflected in the 'Observations' as well as the latter in the Girondine! Thus, was the requirement (Section III, Article 4) that the name of each voter and the names of those he has chosen should be read 'à haute voix' a reflection of Williams's advocacy (supra, 128) of open voting or of an influence which determined his own obvious change of mind regarding the secret ballot?[131]

Ironically, the preamble to the Girondine drops all reference to a Supreme

Being,[132] but includes three clauses (4, 5 and 7) relating to freedom of thought and publication, and ends with the significant assertion (33) that 'a people has always the right to review, to reform, and to change its constitution. No one generation has the right to subject future generations to its laws, and all heredity in functions is absurd and tyrannical.'[133] The extremely detailed regulation of electoral procedures in the Primary Assemblies (whose size, between 450 and 900, would hardly have won Williams's approval), including rigorous scrutiny of lists and voting, coincide in principle with the recommendatons in the 'Observations'. So too does the provision (Titre IX) for the convoking of a National Convention whenever there is any question of reforming the Constitution, and the detailed procedures which guarantee and control it.[134]

The section 'On the People's Censure upon the acts of National Representative Bodies',[135] while not repeating any specific proposal in the *Observations*, is in full accord with Williams's combination of distrust of government with a wish to maximize participation of the citizens in the political process. This attitude of mind is reflected also in the sections dealing with the Executive Council. This body, composed of seven ministers and a secretary, with a fortnightly change of president, is expressly forbidden to modify or interpret law, but empowered to annul unlawful administrative actions and to denounce to 'judiciary censors' any transgression of the judges.[136] Finally, the relations of the Executive Council (whose members are to be directly elected, under strictly regulated procedure, by the Primary Assemblies) with the Legislative Body are so prescribed as to ensure further limitations and counter-checks.[137] All this, together with the apparent absence of any concept of the Executive Council as a coherent and corporate decision- and policy-making body in itself (Paul Bastid concludes that 'ce conseil ne doit pas "vouloir"; il doit seulement "veiller"')[138], seems almost conclusively reminiscent of the submissions of David Williams outlined above.[139] Such features as election of judges and of judiciary censors, and establishment of the jury system, in the very long section on Administration of Justice, are fully in accord with his recommendations.[140]

Both contemporaries and historians proffer divergent estimates of the Girondine Constitution as a theoretical exercise in democracy,[141] but there is no dispute as to its frigid or even glacial reception by the Convention and much of public opinion.[142] The Montagnards derided 'this unhappy child of eight or nine Brissotin fathers' whose complex electoral procedures were designed to smother real democracy.[143] Barère (a member of the Committee of Constitution but pre-eminently a survivor!), while praising its attempt to establish liberty on the widest basis and the potential long-term effect of its ideas, describes how it was condemned as too lengthy and diffuse, containing proposals too clever and too difficult to implement.[144] It is hard to quarrel with a modern judgement that, while representing much that was best in eighteenth-century thinking, it was utterly inappropriate to the revolutionary situation.[145] Indeed its text was so long[146] that Condorcet's voice failed in its reading. Thereafter its consideration by the Convention was unenthusiastically sporadic, and was totally vitiated by the heightening Girondin-Montagnard tension and by military reverses. Ultimately, a new and overwhelmingly Jacobin committee on the constitution was established on 30 May, and the ruin of the Girondine was speedily followed by that of the Girondins themselves.

Much of the criticism directed at this abortive project is equally applicable to Williams's *Observations*. Duverger's point as to potential lack of clarity in the relationship between executive council and assembly[147] is true of both. Alengry ascribes to both Williams and Paine 'a profound aversion toward parliamentary government and a marked preference for a representative regime mitigated by direct government.'[148] Certainly Williams seems resolved first to ensure a rigorous system of checks and balances, *not* between estates of the realm or even primarily between institutions of the constitution but rather between the body of the people itself and every aspect of representation and of governance, and second, to secure the very fullest fruitful participation in self-government. The Girondine's wide diffusion of electoral power – in respect both of recourse to elective offices and of the very large number of relatively small primary assemblies – reflected this approach, but gave much credence to Jacobin charges of decentralisation and federalism.[149] Assuredly, Williams would have detested the 'tyrannie d'assemblée' that was soon to follow.

It is surely not wide of the mark to characterize Girondine and *Observations* alike as seeking to introduce governance without *a* government, as attempting almost to institutionalize spontaneous self-government, but simultaneously – because imbued with such inveterate suspicion both of power itself and of all who would aspire to its exercise – to subject the whole system to so many checks and safeguards as virtually to eliminate all hope of spontaneity. Williams's experience of the British political system had filled him with dislike of a purportedly mixed or balanced constitution which was but a cosmetic presentation of the dominance of Crown and aristocracy, and of the party system as no more than a struggle between 'ins' and 'outs'. His ingrained distrust of all untrammelled exercise of power made him reluctant to countenance its unconditional delegation at an executive, a legislative, or indeed a judicial level. He was prepared to delegate, within the parameters of law and orderly administration, the functional exercise of the expression of the people's will, but not to create an on-going corporate authority which in itself would become a semi-permanent maker of policy. He thought in terms of governmental function, not of a government, of legislative functions but not, above all, of a *sovereign* legislature.

Thus in seeking to institutionalize the expression of the general will in a large and complex society, while clinging simultaneously *both* to a deep-rooted, perhaps subconscious, belief in fundamental law (in terms of innate individual rights rather than of a permanent constitutional code), and also to a desire to model society in accord with the organic analogy which had become a constant feature of his thought, David Williams attempted to construct a model of a body politic bereft of anything which really resembled a head. His belief in organic evolution, with derivative acceptance of the need for regular constitutional adjustment, was firmly implanted; but equally so was the concept of permanent inalienable individual human rights. The two achieved uneasy consonance within a notion of the general will as society's unerring mode of exercising and safeguarding the latter within a changing framework of society which would itself necessitate the former. But in the day-to-day exercise of power, from which there is no escape, he could never free himself from the Scylla and Charybdis of his constitutional dilemma: the tyranny of self-perpetuating and effectively irresponsible governmental power on one side, and Burke's spectre of the 'red fool fury of the Seine' on the other – for Williams shared Rousseau's fear that the general will does not always see the good which it ideally seeks.

There remained, inevitably, problems which would never be resolved, and in more than one sense the failure of the Girondine (the nearest that any scheme embodying so much of his thought came to fruition) is symbolic. Of that failure Williams says only that 'the execution of the King, & the hostile Language & Preparations of the English Ministry, suspended all Constitutional Discussions, & instead of uniting, exasperated the Factions, contending for the Government'.[150] Such disappointing brevity is not really surprising, for he left France before the Girondine's first submission to the Convention.[151] But his lengthy account of the occasion and of the unusual circumstances of that departure suggest an interesting might-have-been. His autobiography explains that within the French Committee of Foreign Affairs Le Brun was the nominal but Brissot the real Minister.[152] Williams deems Brissot, perhaps misled by the protestations of missionaries of the English societies,[153] to have believed war with England to have been unthinkable until the conduct of the English ministry made it inevitable. Indeed, retrospectively, he credits him, stunned as he was by its approach, with having discerned in its outbreak the fate of his party.[154] But, crucially, Brissot 'had felt the force of the Jacobins, in the condemnation of the King'.[155] At meetings which discussed the conduct of England Williams recalls having warned that certain sections of a proposed report were mistaken or impolitic. But next day, attending the Convention, he was appalled to find that Brissot 'had preserved all the Mistakes & all the exceptionable passages; & the Convention, in a fury, declared War against Britain & Holland by Acclamation'. Later, at dinner, displaying mingled regret and fear, Brissot explained: 'It is done, the Committee would have it; if we had hesitated, the Mountain would have taken the business out of our hands.'[156]

Whatever may have been the elements of *naïveté* or even ambivalence on this issue within the Girondin ranks, Williams goes on to relate how, at this late stage, a conference with Roland, Lebrun and Brissot proposed an attempt to re-open negotiations 'by making me (a Citizen of France!) an Embassador to the Government of my own Country'. He explained that such an effort would get no further than his arrest at Dover Castle, but offered to deliver a letter to Lord Grenville in a strictly private capacity. But 'when I came to receive the Letter, I found a Postscript annexed to it giving me something like a Diplomatic Commission – for it informed Lord Grenville that, a friend to both Nations, I was perfectly in the confidence of the French Ministers, & would explain ... the Sacrifices which the Government of France would make to preserve Peace with Britain.'[157] The letter itself, dated 1 February, conveys a note of pessimistic and regretful acceptance of inevitable conflict. But the postscript expresses the hope that 'the philanthropist, David Williams, in conveying to you the disposition of the French people which he has observed, may guide you to more pacific sentiments ...'[158] Some ten days later Williams delivered the letter to Mr Aust, Under-Secretary of State, at Lord Grenville's office. To his chagrin, despite its importance, he received a chilly welcome, his offer to speak to Lord Grenville himself was not taken up, nor did the fact that he left his name and address elicit any communication.[159]

His autobiography explains that 'the Measure I had to propose was, that the Government of England should associate itself in France, with the Girondins instead of the Jacobins; & by them produce internal Peace & a regular Government – without previously defining that Government – What the Consequences of such an Alliance would have been, I need not explain. France must soon have been guided by the Councils of Britain ... happy in a sort of compromise, correcting the Errors of 1790, & *establishing a Constitution similar to that of Britain*' (my italics). The retrospective euphoria is as striking as the revision in constitutional assessment! Yet, while the present age is no stranger to tales of attempted or abortive negotiations which might have re-shaped history, not all is the wisdom of hindsight. For his assertion that the British Government thought only of the opportunity of weakening a rival was shared by many.[160] At all events, he did not attempt to pursue the matter by any written communication with Grenville, 'that the contents of my Letter might not reach France, & send the Girondist Government instantly to the Guillotine'.[161] Thus ended the active participation of David Williams in the affairs of Revolutionary France. The impact of that participation upon both his personal position and his political and constitutional opinions will take us into the next chapter.

Chapter Seven

Recessional: 'British Patriot'

DAVID WILLIAMS lived for twenty-three years after his return from France – years in which his writings on political and constitutional issues (after a period of circumspect silence) were such as to disappoint admirers of his earlier radicalism and also, and increasingly so with age, of his quality of presentation. The charge of apostasy hangs in the air, and one tends to think in terms of a long-drawn-out anticlimax, of shattered illusions and burnt-out ideals. Yet this is unfairly simpliste – at worst, the suggested distinction in this context between apostasy and disenchantment[1] is surely apposite. Insofar as the unmistakeable changes in emphasis in the development and expression of his political and (to an increasing degree) social thought must indeed in part be related to personal circumstances then comparison with some eminent fellow-radicals, Welsh and English, will possibly be instructive.

Of Richard Price, who died in 1791, before the more violent phase of the French Revolution,[2] it has justly been remarked that he was so concerned with checking an over-powerful executive by instituting a fair system of representative self-government that he hardly considered the possibility that the people itself might become tyrannical.[3] While he certainly deplored the spectre of 'a *lawless mob*',[4] his optimistic idealism led him largely to ignore the problems both of definition of 'the people' as fit to exercise political power and of the nuts-and-bolts aspects of representative mechanisms which so preoccupied Williams.[5] Unlike Price, Williams saw at close quarters the problems of the rapid introduction of radical reform. His fellow-Welshman, Morgan John Rhys,[6] shared his distress at the cruelties of Jacobin rule and at what he was to term the eclipse of French liberty by a bloodthirsty Marat and a saturnine Robespierre.[7] But, some two decades younger than Williams, in mid-1794 the warning of imminent arrest served but to trigger an earlier resolve to heed his own clarion cry: 'Embark then for the Western World'.[8]

Of a representative selection of English proponents of reform – Priestley, Godwin, Cartwright, Thelwall, Holcroft, Wakefield and Dyer – the first-named also crossed the Atlantic while the reactions of the others ranged from obdurate adherence to, declaration of, and acceptance of near-martyrdom for their principles, to varying degrees of cautious readjustment in the face of necessity. Perhaps the closest parallel to Williams is Godwin who admitted that, while his *Political Justice* was a child of the French Revolution, the latter's subsequent course was a great disappointment, so that his renewed admiration of the practicality of the English Constitution implied no desertion of earlier doctrines.[9] Perhaps the most immediately forthright contrast is that of Holcroft whose pamphlet written in 1795 as 'one of those "acquitted felons"' presumably thereafter destined to be labelled Jacobin and Leveller, concludes with an impassioned depiction of the plight of the poor in face of the well-to-do and asks: 'Why are the rich tyrants? Because the poor are humbled, and terrified till they dare not speak.'[10]

The touchstones of changing attitudes were the violent events of the summer of 1792 and the outbreak and spread of international conflict. Thus Cartwright and his critic Arthur Young were as one in the belief that the Revolution before the 10th of August was as different from the Revolution thereafter as light from darkness.[11] The trial and execution of Louis XVI, and the declaration of war on Britain, inevitably hardened opinion regarding the old enemy – a term which reminds us that the impact of external war upon internal movements for reform was traumatically different in the case of the French as distinct from the former American adversary. This was no civil war within the British commonwealth, but a struggle against a foe about whom Williams himself had written most savagely as recently as 1778,[12] an enemy who had helped to tear America away from the commonwealth. Yet this does not gainsay the fact that the war with Revolutionary France posed awkward crosscurrents of ideological loyalties for radically minded British patriots. For if the excesses of the Revolution were the occasion of the outbreak of war, even the most level-headed and chastened radical, including Williams himself,[13] could not fail to see that that outbreak in turn was the occasion of further repression of British liberty. Scepticism (expressed by Williams himself and shared by others)[14] as to the real motives of Britain's anti-French foreign policy, and fear of increasingly severe governmental repression of any activity which could conveniently be branded as seditious and unpatriotic, were cut right across by an increasing realisation that what was actually happening in France no longer approximated to the dream of 1789, or even Girondin hopes of mid-1792. It has been suggested that by 1797 the position of remaining English Jacobins resembles that of Elizabethan Roman Catholics made worse by the absence of a credible Rome.[15] Thereafter, the change from Directory to Consulate and Empire, the long war and the sufferings entailed, made relationships between residual movements for internal constitutional reform and patriotic opposition to the military despot thrown up by late-Revolutionary France both complex and ambivalent.

Williams himself had ceased to agitate for such reform. This may not imply any conscious abandonment of principle: one might urge that if politics is a science then its theorist, or practitioner, must learn from any abortive experiments. But it certainly reflects adjustment to his circumstances. Several of his later political works contain passages which can only be described as apologia, but the frankest account of the pressure under which he found himself is that in his manuscript autobiography. He describes himself as received in England, despite professions of loyalty, as 'a Partizan of France', whose neighbours and tradesmen were minutely questioned as to his conduct and conversation by informers and spies. An associate in a literary enterprise seized the opportunity of breaking an agreement.[16] Worse still, 'if my name had been found, in the Lists of any [of] the Societies pretending to be patriotic, I should have been committed to the Tower with Hardy Tooke &c – and the Man who first discerned the features of Jacobinism in Europe;[17] who first wrote against it;

& who, on that account, had the honor of being calumniated in the Jacobin Club of Paris, as the Messenger of Pitt, loaded with four Millions sterling, to save Louis XVI – would have been tried in England for high-treason; & acquitted, to be spit upon as an acquitted Felon, by the foul mouth of a sanguinary Partizan.'[18]

The main features of this highly-coloured recollection are accurate. The morass of the Treasury Solicitors papers has yielded no copy of an agent's report on David Williams,[19] but provides ample illustration of surveillance of suspect societies and of the potential dangers of membership. Indeed a report by none other than John Reeves states that 'the proceedings of these Clubs have been constantly conveyed to the Government from the Autumn of 1792 ... This information has been given by persons who became members for that very purpose.'[20] Thus failure or refusal to join any such organizations now produced an unlooked-for bonus! One list of those examined by the Council includes, in addition to those named by Williams, John Thelwall, William Spence, and also, embarrassingly, two who bore his own surname. The Society for Constitutional Information, the Friends of the People, but above all the London Corresponding Society, were subject to report. The last-named, credited with an avowed intent to overturn the Government, is described as adopting a structure of 'Sections of 30 Members [subdivided] into what they call Tythings or smaller Sections of *Ten* Men each'. Whatever the immediate provenance of the notion, one need not labour the obvious and awkward parallel.[21]

One further piece of evidence suggests the personal, as distinct from general political, pressure under which Williams may well have found himself. A letter from Taunton dated 22 March 1793 reporting, albeit with professed reluctance, a drunken yeoman's toast to Paine coupled with a declaration of resolve to 'go to my neck in Blood and Guts and Garbage for to be in the forefront of the Battle for a Revolution', and seeking official guidance as to a Bill of Indictment, bears the distinctive flourish of the same 'R. Beadon' who wrote to Williams regarding the settlement of the financial claims of his relation Frances Martyn.[22] All in all, Williams very possibly concluded that any attempt further to back up the peace proposals which he had brought from France might be almost as dangerous for him as for his Girondin friends.

Such fears must have been reinforced by the erratic activities and ultimately melancholy fate of one James Tilly Matthews, a London tea-dealer and acquaintance of Williams whom he had followed to Paris. His subsequent attempts to meddle in diplomacy, undertaking to negotiate peace via the Vestry-Clerk of Poplar, gave Williams 'the first suspicion that Matthews was affected in his head'. Another visit to France, posing to Le Brun as an emissary of Williams, led to his arrest as a British spy. Upon return to England, his determination to attract attention led to seizure, examination by the Privy Council, and commitment to Bethlehem Hospital as insane.[23] Yet his relationship with Williams had been sufficiently close for him to write for the return of certain notes and to allude to Bowyer's breach of contract concerning the projected continuation of Hume's *History of England*.[24] The same letter, more frighteningly, reports 'an hours Conversation with Lord H––– from the drift of it I advise you immediately to destroy every paper you may have which relates to France &c'. But the next cryptic remark that 'they on t'other side say the Appeal to the People was yours & here it is also understood',[25] together with evidence from French sources, suggests that although he never mentions it himself yet another anonymous work may well be added to the list of writings of Williams.

In the records of the Convention for January 1793, one after another of his Girondin friends commends an 'appel au peuple' for a judgement of last resort on the fate of Louis XVI: Marat, in turn, repeatedly employs the phrase in his impassioned attack on Brissot, Gensonné, Vergniaud and others as seeking to save the King and incite civil war.[26] The report of Collot d'Herbois to the Jacobins on 3 March 1793 on the 'numerous charges against the ex-minister Roland' states twice that a pseudonymous address to the Parisians, of which Roland was the reputed author, was in fact written by 'un Anglois', an *habitué* of the minister's house.[27] This was undoubtedly the *Appel au Peuple* alluded to by Matthews. A six-page tract by 'Forlis, Ami des Lois', its content goes far to support the belief that David Williams at least participated in its composition. In general, its attacks on the Convention as having arrogated judicial power to which it has no claim, and as having violated the sovereignty of the people in rejecting a direct appeal, are in full accord with his views, if also with those of some of his Girondin associates.[28] Perhaps more nearly conclusive is the parallel drawn with England's regicide which echoes his earlier opinions: 'It is thus that the long Parliament of England, the disgrace of the nation of which it was the scourge, prepared the way for the domination of the scheming *Cromwell* . . . Frenchmen, the bloodied locks of Charles the First still haunt unhappy England . . .' France, in turn, must beware of the indignation of posterity: 'already a judgement is prepared; already the whole of Europe sharpens the daggers of vengeance'. The appeal to insurrection as the only means left of averting the storm – '*levez-vous*; on vous a prêché si souvent & avec tant de succès le saint devoir de l'insurrection'[29] – illustrates with sombre irony the desperation to which his Girondin friends had by now been driven. The circumstantial evidence that David Williams at least contributed to this tract, while strong, is not conclusive; yet the very belief that he had done so would in itself help to explain why, despite his return from helping to draft a republican constitution, he escaped the direct prosecution endured by several erstwhile fellow-radicals.

In all the circumstances – French as well as British – one can surely sympathize with Williams's protestation that 'I withdrew from the Political Arena, not from Fear; though I had some reasons for fear; not from Change of Principles or Connections; but from dispair, occasioned by the Ignorance & Impetuosity of those Reformers, to whom Power seemed to have been delegated only by Chance'.[30] It has been suggested that the virtual disappearance of the Society for Constitutional Information after the repression which followed in 1794 marked the end of the old Commonwealth tradition and the falling of the last leaves of the eighteenth-century tree of liberty, while the seed of the new was planted by Paine.[31] Certainly the failure of the Girondine Constitution – and cause – to which both Paine and Williams contributed was a crucial turning-point. The personal impact of chagrin and of fear on David Williams is hardly in doubt.

Moreover, a favourite project in which he became increasingly and genuinely engrossed brought with it an at least partial change in the nature of (to use his own term) his connections. For among his close associates in what, against the background of war, assumed ever more patriotic overtones, the Literary Fund, was to be John Reeves. Apart from his notorious involvement in the Society for Preserving Liberty and Property against Republicans and Levellers,[32] in 1795 Reeves published his *Thoughts on the English Government* which coincide rather more with those of post-Revolutionary Williams than they contrast with those of his earlier radicalism.[33] While it is clear that their association implied nothing like a complete conversion in regard to political views it surely indicates an increasingly mellow disposition on the part of Williams toward the establishment. This, attributable in part to a patriotism which had always been there but was now buttressed by increasing distaste for events across the Channel, ultimately encompassed a willingness to accept a governmental commission to write press articles, and even to visit France on a fact-finding mission in 1802.

Yet the tenor of his writings, although now sceptical as to any benefits of revolutionary political and social change, is certainly *not* uncritical. More than once he is at pains to rebut any allegation of conscious abandonment of principle. Several printed works, and a number of quite significant unpublished papers, provide ample illustration of the enduring basis, changing emphases, and also in some ways widening conspectus of this last phase of his political and social thought. Before essaying analysis of their content and ideas a word about the individual provenance and impact of his writings may be apposite. The first of these, *Regulations of Parochial Police*, 1797, immediately exemplifies the element of continuity: for the nature of its proposals and the perception of dangerous circumstances which evoked them – in this case the French landings at Fishguard and the projected impact of invasion in terms of civil disorder[34] – are very reminiscent of his *Plan of Association on Constitutional Principles* of 1780, nor are the social undertones entirely different.[35] The book ran through several editions, a copy of the second, sub-titled 'for the preservation of the Lives and Fortunes of Private Families', has a note in ink on its title-page: 'vide Page 26 & infra Pelham'. An enlarged edition appeared in 1803.

All reviews were broadly favourable, though one descried inquisitorial proposals which bore the appearance of trying to combine the affluent against the indigent.[36] Indeed comparison with Bishop Watson's *Address to the People* ... which rebuts any suggestion that French invaders would be joined by hordes of the discontented, with the speedily and passionately written rejoinder of Gilbert Wakefield, and with such other works evoked by the military/security crisis of 1797–8 as that of Erskine and of Joseph Towers (entitled *Thoughts on National Insanity*), brings into stark relief the change at least in emphasis in David Williams's socio-political priorities.[37] All editions of *Parochial Police* were anonymous, as was (at least in form) his contribution in 1798 of the article on Brissot in Vol. II of *Biographical Anecdotes*.[38] His next attempt to tread the stage of political commentary went so far as agreed articles of partnership (with a quarter-share of profits payable to the Literary Fund) for publication of 'The Imperial Gazette'. Its prospectus, indicating October 1800 as the date of first issue, promised 'a Daily Newspaper, conducted upon True Constitutional Principles, and upon an Elegant Scale, devoid of low slander, and Party Scurrility

... whose leading Object is to support the King, the Royal Family, the Laws, the Constitution of the British Isles, and the Administration of the Empire'. Williams's tasks included a weekly review of politics, a sphere in which the Gazette pledged unflinching support of Crown and Government whilst avoiding 'all low paragraphic acrimony against those who oppose their Measures'. Sadly, amidst a welter of other declared intentions, the project seems to have sunk without trace.[39]

Next in order of composition and of first publication came a number of 'Elementary Studies on the Progress of Nations in Political Oeconomy, Legislation, and Government', appearing first in 1802–3 as separate essays in the hope that Members of Parliament might study them and thereby transfer their attention from the intrigues of faction to the truths of political economy.[40] Evidently, his self-imposed role of mentor of politicians was not yet abandoned; but another influence underlay at least the original appearance of these studies. Governmental payment for the writing, printing and circulation of pamplets and articles was not new.[41] What is perhaps disconcerting, after his scathing allusions in his *Royal Recollections* in 1788, is to find David Williams receiving such subvention. Yet his receipt of both encouragement and aid is hardly in doubt. The historian of *The Times* describes *Egeria* (the title of the collected publication) as an attempt by Government to add literary to journalistic propaganda, employing Williams, 'a highly expert Press engineer'.[42] The provenance of a 'Private Paper – requiring immediate perusal', headed 'On the Press', establishes a clear connection. Undated, but certainly submitted during 1802–3 when Pelham (later Earl of Chichester) was Home Secretary, and in Williams's own hand, it expresses his disappointed conclusion that 'though now brought to the true and false principles of *Reform* ... I think *Egeria* must be discontinued ... because the considerations, on which I understand it to be undertaken, are not fulfilled, viz – to circulate the numbers among those who might render it a Text book for discussion, – & for the production of new Topics for writers in the Newspapers'. He regrets the failure to seize this chance to inform and direct the public mind through the Press – a power hardly inferior to that of Government. In the present circumstances, whether negotiations end in war or a temporary and pretended peace, it will be folly for Ministers to allow themselves to be vilified by the inevitable misrepresentations without reply.[43]

The suspension of hostilities with France produced a very interesting report, entitled 'Private Paper. December 1802' drawn from 'Minutes made in Paris in October, November & December – by David Williams' – of which three copies are extant.[44] Combining attempted prognosis of a possible invasion by Bonaparte with analysis of the strengths and weaknesses of the Consular regime (including dark allusions to a projected anti-Napoleonic coup) and advice on the attitudes and policy of British government, it records a visit made during the interlude of peace secured by Amiens. Not without personal interest is the fact that (despite repeated assumptions that it was James Martin) his companion on this visit was almost certainly Frances Martyn. The list of those returning to London on the authority of Lord Hawkesbury's Passport on 16 December 1802, includes very clearly as 'No 51: Mr Williams Mrs Martyn'.[45] The presence of this list among the papers of Lord Whitworth, who had been despatched to Paris as Ambassador Extraordinary and

Plenipotentiary on 10 October 1802, with long instructions regarding the collection of intelligence,[46] and the copies of his report in the Pelham Papers, leave little doubt that Williams acted as a government agent.[47]

After his return *Egeria* appeared in book form in 1803, apparently with minimal impact and without review in a major periodical – though a recent assessment, while critical of its many faults, justly discerns its very real interest as evidence both of continuity and of adjustment of ideas.[48] Thereafter, seven years elapsed before his last production, revealingly entitled *Preparatory Studies for Political Reformers*. Despite the uniform severity of criticism voiced by both contemporary and modern reviewers,[49] it is worth noting that the *Critical Review* accorded it one of the longest notices given to any of the writings of David Williams, significantly, 'more at length than it would otherwise deserve, if it were not from the close relation which many of the reflections have to the critical aspect of . . . the present period'.[50] His touch on the pulse of public opinion had perhaps not entirely gone; contemporaneously Capel Lofft published a short tract *On a Revival of Reform*, and to such a resurgence of interest one may well relate Williams's last composition.

The chief determinant of the general drift of his thought during this last phase of his life was undoubtedly his reaction to the French Revolution. Retrospective analysis of its course ranges from an undated manuscript account of European affairs between March 1792 and the outbreak of war with Britain,[51] to several passages in his last book. *Parochial Police* conveys the deduction made from those events in terms of constitutional thought: suspicion of those who would abandon present institutions 'for the forms of fancy, or the faultless monsters of unexperienced Philosophy'.[52] His article on Brissot, published a year later,[53] while personally orientated, records his general conclusion that as a result of Girondin mistakes (notably that of declaring war) and now Jacobin tyranny, 'the great object of the French revolution, the establishment of a just and equitable constitution, was lost or suspended, and is not to be recovered, probably, by the present generation'.[54] But perhaps the fullest attempt at a rounded assessment, in terms of general political philosophy, is that in Section V of his autobiography. If such French reformers as Condorcet and Gensonné had given less attention to applying 'the calculations of numerical Probabilities & the Art of adjusting mechanic forces, to Political Societies' and more to diagnosis of the realities of their country's constitutional inheritance, then all might not have been abandoned to the destructive passions of the multitude. Upon reflection, 'the transition from Evil to Good, because suddenly attempted, often aggravates the Evil, instead of producing the Good.' Incautious attempts to renew political associations long broken, in order to restore sensibility to all parts of a vast body rendered torpid by disuse, provoked something analogous to a high fever. In more mundane terms, the virtual dissolution of an executive power which had engrossed all authority in the state was the crucial error.[55]

Thus it is not on ultimate objectives but on modes of procedure that Williams must take issue with the Girondins, regretting their errors but honouring their memories. 'They had always in view, a Perfect Constitution, which is an ideal Object. Perfection, in all human pursuits, is like an Asymptote in Mathematics, ever approximating a Curve, but never touching it.' Their obloquy is undeserved, yet it is true not only that they wandered among abstractions but also that they advised and superintended insurrectionary action and – contrary to their original principles and disastrously for their real objectives – assumed the part of demagogues, arousing popular passions and indeed exciting 'the People to acts of Legislation & Government; after the Nation had chosen, or seemed to have chosen a Constitution'. In thus attempting to act as organs of the public will they produced only popular anarchy. Clubs and assemblies presumed to express and to execute the public will: 'destined to be elective & occasional, they became administrative & permanent'. By means of such usurpations 'the Jacobins became the Tyrants of France'.[56]

Much of this was wisdom – and selective wisdom, at that – after the event. His own electoral proposals had been just as complicated and mechanical as those of Condorcet's Girondine to which he had contributed, while his participation in discussion of a new form of government had come after the insurrectionary overthrow of what he now seems to regard as a legitimate and established constitution. But in fairness, the principle of adherence to constitutional propriety, the essential distinction between effective representation and any usurpation of executive power, and the distrust of all sectional pressure groups, however popularly based, had always been present in his thought. He now suggests that although the French Revolution may not have given rise to any new constitutional principles it has abundantly increased the stock of experimental data available for the evolving science of politics, in particular exemplifying the unwisdom of endeavouring to apply the abstract conceptions of individuals to a society which is not yet ready. 'From this Chaos of Good & Evil, or of Principles & Passions, I withdrew into my own private Circle . . .'[57]

That circle may well have contributed to a changing perspective: what had been hailed in 1790 as the approach of a general revolution being now transposed into an assertion that 'in 1789, all Europe was in the condition of the *malade imaginaire*'.[58] Yet much of his analysis is balanced and perceptive. A major and recurrent theme is that democracy descending into anarchy leads not only to the loss of all real civil liberties but also to the ultimate emergence of a military despot.[59] In *Parochial Police* he urges that the state of despondency produced by anarchy 'might have consigned the iron Sceptre of revolutionary Power, to a Baboon, as well as to a Danton, Robespierre, Barras, and Bonaparte'. For the object of fear and execration is not the man but the revolutionary power, the naked and unqualified despotism which recognizes no law of Nature or of nations. The fatal turn was taken when France, having repulsed her invaders, came to the verge of anarchy when the populace first contended with the National Guards, and the Districts thereafter dethroned the King and then proceeded to the September Massacres. Yet 'the crimes and atrocities of the French Revolution are called National, only by ignorance and folly. They are evils to which every nation is liable, and of which every People is susceptible . . .' France furnished not an example but a warning.[60]

Egeria, again declaring premature attempts at major political improvements more harmful than the direct restraints of arbitrary power, discerns at the heart of Jacobinism a spirit of dissolution which has pervaded the whole of Europe, masked with the features of reform.[61] Yet apart from such as Marat or Thomas Paine, ever ready to dissolve societies for reconstruction, even those French reformers whose misfortunes tend to veil their errors were all wiser in their opinions than in their experience – the want of which resulted in a total underestimate of the impact of change. Condorcet is again singled out as an honest but mistaken enthusiast who ignored the potential social effect of the application of his political calculus. Thus their failure derives not from those external factors which are sometimes blamed but from laws of Nature which will ever produce the same effects in similar circumstances. In particular, 'the French reformers organized primary assemblies, municipalities, &c [but] were confounded and lost when it became necessary to check the simple but violent motion of parts that were near, with the compound influence of parts that were distant'.[62] Surprisingly, and in blatant contradiction of his earlier statements, Williams now asserts that 'France commenced her revolution on the model of Britain, which she attempted extravagantly to excel; and, in the extravagant attempt, lost all her own institutions. In the extremity of her rage and disappointment, she "set fire to the four corners of the world".'[63] The ultimate lesson to those who seek for political remedies in the dissolution of political bodies is that their fragments are taken up by some daring adventurer. Since the American War all the world has been in ecstasy for the General Will; but in the event 'the *Public Will* of France became the private will of Napoleon Bonaparte'.[64]

Williams's final work, in 1810, ascribes to the French Revolution a resultant division of opinion between those who would render the mass of the people of no political account and those who would make it everything – a polarisation at utter variance with the laws of Nature. Events in France furnish a dreadful lesson to reformers: usurpations by the *parlements* and the atrophy of the States-General gave opportunity to those wishing to change the constitution (with lawyers to the fore) to appeal to the people. At first they controlled the tempest of their own creation, but then, its patience exhausted, the populace plunged everything in anarchy and dissolution; for the revolution, ill-conducted, had 'generated a monstrous rival in the populace, with whom reform is the signal of dissolution'.[65] Sadly, the number and weight of abuses, and the talents and power of those who sought to preserve them, were in France so great that no laws of political organization then known were able to remove them.[66] Much of this, although indeed the retrospective analysis of one who had not always said the same things at the time, is keenly perceptive.[67]

In contrast with these repeated allusions to the lessons of what he now deems the unsuccessful French Revolution, the significance of its successful transatlantic counterpart receives but occasional reference; yet therein we find an increasing recognition of the economic and social bases of political realities. *Egeria* proffers the striking assertion that 'Britain is the only State in which the modern principles of *political* liberty have had a real, permanent effect ... *America* does not yet offer an example. Its political principles cannot be put to any trial, *until the population of its States overflows on the States themselves, instead of being dispersed by advantageous emigration*' (my italics). Granted the impact of her ideas, yet emulation of her example by European states is misplaced; for she has no classes analogous to those which constitute the greater part of their populations. America has relatively few slaves and 'scarcely any servants, which in Europe form a class of the utmost importance as a perpetual and poisonous spring on the moral of those orders which are the first links of the social chain'. She has no Populace, defined as surplus population, for it is this *super-abundant population*, the general inlet of misery, which first tries the nature and force of political institutions'.[68] With due allowance for a gap of something approaching two centuries, this is impressively reminiscent of the analysis of modern economic historians both as to the significance in early American experience of cheap land, the open frontier to the west, and the relatively favourable bargaining position of labour, and as to the cumulative pressure of population expansion in the countryside of eighteenth-century France.

Discussions of contemporary, Napoleonic France relate to two major themes: military despotism as the almost inevitable end-product of popular anarchy, institutional dissolution, and government by terror; and the picture of Britain as the only real bulwark of liberty and stability against Bonapartist tyranny and/or residual Jacobinism. The 'Private Paper' of 1802 has nothing good to say about the Napoleonic regime: thus 'England alone, by its naval power, by its extensive commerce, by its pecuniary Ability to Support Armies; & particularly by the Example it affords in Legislation, Jurisprudence & the Liberty of adjudging its Government & Governors, bounds the Ambition; and is the severest Satire on the Despotism of his Government.' Williams, who has tried to ascertain the logistics of a proposed sea-borne assault, is certain that Bonaparte had planned to invade England in conjunction with the Emperor Paul of Russia, news of whose death provoked him to throw down the breakfast table and smash everything within reach. Assuredly, Fox 'was deceived, or he deceives in the opinion that a permanent peace with Britain is the wish of Buonaparte'.[69] Ironically, this short-lived peace (1802–3) produced a translation of Williams's *Claims of Literature*, in the context of a French attempt at a version of a Literary Fund.[70] Oddly enough, in the light of Napoleon's known desperate wish to secure recognition, the first benefactors of the 'fonds littéraire français' included his brothers Lucien and Joseph – almost coincidentally with the closer involvement of the Prince of Wales with the Literary Fund.[71]

The virtually contemporaneous *Egeria* devotes three studies to 'Consular Lessons'. These find the root of Anglo-French antagonism neither in Malta nor in Egypt, nor yet in the liberties of Switzerland or Holland, but in the perpetual rivalry between robbery and industry. Williams points the contrast between Napoleonic France and Britain in respect of economic as well as of political and social evolution. The former, instead of draining her marshes, sinking mines, and cultivating the soil to support a growing and contented population, has become a militarised centre of international oppression, rejecting those real and salutary principles of commerce which have originated in England.[72] The contrast is over-simplified. Yet this change in tone from much of his earlier comment on British economic and maritime expansion (which may well reflect his own greater involvement in financial and business affairs)[73] is not unqualified. Neither does he abandon his former criticisms of the English establishment and leadership. The party system, individual *bêtes noires*, and British foreign policy (especially over-reaction to the French Revolution, for 'it is in the nature of inordinate fear to generate the evil it dreads'),[74] all are attacked in his later works. Yet 'with all the Errors, real and pretended, which have been attributed to its Government, and Ministers; that Constitution now stands alone in Europe, as the Depository of practical principles, institutions, and customs, which are the real Elements of political and civil liberty.'[75]

This line of thought, which lies at the heart of all the post-revolutionary writings of David Williams, is not *entirely* new,[76] and is the more understandable against the backcloth of Napoleonic France. But if it may be contended that there was no conscious abandonment of principle for expediency, it would surely have to be conceded that there was much greater readiness, in the sphere of political and constitutional thought, to recognise expediency as a determinant principle in itself. In face of Napoleonic onslaught the soldiers, sailors, and people of the nation will rally round a citadel where everything important to human society is held. For Britain stands alone (America forgotten!) in demonstrating 'lessons of jurisprudence, civil liberty, industry, and political economy [an interesting list, itself indicative of changing priorities], with infinitely more effect than in the declarations of sycophant prefects, or the visions of speculative academicians'.[77] He can now go so far as to declare, combining a phrase reminiscent of an earlier publication with a use of his favourite corporeal analogy which would have pleased his associate Reeves as much as it would have saddened his former admirers, that the nation 'has acquired *Unanimity*; she has purged her political body of those nests of vermin, called political societies, which had nearly burrowed into her vitals, and she now appears in a healthy and vigorous condition'.[78]

Yet alongside this sturdily patriotic orientation of his thought some progressive attitudes survive and surface – if only in the form of reversion to former targets and pursuit of old vendettas! Thus Burke's interpretation of the French Revolution is described as distorted by fantasies, his attitude, exacerbating the very mania it condemns, an English mirror image of Robespierrist Jacobinism.[79] In his very last publication Williams harks back to another adversary, now dead, who had 'directed his great talents to convert Parliament into an organ of his pleasure, and to circumscribe liberty'. Reverting to the moderate-radical lament of the missed opportunity of 1792–3, he condemns a minister who had perceived therein but a choice of methods to profit by French misfortune, and had stained the nation's name by choosing to sow intrigue, corruption and dissension.[80] Confronted by the spectre of Pitt, hated beyond the grave, the old Adam sometimes splits the garments of respectability. Granted that 'the insanity of the French reformers rendered it a question ... whether the necessitous and the profligate had a right to destroy, not only the wealth which had been engrossed by violence, but all that had been accumulated by the gleanings of industry'; yet Pitt won support from people who detested, when once they understood, his real motives for war on the first promoters of French reform. For '*a war to smother French liberty in its cradle will change into a war to destroy English liberty on its crutches*' (my italics). The sentiment is as striking as the imagery, which continues in the assertion that England's own disease is deeply rooted, so that any remedy will be tedious and painful. It has enabled ministers to distance parliament from the people and has rendered near-insuperable the problems of producing a national will.[81]

Indeed, much of David Williams's analysis of the relationship between protracted foreign war, the selfish commercial interests which underlay it, and the contingent repression of British internal liberties, has much in common with the
mainstream of surviving radical and progressive thought.[82] Erskine's justly-famous
tract, in 1797, the contemporaneous *Thoughts on National Insanity* by Joseph Towers,
and William Belsham's *Remarks on a Late Publication* in 1800, had concurred in
condemnation of Pitt's alleged rejection of seriously conciliatory French ouvertures
in early 1793, deliberate identification of any attack on abuses of administration
with an attempt to destroy the constitution from within while giving traitorous
comfort to the enemy without, and failure to define and propose realistic terms of
peace.[83] Williams himself blames inflated claims to maritime dominion, the
influence of pernicious monopolies, and the infectious frenzy of commercial avarice,
combining to produce the proposition that maritime trade must depend on the
pleasure of England, just as much as the counter-claim that the prosperity and
happiness of the Continent derive from a dominant France.

True, British industry and commerce are the major sources of human progress,
yet conceivably the European confederacy which France will soon establish[84] must
offer to English statecraft the opportunity for peace, communications, and
commerce. For France, on her part, must surely grasp that commercial leadership
cannot simply be transferred from England across the Channel.[85] This element of
apparently wishful thinking alongside some keen analysis should not too quickly be
discounted. Cartwright was not alone in sharing the hope of conciliation based upon
commercial understanding.[86] A conflict of over twenty years brought its own
changes: the impact of Napoleon's seizure of nakedly personal power at the turn of
the century, and renewal of war in 1803, may have convinced the liberal-minded
that France was no credible standard-bearer of revolutionary freedom; but the very
duration of the war induced the peace-lover and the realist at least to contemplate
the possibility of coming to terms with a new order in Europe.[87] Yet Williams closes
his last publication with a retrospective avowal of national shame and regret at any
imputation of having induced insurrection, famine, and invasion in neighbouring
states – contrived by a minister who had 'encrusted his face, as he had his heart, with
stone'. The injustice and impolicy of encouraging the devastation of France are
exceeded only by present French efforts to seek the ruin of England.[88]

His appeal to the Prince of Wales as alone possessing the ability and influence to
effect a more magnanimous policy,[89] suggests a theme which will recur. But first, his
discussion of the economic roots of national and indeed all political action is sufficiently striking as to demand attention in itself, as perhaps the most significant
aspect of this last phase of his thinking. A remark in his 'Private Paper' about
Britain's mistaken promotion of manufactures in increasing disproportion to
the means of feeding her inhabitants[90] underlines *Egeria*'s allusion to 'the
impracticability, except in peculiar situations, of increasing food in proportion to
the increase of population' as a general source of moral and political problems.[91] In
fact this was not his first reference to this issue,[92] nor were such *general* concepts
confined to Malthus, who himself alluded to the views on population and subsistence levels of both Godwin and Condorcet in his widely-publicised *Essay on Popula-*

tion[93]. But that work's grim warning had now apparently been confirmed by the first Census of 1801. Thus Williams is concerned lest the problems engendered by unavoidable social inequalities should now be exacerbated by the threat that 'want and misery, which should only circumscribe societies, will penetrate and invade their laborious and useful classes'.[94]

Such fears presumably explain a stark absence of any mawkish sentimentality about institutions which 'by relieving the vicious from the care of their children, enable them to produce more after their own image. By such institutions, the first evil is never diminished, arising from numbers viciously educated ... For who will contentedly or patiently struggle with all the difficulties of bringing up a large family to labour, under the discouragement of hospitals and work-houses, which however piously instituted and humanely conducted, it is to be feared are incautiously filled with the children of the profligate and idle, who are withdrawn from productive labour.'[95] This unattractive exegesis is of course not isolated either in David Williams[96] or in contemporary thought. But his immediately-subsequent attempt to trace the development of the economic substructure of society and its reflection in social classes and political assumptions is surely a remarkable example of an early essay in the materialist interpretation of history. The first crucial phase in such development is identified as that at which 'labour produced a surplus; and the property and command of superfluities became the great objects of contention ...' The transfer of this surplus from its producers and original proprietors to persons and classes whose first offices must have been the preservation of the peace was followed by conversion by the soldier and the priest of a claim for support into an established right of property, while the cultivators of the soil sank gradually into tenants and even slaves. This has occurred because the original proprietors could have regulated their population by their means of subsistence but did not.[97]

Until the final question-begging *non sequitur* much of this seems to anticipate Marx. But Williams's social deductions from this materialist analysis are very different: he looks not forward but back, to an already encountered prescription. Some idealists contend for 'the equal rights of equal beings; whereas every just idea of correct equality is instantly superseded, at the formation of all societies – by the unequal powers bestowed by nature – by the unequal operations of the generative faculty, taxing the same labour with unequal burthens, and creating the distinction of rich and poor – and by all the indefinite though fair efforts of industry, in the alienation of the unequal surplus of equal labour.' It follows therefore that rights, like properties, 'though they may be balanced, cannot be equal; because the just proportions to every man's labour, industry and ingenuity, must be unequal. Rights, however, must be equitable; and properties equitably or equably distributed.' Intemperate claims to impracticable and unattainable equality must be dismissed. During the French Revolution the spectre of a *loi agraire*, seriously mooted by William Ogilvie in 1781,[98] had become the nightmare of the propertied on either side of the Channel.[99] In England Thomas Spence put the question 'whether Mankind, in Society, reap all the advantages from their natural and equal rights of property in land and liberty, which in that state, they possibly may, and ought to expect?'[100] This was not the first time that David Williams had written on such issues,[101] but by now his answer was a rejection of equality not only at a social and economic but also by implication at a political level. What is new is his abandonment of a previous insistence on political equality as a corrective balance in equity against (and indeed designed to ensure acceptance of) economic inequality,[102] in favour of a recognition that in present social circumstances real political equality is a chimera. The problem is to ensure that 'the doctrine of what is called Political Equality be generally understood, and reduced to practical equity. A wise constitution would bring various men . . . to an Equation, who can never be brought to an Equality. All claims should therefore be preferred for equitable or equable, not for equal rights.'[103]

What does he mean by such terms as equable and equity as preferable to equality, and by what criterion is the social justice which is better than *unjustly*-imposed social equality to be determined? His answer goes straight back to the favourite early-modern organic analogy and the values thereby entailed: 'Every member of a wise and equitable constitution possesses his proportion of that influence which is diffused through the whole, as the influence of every member is diffused through the natural body, and to every particle of which it consists; not equally, but in proportion to its capacity of contribution to the general happiness.'[104] Thus increasing interest in economic affairs during this last phase has led not to any deduction that greater social equality is a necessary correlative of greater political equality, but rather to an extension of his reservations as to whether the latter is possible, given the economic and social inequality imposed by the very laws of Nature. These laws, left to their own spontaneous operation, will 'proportion the population to the produce; the wants, passions, desires, and intelligence, to the general circumstances of the political body; and this proportion is the law of political equity; the first law of society'.[105] There is a curious parallel between the ultimate conclusion of his thinking on socio-political issues and that reached earlier in regard to religion. The latter, cut quite adrift from supernatural moorings, and denuded of dogmatic content, had come to rest upon acceptance of unspecified natural laws; in politics we may descry, at a later stage, a similar drift toward an almost determinist acceptance of purportedly natural laws and processes, in place of the radical and even (though carefully circumscribed) democratic beliefs which he had held from the 1770s to the early 1790s.

Several aspects of economic affairs receive attention in these later works (and a number of unpublished papers) including industry and division of labour,[106] the National Debt (where Richard Price is brought into the dialogue but not allowed to say much!)[107], taxation,[108] and restraint of trade and of labour.[109] A much more sophisticated approach is exemplified in the assertion (reminiscent of the once-despised Mandeville) that while merchants seldom intend the public interest, yet every man directing his efforts to produce the greatest good for himself will providentially render trade of the greatest advantage to society, followed by a Smith-like advocacy of the virtues of unrestricted specialisation and exchange.[110] Yet now and then old attitudes surface: 'there is no evil so inveterate as mercantile selfishness; and while it pervades and controls our council, all attempts at parliamentary reform will be of little use – for parliament is a circle within a circle, and the superior influence always carries the inferior with it'.[111]

Yet the evil which (though not new, and first expressed after the Gordon Riots) by now looms largest in his writings, fed both by his current social analysis and the impact on his mind of the French Revolution, is that of the swamping of society and its institutions by a poverty-frenzied populace, whose illiteracy limits its aspiration to that of anarchy: the perennial nightmare of the early-modern Commonwealth idealist. Indeed the central theme of *Regulations of Parochial Police* is the analogy between Paris in 1792 and London in face of putative French attack in 1797: 'When Armies, formed of the best citizens in the lower classes, marched to the frontiers, the industrious suddenly thrown out of employ, the idle, the lazy, the vicious, were drawn, like floating particles towards a vacuum, into the general centre ... Here we may discern the origin and nature of Jacobinism;[112] the disease of every Country in similar circumstances ... The coalition and determination of those dreadful bodies towards the Capital, furnished proper instruments for that spirit of revenge and atrocity with which the Populace in every Capital, in certain circumstances, *would humble, plunder, and destroy all the other classes*' (my italics).

Williams goes on to sketch how any fear of famine (genuine enough at certain stages of the war) would arouse desperation, especially in London. 'All things would be aptly prepared for the generation and birth of Genuine Jacobinism; and it requires a mind tutored in Bedlam, to mistake the materials of which it would be composed. What classes of the People would be first subject to deprivation? And who would first lead them to violence and depredation?' French history supplies the answer. The armies despatched to the frontier, the police unsupported, the lower orders – at best living at subsistence level – rose tumultuously in conjunction with multitudes of discharged domestics. Who dare say that in Britain, where two or three branches of industry, subject to sudden and total interruption, employ a million inhabitants,[113] in similar circumstances the Monster will not rise spontaneously from the amalgamated masses of the idle, unemployed, profligate, and desperate inhabitants of populous cities?[114]

It is thus imperative that internal security regulations should embrace society as a whole, avoiding expensive and fallacious reliance on a standing army. Every parish or district should compile a register of inhabitants and be empowered 'to confine, punish, expel, and otherwise dispose of all vagabonds; to take cognizance of the character and conduct of domestics [and] to visit all public and lodging houses'. *All* householders or, where female, their nominees must assist in forming a police. A committee in each district should register houses of ill-fame.[115] Usage of his favourite corporeal analogy moves from the anatomical to the physiological in commending special surveillance for 'a collateral order, called Servants, incorporated with all families, and pervading the political body in connection with their employers, as the vessels of the lymph every where accompany, affect and influence those of the blood'. A register of servants, based on cards or papers of discharge, must be kept – with wandering servants requiring special vigilance. In particular, all clubs of domestics must be declared illegal; for these cherish, though they may conceal, determined and inveterate feelings of hostility and wishes for revenge.[116]

Finally, such committees, which must include J.P.s, should be authorized to oblige each householder and lodger of good repute to procure appropriate weapons. But those so armed must not belong to any association of domestics and must be wholly under the direction of the committee. In London itself, where any mass assembly may well generate the very evil it is intended to prevent, large parishes such as Marylebone may be sub-divided. Indeed the whole of the City and Westminster should be split up into wards and organised, preferably into basic units of fifty to a hundred families, with representation on a Central Committee of the whole capital. Thereby the respectable, honest, and industrious will be armed without removal from their homes and employments, whilst detaching the idle, lazy, and ill-employed, indeed 'forcing the Political Body to throw out on its surface all its diseased humours, and leaving its active limbs at liberty to repel the assaults of its enemies'.[117] Much of this is closely reminiscent of his Constitutional Associations of 1780,[118] and there is evidence that in certain parts of London attempts at precautionary measures were under way.[119] Yet the much sharper and class-orientated tone of *Parochial Police* is unmistakable and indeed, together with its draconian proposals, evoked comment.[120]

This element of almost pathological distrust appears again, in a wider context, in *Egeria*, where the question is put to Alfred whether the modern emancipation of servants without sufficient regulation, and the present unlimited license of the lower orders to burden the public with a vicious population, do not constitute as great an obstacle as slavery to the effective diffusion of that common sensibility which is a pre-requisite of liberty. Alfred is made to concede 'that the idea entertained by modern philosophers of political liberty, of a state governing itself by a senate, council or *sensorium* [my italics, the word will recur], furnished by the sensibility and will of all the people, is impracticable in the present condition of its *populace* and *servants*'. He goes on to assert that his own political organization had never included the lower orders, attached to the soil in a state of slavery.[121] Thus we are back to the Anglo-Saxon limitation of political rights which Williams, in his radical days, had singled out for criticism. The rationale of his present position may presumably be found in the monarch's reply to Locke's assertion that the lower orders, now emancipated, should justly be included in the political organization of the state: 'But how? That is to me the grand problem of political science. Point out the mode of rendering the condition of the laborious and industrious classes so easy, so comfortable, as to ensure in them sufficient *morality* (for there is no morality in hopeless misery) to confide in them those functions you call their rights ...'[122]

Preparatory Studies for Political Reformers, in 1810, reiterates his reservations and his fear that, their passions once aroused, these classes will always opt for insurrection. A distant and tentative road forward again resembles Godwin in its cautious appeal to the gradual efficacy of leadership by an elite: 'To appeal directly to the people, and to set them in motion before they are minutely and competently instructed, would be to set them in the road of speedy perdition ... I repeat it again and again, the people should be first instructed, and they can, at this time, be instructed only, or principally, by the Press; and in the choice of their magistrates and representatives, they should be induced to place their dependence on the genius, talents, spirit, and patriotism of candidates.'[123] The implicit assumption that the people, if enfranchised, would elect those who were (in every sense) naturally endowed to lead them had of course always been present in David Williams; but the also ever-present assumption of the 1770s and 1780s that the native good sense of the people was already sufficient to make such a choice if only the proper electoral machinery were supplied has now gone. Minute and meticulous instruction from above, looked-at askance in his earlier works, is now a prerequisite and on-going condition – for we cannot in any meaningful sense ascribe to him a general vision of the emergence of a fully *educated* electorate.[124]

Of his earlier political thinking substantial elements remain – notably the belief in gradual, organic change and in the need to purge the imperfections of the present system. His contempt for the interminable contentions and depredations of political factions is as deep-seated as ever. Nor is his appeal to a patriot prince as the only prospect of any transformation in any way new. But as to any hope of reform through an extended and purified electoral system he is utterly pessimistic. Even if the present political parties, the depositaries of corruption, were annihilated, what would be the chances or even the effects of a fair election in society as at present constituted? One passage really says it all: 'Though I am not a professed reformer, I am a warm friend to every real reform; nay, it is my belief and my consolation, that ... society is gradually proceeding in a reforming progress. Why the progress is so slow, why it is attended with such convulsions, and with so much national and private misery, I am not able to explain; perhaps not able to comprehend, if the explanation were made to me. But in the mingled dispensations of providence I see reasons to abstain from all pretences either to political or moral perfection.'[125]

He has long concluded that in attempting to break the bonds of oppression reformers have generally broken those of society itself; indeed the declared purpose of *Egeria* had been to check that tendency. Organic development is as natural in the political as in the physical world; but by the same analogy old states, like old men, are not susceptible of sudden and frequent change. The fundamental problem is 'whether the Mind of a society, like that of an animal, may be so formed as to perceive, resolve, and act from the impressions and inducements of what may be called its body', for we are not yet able to transmit by words the complex ideas of political science as we do those of mathematics. We may dismiss the romances which misled French reformers and the facile way in which Locke, followed by Price,[126] ignored all the problems of practical implementation of their simple asser-tion that societies should be self-governed. The crucial problem, as increasingly complex human society has moved from a merely physical to a moral and political consciousness, is to identify what may properly be called the Public Mind. For the real criterion as to whether a society is a *political* body, possessing a Constitution, or is not, is the degree of 'sympathy and connection of the sensorium with every individual of the assemblage'. The term recurs, but is never defined; Williams's dismissal of Rousseau's 'mystic jargon' is not without irony![127]

As in Nature the ideal, the eternal quest, is unattainable, as are also the point, the straight line, and the circle in geometry, so in politics the art of the real statesman is to reconcile fixed principles with national and domestic actualities.[128] We thus arrive at politics as the art of the possible. The corporeal analogy persists: political like animal constitutions are free in proportion to their sensibility and intellect, which in turn reflect 'the quantity and quality of the organs of general information, and of the capacity communicated to the sensorium of developing a public mind'. But its location or functioning are never clarified. The statement that a constitution lacking an organic arrangement of the people would be like an animal without the sense of general feeling, incapable of judgement,[129] is delusive in its apparently unequivocal import. For *Preparatory Studies* rejects as utterly impracticable the concept of the majesty or sovereignty of the people. Its reader is in no danger of being seduced into illusions of democracy, for 'no condition of society hitherto known would secure its continuance for a day: but a general feeling or sensibility is necessary to the existence of every society; and *the first rights of all its members extend no farther than the expression of that sensibility*' (my italics).[130]

Political tyranny is now defined as the exclusion from political bodies of all instruments of general feeling and information. Where these exist, by receiving and transmitting knowledge, impressions, and reactions, every man is in some degree a politician, whether or not he has or (in a piece of cynicism reminiscent of Soame Jenyns) 'imagines he has' a choice in the determination of power. In heavy reliance on natural analogies, the organs and channels of information in society appear to double for the nervous system within the human body. Meanwhile, if perfection is unattainable balance is surely desirable; partial self-interest, allowing a government to become despotic, is as reprehensible as is public-spirited political frenzy. Thus sovereignty resides neither in the king or nobility, nor yet in the people only, but in the whole organized state, 'in the general sensorium, however denominated, of all its feelings and all its affections'.[131] Unfortunately, it never is denominated. What is insisted on is that, in treatment of the apparent ills of the body politic, 'ignorant practitioners, like ignorant bigots, apply the knife and the caustic, and they always exasperate by endeavouring to extirpate the evils'. Wise states, like healthy bodies, may tolerate and absorb such irritants – as in England's ingestion since 1688 of religious non-conformity.[132] Conformably, by the gradual triumph of sweet reason, the morals of the people may ultimately be purified at their springs; then only will parliamentary electoral precedures be fruitfully reformed.[133]

For the present, the words representative and represented do not really pertain to those primary divisions of the body politic which have *passive* faculties only, exercising no influence in the choice of its councils. Nor does this come amiss in existing social circumstances. The prospect of improvement until those demanding representation 'are capable of a judicious choice, and the morals of the electors are good' is very far distant – perhaps over forty years hence. For who could now contemplate, unappalled, the certain consequences of a correct and faithful representation of the people of Britain at this moment? France sought such an accurate representation, 'not in its first assembly, which was moderate; not in the second assembly, which was not destitute of knowledge and virtue; but in its convention, which was a representation tolerably correct of the general feeling ... of public grievance and public vengeance'.[134] This last statement, at utter variance from his earlier attribution of the excesses of the Convention to its election and coercion by the dregs of the populace,[135] is starkly indicative of his change in stance. 'Have the people of England no general opinion on the subject of grievances, and have they no hope of vengeance?'[136] David Williams now sees a meeting of a genuinely representative assembly, for so long the touchstone of inalienable rights, as opening the lid of a Pandora's box of social discontent, or even as opening the floodgates of social anarchy.

The effectual and beneficent *implementation* of representative government remains then the great problem 'which every tyro affects to resolve, and which every reformer has hitherto found too intricate for his faculties ... Human anatomy exhibits the human nerves. Political anatomy has not yet developed the moral nerves.' Williams himself has now decided that the faculties of sensibility so crucial to political bodies are not to be performed by deputations or elections: the analogy is rather that of sympathy, unhelpfully defined as a merely connecting principle, which should induce an elected member to act, not under mandate, but as he would suppose his constituents to wish – given his situation and information. Not surprisingly: 'To render this principle practical is a difficulty of the first importance to the real Reformer'![137] Posed in such terms he had gone far to render his political problems insoluble. He seems to have been uneasily aware of this himself. 'It will be said that I speak the language of despair, or that I am the indirect apologist of abuse and corruption. I dread incompetent reformers, as I sometimes dread the physician more than the disease. The real progress of society has in no instance been promoted by [emulating] the plan of Medea to renovate her aged father by cutting him up.'[138] For the present form of government may hardly be removed without endangering the Constitution into which it has so assiduously been engrafted.

Certainly it would be folly, as French experience has shown, to give elective power to a people the mass of whom are uninstructed and passive – through long exclusion from exercise of the active faculties of the state – and indeed accustomed to regard politics and parties with contempt.[139] Abstract proposals for reform are not merely ineffectual, they may be positively dangerous as tending to exasperate the people, whether through the Press or public meetings. For 'in this divided state of the community, the people are not susceptible of any general feeling superior to irritation; and all appeals to that feeling are attended with extreme danger.' The distinction in physiology between irritability and sensibility is of infinitely more importance in politics: for in political as in animal bodies those parts which are most irritable are least sensible.[140] Thus the appeal to a reformed Parliament as a means of procuring national unity is but the same deluded sophistry as that which plunged France into anarchy. A perfect commonwealth is an ever-present and laudable ideal, but the problems of its creation are intractable; for 'in politics, we plunge the knife into the living body'. Political experiment, at all times hazardous, may now be fatal.[141]

Much of this leads up to an appeal to the Prince of Wales: for who but the Heir-Apparent can rally the nation and save his aged father the anguish of contemplating his government on the verge of ruin? Such utterances are not new, and certainly must now be related to the context of princely patronage of the Literary Fund.[142] Yet it is hard to comprehend how Williams could have penned the ludicrous encomia of his talents which appear in his later works.[143] Similarly, with full allowance for his stress upon the gradual continuity of effective reform, through what is now termed the revolution of the ages, which may fairly be described as a permanent element in his organic approach to political and constitutional issues, there remains a disconcerting omission. For it is impossible to take at face value his repeated injunctions of the need for an educated electorate as an essential pre-requisite for reform without observing the glaring absence, particularly striking in one who had been a professed and participating educationist, of any genuine pre-scription for its creation. His former contention that public participation in politics was in itself to be a major *means* of education for citizenship[144] has been abandoned, and nothing put in its place. His last work admittedly devotes a Study to the Press, but none to education. His position is not unfairly reminiscent of the dilemma confronting the Russian Czars or American slave-proprietors: they dare not emanci-pate the uneducated, and shrank from educating the unemancipated.

Worse, those passages elsewhere devoted to the topic serve only to deepen one's doubts as to the consistency of his position. The seeker for an exposition of the need for a general extension of educational facilities encounters instead, in *The Claims of Literature*, 1802, a broadside of latter-day Mandeville which – though not the main theme of the work – provides a melancholy illustration of the dead-end to which so much of his social speculation had now come. Therein Williams depicts the apparent increase in misery by the very means intended to relieve it, through the exercise of compassion without judgement. For sadly, '*Charity* in many of its institu-tions ... has had a tendency to dishonour *labour*, the first duty and obligation of man'. The creation of schools (and indeed of manufactories) draws off a potential work-force from agriculture, at once increasing the price of subsistence and encour-aging a vicious procreation. 'If the children preserved by charity, were generally consigned to farmers, under stipulations for certain instructions, and not to schools furnishing them with a little useless learning ... the industrious, the ingenious, and the learned, might be fed better and cheaper; and a useful population increased. By placing them in mechanic, mercantile, speculative, and literary classes, the relative disproportion between those who purchase, and those who furnish, subsistence, is continually increasing.' Thus has charity given premiums for the emergence of dreadful evils; for little but ill may be expected from the children of despair who are educated in literature. Wisdom would say of the majority of such: 'Give them nutricious food, and certain elementary instructions, and inure their bodies to labour.'[145]

The general sentiments, indeed the phraseology, echo Mandeville.[146] True, a contemporary parallel may, again, be found in Godwin, whose treatment 'Of National Education' evinces a fundamental distaste for any such incursion into an area of individual liberty.[147] But there could be no more striking contrast than that with a broadsheet on *The Rights of the Poor*, 1791, by a namesake of his deceased associate Bentley, with its advocacy of Free Schools for poor children of both sexes (with, if need be, removal of children from feckless parents)[148], or with the whole import of George Dyer's *Complaints of the Poor People of England*, 1793, which, ironically, cites earlier works of Williams with approval.[149] Indeed Thomas Cooper's *Reply to Mr Burke's Invective*, 1792, had declared that 'under these Circum-stances of national Ignorance, so prevalent among the lower Classes' nothing is so essential as 'a well formed Plan of public Education. The whole of our conduct toward the Poor, seems to me a System of flagrant iniquity ... Having made them poor and kept them ignorant, we declare them unfit to be trusted ...'[150]

Present-day Williams could only deplore the surplus produce of the charitable institutions, 'with bodies rendered unfit for labour, with sedentary habits, a passion for reading, and an expectation of being provided for and distinguished'. Ideally, a Commission or Board should examine the operation of charities, with special reference to schools for the children of the poor.[151] As for contemporary trends in education in general, Williams alludes to 'a species of revolution, which has lately taken place' and to his own participation therein. More recently, a Mr Florian, of Bath, has undertaken a similar approach.[152] But now, uninformed as to the fate of his efforts, and disappointed in his own, he understands that of late 'a sentimental philosophy of education has been established', by which all branches of learning are made both easy and amusing, whose pupils are speedily qualified for those great universities, the circulating libraries. The sickly spawn of this sentimental education are the most numerous and importunate applicants to the Literary Fund![153]

Suspicion of an element of misanthropy must not make us lose sight of the fact that much of his socio-economic analysis was in the mainstream of contemporary thought. A letter from none other than Thomas Jefferson, dated 14 November 1803, conveying thanks for a copy of *Claims of Literature*, devotes most of its content to the need to correlate education with the economic needs and population trends of society, congratulates Williams on his command of the problem, and endorses his prescriptions.[154] The *Monthly Review* found his comments on the folly of conveying a superficial education in charity schools shrewd, though sarcastic and exaggerated.[155] The admirer of the earlier radical David Williams was now presented with the bitter pill of finding this section (but only this section) of his work awarded the accolade of commendation for much good sense, with but a mild reproof for overstatement, by the *Anti-Jacobin Review*.[156]

Yet, ironically, this last source, but a few years earlier, had attested the fact that his belated apprenticeship in socio-political respectability had not at that point satisfied at least some of the establishment. A poem, of which George Canning was the chief author, first printed in *The Anti-Jacobin* for 9 July 1798, was taken up and made the subject of a large cartoon by Gillray. Entitled 'New Morality; or The promis'd Installment of the High-Priest of the Theophilanthropes ...', this reprints in part the verse, including the couplet:

> 'All creeping creatures, venomous and low,
> Paine, W-ll-ms, G-dw-n, H-lc-ft, praise Lepaux!'

The cartoon depicts, *inter alia*, Paine as a crocodile, Godwin as an ass on his hind legs and reading *Political Justice*, other publications such as 'Pigs Meat' and 'Religion de la Nature', but above – or rather, below – all, a hissing serpent advances over papers entitled 'Williams's Atheistical Lectures'.[157]

Evidently his earlier religious publications, together with his radical political connections, had neither been forgotten nor completely forgiven.[158] Yet any element of exaggerated caricature in his own sketch of the charity schools must not distract us from the very real significance of Williams's failure to follow his insistence that

Plate 9. 'NOT YET RESPECTABLE!' Williams's 'Atheistical Lectures' included in a Gillray cartoon attacking the French Revolution and Theophilanthropy.

the emergence of an educated and hence responsible electorate must precede political reform with any evidence of a disposition in favour of universal elementary education. Admittedly, to regard such a concept as an incursion into individual liberty rather than as a means of social and political amelioration is indicative of the traditional libertarian basis of so much of his thought. Yet well might the reader who has traced the development of the political, social and educational aspects of that thought through more than a score of works of variable quality but very considerable import and impact now share in the ultimate disappointment and disillusion of their author. His almost obsessive corporeal analogy had undergone its own symbolic transmutation: in earlier works it had pulsed with the young blood of progressive, reformist ideals; but with the ageing process, the hardening of the arteries, it figured forth more and more the traditional conservative social values. It would be harsh to speak of a handful of silver or yet of a ribbon to put in his hair; rather should one look for Matthew Arnold's 'petty dust' of time, age, and association. His ideals were not so much abandoned as exhausted. In this context – though not, as we shall see, in that other to which Franklin had directed his remark – the anvil had indeed worn out the hammer.

Chapter Eight

THE CLAIMS OF LITERATURE

IT is perhaps a relief to turn from the exhaustion of the political ideals of David Williams to the triumphant fruition of another early dream. But before we trace the successful establishment of a Literary Fund – of which the launching preceded the French adventure and the initial discussion even that of Margaret Street – there remain the non-political writings and also the personal circumstances of this last phase. Within a year or so of his return from France he moved from Great Russell Street to 23 Brompton Row, Knightsbridge, where he lived for over a decade before taking up residence in the House of the Literary Fund, back once more in Soho, in 1805. But for several months immediately after coming back to England he was concerned about a law suit involving Mrs Martyn.[1] The story must be pieced together from scattered evidence, but the main points seem clear. Her father's will, of 1780, left a substantial income from his estate to Frances, her husband Thomas Martyn, and their putative children; but in default of such issue, lawfully begotten, the legacy was to pass to another branch of the family, while if Frances should live apart from her husband he would be totally debarred.[2] These provisos explain the significance of the rather surprising allusion, in a letter dated 24 May 1793 addressed to Williams (in whose household Mrs Martyn had lived from at latest 1788), to 'Mrs Martyn's Children, who they [i.e., the court] would not decide to be beyond Possibility of having Children'. This letter, from Richard Beadon,[3] which concludes with most affectionate remembrances to Frances and respects to Williams himself, wears the air of an attempt to heal the breach which had opened as a result of failure to pay to Mrs Martyn the moneys due after the death of her father in 1782. Complaint was first made by the Martyns as early as 1785, and the records of the Court of Exchequer rehearse the whole complicated wrangle (including a contention of the Beadons that some moneys had been advanced, partly in payment of Martyn's debts) before ending on 17 June 1793 in an adjournment, presumably in the hope of some settlement between the parties.[4]

This seems to have occurred, for David Williams's papers make it clear that thereafter considerable sums of money were received by Frances.[5] There is no evidence of any fusion of their resources – indeed one record of financial transactions is countersigned 'Frances Martyn' – but insofar as it was a joint household Williams's own financial position would obviously have improved. Thus his papers include references to the purchase and sale of American Bank shares[6] between December 1803 and July 1805 involving several hundred pounds,[7] while a note gives power of attorney to Thomas Whittingham (who was to be one of his executors) 'to receive my Dividends in the three pr Cent Consols' and instructs him to invest a further £300 in those funds – records of receipts on the same page run into hundreds of pounds.[8] But this also brought problems; a note of payment of Property and Income Tax may help explain some indignant comments noted in the previous chapter! Records of furnishings involved in removals, including a large library,[9] and of house repairs and decorations, attest at least a modest competence. This was certainly eroded with the declining health of his last years. Yet sufficient remained in January 1812 for the scale of the funeral arrangements for Mrs Martyn (costing over £42)[10] to testify to a deep and genuine respect, which was unfailingly reflected in much of the correspondence addressed to him.

His sources of income included continued personal tuition, and increasing involvement as political as well as literary adviser to public figures including one episode as public relations consultant to a major business interest. We have already observed his role as governmental literary propagandist and agent.[11] The often overlapping nature of his activities is exemplified by the recurrence of three names – Lord Valentia, Lord Chichester, and Thomas Williams – in the records of the Literary Fund. Two letters from Valentia in April 1807 acknowledge his help in criticizing the work of another, less satisfactory, assistant.[12] But Williams's closest link was almost certainly with Pelham, Lord Chichester.[13] A striking example of the type of work undertaken occurs in the Pelham Papers relating to defence against foreign invasion in the shape of a 'Plan for raising an Additional Force June 13, 1803'. Alongside its unidentified author's original proposals are Williams's notes and criticisms in a separate column. These include the intriguing proposal that the present allegedly female-induced luxury of employing 'the finest men in the Country from 18 to 35 at farthest, for Footmen, shop-men', et al, must be checked: 'A very heavy Tax on such persons from 18 to 45, would indirectly recruit the Services … But the Tax must be very heavy; or the Ladies would pay it.' In general, he suggests the following age-ranges for different types of defensive duty: Army and Militia, 18–45; Army of Reserve, 16–55; for Domestic Security, 16–60.[14]

Equally interesting is an undated document addressed to the Earl of Chichester, headed 'Defence of the Country'. Some typical criticisms of present plans (which, like Pitt's designs for checking the French Revolution, seem calculated to produce the very evil they envisage) include the charge of neglect to harness the 'Spirit of Volunteering'. This, in turn, will further be eroded by any suspicion that people are asked to bear burdens and shed their blood merely 'to keep one Set of Ministers in lucrative Places, or to give others Opportunities & Leisure to dispossess them'. In regard to the war at sea, he has strong views about the interest being shown in two devices brought forward by an American inventor after their rejection by Napoleon: the submarine and the 'catamaran' (a type of primitive torpedo).[15] Williams is in no doubt, first, as to the base cowardice which such an abandonment of all our naval traditions would imply, and second, and most perceptively, as to the peculiarly disastrous impact upon a nation as heavily reliant on international commerce as Britain if by a 'sudden revolution in maritime Warfare … all military Navies were annihilated by Catamarans'.[16] Another undated letter to Chichester alludes to its recipient's possible involvement in peace negotiations – which must bear fruit lest the French succeed in their design of uniting the world against us. Williams intends to repeat what he did the previous year and 'take a little Place at Brighton – where the Perusal of the Manuscripts &c may be consistent with occasional Bathing – a matter of importance to me'.[17]

His advice was also sought by a public figure of a very different type – Thomas Williams, the north Wales, indeed *the*, copper magnate. David Williams relates how, in preparation for a Commons Committee (which reported in May 1799)[18], he was 'three Weeks with him at Bath daily & almost hourly employed in moulding into form, his crude and often contradictory Ideas on the Subject'. But his expectations of several hundred guineas as adequate recompense, and hope of a cottage and garden fit for his retirement when his patron's great concerns in Anglesey were resolved, were dashed. 'The Apprehension & Terror being removed, the Language of Gratitude & Intentions of Compensation seldom occurred.'[19] An offer of a mere £50 from the Copper Company increased his disquiet, which deepened when Owen Williams informed him that his increasingly penurious father had given up French wines at table! Soon afterwards David Williams 'went to France, & the Father to Bath; where he died' – together with all expectations.[20] A projected 'Life of Thomas Williams' came to nothing; but there is very little doubt that *A Letter to the Right Rev. Dr. Warren, on His Conduct as Bishop of Bangor* 'by Shon Gwialan', appearing on St David's Day, 1796, had been written by David at the behest of Thomas Williams in the context of personal, business, and electioneering rivalry.[21]

An attack on the oppressions which allegedly disgrace the diocese relates first to the deplorable appointment of many who are unable to speak the Welsh language – whose tenacious survival the author commends.[22] Indeed, the dignities and benefices in the Bishop's gift were not created for his greedy kindred and dependents – including his nephew 'whose *sensual faculties* would have disqualified him' anywhere else, yet promoted as part of a squalid deal.[23] Still worse, the charitable institutions and schools of the diocese are the rightful property of its poor inhabitants and should not be subject to the Bishop's eccentric whims. Yet by deliberately imposed expenses poor men's children are excluded – presumably because he considers learning inimical to subordination and would banish such a democrat from his diocese.[24] Williams follows this slightly out-of-character defence of the poor's educational rights by accusing the Bishop of reneging on an agreement with the proprietors of the Paris mountain to repair a derelict church,[25] and of refusing to contribute to charity or the poor rate. 'You would rather spend twenty pounds in an election dinner, or a law suit, which you dearly love, than give the value of a loaf to appease the hunger of a poor family.' Typical is his disturbing the tranquillity of the county by his interference in elections, to the detriment of Sir Robert Williams, the present M.P. for Caernarvon.[26] All this, together with his tolerance of the amorous exploits of one curate and in particular of a young dean presented at the church door with their illegitimate fruit, explains why the populace of Bangor have burnt him in effigy – a frightening warning in the context of events in France![27] Finally, a long appendix, 'Disputes with the Mine Companies', rehearses the Bishop's financial and political wrangles with opponents who include, not surprisingly, Thomas Williams, Such conflicts have led, on one occasion, to a scene of indecent violence, involving 'a large detachment of ecclesiastical beef-eaters and mutton-eaters'. This incident indeed led to the trial of the Bishop and sundry gentlemen for Riot at Shrewsbury Assizes in July 1796 – though it took the Jury five minutes to acquit the lot![28]

This pamphlet, while displaying all the old zestful skill in verbal thrusts, was clearly that of a hired lance, albeit with a congenial target; his other publication of 1796, while also the subject of considerable subvention, was of a very different type. But before examining the well-received *History of Monmouthshire* a word is needed about perhaps the most ambitious, though ultimately abortive, of all of Williams's literary projects. A lavishly produced brochure on a 'Proposal for Publishing a complete History of England, superbly ornamented' is still extant. Robert Bowyer, 'Miniature Painter to His Majesty', to whom the work was to be dedicated, proposed a magnificently illustrated reissue of Hume's *History of England*; some sixty paintings by eminent artists, including J. F. Rigaud, would form an exhibition in themselves, before the presentation of Proof Prints to the King and the Prince of Wales. An addition, dealing with the period since the Revolution, was to be written by Williams, whose selection was commended by 'the species of independence he has ever displayed; his peculiar indifference to all political parties, and to the general motives of ambition', which should produce a history of candour and impartiality.[29] Small wonder that *Public Characters for 1798–9* was to allude to a prospectus evidently written by Williams himself![30]

Unfortunately, the brochure is dated January 1792, and we have already remarked the impact of David Williams's acceptance of French citizenship later in the year.[31] Quite certainly this caused Bowyer not so much to withdraw an invitation as to renege upon a quite definite if still verbal contractual obligation, which had evoked a humorous elegy in the *Gentleman's Magazine* as early as February 1792.[32] Thus when James Tilly Matthews, in a letter to Williams, followed his assertion that Bowyer's use of the King's name and of a threatened withdrawal of subscribers was all a lie, despite the exception taken by the establishment, with the forecast that 'you will yet make him smart', he was completely accurate. Bowyer had little option but to settle for breach of contract, for the considerable sum of £315.[33] This was not the last occasion on which Williams's hopes of an ambitious projected publication were dashed;[34] but, more happily, another work of history, whose first inception also dates from 1792, achieved success.

The Introduction to *The History of Monmouthshire*, 1796, explains its origin in the interest and support of some gentry of the county, including 'the late Mr Morgan of Tredegar', the news of whose sudden death while Williams was actually on the road to visit him 'clouded, in a discouraging manner, the first view of the undertaking'.[35] Despite its somewhat cryptic references to a plan and its terms, a letter from Pontypool in August 1794, inviting Williams to spend 'as much of your time *here*, as you can give us, which may *Without interruption* be devoted to the Business, and your own private studies', seems a clear indication of the involvement of the Stoughton/Hanbury family in the continuance of the project. Indeed, a rather curtly worded letter by Thomas Stoughton, in August 1797, addressed to Williams at the home of Dr Hooper, Pantygoitre, alludes to a settlement of 300 guineas which will be made forthwith in person.[36] Certainly, the Preface makes full

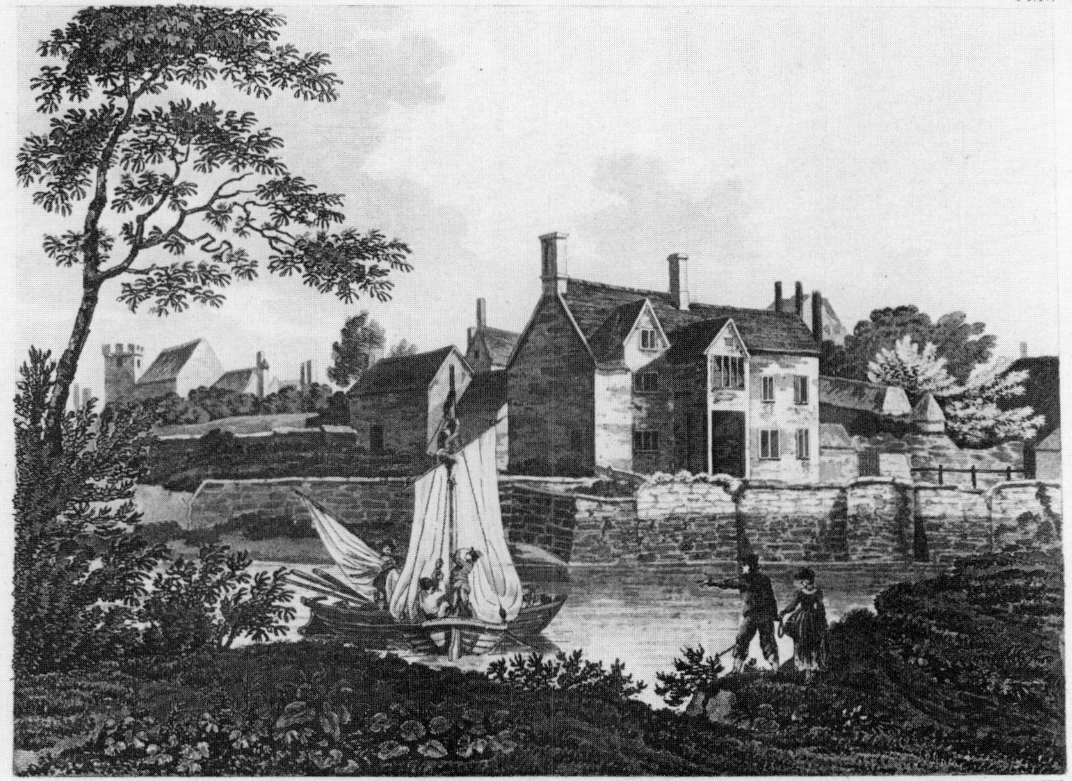

Drawn by the Rev. I. Gardnor. Engrav'd by the Rev. I. Gardnor & J. Hill

VIEW of CAERLEON.

Plate 10.

Publish'd Decr. 14th. 1793 by Messrs. Egerton Charing Cross, Messrs. White Fleet Street & Mr. I. Edwards Pall Mall.

acknowledgement of the help and hospitality received from the families mentioned.[37]

That Preface also records its author's claim to 'so much knowledge of the original language, as to read, speak, and write, one of its original dialects, with facility'. Williams also states plainly that he lacks sufficient time and expertise fully to digest available sources, but will at least avoid antiquarian controversy – the Billingsgate of literature.[38] The list of libraries and of individuals (including Iolo Morganwg) consulted is indeed impressive: a text of 360 pages is followed by 200 pages of appendices, containing transcripts of source-material, verbatim communications from scholars, and a list of patrons and subscribers. The illustrative plates by the Rev. John Gardnor, Vicar of Battersea and an associate in the Literary Fund, received a mixed contemporary reception but are a major reason why the book is highly prized by modern antiquarians. The text itself combines outline history, antiquarian illustration, and philosophical, political, and economic reflections. An increasingly cautious and empirical political approach is encapsulated in the comment that, in the absence of a reliable political compass, it is safer to follow Montesquieu along the shore (risking shoals) than to follow Plato and Rousseau and perish in the ocean. Equally indicative is his emphasis upon both economic *and social* consequences of increasing division of labour.[39]

It is interesting to encounter an explanation of the reverse migration from Britain to 'Armorica' (Brittany), and the assertion that 'the celebrated Arthur has had an actual existence'.[40] Sadly, he believes that the influence of the Druids upon the Welsh character has not entirely been eliminated and that 'irritability, indecision, and credulity, remain the general failings of the natives of Cambria'.[41] As to their tongue, an encomium of its sublimity and power, especially in poetry, contrasts oddly with a later assertion that its continued use is a perpetual impediment to instruction – the people's failure to learn English often giving them 'appearances of folly, stupidity, and inferiority, which exclude them, in a great measure, from all the speculations of industry'.[42] As to their early political progress, Williams is obliged to concede that the mode of activating a whole community without risk of deranging its constituent parts is a Saxon not a British discovery: even Howel the God did not adhere to the elective mechanism.[43]

The Normans followed the Saxons in exploiting the internal divisions of the Welsh – a weakness exacerbated by a deluded tracing of their lineage which would frown at the interruption of the Creation itself.[44] There next comes a lengthy analysis of the Norman-English impact on Wales, with Gwent and borderland illustrations and several references to 'Senghennyth, the present Caerphilly'.[45] Discussion of the limited Tudor impact contains the provocative assertion that translations of the Bible had little effect; more positive was administrative improvement in the Marches, including the creation of an *English* county in Gwent.[46] As to the mid-seventeenth-century Civil Wars, Williams identifies the genesis of religious toleration, despite the extremist episodes, but also a significant political conclusion: 'Men in artificial societies, are more under the impulses of habit, than the guidance of reason; ... it may be a measure of incalculable injury, suddenly to withdraw the instrument of those impulses, and to commit the people at once, to the exercise of their own reason.' To reconcile freedom with the necessary provision of a constitution, amidst the contending factions of a violent revolution, is a problem which Williams now contemplates with awe.[47]

The eighteenth-century's more peaceful ambience (the clash of parliamentary contestants replacing that of swords) has witnessed much neglect of local economic development – especially when contrasted with the growth of Liverpool, Manchester, and Birmingham.[48] But the efforts of the Hanbury family have produced a striking exception: 'By the construction of furnaces and collieries, the formation of rail-roads and canals,[49] a hilly district of great extent will soon be productive of incalculable wealth; and on the banks of the canal from Pont-y-Pool to Newport, a second Birmingham, or a second Sheffield will arise, as by enchantment . . .' But no enchantment is present when Williams moves to a graphic analysis of the social as distinct from the economic effects of industrial development and organisation of labour: 'For the peasant, to persons who will be at the trouble of adopting his language, is more amiable and intelligent than the artificer; the former has his mind unfolded on various subjects, the latter is a machine unfeeling, immoral, and unpleasing. Manufactories, however they may add to the public wealth, certainly degrade and brutalize the people; and, managed as they are, on principles of monopoly, a species of slavery is their constant effect. Children brought up as machines are depraved in body and in mind; and mechanics, substituting intemperance for domestic comforts, are bad husbands, bad fathers, and corrupt or unprincipled citizens.' Having survived the inroads of Roman, Saxon, and Norman, the hills of Gwent will now be invaded by the immorality and rapacity of manufacturing institutions whose magnitude and influence make them arbitrary powers which, like all such bodies, subdue their dependents by depraving them.[50]

This savage indictment, which would have graced the pen of any nineteenth-century philanthropic reformer or even any Chartist,[51] is followed by the contrast with the idyllic prospect from, ironically, Llanwern,[52] of the Bristol Channel with 'the flat and steep holmes, dropped into the water like stepping-stones for the passage of a giant'.[53] Next, an interesting sketch of Monmouthshire's religious denominations finds the Presbyterians not strong enough to form a formal Presbytery, at once the instrument of their power and the ruin of their sect; the Independents greatly moderated in their pretensions to orthodoxy; and the Methodists most active and enterprising, their enthusiasm useful and their general object good.[54] Finally, 'Circulating Libraries, of little treatises on agriculture, would be of more service to the country, than those which furnish political pamphlets to embroil the men, or novels to enervate and inflame the imaginations of the women, destined for sober and domestic duties.' Indeed an 'Oeconomical Society' should help young and poor farmers by the provision of books, machines, implements, and small money grants at minimal interest, and should underwrite rural associations for experiment and improvement. All this would be preferable to the degrading and vicious intrigue of provincial politics and elections, which stimulate only hatred.[55]

Reviewers were impressed. The notice in the *Cambrian Review* is itself of intrinsic interest as an exercise in bending over backwards to be seen as fair while missing no chance of a merited side-swipe. It commends the absence of the expected revolu-

Pl. vi.

Drawn by the Rev.J.Gardnor.

Engraved by the Rev.J.Gardnor & J.Hill.

SOUTH WEST VIEW of USK CASTLE.

Published Dec.24th 1793 by W. & J. Egerton Drawing Sept. Mess.rs Whieldon Fleet Street & Mr J. Edwards Pall Mall.

Plate 11.

tionary reveries in an author now clearly sensible of his former errors, welcomes the cautious disclaimer of any profound linguistic knowledge, and even discerns consummate skill in the blending of national and local history – though patience snaps at the claim 'that Dafydd ab Gwilym would now be rendered David Williams'. As for the illustrations, well, 'they are numerous, and therefore may be deemed good at the price', while the appendix contains much 'entertainment for the antiquarian, thrown in higgledy piggledy, as it were to amend the bargain and fill up the book'.[56] *The British Critic* agreed that such material should have been incorporated in the text but expressed a much higher estimate of the quality of the plates, in a valuable and elegant work marred only by the occasional obtrusion of political theorems and religious prejudices, or of passages of affected description.[57] The *Monthly* and the *Analytical Review* concurred in praising an achievement both in depth of research and in the presentation of history – though the latter observed that the author's ridicule of pride of ancestry would hardly endear him to his countrymen.[58]

Indeed, in such a context, we may raise the question of the strength of any links which still bound Williams to his native land – or at least to his birthplace and family. A persistent oral tradition[59] attests the occurence of visits to Caerphilly, but their frequency and duration are unknown. Yet of continued concern for and very real assistance of his family there remains clear evidence. Four names recur in his correspondence: Vaughan, Pryce, Thomas, and Hedges. In effect, William Vaughan and William Pryce acted as agents for the help given to his family.[60] Letters preserved range from 1781 to 1809 – not large in number (though probably an incomplete record) but incontestably concerned with constant and genuine assistance, such as grants of money to his brother-in-law, Rev. Walter Thomas, and his sister, Joan Hedges, and payment for clothing material for the latter's children.[61] Its provision was not devoid of tact: on one occasion Pryce writes that 'I believe the Waunwaelod people are employed, I dont know wither I must be a petitioner, will you indulge them with a fliech of Bacon, they have no knowledge of my making any application on the subject, I think as Butcher's meat is becoming scarce & dear, it will be particularly acceptable.' By 1809 the same correspondent[62] relates how 'the Family at Wainwaelod go on nearly The Same. I have order'd the Houses to be repaired to prevent Their Tumbling down. The expence I Trust will be Moderate'.[63] Other help sought from David Williams included his insertion in the newspapers of a notice of the death of William Williams, Pantycelyn, and an advance of money to pay a debt incurred in procuring a substitute for his nephew David Hedges[64] as militia man in 1803.[65] This last request refers to all 'that you have and are still doing for them', which suggests that the help given may well have exceeded the amounts still recorded.

During these years the success of his *History of Monmouthshire* was increasingly matched by that of the project which was to be his abiding memorial.[66] Of long gestation, what is now the Royal Literary Fund dates back in conception to Williams's early days in London. His autobiography recalls how, as private tutor of persons preparing for public life, he had reflected on the possible systematization of such tuition in a College protected by the Legislature.[67] He also encountered the peculiar injustice committed with impunity by those who 'tempt ingenious Men, by apparently honorable Engagements ... most dishonorably violated'.[68] In his own annual estimate of the fruits of his labour he has generally thought himself fortunate to receive half the sums promised by verbal agreement – ignoring worthless promises of patronage. For if inventors of such tangible devices as steam engines and cotton mills are somtimes defrauded by adventurers what must be expected by those whose claims are founded on ideas?[69] The first reading of a paper on a Literary Fund to relieve ensuing destitution was made to the original Club set up in Easter Week of 1773. (Indeed Williams attributes to Franklin's influence the switch in his endeavours to a philosophic liturgy which nearly ruined his reputation and his fortune.[70]) A lengthy statement of the case for relief of 'Writers of real Utility, in distress' ends in an outline of the possible Constitution of a Society for a Literary Fund. But Franklin, reflecting the reservations of his fellow-members not on merit but on practicalities, 'pronounced these Words; which have, a thousand times, rung in my Ears. "I see – you will not give up a Noble Idea; I do not say, you will not succeed; but it must be, by much Anxiety & Trouble; & I hope the Anvil will not wear out the Hammer." '[71]

An interview with Adam Smith, a decade later, to challenge his maxim in *Wealth of Nations* that 'Men of Letters were *unproductive* Members of Society' evoked the advice (given perhaps with dry Scots humour) to 'state your Plan to the young Minister. It seems to be a Political Proposition of great Importance.' Pitt's reception was devoid of haughtiness, but as Minister he felt unable to help. The record of Williams's ensuing interviews elsewhere includes two priceless incidents. Mr Fox 'was getting up, at one o'Clock; & though he was hurried in the Offices of a slovenly Toilett, some of which were performed before me – he conversed with perfect good humour – confessing he had been alarmed supposing, from the purity of his early life, that it must have been my Object, to assign him some conspicuous Office in my New Religion. It was with difficulty I could induce him to say or hear anything serious on the subject of Authors. He perused the Paper I gave him – & said Burke is the proper Person to be consulted; his head is as full of Metaphysics, as your own ...' The call on Burke was preceded by a note, but with no more fortunate result: 'at the appointed hour, he entered his Drawing Room, into which I had been shewn, like a Maniac; & uttering execrations on Authors & Scribblers, he approached me with such Gesticulations, as a Welsh Constitution interpreted into hostile Signals; & I prepared for Battle – But the gesticulations were Oratorical; & he looked fiercely in my face & said, Authors, Writers, Scribblers, are the Pests of the Country ... His Fury infected me "Who, & what are you to use such Language? If you had not been a Man of Letters; you would have been a Bog-trotter. You are not a Gentleman; & I will quit your house." He cooled, at once, like an intoxicated Person on receiving a Blow, made an Apology, that he had mistaken me for another Person of my Name – but I was rolling downstairs, like a true Welshman, & thus terminated my Intercourse with Mr Burke.'[72]

After a fruitless approach to his erstwhile acquaintance Banks, now prominent in the Royal Society, Williams despaired of immediate success, having failed to enlist any person of major standing and popularity and borne out the succinct contention of an aged and experienced book-seller, 'Good God! Sir, no body will meddle with authors'. An attempt in October 1786 to associate Artists with Men of Letters in publicising the projected scheme had no impact.[73] The tragic and quite fortuitous triggerpoint for an effective launch was almost certainly the death, broken-hearted, imprisoned at the age of seventy-seven for a minor debt, of Floyer Sydenham. Eight gentlemen subscribed a few guineas each to finance a regular advertisement which first appeared on 10 May 1788. This time an actual Constitution was established, with Committee and Officers, and Coutts as banker to hold subscriptions. Yet although the melancholy fate of an eminent scholar sufficed to bring together a few subscribers, Williams relates how the attitudes displayed were sometimes uncongenial: 'The Language & frequently the Minutes of those who offered their Assistance, were those of an Hospital; & often gave me Offence'; Franklin's prophecy echoed in his mind as he strove to establish the Society on the right foundations.[74] The list of original subscribers includes James Martin, M.P.,[75] Hugh Downman, J. F. Rigaud, and Dr Thomas Dale. The last-named, W. T. Fitzgerald, and W. Boscawen, receive special commendation for their later service.[76] A letter to Dale from Rigaud in November 1790, approving the intention of making their old Club subordinate to the object of the Literary Fund, points to an element of continuity.[77] The 'Minutes of General Committee' record a meeting on 10 May 1790 with the Rev. Mr Gardnor in the Chair and Dr Dale acting as Secretary; that of 18 May elected a Committee and established the principle that service was completely honorary, confirming Williams's own allusion to 'gratuitous Officers, directed by the Founder'.[78]

It was later resolved to publish accounts of the Fund's activities, and the first of these, printed in 1799 by John Nichols, another supporter, relates the gradual achievement of stability.[79] But the Society had already encountered criticism and was soon to survive an internal squabble. Derision surfaced in a footnote attack on William Boscawen in a long, anonymous, and successful satirical poem, *The Pursuits of Literature*.[80] In a rather oblique allusion to the Fund the qualification for relief is defined 'for a Poet, that he has never disposed of twenty copies of any one poem of his own composing', and a flood of applications is envisaged.[81] A fierce rejoinder by a contributor to the *Gentleman's Magazine* in 1798 can only ascribe such vilification of a benevolent institution to 'a base and unfeeling heart'.[82] Meanwhile, efforts to bolster the funds had included projected theatrical productions, involving Thomas Morris and David Williams himself as managers,[83] and a proposed monthly, 'The Review'. First mooted in the Minutes for 20 June 1799,[84] the scheme progressed as far as a declaration that it would first appear on 1 May 1801. A critical compendium of contemporary science and literature, its honorary trustees would remit a legally-defined portion of its receipts to the Fund, while its editors, all other things being equal, would prefer to 'provide employment for distressed Writers'. Despite explicit reference to those members of the Fund who had subscribed for the Review,[85] no trace of its appearance has been found.[86]

More success attended the decision, in May 1800,[87] to publish a History of the Fund – though this also led to a major quarrel. *Claims of Literature* duly appeared and was presented to both the King and the Prince of Wales in circumstances not entirely clear.[88] At a subsequent meeting a Fund Vice-President, Sir James Bland

Burges, launched a bitter attack on the moral, religious, and governmental principles expressed in that portion of the work which the Founder had written. The fifty
or so members present were reportedly astonished, for as Williams himself is at
pains to stress, the contents had even won the approval of John Reeves – whose
original appointment as nominal collaborator had been qualified by a clear recognition of the Founder's unique qualification to write the History.[89] Boscawen,
Fitzgerald, and others closed ranks and Sir James, failing even to secure appointment of a committee to consider his charges, announced his resolve to retire. In a
most revealing passage Williams confesses his relief at the avoidance of a protracted
contest: Burges had 'never possessed the esteem of the Society. I have a pride in
saying I did; & in losing it, I should have lost a Pearl, to me, of great price.'[90]

The clash involved principle as well as personality. Sir James, says Williams, had
from the first endeavoured to pervert the Society 'by mingling religious & political
Enquiries with the cases of the unfortunate Claimants'. Such bigotry was resisted by
Boscawen and Fitzgerald, the more nobly since they shared the political and religious views of Burges. 'But I was the rock, on which Sir James was to split' in his
efforts to banish all mercy and candour whenever any disloyal or profane indiscre-
tion could be imputed to a claimant. 'Is it to be supposed, that I would tamely have
suffered a liberal & independent Institution to be converted into a gloomy &
suspicious Court of Inquisition? Or that a Court-Reptile should wound his snares
around their Committees [as] Grand Inquisitor of the Literary Fund?' In Courts the
Law dictates; but in benevolent institutions the heart must speak. The last and best
legacy Williams can bequeath to his colleagues is the earnest wish that they should
'continue to act, as they have ever done; their Judgement contending & sometimes
contending in vain with their Humanity'.[91]

In this context the astringent notice of *Claims of Literature* in *The Anti-Jacobin
Review*[92] is of particular interest. The personification of ideas so as to render them
universal philanthropists and benefactors is surely more eccentric than intelligible?
Nor would the *Anti-Jacobin* 'wish to see literary men considered as a separate class
...; still less do we wish to witness a Government chiefly composed of such characters; – the experiment has been tried on a large scale in another country; and we are
not enamoured of the result'. In short, the overstated views of David Williams,
though quite in character, do nothing to serve the Society or to 'weaken any of the
objections which have occasionally been urged against it; and, as they contain much
objectionable matter, it would have been an act of wisdom and of policy in the
Committee, wholly to reject them'. But in truth those objections are misdirected 'to
a charitable institution of this nature, which certainly holds out no encouragement
to a man to become an author. It is only intended to relieve distress, and, in the
accompaniment of that laudable object, great discrimination, we are happy to find,
is invariably observed.'[93]

In considering the conduct of the Fund we can but touch on certain aspects: the
Founder's colleagues, the cases helped, the annual dinners with their convivial-
patriotic tone, and the acquisition of a House as headquarters in which Williams
spent his own last years. Among the names which recur in the records, besides those
already mentioned, are those of the Rev. Yates (later to be co-executor with Whitt-

ingham), Captain Morris (his biographer, the date and circumstances of whose estrangement from Williams remain unknown), and John Reeves, whose prominence came late but was thereafter steadfast, including considerable service as Treasurer. Vice-Presidents of note included Thomas Williams, M.P., Burges, and Valentia. The death of the first-named led to replacement as Vice-President in January 1803 by Lord Pelham (later Chichester), whose name was to figure largely not only in the correspondence of David Williams and in the general affairs of the Fund but also as playing a crucial role in liaison with the Prince of Wales and in the acquisition of a House.[94]

As to the 'Cases in which Relief has been Administered', Boscawen in 1802 reported from the Minutes of Dr Dale, Registrar, that in twelve years some £1,680 had been donated to 105 persons.[95] The first extant *Account* of the Society, 1799, which prints the Constitutions, makes reference to individuals – such as 'No. LXVI. Twenty-five pounds being voted for the widow and children of the late Robert Burns, the *Scotch Bard*'.[96] But that for 1801 explains the cessation of this practice not only as a needless expense but as 'a violation of that delicacy, which is necessary to render the beneficence of the Society acceptable to minds made peculiarly irritable by misfortune'.[97] Relief was not indiscriminately granted: the first application, that of a military gentleman who was impressively quick off the mark, was summarily rejected, and the first request of a novelist was coolly received. The notion of writers of *utility* was not readily abandoned. Whilst eschewing bigotry, both Williams and Boscawen in *Claims of Literature* insist that 'authors of slanderous, of immoral, or of impious works, have, in general, been speedily detected, and ignominiously repelled'. The Minutes convey an impression first, that men of the cloth received kindly consideration, and second, that in cases of repeated importunity the heart often (but not always) overruled the head; a lady whose first disappointment was expressed in terms unfit for the ears of the Committee was later helped, but Iolo Morganwg came once too often to the well.[98]

Early recipients of relief included 'Mr De Lolme, in consideration of his excellent Publication on the Constitution of Great Britain',[99] and the more radical political pamphleteer, John Oswald.[100] Notable poets, or their families, received help, among them Coleridge (nominated by James Martin), Cowper, and George Dyer. Grants were made to the bereaved dependants of the historian Bisset and of Thomas Holcroft.[101] At the 1822 banquet Viscount de Chateaubriand, then French Ambassador, made public avowal of the relief he had received when a struggling exile in London; the Minutes for 20 June 1799 indeed award ten guineas to this 'noble French Emigrant, & Author of "Une Essai Historique et Politique, sur les Revolutions anciennes et modernes", published in London: he being in great distress'.[102] But in our present context pride of place must perhaps (and not unfairly, given its frequent recurrence in the Minutes) be given to the name of a fellow-countryman and purported relative of Williams, Iolo Morganwg or Edward Williams.

The first items in the one-sidedly preserved[103] correspondence between the Welshmen attest to its rather wobbly nature. Writing to Iolo at 2 Star Court, Chancery Lane, Williams asks to meet him before the Fund Committee deliberates the following day. The date, 22 December 1794, is puzzling, for the Minutes for *19*

December record a decision 'that Ten Guineas be given to Mr Edward Williams, the Welch Bard; & the Revd. D. Williams is desired to deliver them'.[104] By 7 April 1795, this time from 23 Brompton Row, Williams is writing to express surprise that, two months after receiving a note that Iolo was to call next day, he is still waiting to give him the money! Clearly, it did change hands for by 13 May Williams was reminding Iolo of the need for a letter of receipt.[105] Iolo's forgetfulness seems to have extended also to a promise made to forward material for the *History of Monmouthshire*, of which several letters during 1795 remind him, in tones of increasing exasperation, for 'whatever little Information you may have obtained ... will be of no use to me, if deferred until my Work be completely printed'.[106] An early allusion to poetic licence in making promises has, by December, been replaced by a cutting reprimand: 'It has ever been the pride and satisfaction of my life, never to have intercourse with Great Men, who affect the privilege of disregarding Promises, & leaving Letters Memorials &c unanswered. But I have unwittingly stumbled on one in you ...'[107]

Presumably material belatedly received is that which appears in the Appendix of the *History*. But David Williams bore no permanent ill-will, and was instrumental, some years later, in procuring a grant of £20 for Iolo on the ground that he was now in great distress – though yet again the absence of acknowledgement produced a panic-stricken query lest ill had befallen the recipient or the banknote itself in transit.[108] This aid was given by a meeting with Burges in the Chair, but the connoisseur of irony will discern a real gem in the Minutes for 19 April 1804: a grant of fifteen guineas to this 'translator of many curious Welsh M.S.S.' was made by a Committee presided over by John Reeves![109] In August of the following year Williams combines assurance of the Fund Committee's goodwill with comments on his and Iolo's health: 'I set out on Sunday for the Seashore; to recover my health; if I can, by Sea-Air & Sea-bathing – I have had some thoughts of Newton in your Neighbourhood, on account of it's retired and quiet situation; but the journey is too long – I believe I shall fix at Brighton ... Your account of your own health is deplorable. Your Diet & Beverage are not sufficiently stimulating – you depend too much on Opium, Foxglove &c.' He thanks Iolo for some papers on Welsh anti- quities[110] and sends best wishes from Mrs Martyn.[111] His forecast of generosity was correct; on 17 October 1805 a ten-guinea grant ensued.[112] But the following May, despite the presence of David Williams, yet another request from 'Edward Williams having been three times liberally relieved' was refused.[113] Further grants *were* made in 1809 and 1812,[114] but the limits of audacity were surely reached in Iolo's enquiry in 1814 whether the rules of the Fund would stretch so far as to provide 'a little Trade-Stock' for his son so as to protect him from 'being tempted and of course ruined by the syren songs of literature'.[115]

Alongside these benefactions which were its *raison d'être* the members of the Society did not forget the habits of sociability which many brought with them from earlier Club activities.[116] A proposed Annual Dinner of the Friends of the Society, first mooted in January 1793, speedily assumed 'the Conviviality of an Annual Festival'.[117] Patriotic toasts, recitations and musical compositions by talented members of the Fund, were backed in due course by the hiring of a horn and clarinet band as a feature of the entertainment.[118] Draft programmes for 1797, 1799 and 1800 convey the general atmosphere in a selection of toasts. 'The Republic of Letters, the Aristocracy of Talents & the Monarchy of Reason', and 'May the blossoms of Genius escape the Frost of Neglect', may fairly represent the ethos of the Fund; while 'Our brave Tars', 'The Hero of the Nile', and 'May an invading army find every Briton a Soldier', evince a strongly patriotic flavour. Again, 'Our Native Country, the Asylum of Liberty', 'May the Demon of Anarchy fall, like Lucifer, never to rise again', and 'The Constitution of England, untempered & unimpaired by French Quackery', suggest an ambience politically far removed from that of David Williams's earlier years.[119]

In regard to one toast, to the health of the Founder himself, the *Times* in 1807 observed a curious circumstance, that when it 'is drunk, as it always is with great warmth and respect, he contents himself with mere thanks, and never says anything on the circumstances and prospects of the Society, or of his wishes to serve it, though it is well known, that from his unwearied and indefatigable exertions, it has chiefly risen to its present high state of respectability and prosperity'.[120] Among the glees and verse contributed by Morris, Boscawen, Pye (Poet Laureate) and others, a composition of Fitzgerald is typical in its combination of tribute to the Founder and the Fund and of patriotic fervour; extolling

> 'British Liberty – that draws the Line,
> 'Twixt wild Democracy, and Right Divine;
> With equal zeal the Monarch's power maintains,
> And guards the Subject from despotic chains';

and concluding with the deservedly much-quoted eulogy:

> 'And He, who first this noble fabric rais'd,
> Shall with no common gratitude be prais'd:
> Time, that destroys the Hero's trophied bust,
> Shall spare the bay that blossoms o'er his dust.'[121]

Unfortunately, the Founder's part in procuring the patronage of the Prince of Wales and the consequent lease of a house in Gerrard Street, which marked a major upsurge in the prestige and fortunes of the Fund, caused some friction – though nothing like the Burges incident. There is little doubt that royal interest and benefi-cence followed the appointment as Fund Vice-President in 1803 of the Earl of Chichester.[122] As Chairman at the Anniversary Dinner on 25 April 1805 that nobleman informed the members that the Prince 'has been graciously pleased to direct Col Macmahon, this morning, to call on your Founder (David Williams) – to desire the Society might be informed that His Royal Highness would order the Revenue of the Duchy of Cornwall to be charged with the Sum of Two Hundred Guineas a year' for discharge of the rent of a proposed House. 'The Prince has also, in the most delicate manner expressed his ... Opinion & Wish that the Founder should have Apartments in the House, & such a direction & superintendence of the uses of it, as in the present Circumstances of the Society may be necessary.'[123] This last proviso raised some hackles; yet only the reality of the link between this muni-ficence and the personal involvement of David Williams explains the very evident anxiety of a Special Committee Meeting in August 1816 as to the Prince's pleasure regarding the House after the Founder's death.[124]

In fairness, the initial approach had indeed been made by Williams himself, following Committee discussion of the expediency of hiring or purchasing a House.[125] A long letter to Chichester, dated 19 February 1805, deprecates the need to meet in taverns and urges the advantages of a fixed location for the Fund: 'If the Prince of Wales were to bestow on it a place of abode in the neighbourhood of his Palace, I have no doubt that the Fund would soon support a College for decayed and superannuated Genius the most pitiable of all objects.'[126] The General Committee learned the details of royal intentions on 18 April when a 'House Fund' was set up, and a 'Committee fully empowered to take a House' was established a week later.[127] Subsequent Minutes record a near-miss of 52 Leicester Square (despite the Prince's readiness to pay the extra rent) and a decision that the cost of rooms in Pall Mall would be too high.[128] Not all the details of the actual decision on 36 Gerrard Street are clear: an indenture for its lease was not in fact signed until 20 September, when the General Committee was informed;[129] but removal bills leave no doubt that Williams had moved in during July, the 'First Cart' leaving Brompton Row on the 9th.[130]

Whether his colleagues suspected a unilateral *fait accompli* or whether their reservations were directed solely to what some regarded as the overambitious plans of the Founder, disquiet surfaced. Reporting to the Committee on 17 October, Williams felt constrained to cite 'a Species of *honorable Contract* ... between the Earl of Chichester & the House Committee',[131] to point to his own severe illness at the crucial time, and to stress that the decision on Gerrard Street was taken by the Earl.[132] Not all doubts were allayed. Fitzgerald, writing to another Fund stalwart, Yates, took exception to what he saw as the Founder's implication 'that every thing good was done by him, & every thing the reverse by the Committee', for its members have, more than once, saved the Society from utter ruin. There is at present a real danger that 'by endeavouring to do too much, you will *do worse than Nothing*'. Williams deserves 'all the Merit of Founding, & cherishing the Literary Fund, but let him be content with that honourable Praise, & not say, or insinuate that the Society has never been *efficient but through him*.'[133]

A paper presented to the Committee by Williams in March 1806 defends his objectives and his personal position regarding 'Uses of the House'. His original scheme envisaged 'Temporary Relief to Temporary Distress. Annual Income to other Species of Misfortune – & a Collegiate Retreat for a few of those Literary Benefactors of Mankind, who having outlived their Connections, cannot be benefitted by Donations & Annuities' which, in the hands of servants, produce a level of care but dubiously preferable to the Parish Workhouse. 'The Care of the House, & of its respectable though unfortunate Inhabitants should itself be a Literary Benefit – It should be conferred on a Man of Letters – to whose Circumstances, the appointment would be a convenience; & possessing the Character, the Temper, & the Literary Sympathy, from being an Author which are the necessary Qualifications ... To prepare for this Event, has been & is the object of Mr Williams in obeying the commands of the Prince of Wales by coming into the House – & he is willing gratuitously as he has always served the Society – to receive Powers [and] Regulations which he may execute as Examples to those Persons who may succeed him as Beneficiaries.' He disdains any imputation of personal calculation in all this.[134]

The issue remained sensitive, and a few months later the Founder suggested that a Visitor and a Treasurer join him in discharging needful regulations (though not to interfere in the choice and dismissal of servants!), with particular attention to economy. For the present pattern of expenses, now partly paid by Mr Williams, will *all* be borne by the Society when he quits the House. In looking ahead to the time when the care of the House, free of all expenses, shall be bestowed as a valued benefice upon a poverty-stricken author of great literary merit, and in clinging to his vision of 'a College, or Retreat for aged and respectable Authors', David Williams is at pains once more to rebut 'an erroneous opinion already very prevalent, that he is himself a beneficiary'.[135] At all events, and whatever the relative weight of argument, personal esteem, or even inertia in the transition from an *ad hoc* to a permanent arrangement, he was to stay in Gerrard Street until his death.

His circumstances became increasingly distressing in regard both to his health and, consequentially, his income for some six or eight years prior to his demise. Now into his seventies he was starting, in his own words, to outlive his Connections. The death of his sister, wife of the Rev Walter Thomas, in 1809 (by which time her daughter Mary Watkins[136] had joined the Gerrard Street household), was followed by that of Mrs Martyn in 1812. Several letters from another London correspondent of Iolo yield independent testimony of Williams's own declining health: in March 1811 'not equal to any kind of business whatever', in August 1813 'still in weakly Health – but he walks about in fine weather'.[137] A reported improvement a couple of months later brought a long letter expressing pleasure, amongst much else, from Iolo to Williams himself in January 1814; but time was running out.[138] Sadly, not only time – a letter from the Founder to Chichester (in the date of which the crucial digit is alas indecipherable) contains an inference which is unmistakable: 'Your Lordship's Views, might determine my place of Abode, for a little better Air – & to escape the Inconvenience of Repairs which are now driving me out of the House . . . These Considerations are of serious importance to a Man, whose Peace of Mind greatly depends on living strictly within a very narrow Income.'[139]

The clearest testimony not only of continued decline in his health and financial circumstances but also of the near-veneration with which he was by now regarded, is minuted by a special Committee Meeting of 25 July 1815. Its membership resolved that the Society should 'earnestly request his acceptance of a present of Fifty Pounds as a Testimony of their respect; and do further solicit him . . . to receive, at the expiration of every six months, a donation from their Fund, of a similar amount.' This decision has been taken after 'deeply commiserating the situation to which, at his very advanced age, he is reduced by six years of suffering under a severe paraletic affliction which hath rendered him totally incapable of any Literary Exertion, & hath of course deprived him of a considerable portion of his usual Income'. The signatories of this commitment to 'administer every possible comfort to the declining years of the respected Founder, whose disinterested, impartial & generous conduct, while able to act in the concerns of the Institution was eminently conspicuous', include Fitzgerald, Yates, Symmons, and Reeves.[140]

A letter from Sir Benjamin Hobhouse (in whose offices the committee met) had emphasized to Yates that the prior agreement of Williams was essential to this proceeding, that he had better not be present when it was considered, and that to be consistent with the rules of the Society the greatest secrecy should be observed.[141] Thus, with gentle if sombre irony, Registered Case No. 335 of the Fund is recorded as 'Revd David Williams, Founder of the Society, and Miss Mary Watkins, his Niece'. Some weeks later Chichester wrote to 'concur most heartily with what they have done & lament only that in his declining years he should feel as I know he does the want of such assistance'.[142] This combination of personal esteem and considerable delicacy of treatment endured beyond the death of Williams himself to include his niece, whose tender assiduities during the length of time in which he was unable to walk or move without help were well known.[143] A Special Committee Meeting on 1 August 1816 expressed its warm approval of her exemplary attentions to her uncle, requested that she defer removal from the House until it was completely convenient, and asked that she accept the sum of Fifty Guineas 'which would have been given to Mr David Williams, if he had survived till the 25th of July'.[144]

One of her uncle's last letters, its recipient identified only as a Church of England clergyman dwelling in the country, suggests an image of the Philosopher approaching death, but also brings in question whether Mary Watkins was the only native of his birthplace to comfort the London Welshman's last days. Williams describes himself as nearing his end and desirous of concluding his days in peace: 'I have outlived almost all my relations, and all my acquaintance; and I am desirous to exchange the most sincere and cordial forgiveness with those I have in any sort offended. I had once a great regard for you; why it was not continued I have forgotten. Indeed a paralytic stroke has greatly destroyed my memory, and will soon destroy me ... I greatly esteemed you and your worthy father; and I hope you will only remember what you saw commendable and good in me ...' The recipient of the letter was apparently thereafter a regular visitor for the last two years of Williams's life – but is not named by the *Cambrian Register* which prints it.[145] Yet the allusion to respect for father and son suggests a lead, especially when we learn that Thomas Williams, a son of the namesake who had taught him so many years ago in the Cwm, after succeeding his father at Watford, had then taken orders in the Church of England and become a vicar in Hampshire.[146] Conjecture becomes near-certainty in the context of a letter of Mary Watkins in October 1818 which has a postscript: 'I leve town tomorrow my address – Revd Mr Williams – Vicar of Romsey – Romsey Hants'.[147]

David Williams was buried in St Anne's, Soho, on 6 July 1816.[148] His Will expressed a wish to be interred 'in as plain and ffrugal a manner as the rules of decency will admit of', bequeathed all manuscripts in his possession to the Rev Richard Yates and Thomas Whittingham, his executors, and gave 'all my Bank annuities and also all my ffurniture & printed Books plate and Linen and all the residue of my Estate' to his niece.[149] The letter of Mary Watkins cited above requested its unnamed recipient to 'have the *kindness* to give orders to fix up the picture of your *old friend* and *my good Uncle* and not Let him keep company with the *Lumber*'. Almost certainly this explains the report by Yates to the General Committee on 11 November 1818, of her wish to present to the Society the full-length portrait by Rigaud which is now with the Society of Authors.[150]

That presentation, and indeed the fact that David Williams died in the House of the Literary Fund, may well be seen as appropriately symbolic. For although it could in no way have been foreseen by him when his concept was first outlined some forty years ago, his was surely precisely the type of meritorious case envisaged – whether the criterion be that of the pursuit of ideas for their own sake, with scant regard for their implications in terms of personal advancement, or that of the ill-health and relatively straitened circumstances of his declining years. Moreover, despite his more dramatic, sometimes flamboyant essays at originality within the fields of religious philosophy, education, and political and constitutional thought, it was indeed to be the Literary Fund which did most to 'spare the bay that blossoms o'er his dust'. Justly so, for the contribution of David Williams toward the nurturing of this, 'the offspring of his own heart',[151] is surely hard to overestimate, in terms not only of personal endeavour but of constituting a focal point of a complex and extensive network of personal relationships.[152] The anvil had not worn out the hammer before the artefact was truly shaped. The Founder himself had written perhaps more surely than he knew in *Claims of Literature*, in declaring his conviction that therein, 'in proportion to my attention to its proceedings, I had rendered my country the most important service.

> "I'd weigh it as the action of my life,
> That must give name and value to the whole." '[153]

Chapter Nine

Conclusion: The Anvil and The Hammer

ASSESSMENT of David Williams as an author, as a thinker, as a man, in the context of his own era and in that of the history of ideas, is a daunting task. So many-sided was his long career that it is difficult to establish a permanently valid vantage-point. Evaluation of his life and thought encounters paradox and irony – in a philosopher who eschewed metaphysics, an educationist who ceased to enjoin innovation after he had ceased to teach, and a political thinker who eschewed party, but perhaps most notably in the endurance of the least dramatic of his early concepts as a permanent memorial when other more colourful ventures were forgotten. Williams was a Welshman who, despite continuing regard for his family roots, became almost completely anglicised; a thinker of undoubted perception if not of the first rank who published many books (several thought worthy of translation) yet never quite produced a great work; and a radical political philosopher whose ultimate drift toward conservatism derived from *increasing* recognition of the significance of the changing economic and social bases of society.

The key to this last development, as to so very much else, lies in personal circumstance. In a sense, the wheel had turned full circle: the partial resemblance in format between his last writings and his first, *The Philosopher*, is symbolic. The optimist apprentice of 1771 had become the disillusioned veteran of the early nineteenth century, but the stance of disinterested observation had been resumed. Meanwhile, theory had been tempered by experience: he had run his own school, set down and offered for public appraisal his own religious credo, and even ventured briefly (in unusual circumstances) into the political arena. Indeed, the impact of experience is crucial for an overall appraisal of his thought. In approaching a thinker who wrote on religious philosophy, education, and politics, one would normally look for an integrated core of common ideas and principles;[1] but in the case of David Williams one will search in vain for any definitive exposition of his basic philosophy, which must therefore be inferred from the numerous reflective passages scattered through his works. We can at most identify a basic attitude of mind and trace the shaping of his thought upon the anvil of experience.

What remained at the heart of the thinking of his fellow-Welshman, Richard Price, was progressively eroded from that of David Williams. Yet, ironically, we may suggest that what some contemporary critics regarded as his obsession with an organic, anthropomorphous analogy of society and politics is almost a subconscious transfer of a concept which he had determined to excise from his religious philosophy. What has been termed a nostalgia for religion not only survived his gradual

Plate 12. DAVID WILLIAMS, a later portrait attributed(?) to John Hoppner

abandonment of dogmatic theology, as was typical of many contemporaries, but also influenced his approach to social and political thought. Nonetheless, to revert to J. M. Robertson's most apposite concept of experiential rationalism,[2] it will be difficult to define more precisely the position of Williams against the background of the philosophical, religious, and political trends of his age. Indeed it could well be argued that his career and his writings encapsulate many of the unresolved tensions of a dynamically changing era. He himself would surely never have wished to be assigned to any school of religious or political philosophy any more than he could ever bring himself to join a political party or faction.

Less kindly, one cannot shirk the fact that a disinclination to think through, and to present logically, his ideas detracts from much of his work. Many passages of sustained presentation of an argument break off just when one hopes for a coherent expression of a rounded philosophy. Sadly, it is when Williams decides to write at length that his defects become most obvious. He is at his best when essaying combative analysis of a particular issue, bringing to bear in the cut and thrust of debate a keen brain and an incisive style. Thus his shorter books were his most effective. Some of his longer works have been thought ill-ordered and flabbily-written, and a contemporary critic shrewdly remarked that certain discursive and inflated passages appear to contain more than they do.[3] Undoubtedly, Dryden's lines are sometimes apposite:

> 'Words are like leaves, and, where they most abound,
> Much fruit of sense beneath is rarely found.'

Yet recognition of this failing brings its own dangers – for embedded within some sections of rambling verbiage in such lengthy works as his *Lectures on Education* are pieces of genuine and valuable analysis.

Assessment of the originality and the influence of his thought must recollect first, his own salutary warning that in the realm of ideas there is nothing really new, and second, the real possibility that the most forward-looking concepts may sink without trace and reappear from a very different source in a later age. Subject to these caveats, one might suggest that the most original contributions of David Williams lay, in the field of religion, in his attempt to institutionalize and furnish with a liturgy a social and non-dogmatic religious philosophy; in that of education, in the assembly of a body of precepts in teaching method and curriculum content based on experiment, observation, and deduction, and above all on the reaction of the pupil; and in that of politics, in recognizing the *difficulties* of implementing the representative process so as fully to reflect *collective* while simultaneously safeguarding *individual* and eliminating selfishly sectional rights and interests. These difficulties were not so much resolved as progressively subsumed within an analogy of the body politic – yet this in itself has been identified as a claim to originality as a precursor of an organic/collective or indeed sociological approach to politics.[4]

The importance of David Williams as a thinker, and indeed what has been termed the studied impersonality of most of his writing, must not cause us to forget the very considerable impact of his personality. Julia Wedgwood was not alone in her reflection that he 'was one of those men who produce more effect on their contemporaries than posterity can readily account for'.[5] He was a tall, commanding figure – rather slender in his younger days in which he was accounted handsome – with a long, aquiline countenance. His speech and delivery were clear and persuasive rather than powerful and impassioned. His dress was fastidious though rather colourful in taste for the clerical aura which continued to surround him long after his formal abandonment of the ministry. His friend Thomas Morris describes him as devoid of 'provincial' (presumably Welsh) characteristics, but he himself pleaded guilty to at least one reputed national trait in relating his interview with Burke! Certainly he seems to have been unable to suffer fools gladly. There is also evidence that while he made valued and lasting friendships these could be broken by some real or fancied offence – the breach with Morris is a striking instance.

In some respects he was his own worst enemy. For although in general highly esteemed, there persisted a vein of criticism of his motivations and morality which derived (so several who knew him best insisted) not from any deep-seated defects but from his own careless or even provocative contempt for appearances and for public opinion. On several occasions Williams himself was almost at pains to lay claim to such misinterpretation: indeed the title of his manuscript 'Incidents in my own Life' as at first drafted included the phrase 'which has been often misrepresented'. With an undoubted attraction towards and for the opposite sex, and with all the instincts of a family man, the tragic loss of his wife and child need hardly be laboured. An eminently sociable and even 'clubbable' person, in some respects he remained a constitutional non-participant on principle. His persistent refusal to adhere to any political faction was totally consistent with his declared beliefs – yet he did not even join the Society for Constitutional Information with its commitment to political and constitutional education (but also, on reflection, with rather high fees). The avowal that he was never invited to join any lodge of freemasons, despite the large number of their members among his associates,[6] may perhaps be related to the piquant suggestion of one modern biographer that Williams would surely on principle have rejected the anthropomorphic concept of a 'Great Architect of the Universe'.[7]

The charges of egotism were not devoid of truth; nor was Williams ever inclined to understate his own significance. It is hard to tell whether it was this trait, or a possible and understandable tendency of his relatives to recount his achievements, which evoked the jingle still extant in oral tradition in Caerphilly when Dr T. W. Thomas wrote some three-quarters of a century ago:

> 'Ewa fawr, o Loeger,
> A'i got fawr, a'i standin' coler',

which may be loosely part-translated as

> 'Big uncle from England,
> With his great coat, and standing collar'.[8]

A contentious streak in his nature was ever liable to convert a friendly acquaintance into an opponent. Yet in every sphere a critic may be found who pays tribute to a quality of personal integrity which was clearly discerned. Particularly impressive is the esteem and affection displayed by his colleagues in the Literary Fund during his declining and presumably least memorable years.

In previous chapters our treatment of those major themes recurrent in his works has related them to the circumstances which evoked each publication and which influenced the evolution of his ideas. It remains to ponder any pattern of synthesis and enduring impact. The title of his first major work, *The Philosopher*, annexed by hostile critics as a favourite gibe, was almost certainly meant to signify the adoption of a detached, judicious, and balanced approach rather than to indicate any pretensions to a distinct and systematic body of philosophical thought. Of this his persistent rejection of metaphysics was perhaps unconsciously symbolic. It may indeed be suggested that Williams saw himself not as a philosopher but as a thinker of philosophic disposition. For his many philosophical passages were orientated toward educational, religious, and political issues, and it is not easy to identify a constant and fully integrated philosophical and psychological foundation of his thinking.

Certainly he was not in his own right a powerful or even always consistent philosopher. Neither may he be assigned with confidence to any one philosophical school. Many of his political attitudes have been related to the Real Whig or Commonwealth tradition of the late-seventeenth to mid-eighteenth centuries. But in a wider context he reflects many aspects of a tradition stretching right back to the Commonwealth idealists of mid-Tudor England and to the Erasmian basis of their thought: of this his frequent citations of More (and of Bacon) are significantly indicative. The assertion that 'thou knowest well there is in all things a measure and a mean' would have won his warm approval. Yet many passages in his work – and those some of the clearest and most unequivocally expressed – look forward to Benthamite pleasure-and-pain utilitarianism. Yet this in turn had been in part anticipated by Wollaston, and derives from the psychology and philosophy of Shaftesbury and Hartley[9] together with a mainstream current of thought in which such as Priestley find their place. Again, certain aspects of his thinking anticipate Comte and Herbert Spencer: the experiential rationalist not only becomes the experiential moralist, but sometimes sounds like a positivist or determinist. If Williams never represented any specific school he does represent, and to a limited degree may have contributed towards, a crucial phase of transition – although he himself might have recoiled at the terminology, Vereker's suggested transition from Metaphysical to Empirical Optimism springs to mind.[10]

His philosophy cannot always be derived from a clear psychological base; having rejected the theological he seems reluctant to plump for the nakedly materialist. If what has been written of Locke, that system tends to emerge out of rather than control what he wrote, is also pre-eminently true of David Williams, so too is another attribution: that moral rules are either laws of nature or derivative therefrom.[11] Williams, though never defining what he means by Nature or her laws, clings always to the idea of a Supreme Being or Intelligence (whether identical with, or working in and through Nature is not always clear) establishing a code of morality which the whole apparatus of pleasure-and-pain based sensational and reflective experience is geared ideally to enforce. Alengry's pointing ahead[12] to

Spencer is particularly apposite. The assessment of his thought as combining 'the Benthamite principle of happiness with those doctrines of natural rights and of an intuitive moral sense which Bentham denounced as prime fallacies', and the characterization of his philosophy as an incongruous mixture of Natural Rights and physiological metaphor, come very near the mark. So too does Spencer's insistence that the happiness achieved by Man must be willed by the Creator not the State, while the notion that, perfect equilibrium and adaptation once attained, Man will automatically do for himself what he ought to do, and government will fall away like a discarded garment,[13] is directly evocative of one of Williams's more visionary insights – shared of course with Godwin.

Insofar as one can identify a permanent and distinctive basis of the philosophy of David Williams it must surely rest in his concept of natural, gradual, and balanced organic evolution. The individual's rights and potentialities, and the institutions of society (including the constitution of the State itself), alike derive from natural laws and realities: the striving for perfection is but a search for personal and social adjustment to changing circumstances in accord with Nature's own guide-lines of pleasure and pain. This cast of mind, confirmed and deepened by experience, was always there. Effectively, it reflects an early modern code of values combined with a more forward-looking theory of cognition – the two perhaps uneasily yoked by replacing the supernatural, theologically defined godhead which sanctioned and sat in judgement on the first with a supreme intelligence which endowed with moral validity and purpose a purely sensational and reflective theory of cognition and derivative action.

In any résumé of the diverse aspects of the work of David Williams his importance as an educationist should perhaps come first, for it is probably in this context that one encounters the fullest and clearest expositions of his psychological and philosophical beliefs. Yet immediately we meet another paradox. His grasp of the psychological bases of the learning process, combined with his practical experience and perceptive reflection thereon, has the most impressively innovative and progressive impact upon his prescriptions as to teaching method and content. Yet his concept of the place of education in society remains almost completely traditional. Overall, the limitations in his general educational philosophy are as striking as the insights in his teaching method. That said, it is impossible to withhold recognition of a genuinely creative thinker on the theory of the educational *process*. Though publishing but two works devoted to education, Williams was held in uniformly high regard as a teacher and as a remedial tutor of adult students. He had clearly pondered the writings of previous educationists ranging from Bacon through Milton, Comenius and Locke, to Rousseau and Helvetius. But, while at pains to acknowledge indebtedness and to grant more generous recognition than he ever accorded to either precursors or contemporaries in the realm of constitutional and political speculation, he was never a mere imitator. Indeed he is most highly rated by modern educationists for his discerning and incisive critique of Rousseau. That critique was based upon experience, and it was reflection upon that experience, which included what can only be described as calculated pedagogical experiments, which produced his own distinctive contributions to educational theory.

His Renaissance-style concept of the general purpose of education looked not to the mere inculcation of knowledge but to the fullest development of the personality in all its aspects. Yet if education was envisaged as in and for society, designed to produce the complete and happy citizen, this was to be within the ambit of existing society. It was an instrument of personal development and indeed of moral guidance, but not of social evolution. Yet in teaching *method*, while some of his contemporaries correctly observed that his school-based experience was short-lived and that a fully worked out scheme was not presented, David Williams ranks as a major pioneer in the realistic development of a child-centred approach and curriculum. Whilst the partial debt to Locke and to Rousseau was fully acknowledged, he brought to his conclusions a valid experience which enabled him to distinguish between the practicable and the visionary or naïve. It cannot be too highly emphasized that what he evolved was a child-centred method conceived of as an intelligent correlation between the instincts and potentialities of individual pupils and a range of clearly enunciated educational objectives – not a child-reliant abandonment of method. Pupils were to be led and persuaded, if necessary by example rather than precept, to pursue such valid objectives.

David Williams's recommendations as to the curriculum have evoked from modern commentators almost unqualified expressions of admiration, and justly so. His views derived directly from his apprehension of the psychological fact that learning was a unitary process. By present standards some of his assessments of the learning capacities of young children seem sanguine; but by those of his own age he brought a gust of realism. Here again, the debt to certain predecessors was acknowledged, yet his emphasis upon a practical and varied approach, geared to the interests and aptitudes of the pupil, upon the advantages of experiment and illustration, of what would now be called group-work and of projects, together with some integration of subjects and even perhaps the introduction of new ones, are all impressive. Equally so is his suspicion of any 'gimmickry' or of learning made easy – alluded to in one of his last excursions into this field.[14] Innovation for its own sake, and any tendency to compensate for the defects of established methods by substituting none, provoked scathing comment. His belief in the validity only of considered, tested and gradual change was as strong a characteristic of his educational as it became of his political thinking. The differing super-optimism of Rousseau and of Helvetius respectively was placed alongside reality and exposed. Yet the very fact that his educational prescriptions were based upon experience imposed its own limitations of insight; for that experience was gained in a school for the sons of the well-to-do, followed by private tuition of adults of the same class.

His explicit recognition[15] of the existence of 'blockheads' among that order was presumably accompanied by a realization that high intelligence must sometimes exist among the children of the poor. Yet his scepticism about educational provision for the lower orders is both depressing and puzzling when set alongside the optimistic radicalism of at least his earlier pronouncements about the political participation of the people. Perhaps his own rise from comparatively humble origins convinced him that sufficient opportunity for the advancement of real ability already existed? Certainly a general presumption that education should be related to one's likely prospects in life comes through. If the minds of workhouse children must not be forced beyond their capacities, neither must their imaginations be stimulated above their destination in the social order. Even in the sphere of politics, the assumption that properly instructed participants in democracy would follow the lead of the intellectually elite was almost always there.

Almost certainly, Williams took no cognizance of education as fulfilling a socially egalitarian objective. Despite the very considerable originality of his thought regarding educational method and content, he remained a prisoner perhaps not so much of his age as of his social milieu – with no contact with such differently motivated if pedagogically less adventurous efforts as those commenced within his own native valley by Morgan John Rhys. He had but little sympathy with those progressive trends which ran from the seventeenth century to his own day,[16] let alone those of the nineteenth century. There is thus perhaps a measure of poetic justice in the fact that, in his own country at least, his very real advances in teaching method seem to have sunk without trace or acknowledgement, and that later developments sometimes resemble but do not emanate from his work. For when those later movements burgeoned they did so within the context of a trend toward an extension of education in which David Williams had no share.

Just as his educational writings reflect his activities as a teacher, so those devoted to religious philosophy derive from his experience first as nonconformist minister and then as 'Priest of Nature'. Here again questions of originality, impact, and later influence will arise. But the issue of motivation is rather different. In regard to personal as distinct from educational and professional influences the effect of his tragedy both as husband and as father cannot be dismissed but is impossible to evaluate from internal evidence in his writings. Equally difficult to assess and impossible to discount is the persistent charge of ambition – or perhaps more fairly of a wish for 'singularity', for there is little reason to doubt his own frequent assertions that had financial and careerist advancement been his objective then well-worn tracks proffered a safer and more rewarding route. His published views upon religion and progressively less successful endeavours to crystallize them in an acceptable form of public worship are therefore almost certainly an accurate reflection of his own beliefs – though tinctured unmistakably by disappointment and frustration.

While Williams retrospectively attributes a lack of enthusiasm for his religious vocation to the very moment of its undertaking, any public disavowal of the dogmatic content of Christianity came only in his late thirties, and he is at pains to explain that its abandonment did not precede his leaving Highgate. Yet despite these protestations Arian, even Socinian, tendencies undoubtedly preceded the move to London – the former dating perhaps from his student days, the latter from his introduction of an 'Octagon-type' Liturgy while still in the West Country. The formal breach once made, his writings exemplify the tensions between a residual yearning for religious faith made manifest in moral conduct and a steady erosion of belief in any religious dogma and progressive abandonment of all confidence in an afterlife. His tenacious adhesion to the social and moral functions of religion has important implications for the corporate worship which he never ceased to enjoin.

In hindsight, the problem at the heart of his religious philosophy was that of reconciling a belief in permanent moral values, deprived of any sanction of an omniscient Deity administering rewards and punishments in an afterlife, with a materialist exposition of the process of human cognition and motivation. The two were brought into incongruous if symbolically appropriate harmony by the transfer of the notion of pleasure-and-pain based incentives *from* anticipated dispensation by a vengeful Deity in the hereafter *to* an apparatus of reactions to stimuli within this world. The linchpin of the argument is firmly planted in the *a priori* assumption that the supreme life-force has correlated such reactions to the natural production of morality. As to that Supreme Being itself, Williams, eschewing an attempt at definition, often came close to identifying God with Nature, whose very laws exemplified the existence of some Supreme Intelligence. Yet again, he never tried to define Nature or clearly to enunciate her laws. Certainly, the inference that natural forces may be equated with all virtue at a moral level raises obvious problems. Despite his origins, one suspects the emergence of the town-dweller's idealized picture, of a stylized concept in which indeed 'True God is Nature to advantage drest'.

In evaluating his religious philosophy and suggested forms of worship against the heritage of contemporary thought we shall not find much that was entirely new. His idealization of Nature and its near-identification with the godhead had long been anticipated by Wollaston, while his later explicit abandonment of all belief in an afterlife was fully matched by contemporary thought, especially in Holbach. His first revised Liturgy had been anticipated at the Octagon, while Lindsey had preceded by a year his Margaret Street venture in stepping outside the ambit of orthodox Christian worship in London itself. Although his diminishing congregation became but an audience of lectures his insistence on the need for corporate, social worship was reiterated in his last avowedly religious publication in 1789; yet by then it was equalled by that upon unrestrained freedom of enquiry, thought and expression. Despite his earlier pejorative use of the term 'free-thinker' we may trace a steady move toward advocacy of complete liberty in regard to philosophical and even moral speculation. Such freedom, at first a prerequisite of genuine religious progress, finally became an object of veneration in itself.

This indeed is perhaps the key to his views on the relationship between religion and politics, in which context David Williams never was in full accord with the normal dissenting tradition. For the very acceptance of a principle of toleration implied at least a power not to tolerate to which he was utterly opposed. To be fair, much of his interpretation of Puritan religious and political endeavours was uncomfortably near the mark, and cannot have endeared him to his erstwhile colleagues. Recognition of recent historical trends in the relationship between government and established religion led him, in practice, to be wary of any activity likely to stir up sleeping dogs or to turn back a tide of *de facto* tolerance which had swept in largely unperceived, and in theory to reject all governmental interference in religion – unless it be to safeguard individual freedom against the tyranny of sects. Certainly as the residual habits of his former vocation (whose persistence he ruefully conceded) faded away, so he came to adopt an almost completely rationalist position, and a suspicion of all organized religion as all too likely to circumscribe freedom of thought. John Taylor relates a story of Williams in his later days which is at least indicative: 'observing him in a very light grey coat, I could not help expressing my surprise, "Why," said he, "I wore the garb of hypocrisy so long that I was ashamed of it, and have now cast it aside".'[17]

What then was novel in his contribution, and what, if any, was his legacy? One must accept the justice of his own contention that he put to the test the practicability of an undogmatic form of social worship. This attracted widespread notice – admiring, sceptical, and sometimes derisive. Some at least of the international publicity achieved was self-sought, but much of it fell on receptive and appreciative ears. Yet it is difficult to quantify any permanent influence. A clear line of descent has been descried between the Margaret Street venture and both the cult of the Supreme Being and the movement known as Theophilanthropy in France (with short-lived imitative offshoots in England and the U.S.A.), and also the genesis of Iolo Morganwg's Gorsedd, returning to his native Wales. On the basis of known evidence it seems hard to determine the extent to which these owed their content and format directly to David Williams rather than to a shared derivation from un-doubtedly influential contemporary trends. But that several informed observers imputed such a direct and considerable influence extending over a couple of decades is unquestioned.

Finally, to turn to political and constitutional issues, any coincidence between his evolving rationalist approach to religious philosophy and his views in this sphere may well reside in his inability completely to abandon an ingrained religiosity of thought. Thus he clings to a concept of the body of society and its members as *feeling* a sense of union and collective happiness which sometimes seems as much to transcend as to comprehend individual political rights. In terms of both number and volume of writings this was the field in which David Williams published most. Although such publications spanned four decades it could perhaps be argued that his most striking and stimulating contributions came during little more than one: 1782–1793. But despite an apparent pattern of development to a peak of radical reformist speculation, followed by more conservative reconsideration, it cannot be too strongly emphasized that many specific criticisms and suggested constitutional innovations were clearly present in his earliest writings, while the caveats of his last phase were quite explicitly enunciated in his central and most radical works. Thus the interplay of enduring basic principles, evolving proposals for constitutional reform, and the influence of changing circumstances is both absorbing and ex-asperating.

Here, as elsewhere, Williams was a perceptive and stimulating rather than an always consistent thinker. The unresolved tensions within his thought were those of the age in which he lived. His undoubted flashes of originality may tempt us into reading into his words more than he certainly meant. He finished as he had com-menced, in advocating a science of politics, but the confidently declared hopes of success had long waned by 1810. His purportedly scientific approach rested first on the claim to exercise a detached, impartial, and philosophic judgement, remote from party allegiance and sectional interest; and secondly on the affirmation that the essential functions of the representative and governmental process derive from ascertainable laws. Though never able fully to identify these laws, he claims nonetheless to have made a genuinely original contribution to the science. An undated document among his papers acknowledges 'the various Hints on Liberty which are scattered through Montesquieu, Blackstone, De Iolme, Price, the American Adams', but goes on to assert that, compared with *Letters on Political Liberty, Lectures on Political Principles*, and *Lessons to a Young Prince*, whose principles were partly reduced to practice in the French Constitution, though not yet fully understood, 'all the other Works, such as those of Burke, Paine, Mackintosh, Cartwright are polemic – they contend on *known* principles – but they make no advance in the Science'.[18] Again, he predicts that all the mistakes of rulers cannot negate the validity of fundamental laws which, when the diffusion of Political Science has sufficiently enlightened governments, will emerge 'with as much certainty & what may be called Geometrical Truth, as the phenomena of metals or minerals', producing 'a political Theory on Scientific principles; which might be reduced to analytic Formulae'.[19]

What these were he never quite discovered, even to his own satisfaction, and any down to earth scrutiny of his political writings may more fruitfully relate his ideas to the process of transition from an inherited Commonwealth tradition, with its emphasis on individual *civil* rights and those constitutional and governmental limitations so essential to their preservation, towards an emergent neo-democratic concept of *political* rights. But behind this lurks the contingent question of any necessary economic and social preconditions for, or any potential derivations from, the extension of political democracy. Identification of this problem was not new, dating at latest from the mid-seventeenth century, but with it David Williams was never entirely happy. Throughout his work there runs a normal Real Whig suspicion of government and of the motives of those who engage in politics, and an abhorrence of all untrammelled power – even in the hands of an elected assembly, let alone a body which is the pawn of connection and corruption. Yet alongside this persists a yearning, manifested in recurrent recourse to the corporeal analogy of society, for an almost telepathic communication of the people's will to the processes of governance. Despite his dread of all *direct* democracy and of any type of government by assembly, he has a vision of the participation of the will and the feeling of the whole body of society in its own self-governance. One might almost postulate a democratized version of an early modern concept but without any egalitarian implications for the *social* aspect of the body politic. Despite their occasional partial reconciliation in an interesting and stimulating way these issues created unresolved tensions within the political thought of David Williams.

Within the Real Whig tradition, much has been written about the problems of definition of the concepts of mixed government, a balanced constitution, and the separation of powers. But adoption of the broad distinction that the essence of mixed government surely lies in the origin and the basis of power, while that of balance and separation relates to its functional exercise, substantiates Williams's contention that in contemporary England the *fiction* of balance and separation was used to gloss over the fact that the basic reality of power was not *mixed* but concentrated in the hands of an oligarchic aristocracy. His prime concern was to relate the institutions and the functions of government to a much broader base of consent, consultation, and participation. He was preoccupied not with any metaphysical origin of power – like Locke, he was concerned less with the derivation of sovereignty than with its limitations – but with its location and its exercise.

Yet the definition and implementation of political democracy, to which at one stage he certainly committed himself, posed its problems. Even if a discernible reluctance (grudgingly overcome) to enfranchise *all* males could satisfactorily be resolved, there remained the method and the purpose of democracy. Williams, like many of his generation, was suspicious of the notion of sovereignty but believed that it might safely be located in the body of the people. But when it came to its exercise the twin problems of effective communication of the public will and protection of inalienable individual rights were ever-present. The 'system of Alfred' was the model for his repeated advocacy of modes of consultation and election by which the wishes of participant citizens could influence those who performed the functions of representation, legislation, and government. As to strictness of accountability, his prescriptions ranged from an unequivocal mandation of delegates to an informed exercise of the individual representative's conscience – such indecision reflecting his comprehension of a genuine problem. But on one thing he was very clear: direct democracy, defined as the exercise of power either by or under the immediate influence of a large body of people, was anathema.

The spectre of a tumultuous assembly derived from an inherent doubt as to the fitness of the lower orders (whose natural aspiration was anarchy) to participate in any exercise of authority, and from an identification of their potential as yet another sectional interest, distinctive only in its size and nightmarish quality. Such fears were reinforced by the events of 1780 and of 1792–3 alike. Within a British context David Williams brought to bear a more cautious and sceptical mind on the problem which confronted Rousseau: how the collective or general will of the people could accurately be ascertained and implemented without infringement of individual liberties and of constitutionalities. He lived on the threshold of the establishment, in optimistic liberal/radical minds, of an almost implicit assumption that democracy would always square with the full protection of individual civil and political liberties. But his experience in France only deepened his innate reservations.

To David Williams the essence of democracy was the realization of individual civil and political rights as part of the achievement of one's full social and moral potential. But if these rights derived neither from the aegis of a secular Leviathan nor yet from the designs and sanctions of an anthropomorphic Deity then Man was left with an equally *a priori* assumption of derivation from Nature and Nature's Laws. And all rational observation of realities confirmed that diversity and in-equality were facts of Nature. Democracy, therefore, as a reflection of man's inalien-able and natural rights did not in any sense infer social and economic equality.[20] Meanwhile, his appeal to individual effort and suspicion of state intervention in social and economic affairs typified a laissez-faire approach. He thus contrived to combine an almost obsessive adherence to the concept of the organic unity of society with a persistent concern for individual political and civil rights (as indeed essential features of its health), a recognition of the inevitability of constant, ideally gradual, change, and even a definite perception of some of the social and economic effects of industrialization – but all without any discernible acceptance of any contingent implications for the range of obligations of the state.

His recommendations in *Letters on Political Liberty* may indeed have anticipated nearly all of the People's Charter, but Williams would never have agreed with the sentiment of the Rev J. R. Stephens that 'this question of universal suffrage is a knife-and-fork question, a bread-and-cheese question'. Political freedom was an end in itself, without the derivative collectivist social obligations envisaged by very many Chartists. *Not* that David Williams was devoid of humanitarian conscious-ness. But social desiderata were to be accomplished through general moral progress, which in turn would be reflected not in or by an extension of governmental inter-vention but by the very reverse. Use of democratic political power deliberately to institute social and economic change would have seemed to imply an infringement of those very liberties he wished to guarantee, and to flout the manifest prescriptions of Nature. His acceptance of gradual and organic constitutional change as imple-menting inalienable individual *political* rights within an evolving society did not encompass any derivative change in the social order itself.

Thus, despite the obvious change of emphasis in his later years, any imputation of conscious abandonment of earlier radical principles cannot go unqualified. If he had always been suspicious of the more irresponsible elements among the lower orders so too had he always assumed that, given full democratic rights to communi-cate their wishes by consultative and electoral processes, the people, responsibly defined and motivated, would naturally choose to be represented and governed by a meritorious elite.[21] Equally basic was his insistence on gradual and tested readjust-ment rather than precipitate change. The influence of perhaps embittered and disappointed experience, as well as that of circumstance, cannot be discounted. Yet the patriotism expressed in a desire to close the ranks which is so clearly evident in his later writings had also been present at an earlier stage – notably in *Unanimity* when the nation had felt threatened by the same French enemy.[22]

Certainly the biggest and at first most surprising disappointment for one who seeks to extract a coherent political philosophy from the work of David Williams is the failure of a notable educationist to locate any concept of a systematic extension of national education in the process of creating an informed and active democracy. Yet in this he was at one with Godwin and Priestley. Indeed if his versatility typified many Enlightenment philosophes so too did the elitist element in his thought. Essentially, education in the fullest sense was for the better-off; the poor stood in need of moral instruction. Education was the route to improvement and happiness – but mis-handled it could endanger both economic productivity and the social order. Conformably, the radical approach to religious dogma did not extend to the social order. Fear of the hereafter was indeed to be expunged, but not acceptance of one's place in society.[23] Yet, all in all, it may be unfair to expect too much, and is probably unjust as well as unhistorical to judge David Williams as a renegade democrat or a Chartist manqué. While not in the first rank of political philosophers he is surely of great significance[24] not as presenting a fully-worked-out and logically integrated body of political theory but as embodying (often in his reaction to specific crises, sometimes in more general works, and very often with most penetrating insight) the most important political and constitutional issues with which the best contemporary minds were grappling in a time of crucial transition. In particular, he stands out as grasping (though not resolving) some of the permanent problems of an increasingly complex society in the reconciliation of individual civil and political liberties with collective wishes and individual social rights. True, he subsumed his difficulties within the organic analogy of society, yet others often pushed them aside in a simplistic assumption that democracy would always coincide with individual liberties.

In attempting a final overall assessment it would first perhaps be fitting to reiterate that in education and in religious philosophy he was practitioner as well as theorist, while his idea of rendering assistance to impecunious but meritorious authors bore final and permanent fruit in what is now the Royal Literary Fund. Yet politics remains the problem: he wrote more on this than on anything else but made no personal mark – at least in England – in the political arena. While conceding the near-inevitability of compromise and association for effective political action he eschewed and even condemned party politics. One may hardly infer complete absence of personal ambition; Williams was ready to act as a not too far behind the scenes adviser in revision of the Constitution of Revolutionary France, and there are occasional indications of willingness at least to be consulted within his own country. Yet not only did he reject association with any political group or faction but he also refrained even from joining the Society for Constitutional Information. Was he, in politics, the victim of a Frankenstein-like monster of his own first literary creation: the detached and disinterested Philosopher? For surely, on balance, constitutional and political affairs were his major enduring interest, and although he wrote no one great work, *Letters on Political Liberty* in 1782 perhaps came near the mark.

His own self-assessment in his manuscript autobiography disclaims 'that species of Ambition which must be the actuating Principle of every Man, who rests his happiness on his Literary Fame'. He explains that since literature was never his employment his books emerged in slovenly fashion, often without revision or correction. 'Some of the most popular & most saleable were taken from me, transcribed with some little interpolations, & long attributed to others, before my name was ever associated with them.' He confesses 'a strong & almost unconquerable Disposition to Satire; unconquerable even by a mild & candid temper; & I attribute it to an early force on my inclinations, in favor of a Profession, which had to my Imagination, very strong Points of Ridicule. In that ridicule I perpetually indulged myself; & if my Temper had allowed it, I might have been an eminent Satirist ...' Yet he insists that in various branches of literature he has remained an amateur. He goes on to disclaim any passion for languages, being more inclined to devote himself to Mathematics.[25] Too much should not be read into these retrospective musings, in pages misnumbered in the original copy of his manuscript[26] and possibly unfinished. But while the avowal of distaste for his first vocation is not surprising, his professed attraction toward satire is interesting in the light of the fact that his most lucrative production was probably *Royal Recollec-*

tions, as is his reference to Mathematics in view of his persistently declared wish to reduce politics to scientific and neo-mathematical principles.

The many and varied verdicts of his contemporaries range from the scathing indictments of Benjamin Thomas and of the author of *Orpheus*[27] to the eulogy of Morris – written at the high tide both of personal friendship and of repute as an author and political philosopher, yet also a perceptive critique. Its subject is described, despite his strict sense of honour and virtue, as 'so careless about public opinion as even to appear pleased with false rumours concerning him ... In his friendships he is warm and steady – but they have been principally with women of sense, taste, and beauty; for he has always been very sensible to female charms ... As a citizen, though no man sees abuses with a quicker eye, he hates all demagogues, and all leaders of petty factions for private views. In the first interposition of the Dissenters, on the rumour of the French Revolution, he frequently foretold to me the evils it would occasion, and the injury it would do to the general interest of liberty.'[28] Morris regrets his friend's inability to accept the principle of Revelation in religion, adding the intriguing attribution of such regret to Williams himself, 'as he might be handsomely provided for, if he could accept the ecclesiastical patronage of a former pupil'. He goes on to liken his literary style to that of Addison, and to forecast that he will outshine Hume (of whom in many things he owns himself the pupil), before ending with a glowing account of his personal characteristics.[29]

The same biography evoked a review which contains an astringent but also genuinely discerning contemporary estimate of its subject, concluding that, endowed with considerable talents, 'he might have been a great man, but he has chosen to be a singular one. He might have enlightened the world, but he is willing only to dazzle it.'[30] A very lengthy notice of *Preparatory Studies* in the same periodical, the *Critical Review*, has much trenchant analysis of general applicability. Thus 'we do not know what ideas the author may affix to the term *nature*', while his near-obsession with the analogy between the body politic and the natural body may raise as many problems as it solves. For the human body is composed of parts which cohere spontaneously, possessing one mind, one will, one sentiment of interest, in contrast with 'the body politic, which is compounded of such a multiplicity of divided selves ...' But perhaps its unkindest cut is the allusion to a *metaphysical* tone which pervades the work and renders many passages obscure! Yet even this critique of an anonymous work can 'discover rays of no ordinary sagacity, but which are much obscured by the cloudy medium through which they are conveyed'.[31]

During the present century, the understandable pride of fellow-Welshmen such as Dr T. W. Thomas and H. Prosser has been followed by the more sceptical and scholarly assessments of Professor David Williams and, much more recently, of Professor Peter France. With much of the criticism expressed, especially in respect of the uneven quality of writing, it is impossible to disagree. Perhaps David Williams was one of those people destined to receive, in the judgement both of contemporaries and of posterity, either much more or much less than they deserve. Any attempt at impartial assessment of his career must surely admire his immense versatility: as teacher and educationist; as religious philosopher and liturgical innovator; as political analyst and constitutional adviser; as historian and satirist;

as consultant to men of stature in politics and industry. For in all these roles he made a considerable if variable mark. Perhaps this very versatility was at once his making and his undoing. Some of his most effective works were *pièces de circonstance*. If undoubtedly a man of many parts, it is not easy to make of those parts a fully integrated philosophy; his career seems more impressive than its permanent achievements. Yet in aggregate those achievements have themselves been under-estimated. In terms of his impact in the realm of ideas David Williams, while not of the very first rank, was undoubtedly a major figure. It has been observed that in many ways he typified his age, yet also that certain of his concepts failed because they were too far ahead of their time; both comments are just.

The whirligig of time has not dealt kindly with David Williams. His Margaret Street Chapel has now become the Catholic Church of All Saints, while the site of the Great Russell Street home of a constitutional 'non-joiner' is now occupied by the headquarters of the T.U.C. But the problems which lay at the heart of his thinking – of the evolution and inculcation of a code of morality devoid of fear of punishment in this world or the hereafter, and free of the parameters of religious dogma; of the development of an educational method which shall match the fullest respect for the personality of the individual child with all the realities of the adult world of which he or she will ultimately become a part; of the balance between individual and collective liberties, rights and duties within a democratic society – remain as contingent and challenging now as in his day. Yet one's last word should perhaps be essentially personal. He penned his own epitaph – more than once. We have noted[32] his parting reference to the Margaret Street venture as that 'which may honorably distinguish my life, and make me lie down in my grave with the consciousness of some effort for the interest of society', and his later characterization of the establishment of the Literary Fund as the action of his life 'that must give name and value to the whole'. But to the present writer, more generally apposite is the observation in his autobiography that 'Perfection, in all human pursuits, is like an Asymptote in Mathematics, ever approximating a curve, but never touching it'.[33]

Appendix I

Mary Watkins

The precise nature of the family relationship between Mary Watkins and David Williams (involving the cognate question of the number of his sisters) has puzzled more than one biographer. Despite some persistent and understandable uncertainty the number of sisters who, unlike his brothers, survived into adult life was *two*. Dr T. W. Thomas referred to three sisters,[1] and Professor David Williams noted the apparent conflict between statements as to bequests of papers and property, as between the daughter of his sister, Mrs Watkin Abram, and his sister, the wife of Walter Thomas, minister at Llanfaches and elsewhere.[2] The first-mentioned, Mary Watkins, was his housekeeper for many years; the relationship with the Rev Walter Thomas is well documented; and there is the fullest evidence as to his sister Joan, who married Edward Hedges and whose descendants still live in Caerphilly.[3] The case for dismissing David Williams's own very clear reference to *two* sisters[4] as a slip of the pen seems very fair, but does not resolve the apparent inconsistency noted by Professor David Williams. A study of the Eglwysilan Parish Registers does so, while the Wills of David Williams and of Mary Watkins confirm and explain the position.

A register entry for 1758 records the calling of the banns for 14 May, and the marriage on 20 July, 'between Watkin Abraam[5] & Anne William, both of this parish'; the signature of 'Ann William' is very clear.[6] But entries for 1775 include the 'Banns of Marriage between Walter Thomas and Anne David both of this parish' and the marriage itself on 31 October. (The entry was witnessed by Edward Hedges, who made his mark, and whose marriage to 'Ioan David' had occurred on 3 June 1769.) But the crucial fact is that the signature of 'Ann ~~William~~ David' (the alteration attesting continued indecision in chosen surname), bride of Walter Thomas is in a hand which seems identical with that of the entry for 20 July 1758.[7] The conjecture of widowhood and of re-marriage after an unexplained resumption of her maiden surname (whether William or David!) seems irresistible – and is given further credence by the record of the burial of 'William the Son of Watkin Abraam' on 26 January, 1763, followed on the same page of the register by that of the baptism of 'Mary the D. of Watkin Abraam by Anne his Wife 19th of Febry'.[8] Much later, a letter from Caerphilly dated 26 November 1809, informing David Williams of a message from Walter Thomas reporting the death of his wife, contains the request that 'you will have the Goodness to Communicate this to Miss Watkins'.[9] Finally, any remaining doubts are resolved by the Will of David Williams, which bequeathed 'all the residue of my Estate and Effects unto my Niece Mary Watkins daughter of my deceased Sister Ann Thomas',[10] and by the Will of Mary Watkins herself.[11]

Appendix II

The David Williams Manuscripts

The full story of the line of descent, and indeed the ultimate fate of many, of the David Williams manuscripts will probably never be known. The basic outline was meticulously established by Professor David Williams some thirty years ago,[1] but one may usefully proffer some additional information and raise if not resolve some questions. By his Will David Williams bequeathed 'all Letters and Copies of Letters papers and Manuscripts whatsoever which may be in my possession at the time of my decease unto the Reverend Richard Yates Chaplain of Chelsea Hospital and Thomas Whittingham of Kentish Town ... to be by them disposed of according to their discretion'.[2] It seems a fair inference that that discretion led to the papers remaining in the hands of Mary Watkins. For by her Will, proved in March 1845, Miss Watkins made several bequests to her Thomas, Jenkins (by marriage), and Hedges relatives, the most crucial being that of all residue to 'my dear Brother David Thomas of Evelisaf ... near Cardiff'.[3] Assuredly, it was some knowledge of the implications which led to the visit of Evan Evans, the Caerphilly banker and antiquarian, dated by his son (who accompanied him) at about the middle of the forties, 'to Gwaelod-y-Garth, to the house of a Mr David Thomas'.[4] For most certainly the papers there discovered in the carpenter's shop had not been supplying the needs of the glue-pot for thirty years!

Precisely what happened to these papers thereafter is something of a puzzle. The explanation that Evan Evans, after making an exact transcript of the manuscript autobiography, returned it to its owner (who presumably required it for the carpenter's shop?) seems odd. This transcript, held by Walter Evans in 1890, is now in the National Library of Wales. But the original manuscript was, when 'Morien' wrote in 1890, owned by Thomas Jenkins, Pantscallog, Dowlais, a great-grandson of a sister of Williams, and was purchased for Cardiff Public Library in 1906. The collection of documents found at Gwaelod-y-Garth returned only temporarily, if ever, to that location. There is no doubt that they constitute the material held by Evan Evans and subsequently by his sons.[5] Of these the family of Joseph gave some at least to the father of Dr T. W. Thomas, and these make up the collection which now bears his name at Aberystwyth; the son Walter's share reached the same haven in 1951. But the matter is complicated by the presence in the Pantscallog (Jenkins) Collection of a letter which bears on its dorse the casual scribbling and the autograph of 'Thomas Thomas Gwaelodygarth':[6] evidently not all of the material rescued from the glue-pot had either been returned or held by the Evans family in a box at the bank.

Sadly, documents seen by 'Morien' in 1890 soon afterwards disappeared. A collection sold at Sotheby's – for an unidentifiable vendor to untraceable purchasers – in November 1893 included letters from Brissot, Franklin, Garrick, and Thomas Jefferson,[7] among others. This infuriating catalogue typifies the treatment often accorded to the Williams papers. Thus, the Franklin Papers held by the American Philosophical Society include a letter to David Williams, dated May 9, 1774, bearing an addendum: 'Caerphilly. Wales. (Undecipherable) 6th 1878. Presented to Mr Franklin W. Smith of Boston U.S.A. as a souvenir of his visit to Caerphilly Castle on this day Joseph Evans.'[8] One can but hope that there were not too many such transatlantic visitors and that the demand for souvenirs had not replaced that of the glue-pot.

My own personal enquiries – for descendants of the Hedges family still live in Caerphilly – yield no fruit. But surprisingly the Victoria and Albert Museum proved more rewarding. The Forster Collection contains several letters from Williams to Garrick and others,[9] but also a full assembly, cut and mounted, of the pages of the hitherto untraced pirate quarto edition of the *Letter to David Garrick*.[10] This copy, the *Liturgy on the Principles of the Christian Religion* now in Dr Williams's Library, and the article on 'Jean Pierre Brissot', are the only additions I am able to make to the exhaustive list of extant printed works compiled by Professor David Williams in 1957.[11] Finally, the Pelham Papers at the British Library contain several documents, one previously mis-attributed, which were written by David Williams. We may but hope that time will fill more gaps. One would also like to know the exact provenance of the second portrait of Williams. The Rigaud portrait went to the Literary Fund and is now with the Society of Authors; yet a letter from 'Morien' to the *Western Mail* makes explicit reference to another *'original* oil painting' – the word italicised being queried by another 'Contributor'.[12] Now the Will of Mary Watkins quite clearly bequeathed 'unto David Moore of . . . colas Inn Esquire the portrait of my said uncle . . .',[13] and while 'Morien's account of its provenance is different there is little doubt that this portrait, which he located at Gwaelod-y-Garth, is that now held by the National Museum of Wales.

Appendix III

THE BEADONS, THE MARTYNS, AND THE ST ANNE'S CONNECTION

A pertinent reminder of how relatively small a world was the London and indeed the England of David Williams – at least at that level of society in which he moved – is furnished by recurrent references to a West Country family, the Beadons, of whom one lived in his home for a quarter-century, and to the parish of St Anne's, Soho, in which he resided for so much of his time in London. The Rev Samuel Squire, whose history of the Anglo-Saxons was cited by Williams, was rector of St Anne's, a position he retained after becoming Bishop of St David's; on his death in 1766 he was buried in the church.[1] But while rector of Oakford in Devon his daughter Margaret had married Robert Beadon. Among the children of this match were Edward (father of Frances, later Mrs Martyn) and Richard (who pursued a clerical career of great distinction).[2]

In 1759 Frances married Thomas Martyn (almost certainly of Awliscombe, Devon, born 1737)[3] who not surprisingly thereafter became curate at St Anne's. However close her later relationship with David Williams, her marriage left Frances no stranger to contention. Her husband engaged in a prolonged vendetta with his equally obdurate rector, Dr Richard Hind (who had succeeded Squire) – as histories of Soho, the records of St Anne's, the Press, and even a publication by Martyn himself abundantly attest. At issue between them was the edifying question of whether the curate's duties included the burial of non-parishioners without additional payment and/or by whom any such recompense should be made, but even more dramatically the notorious occasion on which Hind complained that 'Mr Martyn had insulted me in the Face of my Parish, by taking Possession of my Pulpit, and preaching in opposition to me'.[4]

This was the incident lampooned in an undated and scurrilous print which depicts the rector as emerging from beneath a table to remonstrate with one paying close court to a lady in bed. The couplet adjoined –

'Hold! hold! exclaim'd th'enrag'd Divine!

Descend! descend! the Pulpit's mine'

– and the contemporary manuscript notation of the names and offices of Hind and Martyn leave no doubts of identification but certainly raise questions as to the varied levels of clerical rivalry in the parish of St Anne.[5] The prolonged squabble (which had commenced as early as November 1774 when Hind attempted to give his curate notice to quit) went to litigation, which Martyn won, at the Court of King's Bench, and is further reflected in *An Address to the Inhabitants of the Parish of St. Anne, Westminster*, by Martyn, which ran to a third edition in 1777, as well as in the Vestry

Minutes for 1778. In this last year Hind left for livings in northern England, while almost simultaneously the name of his curate ceased to appear in the parish records.[6]

Meanwhile, if the admittedly imperious rector was unhappy with his curate, we have seen[7] that Frances Martyn's family were becoming increasingly concerned about her husband and clearly envisaged the breakdown of her marriage. Exactly what happened after 1778 remains, as yet, a matter for conjecture, but relations with the Beadons after Frances became settled at Great Russell Street were obviously soured by the impending litigation on the financial dispute considered earlier.[8] Yet assuming some restoration of amicable family relations after the settlement of 1793, David Williams, ironically, was now extremely well (if indirectly) connected. For Richard Beadon was archdeacon of London between 1775 and 1789 before becoming Bishop of Gloucester, and then of Bath and Wells from 1802 to 1824.

Finally, of course, David Williams returned to the Soho in which he had already lived for several years in Frith Street and in Meard Street respectively, when he moved from Brompton Row to the House of the Literary Fund in Gerrard Street in 1805. From that house Frances was buried in St Anne's in January 1812, and David Williams himself in July 1816.[9]

Notes

Introduction

[1] Although only illness precluded a magisterial study by one of the greatest of Welsh historians.

[2] Most notably, those of his namesake and, more recently, Peter France – see Bibliography.

[3] University of Wales Press, for Welsh Department of the Board of Education, 1961 reprint.

[4] Roddier's monograph, *Rousseau en Angleterre*, over thirty years ago, seized on Williams's highly individual amalgam of ideas and on his life-long preoccupation with the 'great central problem' of politics. More recently, in 1968, Jacob Viner included him in his identification of a group of social-reformist writers in the 1770s and observed an affinity with Godwin, while Bonwick's study of *English Radicals and the American Revolution* (1977) accords him considerable space. Yet his name does not occur in *The Eighteenth-Century Commonwealth*, by C. Robbins, nor in the magisterial study of Richard Price by D. O. Thomas, while he wins but a few brief references in H. T. Dickinson, *Liberty and Property*, and in A. Goodwin, *The Friends of Liberty*. Most recently J. A. W. Gunn's *Beyond Liberty and Property*, 1983 (and again trans-Atlantic), devotes a whole chapter to 'David Williams: Organicism and Reform' and places him 'in the vanguard of the political thought of the time' (228).

[5] N.L.W., MS 10333E(77); a letter regarding his bequest of books to his sister (N.L.W., MS 5452D, Henllan 1, Thomas Rees to W. D. Jeremy, 8 December, 1869) refers to 'heaps of them' as still in the possession of her grandson, while the first seven pages of C.P.L., MS 1.153 look very like an attempt at a semi-classified catalogue.

[6] E. Waring, *Recollections and Anecdotes of Edward Williams*, 49.

[7] Infra, 192.

[8] Although that of Professor David Williams, in *N.L.W.J.*, X(2), 131–36, must surely be very near the mark.

[9] Infra, 10. For other additions see 113, n. 2 and, less certainly, 139.

[10] See Appendix II.

[11] J. M. Robertson, *A History of Freethought*, II, 758. This seems much more appropriate than the still-surviving tendency to label Williams a 'rational Dissenter'.

Chapter One

[1] D. Williams, 'Incidents in my own Life' (hereafter 'Incidents'), 1, 1a.

[2] *Western Mail*, 22 February, 1911. The eulogy on the base of the obelisk, with pardonable but inaccurate over-statement, describes Williams as having 'devoted the greater part of his life to the helping of the poor, the expounding of the principles of popular education', and with more justice as having shielded Benjamin Franklin, and drafting 'the first constitution of the French Revolution' (French *Republic* would be better – see below, 124–31).

[3] 'Morien', *Western Mail*, 22 May 1890; H. P. Richards, *David Williams*, 6.

[4] Glamorgan C.R.O., Eglwysilan Parish Registers, P/1, I, 33dorse; T. W. Thomas, in *Pebyll Seion*, ed. C. T. Thomas and E. Bush, 113.

[5] D. Williams, 'Incidents', 1.

[6] E. T. Chappell, *Historic Melingriffith*, 23–6, 40; infra, 167.

[7] D. Williams, 'Incidents', 1–2.

[8] Ibid., 1; *Annual Biography*, 1818, 17; T. W. Thomas, *Pebyll Seion*, 114; Glamorgan C.R.O., Eglwysilan Parish Registers, P/1, II, 9.

[9] T. Rees, *History of Protestant Nonconformity in Wales*, 362–3, n. 2; H. P. Richards, *Caerphilly* (Jnl. of Caerphilly Historical Society), No. 4, 25–33.

[10] J. Morgan Jones, 'Calvinistic Methodists and Groeswen ...', *Western Mail*, 18 and 19 November, 1897.

[11] N.L.W., MS 5453.C (Henllan 2. Letter-Book &c) 1771 Sept 30; MS 10329.B (W. J. Evans), 140 (extract diary, 26 November 1766).

[12] Indeed, writing from personal acquaintance in later life, F. A. Wendeborn, a German *prediger* or pastor in London, states that the boy's overt resistance to this imposed and distasteful future vocation led to expulsion from school, only his father's dying plea securing a resumption of his studies for the ministry: *Der Zustand des Staats, der Religion, der Gelehrsamkeit und der Kunst in Grosbritanien*, Berlin, 1785, Vol. 3, 369 (trans. Robert James).

[13] *D.W.B.*, 1031; T. Rees, loc.cit.

[14] Infra, 27.

[15] See H. P. Roberts, 'The History of the Presbyterian Academy, Brynllywarch-Carmarthen', *Trans. Unitarian Historical Society*, Vol. IV, Part 4 (Oct., 1930), 343–4: Samuel Thomas was an avowed Pelagian if not Arian, while Evan Davies was not considered 'sound'.

[16] T. Rees, op. cit., 362–3, 495–6.

[17] Infra, 4, 44.

[18] Dr Williams's Library, Presbyterian Fund Minute Book (Microfilm 83), Entries for 1753 to 1758.

[19] *Cambrian Register*, Vol. 3, 529; D. Williams, *Treatise on Education*, 184, and *Lectures on Education*, I, 95, 98–9.

[20] Eglwysilan Parish Registers, IV, 10, 47, 65 (see also Appendix I, II); D. Williams, 'Incidents', 2; infra, 167.

[21] T. Morris, *A General View of the Life and Writings of the Rev. David Williams*, 23.

[22] C. J. Phillips, 'The Life and Work of David Williams', London Ph.D., 7.

[23] D. Williams, 'Incidents', 3.

[24] *Annual Biography*, 1818, 18–19.

[25] D. Williams, 'Incidents', 3.

[26] B. Thomas, of Malmesbury, his fellow-student, in *The Political and Religious Conduct of the Dissenters Vindicated* (1777), 49–55.

[27] *Cambrian Register*, Vol. 3, 529–30.

[28] Cuttings from an as-yet unidentified newspaper, bound in with a volume of pamphlets held by the Royal Literary Fund, consisting of letters by 'Sappho' dated 19 June, 21 August, and 23 September 1777(?), with two pseudonymous rejoinders. The conjecture of the unidentified collector of these cuttings that 'Sappho' was 'a Mrs Nation a very sensible woman at Exeter who had been one of Mr Wms Hearers ... to whom Wms had paid his addresses' (R.L.F., loc.cit.) is given additional credence by the presence in the Register of the Mint Meeting House, Exeter, of four baptismal entries for branches of the Nation family during the ministry of David Williams: P.R.O. RG4, 336, p. 17. Williams's first administration of baptism is recorded in May 1762, and his last in November 1769.

[29] Manuscript note by the collector of the 'Sappho' cuttings; R.L.F.

[30] Hand-written note in a copy of J. Cornish, *A Blow at the Root of all Priestly Claims*, 1775, 3; infra, 8–9 for more on anonymous letters.

[31] *Public Characters of 1798–9*, 508; F A. Wendeborn, op.cit., Vol. 3, 369–70.

[32] D. Bogue and J. Bennett, *History of Dissenters, from the Revolution to the Year 1808*, II, 168–75; *Public Characters* .... loc.cit.

[33] B. Thomas, op.cit., 47–56; 'Sappho' Letters, R.L.F.

[34] F. A. Wendeborn, loc.cit., trans. Robert James.

[35] Infra, 24, 33, 39.

[36] A. Brockett, *Nonconformity in Exeter 1650–1875*, 156–8.

[37] *Annual Biography*, 1818, 18–19.

[38] F. A. Wendeborn, Vol. 3, 370; T. Morris, *General View*, 4–5.

[39] *Gentleman's Magazine*, LXVIII, Feb. 1798, 126; March 1798, 215.

[40] D. Williams, 'Incidents', 3–4.

[41] Infra, 11; *Essays on Public Worship*, 3.

[42] F. H. W. Sheppard, ed., *Survey of London*, XXXIII, 2, 7, 15, 153, 174, 252; XXXIV, 405–6.

[43] F. H. W. Sheppard, op.cit., XXXIII, 151, 174; XXXIV, 406; E. B. Chancellor, *The Romance of Soho*, 162; E. F. Rimbault, *Soho and its Associations*, 100.

[44] *Daily Telegraph*, 5 February 1872, which pictures Chateaubriand going to bed in his clothes, to save fuel.

[45] Information from the Rev. Michael Hurst-Bannister.

[46] Sir W. N. Wraxall, *Historical Memoirs of My Own Time*, I, 136, 155–6.

[47] D. Williams, 'Incidents', 3.

[48] Percy Fitzgerald's *Life of David Garrick* concurs that Williams was known to Goldsmith and others of his coterie; 402.

[49] Victoria & Albert Museum, Forster Collection, MS 213.48.F.11(3).

[50] Victoria & Albert, Forster Collection, MS 213.48.F.11(3).

[51] 'L.D.G.', in *Notes and Queries*, 1st Ser., VI, 18 Dec. 1852, 577.

[52] N.L.W., MS.10338E (89, 90); supra, 5.

[53] Forster Collection, MS 213.48.F.11(1).

[54] D. Williams, *Letter to David Garrick*, 3–5; T. Morris, op.cit., 5–6.

[55] Forster Collection, MS 213.48.F.11(5).

[56] Loc.cit. (6).

[57] P. Fitzgerald, op.cit., 404–5.

[58] 'B.D.', author of the notice which appeared in the *Gentleman's Magazine*, 1816, and *Cambrian Register*, 1818 (the presence of a manuscript draft of this among Williams's papers suggest that it was almost an 'authorized' account); *Monthly Review*, LIX, 72, in a review of the later 'pirate' edition, infra, 10.

[59] Victoria and Albert, Forster Collection, MS 213.48.F.11(2).

[60] J. Boaden, ed., *Correspondence of Garrick*, I, lv.

[61] D. Williams, *Letter to David Garrick*, 3–7, 9–13, 24–7, 32–4.

[62] *Critical Review*, Vol. 33, 1772, 53.

[63] *Monthly Review*, XLVI, Jan. 1772, 263; LIX, Jly–Dec, 1778.

[64] It was printed and published by J. Williams, Fleet Street, and G. Corrall, which may explain the incorrect assertion of a manuscript note on the B.L. copy of the first edition, apparently in the hand of Kemble, that the Rev. David Williams was the editor of a second edition.

[65] Almost certainly George Colman, manager of the Haymarket.

[66] Victoria and Albert, Forster Collection, MS 213.48.F.11(20ff).

[67] *Monthly Review*, LIX, Jly–Dec. 1778, 72.

[68] Forster Collection, loc.cit. (8).

[69] Ibid., (9).

[70] Anon., *Orpheus, Priest of Nature, and Prophet of Infidelity*, 24–5.

[71] *Correspondence of Garrick*, II, 308–9.

[72] The story was rejected by C. F. Taggart (*The Athenaeum*, No. 2116, 16 May 1868, 704) and by the Rev. A. Gordon (*D.N.B.* article on Williams), but was accepted by Garrick's biographer (P. Fitzgerald, op.cit., 405). See also D. Williams in *N.L.W. Journal*, X, (1957), 123.

[73] C.P.L., MS.1.153, 11–1.2

[74] N.L.W., MS.10338E(93).

[75] Infra, 36, 38.

[76] *Critical Review*, Vol. 31, 1771, 63–5, 395–8; Vol. 32, 1772, 68–71.

[77] Resembling More's *Utopia*, to which it alludes, or Starkey's *Dialogue* …

[78] See J. H. Plumb, 'Political Man', in *Man versus Society in Eighteenth-Century Britain*, ed. J. L. Clifford, 14–16.

[79] See Almon's *Political Register*, commenced 1767, or M. Peters, 'The "Monitor" on the constitution, 1755–1765', *E.H.R.*, LXXXVI (1971), 706–27.

[80] *Critical Review*, as n. 6, p. 17; *Monthly Review*, XLIV, Jan. 1771, 35–41, 493; XLV, Jly. 1771, 261–9.

[81] N.L.W. MS.15269C(3); letter to Williams from Cambridge, 26 October 1772.

[82] *The Philosopher*, I, iii-iv, xix.

[83] Ibid., I, 24–5; II, 15.

[84] Cf. Samuel Johnson's allusion in *The False Alarm*, 1770 (anonymously published), to 'the constant fomentors of sedition, and never-failing confederates of the rabble' (52).

[85] D. Williams, *The Philosopher*, I, 48–9.

[86] E. Burke, *Thoughts on the Cause of the Present Discontents*, in *Writings and Speeches*, I, 530.

[87] D. Williams, op.cit., I, xi-xii, xvi–xvii; see also II, 61.

[88] E. Burke, op.cit., 437, 441, 478.

[89] D. Williams, op.cit., I, 16, 52, 67; II, xii, 69.

[90] Ibid., I, v, 7–14; I, v, xvi; II, v–vii, xvii–xxix.

[91] Ibid., I, 5–7, 15, 51.

[92] E. Burke, op.cit., I. 530.

[93] Though Burke attributes to the 'cabal' (the alleged 'interior ministry') the successful propagation of the doctrine 'that all political connections are in their nature factious, and as such ought to be dissipated': ibid., 525.

[94] D. Williams, op.cit., I, 48–51.

[95] Ibid., I, xii-xiii, 50.

[96] D, Williams, *The Philosopher*, I, 53–6.

[97] The feud dated from the early 1760s, but the recent hubbub was triggered by the return of Wilkes from four years' exile to almost immediate victory in the Middlesex county election. In May 1768 his supporters had participated in the riot (or, according to view-point, 'massacre') in St George's Fields where some half-dozen were killed by troops. Wilkes's election as alderman of the City of London further strengthened his base. His expulsion by the Commons in February, 1769 was followed only by his return unopposed in the consequent by-election, renewed expulsion accompanied by a declaration of ineligibility, and finally, in desperation, by the declaration that a heavily defeated rival candidate was duly elected. By 1771, indeed, the confused and confusing ministerial general post which had bedevilled the 1760s had been followed by the ministry of Lord North (thereafter for more than a decade a congenial target for the would-be constitutional reformer). But most of the specific references of Williams relate to the Grafton ministry – towards its end hag-ridden by Wilkes. On Wilkes see, among others, G. Rudé, *Wilkes and Liberty*.

[98] Indeed, during 1770 the original 'Wilkite' body had split. Fear of mob violence, realization that the hero was a charlatan, and the emergence of a more genuinely radical wing, sufficed to produce the type of division which was to hamstring the 'Association' movement a decade later.

[99] D. Williams, op.cit., II, 5–8; here again, the argument is in close accord with that of Burke, op.cit., I, 496–501.

[100] D. Williams, op.cit., II, x–xi; also I, 69.

[101] Ibid., I, 65; see also II, x.

[102] Ibid., I, 68–72; Burke's diagnosis (op.cit., I, 491–6) in many ways runs parallel with that of Williams, but leads, as we shall see, to a very different prescription!

[103] D. Williams, op.cit., II, 47–53.

[104] Amendment 2 in the 'Bill of Rights' Amendments, 1791.

[105] D. Williams, op.cit., II, 56–9.

[106] Williams observes, shrewdly, that British policy had reached its nadir in its ridiculous attempt to establish governmental claims 'by asserting and withdrawing them, in an equivocal and undetermined manner', an obvious allusion to the Declaratory Act of 1766 (*The Philosopher*, I, 57–61). See I. R. Christie, *Crisis of Empire*, 62–4.

[107] D. Williams, op.cit., II, 81–3; cf. N. Machiavelli, *The Prince*, Chapter 5.

[108] Infra, 19–20.

[109] D. Williams, op.cit., II, 84–90.

[110] Ibid., I, xiv; see W. R. D. Jones, *The Tudor Commonwealth 1529–1559*, 18–23.

[111] D. Williams, op.cit., I, 52–3.

[112] Infra, 73.

[113] D. Williams, op.cit., I, 33–5.

[114] Another comment which was to be strikingly apposite in the context of the constitution-making of the United States.

[115] D. Williams, op.cit., I, 35–39.

[116] Ibid., I, 39–40.

[117] Ibid., II, 18–22.

[118] Ibid., II, 22–27; while the main drift of the argument is by now very different, this last point closely resembles the starting-point of Burke in his *Thoughts on the Cause of the Present Discontent* (I, 436–41).

[119] D. Williams, op.cit., I, 21–2, 29–30; see W. R. D. Jones, *The Tudor Commonwealth 1529–1559*, 13–17.

[120] D. Williams, op.cit., I, 46; J. Ponet, op.cit., A.i–A.viii.b, B.iii–C.vi.b, C.viii–C.viii.b, D.vi, E.vi-ii–E.viii.b, F.i–F.viii, but above all G.i.b–G.vi.b: 'common wealths and realms may live, when the head is cut off, and may put on a new head'.

[121] D. Williams, op.cit., I, 41–5; II, 14.

[122] Sir J. Mackintosh, op.cit., 305.

[123] D. Williams, op.cit., I, xii.

[124] Ibid., I, 17–18; W. Tyndale, *The Obedience of a Christian man* (1528) in *Works*, ed. T. Russell, 1831, I, 199–200.

[125] D. Williams, op.cit., I, 17–18, 20; II, xii, 8, 77.

[126] Op.cit., 228; see also M. Peters, in *E.H.R.*, LXXXVI, 1971, 716.

[127] D. Williams, op.cit., II, 18–23.

[128] Ibid., II, 9; see E. C. Black, *The Association. British Extra-parliamentary Organization 1769–1793*, 4–5, 11–14.

[129] D. Williams, op.cit., II, 9–10, 13–14.

[130] Ibid., II, vi–vii.

[131] C. Macaulay, *Observations on a Pamphlet Entitled, Thoughts on the Cause of the Present Discontents*, 1770, 5.

While Williams would have shared Burke's fear lest 'the House of Commons should be infected with every epidemical frenzy of the people' (*Present Discontents*, 492), he could not endorse his resistance of any proposals to shorten the duration of parliaments and his lack of 'any sort of reliance upon either a triennial Parliament, or a place-bill ... To say nothing of the horrible disorders among the people attending frequent elections ...' (516–7).

[132] D. Williams, *The Philosopher*, II, 27–8.

[133] Hulme, though a rather obscure figure, is sometimes accorded more space than Williams in histories of political ideas. Even within the conspectus of the same general body of thought, the similarities are striking: notably, the repeated observation that, in default of public action, a subservient or a suborned parliament may itself be a threat to liberty (op.cit., 116, 145–7); the insistence that 'where annual Election ends, there Slavery begins' (title-page, 7, 115, 161); the prescription of an electoral procedure, including the ballot (158–60); the balanced approach to the American problem (180–1); and others we shall soon observe. Hulme's emphasis on the Saxon tithings system for provision of *police* (13) was to be a major preoccupation of Williams.

[134] The average price of a pocket borough in 1761 was £2,000 per seat; L. B. Namier's *Structure of Politics* cites material relating to the 'convivial' aspect of polling which makes 'Eatanswill' sound non-fictional (78–9, 164–5).

[135] J. Almon, op.cit., 18–21. The objection to '*annual tumults, annual perjuries,* and *annual corruptions*' is countered by the observation that even the resources of bribery are not unlimited! (35–6).

[136] D. Williams, op.cit., II, 11–13, 16–17, 28–30.

[137] Ibid., II, 34–7; his later views on mandation were to undergo some modification.

[138] Ibid., II, 38–9; A. Hamilton, J. Jay and J. Madison, *The Federalist*, 71–2; see Caroline Robbins (op.cit., 9) on Commonwealth belief that members should be rich enough to scorn bribes; but Hulme (op.cit., 161) commended the abolition of the 'landed qualification for members to serve in parliament'. The Massachusetts Constitution of 1780 explicitly associates the doctrine of the separation of powers with the need for maximum safeguard against human frailty, 'to the end that it may be a government of laws and not of men'.

[139] O. Hulme, op.cit., 112.

[140] D. Williams, op.cit., II, 37–41.

[141] Infra, 72–5, 122–4.

[142] See E. C. Black, op.cit., 13.

[143] See I. R. Christie, *Wilkes, Wyvill, and Reform*, 36.

[144] See E. C. Black, op.cit., 14.

[145] Hulme is equally clear that 'the only effectual remedy the people of England have now left ... is to enter into legal associations, in defence of their constitutional rights, and liberties' (op.cit., 161) – such associations to require of parliamentary candidates pledges in line with contemporary radical thought (161–4).

[146] D. Williams, op.cit., II, 41–6, 95. This last phrase is uneasily reminiscent of that employed, ill-fatedly, by Lamartine in debating French presidential electoral procedures after 1848! But it is wholly consonant with the evolutionary approach of Williams to constitutional issues.

[147] Ironically, Williams is almost a paradigm case of the contention that 'the American constitution employs many of the devices which the Real Whigs vainly besought Englishmen to adopt and in it must be found their abiding memorial' (C. Robbins, *The Eighteenth Century Commonwealthman*, 4).

Chapter Two

[1] D. Williams, *Essays on Public Worship*, 24–5; Appendix, 9.

[2] Ibid., Appendix, 9–13.

[3] J. Jebb, in N. L. W., MS.15269C (3); D. Williams, 'Incidents', 4; supra, 5; D. Williams, *Liturgy on the Principles of the Christian Religion*, v; T. Morris, *General View*, 7; *Critical Review*, Vol. 6, (Dec. 1792), 457–9.

[4] *Critical Review*, Vol. 36, 1773, 77; *Monthly Review*, Vol. XLVIII (Dec. 1772–Jly. 1773), 227–33.

[5] *Liturgy*, 1, 30, 39–47, 49–59, 75, 87; the only copy extant, once owned by James Martin, is now in Dr Williams's Library – see D. Williams, *N. L. W. Journal*, X(No 2), 125–7 for a full account of the complicated story of the publications of *Essays* and *Liturgy*.

[6] D. Williams, *Liturgy*, vii, x–xiv; a copy of the 'Octagon Liturgy', so-called after the shape of the place of worship in which it was established, published in 1763, is in Dr Williams's Library.

[7] *Monthly Review*, Vol. LII (Jan.–Jly, 1775), 428–30; *Critical Review*, Vol. 39 (1775), 65–6.

[8] T. Morris, op.cit., 8; 'Minute Books ...', Dr Williams's Library, RNC, 38. 105–7, Vol. 2 (106), 141, 172.

[9] D. Williams, *Essays*, Appendix, 21, 28–31.

[10] D. Williams, *Sermons . . . upon Religious Hypocrisy*, I, i–iv; II, 42–3.

[11] D. Williams, *The Philosopher*, III, 4–5; *Essays on Public Worship*, 3.

[12] *Essays on Public Worship*, 46–7; Benjamin Thomas (supra, 4, infra, 44) makes several kind allusions to these *Essays* in his *Letters to the . . . Lord Bishop of Landaff*, 1774 (24, 46, 50), including a virtual quotation of this 'western regions' passage.

[13] *The Philosopher*, III, 78–9; Hume, in *Dialogues Concerning Natural Religion*, 1779, makes an identical point on abandonment of human analogy (203).

[14] D. Williams, *Essays on Public Worship*, 12–14; *The Philosopher*, III, 99–100.

[15] Enno van Gelder, H.A., *The Two Reformations in the Sixteenth Century* (a stimulating over-statement), 367.

[16] D. Williams, *Sermons . . . upon Religious Hypocrisy*, I, 17–18, 54–5, 144–5, 166, 168, 171, 179; II, 34, 11.

[17] Ibid., II, 34, 115.

[18] D. Williams, *Lectures on the Universal Principles and Duties of Religion and Morality* (1779), I, 47–8.

[19] D. Williams, *Sermon preached at the Opening of . . . Margaret-Street* (1776), 13–14; *The Philosopher*, III, 112–14; *Lectures on . . . Religion and Morality*, I, 45–7.

[20] *The Philosopher*, III, 48–9, 52–6; *Sermons . . . upon Religious Hypocrisy*, I, 14–15 (cf. Bishop Butler's reproof to John Wesley: R. E. Davies, *Methodism*, 75).

[21] *Lectures on . . . Religion and Morality*, I, 80, 201–2.

[22] Ibid., I, 136; II, 150–3.

[23] *The Philosopher*, III, 27, 68–9, 83, 87, 120–3, 128–9.

[24] M. R. Watts, *The Dissenters: from the Reformation to the French Revolution*, 465, 469, 477.

[25] D. Williams, *Sermons upon Religious Hypocrisy*, I, 109–10; II, 28, 32, 99–100, 115, 153.

[26] D. Williams, *Essays on Public Worship*, 9–11, 27–9, 32–3; 'Letter', p. **; *Sermon*, 11, 13; *Lectures on Religion and Morality*, I, 37, 41, 108–9, 120–1, 141–2.

[27] Ibid., II, 22 (also I, 107); his use of 'metaphysics' was invariably pejorative, exemplifying one modern definition as 'loosely and vaguely applied to anything abstruse, abstract'.

[28] D. Williams, *The Philosopher*, III, 57, 121, 130; *Essays on Public Worship*, 16–21 (he particularly likes the Utopian agreement in 'worshipping the divine essence'); 64–5, Appendix 5–6.

[29] *Sermons upon Religious Hypocrisy*, I, ii, 4–5, 12, 26, 117; II, 41–2; *A Sermon preached at the Opening of a Chapel*, 6, 8.

[30] In *An Essay on Crimes and Punishments*, 1782, Manasseh Dawes (elsewhere a critic of Williams) cites this passage at greater length, in a very close paraphase and with evident approval (166–7).

[31] D. Williams, *Lectures on Religion and Morality*, I, i, iv, 4, 9, 14–16, 18, 70, 87, 97–8, 131, 135–6, 140–2, 162, 173, 188–9, 228; II, 51, 147–8, 213–5.

[32] *The Connoisseur*, No. 9 (March 28, 1754), pp. 16–17.

[33] William Wollaston, op.cit., 1726 edition, 35–8, 45, 51, 55, 69, 114–20, 124, 179, 193, 206.

[34] D. Williams, *The Philosopher*, III, 86, 99, 120–1, 124–7; *Essays on Public Worship*, 3, 9–10, 60, Appdx., 18; *Sermons upon Religious Hypocrisy*, I, 57, 102; *Lectures on Religion and Morality*, I, 30.

[35] *Sermons upon Religious Hypocrisy*, II, 60.

[36] *Lectures on Religion and Morality*, I, 61–2, 92, 112, 138, 153, 156.

[37] Ibid., I, 161–70, 186–7, 237.

[38] One sympathises with the comment of the *Monthly Review* (LXII, Jan.–Jne 1780, 104) that 'we seldom observe any *beginning* or *middle* in Mr Williams' productions. He appears to be always some where or other *about* the end.'

[39] D. Hartley, *Observations on Man . . .*, 1749, I, viii, 512; II, 338–9, 382, 447; Basil Willey, *The Eighteenth Century Background*, 70, 74, 137, 143–4, 152; F. L. Baumer, *Modern European Thought*, 175–6, 183; C. Vereker, *Eighteenth-Century Optimism*, 67–71; D. Williams, op.cit., III, 55.

[40] D. Williams, *Lectures on Religion and Morality*, I, 170–1, 173, 178–9 – the crucial implications of all this for education will concern us in Chapter 3.

[41] Ibid., I, 184–5, 190–2, 193.

[42] Ibid., I, 219, 225, 228–31.

[43] Ibid., II, 20, 25–6; see, particularly, More's *Utopia*, 112.

[44] D. Williams, *Lectures on Religion and Morality*, II, 27; see L. Radzinowicz's *History of English Criminal Law*, I, 1, for Romilly's concurrence on such severity, also D. Hay, *Albion's Fatal Tree*, 17–63; also infra, 213, n.67.

[45] *Lectures on Religion and Morality*, II, 14–15, 27–30, 80–8.

[46] Ibid., II, 130–1, 212–3, 216.

[47] D. Hartley, *Observations on Man*, I, vi–vii; J. Priestley, *The Doctrine of Philosophical Necessity Illustrated*, xxx–xxxi.

[48] His own *Disquisitions relating to Matter and Spirit*, also in 1777, and *Free Discussion of the Doctrines of Materialism, and Philosophical Necessity*, 1780; anon., *A slight sketch of the Controversy ... on Matter and Spirit*, 1780; M. Dawes, see note 51.

[49] See *Monthly Review*, LXII, Jan.–June 1780, 223–4. Amidst the extraordinary ramblings of *The Life of John Bunckle, Esq.* (by Thomas Amory) a section on religion (1770 edn., III, 258–80) lends colour to this gibe.

[50] M. Dawes, *An Essay on Crimes and Punishments*, 1782, 138–9.

[51] M. Dawes, *Philosophical Considerations: or A Free Enquiry into the Merits of a Controversy ... on Matter and Spirit and Philosophical Necessity*, 18–19, citing D. Williams, *A Treatise on Toleration ...* (Trans. Voltaire), 1779, 88–9.

[52] See Basil Willey, *The Eighteenth Century Background*, 178–80.

[53] D. Williams, *Lectures on Religion and Morality*, II, 216.

[54] Clarke's own copy, with interleaved manuscript amendments, was given to the British Museum by his son in 1768 (B.L., C. 24. b21). See A. Elliott Peaston, *The Prayer Book Reform Movement in the XVIIIth Century*, 59, 71, 78–9.

[55] T. Lindsey, *A Sermon preached at the Opening of the Chapel in ... Essex-Street*, 1774, 28–32.

[56] Supra, 24.

[57] S. G. Fisher, *The True Benjamin Franklin*, 99–100.

[58] D. Williams, op.cit., I, i–ii, and 'Incidents', 6–7.

[59] D. Williams, 'Incidents', 6–7. The story leaves the American editor of *The Papers of Benjamin Franklin*, W. B. Willcox (Vol. 21, 119–20) 'very sceptical', but his dismissal of 'uncorroborated recollections of the old' as shaky evidence ignores other near-contemporary testimony which mentions the incident.

[60] *Papers of Benjamin Franklin*, Vol. 22, 173–4.

[61] See *Annual Biography*, 1818, 22–3; T. Morris, *General View*, 10–12; anon., *Orpheus, Priest of Nature*, 17–18, 20–1; *Memoirs of the Late Thomas Holcroft*, ed. W. Hazlitt, III, 67–70; Thomas Somerville, *Own Life and Times*, 215–6.

[62] T. Morris, *General View*, 13; D. Williams, 'Incidents', 8.

[63] D. Williams, *A Sermon preached at the Opening of a Chapel*, 1776, 23–5.

[64] *A Liturgy ...*, vii.

[65] D. Williams, *The Philosopher*, III, 10, 120–1, 130–1; the anonymous *Sentiments for Free Devotion*, c. 1771, had accused him of lack of logic in this (4–6, 14, 21).

[66] *A Liturgy ...*, x–xii.

[67] Ibid., 3, 19, 21.

[68] As in 'The Citizen of Heaven':

'His hands disdain a golden bribe,
    And never gripe the poor;
This man shall dwell with God on earth,
    And find his heaven secure.'

[69]
'Beasts wild and tame,
    Birds, flies, and worms,
    In various forms,
Exalt his name.' (80, cf. 'And worms attempt to chant thy praise',
R. E. Davies, op.cit., p. 111.)

[70] *A Liturgy*, 50–1, 53–6.

[71] Ibid., 95.

[72] Ibid., 73, 102, 105.

[73] An unnamed correspondent of *The Morning Post*, 13 April 1776, asks the question: 'Is a man to be molested for preaching only morality? Aye; but he does not preach *Christian* morality? And are there two sorts of morality? If there are, Mr Williams deserves well of the public, for giving it a choice.'

[74] F. A. Wendeborn, *Der Zustand des Staats ...*, Vol. 3, 371 (trans. Robert James).

[75] Published in 1781 but purportedly written earlier. Its author, as well-informed and skilful as he is hostile, discerns the early signs of ambition in his subject: 'foremost in every rebellion at School: he had some project of his own to lead the boys from their Business; and when he entered on his religious Office he stript himself gradually of one principle and doctrine after another, till nothing but naked nature was left.' The term Priest of Nature (while its ascription to Williams's own vanity is inherently plausible) he attributes to a monthly club called 'sacramental' which had toasted his lectures to inebriation! (op.cit., (3), 15n. 13, 5–6).

[76] *Orpheus*, 6–9: 'Philosopher' and 'Enthusiast like' are obvious barbs!

[77] Ibid., loc.cit.; Wendeborn, loc.cit.; *Annual Biography*, 1818, 26; *Public Characters of 1798–9*, 510.

'Morien' (*Western Mail*, 27 May 1890) stands alone in his clear inference that it was to Caerphilly that Williams fled.

[78] Supra, 1; T. Morris, *General View*, 10; infra, 39, for possible explanation of the 'cavern' story.

[79] Infra, 52, for consideration of the fragmentary evidence concerning what was all too probably her tragically brief life.

[80] Apparently, a reference back to some of the early Dutch Anabaptists.

[81] *Orpheus*, 11–14.

[82] D. Williams, 'Incidents', 8–9.

[83] Infra, 45–6 for the later contribution of Melville.

[84] Confirming the prescience of Rousseau's remark to Bentley, when informed of the project: 'Depend upon it, you will not have many women' (*Journal of a Visit to Paris*, ed. P. France, 61).

[85] T. Somerville, *My Own Life and Times 1741–1814*, 217–8. This was written well after the event, but is not the only source to countenance the smear.

[86] Williams refers to Banks ('Incidents', 16) but hardly as a major contributor to the enterprise.

[87] A Librarian of the British Museum.

[88] Despite a modern suggestion of the converse, that 'Bentley would not accept the belief in an after-life which was a cardinal point in Williams's doctrine' (D. Williams, *Welsh Review*, V, 40), Holcroft is probably right.

[89] T. Holcroft, *Memoirs* ..., III, 68–9.

[90] J. Taylor, *Records of My Life*, II, 398–9; oddly, the chapel was shared with the Methodists, who ultimately triumphed (see *Orpheus*, 17 n.1).

[91] Anon., MS bound in with a pamphlet collection, R.L.F. The newspaper or periodical remains, as yet, untraced.

[92] 'Sappho', 19 June 1777.

[93] Ibid., 21 August 1777.

[94] Ibid., 23 Sept., 1777.

[95] Personal knowledge is asserted by the collector of the cuttings.

[96] *London Magazine*, Vol. LXXX, 271.

[97] *Critical Review*, Vol. 42 (1776), 271–80.

[98] *Monthly Review*, Vol. LV (July–December 1776), 133–9 (see B. C. Nangle, *The Monthly Review. First Series*, 23–4, 222); infra, 209, n.137, re. Kippis.

[99] *Monthly Review*, Vol. LXII (Jan.–June 1780), 1–12.

[100] D. Williams, *Lectures on Religion and Morality*, I, i–iii.

[101] 'Incidents', 9; D'Holbach's *Système de la Nature* was published in 1770; ironically, Bogue and Bennett (*History of the Dissenters* ..., II, 199) thought that Shaftesbury's own ideas 'entitle him to a high rank in the list of infidels'.

[102] 'Incidents', 9–10.

[103] Supra, 24. See Anne Holt, *Walking Together*, Chapter VII.

[104] The *Morning Chronicle* for 9 April 1776 confirms this comment: 'His delivery was exceedingly engaging. The attention of the audience was on the stretch', though less than a hundred were present.

[105] Letter dated 12 April 1776 (J. Boardman, *Bentleyana*, 19), which states that Williams, *author* of the Liturgy, will depend on the reception accorded it and his course of lectures for a society and a subscription.

[106] *Bentleyana*, 22; 'R.B.', *Thomas Bentley*, 18–19, 51–2.

[107] *Selected Letters* ..., ed. A. Finer and G. Savage, 275.

[108] *Life & Works of Josiah Wedgwood*, E. Meteyard, II, 419; Wedgwood MSS, Keele University Library, 18508–25, Wedgwood to Bentley, 13/12/1773.

[109] Wedgwood MSS, Keele, 18759–25, Wedgwood to Bentley, 21/5/1777, and 18767–25, Wedgwood to Bentley, 24/6/1777.

[110] Ibid., 18619–25, Wedgwood to Bentley, 19/10/1775 – though the time of year is not quite right!

[111] Ibid., 18666–25, Wedgwood to Bentley, 4/5/1776.

[112] Ibid., 18675–25, Wedgwood to Bentley, n.d.; 18690–25, Wedgwood to Bentley, 10/9/1776; 18748–25, Wedgwood to Bentley, 19/4/1777.

[113] Ibid., 18826–25, Wedgwood to Bentley.

[114] Wendeborn (op.cit., 372), in contrasting such as attended out of mere curiosity (their unwillingness to subscribe protecting both character and purse) with a few loyal friends and subscribers, is the only source to declare that among these latter 'were to be found a few rich Jews'.

[115] Supra, 36–9.

[16] Wedgwood MS, Keele, 18563–25, Wedgwood to Bentley, 10/11/1774, and 18576–25, Wedgwood to Bentley, 26/12/1774.

[17] Ibid., 18866–26, Wedgwood to Bentley, 5/12/1778; 18867–26, Wedgwood to Bentley, 14/12/1778; 628–1, Bentley to Wedgwood, 17/12/1778; and 18869–26, Wedgwood to Bentley, 21/12/1778.

[18] Ibid., 10475–59.

[19] Thus William Hodgson, writing to Franklin in March and May 1780, describes Williams's story of desertion at the launching of Margaret Street as a gross falsehood, and asserts that he has been told that his presence would no longer be agreeable at Slaughters (See N. Hans, *Proceedings of the American Philosophical Society*, Vol. 98, No. 6, 1954, 410–11).

[20] Anon., *Orpheus*, 20–1, 23.

[21] Ibid., 28–30.

[122] Ibid., 37–40: *The Connoisseur* for 21 February 1754 had defined the Demi-Rep, whose conduct is such that 'as long as the last failing remains a secret, the lady's honour is spotless', everyone thinking 'what nobody chooses to call her. It is absolutely necessary that every lady of this order should be married.' (Reprint, W. P. Nimmo, London, 1877, 7–8.)

[123] *Orpheus*, 40–1.

[124] 'Incidents', 10–14; infra, 210, n.178, for the incident involving Thomas Day.

[125] Ibid., loc.cit.

[126] Ibid., 9 dorse.

[127] *Lectures on Religion and Morality*, II, 21, 23; one should not underestimate the reality of fear of a debtors' prison.

[128] T. Morris, op.cit., 13–14.

[129] Samuel Heywood, in *The Right of the Protestant Dissenters to a Complete Toleration asserted*, 1789, cited a description in 1733 of 'a church in this town ludicrously called *The Qualifying Office*', where fee-paying and purely formal communicants took the sacrament, as still true (op.cit., 70).

[130] See Ursula R. Q. Henriques, *Religious Toleration in England*, 3, 15, and Bernard L. Manning, *the Protestant Dissenting Deputies*, 2–5.

[131] See Roland N. Stromberg, *Religious Liberalism in Eighteenth-Century England*, 48.

[132] Ursula R. Q. Henriques, op.cit., 31.

[133] Indeed, Raymond V. Holt's summation (in *The Unitarian Contribution to Social Progress in England*, 275–6, 308) of the special characteristics of Unitarianism (distaste for doctrine and metaphysics, stress on morality) suggests much that coincides with Williams's cast of mind; but so does R. N. Stromberg's 'Definition of Deism' (op.cit., 52–69) – to an even greater extent.

[134] D. Williams, *The Philosopher*, III, 23–5, 108–9, 115–7.

[135] *Essays on Public Worship*, 48–9, 58–61, Appendix, 'Sermon', 25.

[136] See A. Lincoln, *Some Political and Social Ideas of English Dissent 1763–1800*, 14; R. N. Stromberg, op.cit., 47; G. Rudé, *Hanoverian London 1714–1808*, 109.

[137] A. Lincoln, 204; Andrew Kippis, in *A Vindication of the Protestant Dissenting Ministers*, 1773, defends the petitioners against 'objections to the *Matter*, the *Manner*, and the *Time* of their late application' (116). In his *Essays* (43–5) Williams deprecates celebration of Blackburne's *Confessional* as 'a wonderful book' from which the petitioners draw their maxims of liberty.

[138] Minute Books of the Body of Protestant Dissenting Ministers, Dr Williams's Library, MS R.N.C., 106, pp. 110, 139.

[139] 'State of the Dissenting Interest' ('Thompson's List'), Dr Williams's Library, MS R.N.C., 38.6, p.49.

[140] A. Lincoln, 224–5; a more liberal declaration than that of 1779.

[141] A. Kippis, op.cit., 5–6.

[142] Lincoln (229) assigns to their actions pride of place among reasons for failure.

[143] Minute Books ..., 115–6 (10 June 1772); 134–9 (28 April 1773).

[144] E. Hitchin, *Free Thoughts on the Late Application*, 8–10.

[145] Ibid., 32.

[146] Israel Mauduit, *The Case of the Dissenting Ministers*, 57–8.

[147] '*A Reply to the Reasons offered by Thirteen Dissenting Ministers, against The Present Application to Parliament* (in 'A collection of the several papers relating to the application made to Parliament in 1772 & 1773'), p. 4.

[148] See John Fell, *Genuine Protestantism; or, the Unalienable Rights of Conscience Defended*, 1773, 45, 64, and *A Fourth Letter ...*, 1775, 45.

[149] D. Williams, *Essays*, 45.

[150] Ironically, while Blackburne remained in the Church the failure of the venture caused his collaborator, Lindsey, to become an overt Unitarian.

[151] Notably, Benjamin Thomas, whose *Letter to the ... Lord Bishop of Landaff*, 1774, has kinder references to

Williams than his work of a few years later, and Henry Mayo (*London Magazine*, XLIV, Jan. 1775, 5–8) who deplores the recent dishonourable attempt at partial toleration and advocates complete repeal.

[152] D. Williams, *Letter to the ... Protestant Dissenters*, 1–8, 11–15.

[153] Ibid., 17–18; B. L. Manning, *The Protestant Dissenting Deputies*, 22, describes its establishment as 'a pure act of charity without political motive'.

[154] See P. D. G. Thomas, *Lord North*, 147–9, for total confirmation of a quite deliberate decision not to fight in the Commons but to rely on the Lords.

[155] D. Williams, op.cit., 18–20, 22–5, 28; John Palmer's *Free Thoughts on ... the True Principle of Protestant Dissent*, 1779, makes very similar points.

[156] An obvious reference to *Observations on Civil Liberty*, 1776.

[157] D. Williams, *Letter ...*, 30–3, 34–5, 40–1.

[158] *London Magazine*, XLVI, 1777, 427; *Critical Review*, Vol. 44, 1777, 70–1; *Monthly Review*, LVII (Jly–Dec. 1777), 325.

[159] Supra, 4.

[160] B. Thomas, op.cit., 8, 29–30, 59–63, 82–90.

[161] Including the writing of letters to Savile himself, Sir Henry Houghton, Col. Barré, Charles Fox, Burke, and Wilkes – as likely to support it.

[162] D. Williams, *Intellectual Liberty*, 1, 4–5, 6–8, 11–12.

[163] Ibid., 16, 20–5, 27–31, 33, 36–8. The work received rather tepid reviews, and a published reply, by Manasseh Dawes (*Essay on Intellectual Liberty ...*, 1780), defending Savile though not unfavourably disposed to Williams. The Girondin Lanthenas, in his *De la Liberté Indéfinie de la Presse ...*, 1791, (10, n.1) pays tribute to Williams's advocacy in '*De La Liberté Intellectuelle*' of complete freedom of expression. Another French source (*Lettres de Madame Roland*, II, 699) asserts that Lanthenas derived his views in part from Williams.

[164] *General Advertiser*, 28 April 1779 prints a long letter, and the *Monthly Review*, Vol. LXI (Sept. 1779), 238, describes the 'Remonstrance des Naturalistes' itself, both by 'D. C. Avocat' of 3 Market Street, Oxford Street – who terms himself 'a Cosmopolite, who has lived above 13 years in this country' and whose native tongue is French. *Westminster Magazine* (XCII, June 1780, 327) asserts that the worshippers at Margaret Street know nothing of, resent, and reject the petition and the book, and concludes that the author 'is probably an impostor or insane'. The 1781 reprint alludes to this attack (v).

[165] Anon., *A Petition ...*, vi-xii; 71–2, 88.

[166] Sir John Ballinger, recording its acquisition from the Pantscallog collection of Williams material (*City of Cardiff Public Libraries Forty-fifth Annual Report*, 1906–7, 26) believed that he probably wrote it. But there remains a very real possibility that it was written by a French adherent.

[167] 'Constitutions of a Philosophical Society', 1–2.

[168] *Orpheus*, 17 n. 1.

[169] *Annual Biography*, 1818, 26–8.

[170] Letter in N.L.W., MS. 10331.E (64–7).

[171] One other acknowledged, and much later, publication on religious philosophy will concern us in Chapter Five.

[172] The hostile notice of his *Lectures on Religion and Morality*, in the *Monthly Review* (Vol. LXII, Jan.–Jne, 1780, 6, 106), found peculiar beauties, varied and striking excellencies, and many valuable observations therein.

[173] J. M. Robertson, op. cit., II, 758, 787.

[174] See R. V. Holt, op.cit., 287.

[175] Op.cit., Vol. 42 (1776), 272.

[176] *The Rise and Dissolution of the Infidel Societies in this Metropolis: Including, the Origin of Modern Deism and Atheism*, 25, 83, 90.

[177] David Bogue, *Essay on the Divine Authority of the New Testament*, 267–8.

[178] D. Williams, 'Incidents', 11, 11 dorse, 12–13; *Journal of a Visit to Paris*, ed. P. France, 59–61. Unfortunately Rousseau's reaction to verse sent by Thomas Day, unflatteringly described by Williams as of literary talent but insatiable ambition, was very different: 'But what is this Poem, dedicated to *Me*, without *My Permission*'. His scathing comments were duly reported and, predictably, severed relationships between Williams and Day – already strained by what the first-named considered counterproductive letters to the press.

[179] See E. Robinson, 'R. E. Raspe ...', *Annals of Science*, II (1955), 142–4. Incidentally, Williams remarks that numbers of 'those Persons, & several of my own Congregation, were Free-masons – but I was not; nor was I ever invited to become a Member of any of their Lodges' ('Incidents', 16).

[180] *Annual Biography*, 1818, 23–4.

[181] *Orpheus*, 36–7.

[182] Infra, Appendix II. The letter dated 17 July 1776 which was sent with Bentley to Rousseau is also lost, but a transcript survives in N.L.W.MS 15268C (copy of 'Incidents').

[183] No obvious evidence of Rosicrucian influence can be found in Williams.

[184] D. Williams, *Lectures on Education*, 1789, III, 298–304.

[185] *Journal des Sciences et des Beaux Arts*, 1 December 1777, cited in *Nouvelles Ecclésiastiques ou Mémoires*, 27 February 1778, 35–6.

[186] A letter to the *Morning Post*, 2 November 1776, described Williams as 'this bold and dangerous man'.

[187] J. W. von Archenholz, op.cit., I, 176–7.

[188] Infra, Chapter Six.

[189] D. Williams, *Lectures on Education*, III, 306.

[190] Abbé Grégoire, *Histoire des Sectes Religieuses*, I, 358–63. Grégoire errs in identifying Williams as former minister of a Dissenting church in Liverpool at which he first attempted a Socinian liturgy (though the wording of the source cited, *Public Characters of 1798*, 508, makes clear how this confusion with Bentley arose). He also likens Basedow's 'Philantropin' to Williams's cult and draws parallels with Frederick the Great's 'Pantheon'.

[191] A word which is almost impossible to translate; the allusion is to the 'decade-based' revision of the calendar during the dechristianisation era of the French Revolution: see J. H. Stewart, *Documentary Survey . . .*, 508–12.

[192] A. Mathiez, *La Théophilanthropie et le Culte Décadaire*, 8, 123, 392–5, 399, 708 – alas, he repeats the Cardigan birthplace error and, much worse, describes Williams as 'a former methodist minister'!

[193] A. Aulard, *La Séparation de l'Église et de l'État*, 147–8; *Le Culte de la Raison et le Culte de l'Être Suprème*, 210, 330, 345–7.

[194] Infra, 92–6 for his later, more extreme opinions.

[195] J. Walker, op.cit., 1–2, 4–5, 6–9, 16.

[196] J. Bogue, op.cit., 268.

[197] D. Williams, 'A Priest of Nature', *Welsh Review*, V, No. 1, 36–41.

[198] Ibid., loc.cit; W. Philip Williams, *Welsh Outlook*, 1926, 90; Gwyn A. Williams, *The Search for Beulah Land*, 17, 24.

[199] See C. M. Lombard, *Notes & Queries*, New Ser., CCIV (1959), 37–9.

[200] Iolo Morganwg, listing religious innovations (N.L.W., MS 13146 Llanover 59 (102)), placed 'The British Theists/Margaret Street Society' directly before 'Theophilanthropists of France'. Abraham Rees's *Cyclopaedia* (1819, XXXIX, 'Theophilanthropists') records acceptance of a connection.

Chapter Three

[1] *Orpheus*, 6(n. 4).

[2] Supra, 23–4.

[3] 'Incidents', 4.

[4] Op.cit., 1818, 25.

[5] *Treatise on Education*, 194–202.

[6] A wall-plaque records the some time residence of Tobias Smollett, and also the presence of a china-manufactory at its northern end from the 1740s to the 1780s – indeed for some time Bentley lived nearby.

[7] *Annual Biography*, loc.cit.; *Cambrian Register*, Vol. 3, 530–1; *Public Characters of 1798–9*, 509–10.

[8] D. Williams, *Treatise*, sub-title.

[9] Ibid., 202, 208.

[10] The portrait painter, whose subjects included Williams himself.

[11] N.L.W., MS 10336E (7).

[12] Westminster City Library, St Anne's Soho Baptisms Register, Vol. 3 (1768–1818), 28.

[13] Greater London Record Office, P74/LUK/164 (Micro. X26/12). Tantalisingly, for any presumption of the early death of her child, *Maria* Williams was buried at St Luke's on 18 *September* 1775.

[14] N.L.W., MS 10333E (13).

[15] N.L.W., MS 10336E (7).

[16] Op.cit., III, 194; W. Shakespeare, *King John*, Act III, Sc. IV, 11.93–8.

[17] Wedgwood MS, Keele University Library, 18555–25 (30/8/1774).

[18] D. Williams, *Lectures on Political Principles*, a.3.

[19] N.L.W., MS 10337E (52).

[20] *Cambrian Register*, Vol. 3, 531–2; H. Prosser (*Wales*, II, 1912, 568) suggests that his students included the Marquis of Camden's son.

[21] D. Williams, *Lectures on Education*, III, 112; J.-P. Brissot, *Memoires* I, (1754–1784), 389–90.

[22] *Critical Review*, Vol. 38, 211–15; *Monthly Review*, Vol. LI, Jly–Dec. 1774, 255.

[23] 'A.B.C.', in *Monthly Review*, as above, 406.

[24] *Critical Review*, Vol. 69 (1790), 489–96; *Monthly*, New Ser., Vol. I, 1790, 361–71; Vol. II, 1790, 30–38; see B. C. Nangle, *The Monthly Review. Second Series . . .*, 20–21, 226.

[25] *Lectures*, I, 59, 72.

[26] *Treatise*, 184.

[27] D. Williams, *Lectures*, I, 95.

[28] Ibid., I, 22, 130–1; II, 282–4, 289, 297; III, 250–1, 271, 284–5, 293–4.

[29] Infra, 83, 127, 150–1.

[30] *Treatise*, 1, 15.

[31] *Treatise*, 1–2; *Lectures*, I, 50–1, 201; II, 92, 288.

[32] D. Williams, *Treatise*, 64–5.

[33] Ibid., 69; in *A Treatise on Man, his Intellectual Faculties and his Education* (English translation, 1777), Helvetius declares that 'inequality in minds or understandings, is the effect of a known cause, and this cause is the difference of education', which 'makes us what we are' (Vol. I, 13, 92, 254; Vol. II, 395).

[34] D. Williams, *Treatise*, 70–4.

[35] D. Williams, *Lectures*, I, 44–5.

[36] Ibid., II, 228.

[37] *Treatise*, 35–9; see John Milton, *Of Education. To Master Samuel Hartlib*.

[38] *Treatise*, 41–3, 70, 91.

[39] N. Hans, *New Trends in Education in the Eighteenth Century*, 184.

[40] *Treatise*, 55; J. J. Rousseau, *Émile*, introd. P. D. Jimack, ix.

[41] *Lectures*, I, 84–5, 87; *Treatise*, 56. A. V. Judges, 'Educational Ideas, Practice and Institutions', *New C. M. H.*, Vol. VIII, 162, alludes to the element of 'anti-intellectualism' in Rousseau.

[42] D. Williams, *Lectures*, I, 120.

[43] Ibid., I, 129–30, 141, 145, 180.

[44] Ibid., III, 2–5.

[45] Ibid., II, 115–16. The comment that Rousseau had never been a parent is true only in the sense that he fostered out his several offspring.

[46] Ibid., III, 30, 42. Thus Jacques Pons, in *L'Éducation en Angleterre entre 1750 et 1800 . . .*, which discerns both qualities and shortcomings in Williams, overstates his case in identifying 'one of the rare disciples of Rousseau, who stayed faithful to the master throughout his life', and in claiming that his experimental group-work and the better parts of his *Treatise* were alike but imitations of *Émile* (op.cit., especially 42–3 and 71–3).

[47] D. Williams, *Lectures*, II, 24, 312, 316, 318–9; see J. E. Sadler, *J. A. Comenius and the Concept of Universal Education*, 29, 73, 108.

[48] J. A. Comenius, *Orbis Pictus* (English translation), 90.

[49] J. E. Sadler, Introduction to *Orbis Pictus* (facsimile edition), 20, 81.

[50] J. E. Sadler, *J. A. Comenius . . .*, 39, 257, 280; on Comenius see also G. H. Turnbull, *Hartlib, Dury and Comenius*.

[51] D. Williams, *Lectures*, II, 314.

[52] J. E. Sadler, Introduction to *Orbis Pictus*, 75.

[53] See G. W. Thomas, 'A Study of the Developments towards the Principles and Practice of Modern Education as shown in the Dissenting Academies in England', University of London M. A. Thesis, 1949.

[54] Supra, 4.

[55] Dr. Williams's Library, MS R.N.C.38.15.

[56] D. Williams, *Lectures*, I, 153–4; II, 2–3, 63, 155.

[57] Ibid., II, 296.

[58] Yet Pons (op.cit., 72), while admiring the patience of 'ces braves gens' who presumably sat through the fifty-four lectures, rightly observes that they constitute not so much a theoretical treatise as a series of reports on the author's educational experiments.

[59] D. Williams, *Lectures*, I, 52, 55, 62, 65, 74; *Treatise*, 95, 99–101.

[60] *Lectures*, I, 100–2; II, 121.

[61] Ibid., II, 286–7, 309, 316.

[62] Ibid., III, 55, 57.

[63] The translator of *Orbis Pictus* (97) deplored the fact that we 'do teach children, as we do Parrots, to speak they know not what'.

[64] D. Williams, *Treatise*, 11, 51, 121, 187; *Lectures*, I, 96–7; II, 312.

[65] D. Williams, *Treatise*, 242–3.

[66] Infra, 59.

[67] *Lectures*, I, 13, 80, 230; II, 62, 90, 158, 311. A chapter on 'Punishments' in Vol. III develops the theme that 'punishments having been the motives of action in modern states, they were adopted as instruments of education', and contends that 'in proportion to the wisdom or goodness of a law, sanctions lessen in number, magnitude and severity', citing Bacon's observation that 'states had been too busy with laws, and too remiss in education' (III, 84–92).

[68] *Treatise*, 25–6; *Lectures*, I, 131–2; II, 46. His dedication of Vol. II to the Duchess of Northumberland remarks that her daily and assiduous superintendence of her children evoked both respect and astonishment.

[69] *Lectures*, II, 63–4, 70–1, 74–5, 84, 137.

[70] Clearly, an allusion to rabies.

[71] *Lectures*, II, 292–3.

[72] Ibid., I, 232–3, 235; II, 141–3; III, 57, 60–2, 272–3.

[73] Ibid., I, 240–2, 245, 248, 260; III, 67.

[74] D. Williams, *Treatise*, 9–10; *Lectures*, I, 222; II, 266–7, 317.

[75] *Lectures*, I, 49–50, 132, 213–4. Comenius devoted a chapter of *The Great Didactic* to the proposition that 'A Man can most easily be formed in early youth, and cannot be formed properly except at this age' (209, 409). The opportunity of appropriate educational activity, once lost, is hard to recover; moral education, especially, depends on first impressions (see J. E. Sadler, op.cit., 197). John Locke, in *Some Thoughts Concerning Education*, urged that 'the little, or almost insensible, impressions on our tender infancies, have very important and lasting consequences', and that children should be handled as rational creatures (20, 36, 59).

[76] D. Williams, *Lectures*, I, 217; II, 72–3, 114.

[77] Again, as in Locke, reasoning 'such as is suited to the child's capacity and apprehension' (*Some Thoughts Concerning Education*, 65).

[78] D. Williams, *Lectures*, II, 154, 295–6, 303–5.

[79] Williams is at one with Helvetius in dismissing Rousseau's assertion that children '*are till ten or twelve years without judgment. Till that age therefore all education is useless*' (*Treatise on Man*, II, 31–2).

[80] D. Williams, *Lectures*, I, 122; II, 306–8.

[81] See W. Boyd, *Emile for Today*, 9, 18, 22, 38, 40–1; P. D. Jimack, op.cit., xiv–xvi.

[82] Possibly Bentley, on the occasion of his visit – supra, 47.

[83] *Lectures*, III, 1–3.

[84] *Treatise*, 112.

[85] Ibid., 116–21, 126, 135–6, 139, 140, 162, 171.

[86] Infra, 155–6 for the full significance of this.

[87] *Treatise*, 191, 193.

[88] *Lectures*, I, 83–4, 133.

[89] Ibid., III, 24, 29.

[90] See N. Sykes, *Church and State in England in the XVIIIth Century*, 334–5.

[91] D. Williams, *Lectures*, III, 31–2, 34–7.

[92] Ibid., III, 34–7.

[93] Ibid., III, 78.

[94] Ibid., III, 211–4.

[95] Supra, 58; *Treatise*, 49.

[96] *Treatise*, 242–3, 254–5.

[97] Thus Locke believed that 'there ought very early to be imprinted on his mind a true notion of God, as of the independent Supreme Being, Author and Maker of all things', avoiding 'being unseasonably forward to make him understand the incomprehensible nature of that infinite Being, his head ... filled with false, or perplexed with unintelligible notions of him'. Indeed 'it would be better, if men generally rested in such an idea of God, without being too curious in their notions about a Being, which all must acknowledge incomprehensible' and avoided 'making God like themselves'. Nonetheless, 'the Lord's prayer, the creed, and ten commandments, it is necessary he should learn perfectly by heart ... even before he can read' (*Some Thoughts Concerning Education*, 99–100, 114).

[98] D. Williams, *Lectures*, II, 46–7; III, 291, 297, 330.

[99] *Treatise*, 118.

[100] D. Williams, *Lectures*, I, 75–7.

[101] D. Williams, *Lectures*, II, 115, 190–2, 208, 211.

[102] *Information Gazette*, 11, reviewing a German research monograph of the previous year (still shelved in the Bodleian) on the educational reforms of 'Dr' Williams.

[103] N. Hans, *New Trends in Education in the Eighteenth Century*, 163, 165, 181, 209. Near-contemporary are C. J. Phillips, 'The Life and Work of David Williams', University of London, Ph.D. thesis, 1951, and G. W. Thomas, 'A Study of the Developments towards the Principles and Practice of Modern Education as shown in the Dissenting Academies in England' (106–116), University of London, M. A. Edn., thesis, 1949. W. A. C. Stewart, *Progressives and Radicals in English Education 1750–1970* (1972), 4, 23–31, 40, 66. W. A. C. Stewart and W. P. McCann, *The Educational Inheritors, Vol. I; 1750–1880* (1970) 35–6, 52.

[104] See J. W. Yolton, *John Locke and Education*, 16, 24–6, 37, 91.

[105] D. Williams, *Treatise*, 20–3; *Lectures*, II, 228.

[106] Supra, 59–60.

[107] In which, he notes, the infliction of rote-learning (including religious knowledge) enforced by punishment has scarred every feature of the mind, and whose demerits he states his future intention to record.

[108] D. Williams, *Lectures*, I, 24; II, 126–8.

[109] Infra, 229, n.6.

[110] Infra, 155–6.

Chapter Four

[1] As late as April, 1780, Thomas Day was to allude to 'the pernicious civil war': *Two Speeches by Thomas Day*, 10.

[2] In *Lectures on the Universal Principles and Duties of Religion and Morality*, 1779.

[3] *Monthly Review*, LIV, Jan–Jne 1776, 167–8; *Critical Review*, Vol. 41, 1776, 73; *London Magazine*, XLV, Feb. 1776, 102.

[4] The pamphlet's confused impact stands in marked contrast with the phenomenally successful *Royal Recollections on a Tour to Cheltenham*, 1788 (infra, 134–40), Williams's only other extant essay in this genre.

[5] D. Williams, *Morality of a Citizen*, 5–11.

[6] Ibid., 12–13.

[7] Ibid., 16–19; see Bernard Bailyn, *Ideological Origins of the American Revolution*, 103–4, for colonial fears of placemen, and 112–16 for fears of military force and the alleged parallel between the St George's Fields (1768) and Boston (1770) 'Massacres'.

[8] The Septennial Act was a focal point of radical attack, as tending to protect the independence of the Commons not from the Crown but from public opinion – see Betty Kemp, *King and Commons 1660–1832*, 4, 43.

[9] D. Williams, *Morality of a Citizen*, 21–3.

[10] Ibid., 24–5.

[11] Ibid., 27–8.

[12] See Robert E. Toohey, *Liberty and Empire. British Radical Solutions to the American Problem, 1774–1776*, 34.

[13] Its first page enunciates the analogy between the state and the human body which was to become increasingly characteristic of Williams's thought; F. Alengry, *Condorcet. Guide de la Révolution Française*, 5n. 1, describes him as 'a neglected pioneer of the *Organic Theory of Society*'. For a recent and perceptive critique of this aspect of the thought of David Williams, see Chapter V of J. A. W. Gunn's *Beyond Liberty and Property*.

[14] A crucial phrase, which touches the fundamental problem – see Bernard Bailyn, op.cit., 79.

[15] D. Williams, *Unanimity*, 8–10.

[16] Ibid., 2–7.

[17] Day's poem *The Desolation of America*, 1777, expressed liberal horror at enlistment of 'the fell Indian' among Britain's murderous allies.

[18] D. Williams, *Unanimity*, 10–15.

[19] The English edition of *The Constitution of England*, 1777, remarked on the mildness of the exercise of criminal justice (143).

[20] See Douglas Hay, *et al.*, *Albion's Fatal Tree*, 17–63, and, for a rather different slant, Jacob Viner in J. L. Clifford, *Man Versus Society in Eighteenth-Century Britain*, 38–9.

[21] D. Williams, *Unanimity*, 17–28. Priestley, in 1774, in *An Address to Protestant Dissenters*, 13–14, had forecast the ruin of the whole empire.

[22] See Colin Bonwick, *English Radicals and the American Revolution* (xv, xviii, 112) – which takes more note of Williams than any other treatment.

[23] Infra, 79.

[24] Printed in M. Beloff, ed., *The Debate on the American Revolution*, 94.

[25] I. R. Christie, *Crisis of Empire*, 85. Bonwick believes that Radicals were probably never more isolated than at the outbreak of war (op.cit., 84). See also P. Langford in *London and the Age of Reform*, ed. J. Stevenson, 74–5.

[26] See J. H. Plumb, *In the Light of History*, 75, 81.

[27] Others who used the same device of contrasting conflict with America with war with France included Charles James Fox – see John Derry, *English Politics and the American Revolution*, 159–61.

[28] I. Minis Hays, *Calendar of the Papers of Benjamin Franklin . . .*, Vol. II, p. 225. Nicholas Hans (*Proceedings of the American Philosophical Society*, Vol. 98, No. 6, pp. 411–15, 421–3) deals fully with such contacts.

[29] C. Bonwick, op.cit., 157.

[30] *Letters to a Young Prince*, 1790, 63.

[31] *Critical Review*, Vol. 45 (1778), 308–9; *Monthly*, LVIII, Jan–June, 1778, 313–14.

[32] J. W. Osborne, *John Cartwright*, 9, regarding his *American Independence: The Interest and Glory of Great Britain*, 1774.

[33] See John Brewer, *Party ideology and popular politics at the accession of George III*, 20, 215.

[34] See M. J. C. Vile, *Constitutionalism and the Separation of Powers*, 120, and John Derry, op.cit., 108.

[35] *Parliamentary History of England*, XVIII, Cols. 436–46, speech in debate on 16 March 1775.

[36] On these issues see M. Beloff, op.cit., 6; G. H. Guttridge, *English Whiggism and the American Revolution*, 61; M. J. C. Vile, op.cit., 181; and J. W. Gough, *Fundamental Law in English Constitutional History*, 3, 192–3.

[37] See W. B. Gwyn, *The Meaning of the Separation of Powers*, 118.

[38] R. E. Toohey, op.cit., xii. Ironically, but typically, Williams's name is not present in the membership of the club of 'Honest Whigs', which included Burgh, Priestley, Franklin, and his fellow-Welshman Richard Price (see D. O. Thomas, *The Honest Mind. The Thought and Work of Richard Price*, 142–3; Thomas, like Robbins, makes no reference to David Williams).

[39] *St James's Chronicle*, February 1–3, 1780. On the whole concept of Association see E. C. Black's magisterial work, *The Association; British Extraparliamentary Organization 1769–1793*.

[40] D. Williams, *Plan of Association*, 2–6; in fact 18 Geo III, c.60 did but remove two galling disabilities seldom enforced; see E. C. Black, 133.

[41] *Plan of Association*, 6–7; E. C. Black, 142–7.

[42] This identification of Methodism with intolerance gains depressing credence from some statements of John Wesley: see E. C. Black, op.cit., 157–8.

[43] D. Williams, *Plan of Association*, 9–13.

[44] Ibid., 13–16.

[45] Ibid., 17–20.

[46] Ibid., 18–24.

[47] In a notable speech in the Lords, reported in the *Morning Chronicle* for 5 June, Lord Shelburne, after declaring that 'the police at Westminster was an imperfect, inadequate, and wretched system', and pointing to the virtues as well as the notorious dangers of 'the Police of France', went on to urge: 'Let the appointment of Magistrates be elective; let the people have a power to vote for them, and chuse them by their suffrages . . . and the end of such a police would be most fully answered.' He commended also the existing arrangements in the City of London for policing in Wards & Parishes.

[48] *Plan of Association*, 25–30.

[49] Ibid., 28–33; N.L.W., MS 10337E (50).

[50] *Plan of Association*, 35–6.

[51] Ibid., 43–5.

[52] See W. R. D. Jones, *The Tudor Commonwealth 1529–1559*, 13–17.

[53] D. Williams, *Plan of Association*, 44–55; its continuance as a touch-stone in terms of political ideology is symbolized in the re-printing no fewer than eight times in the eighteenth century of editions (in whole or part) of John Trenchard's *History of Standing Armies in England*, including one in 1780 – see Lois G. Schwoerer, '*No Standing Armies!*', 188–200; J. G. A. Pocock, *Politics, Language and Time*, 120–1; and W. B. Gwyn, *The Meaning of the Separation of Powers*, 84–5.

[54] *Plan of Association*, 55–9.

[55] E. C. Black (*The Association*, 160) points out that effective police systems were traditionally equated with continental, particularly French, despotism, so that riot was the price paid for freedom.

[56] *Plan of Association*, 61–7.

[57] *The Last Journals of Horace Walpole*, ed. A. Francis Steuart, II, 306–12; *Georgiana*, ed. Bessborough, 47; she also deplored governmental irresolution.

[58] Sir W. N. Wraxall, *Historical Memoirs of My Own Time*, I, 320–36.

[59] See E. C. Black, op.cit., 131–2 and J. W. Osborne, *John Cartwright*, 27.

[60] See C. Reith, *The Police Idea . . . in the Eighteenth Century and After*, 82–5, although he does not mention David Williams's pamphlet.

[61] William Jones, op.cit., 2nd edn., 8–10, 17, 34–5, 37–8, 56–7.

[62] Thomas Morris, *General View*, 15–16 (Jones's *Inquiry* received the accolade of the Society for Constitutional Information: P.R.O., T.S. 11/1133 (7392) 'Resolutions and Orders', I, 83, March 1782); *Monthly Review*, LXIII, Jly–Dec. 1780, 143; *Critical Review*, Vol. 50, 1780, 65.

[63] D. Williams, 'Incidents', 17 dorse; *Letters on Political Liberty*, 5–6.

[64] De Lolme had already written on the significance of 'the principles of politics' as a 'Science': *The Constitution of England*, 390–1 (n.(a)).

[65] *Letters on Political Liberty*, 2, 4–5, 11, 72, 76.

[66] Cartwright's *Take Your Choice!*, 1776, had depicted a House of Commons of 'idle school-boys, insignificant cox-combs . . . and toad-eaters, profligates, gamblers, bankrupts, . . . public plunderers . . .', p. x.

[67] *Letters on Political Liberty*, 75, 85.

[68] Ibid., 2–3, 13, 27–9. His estimate of De Lolme was not shared by Bentham, who remarked in his *Fragment on Government*, 1776, (p. 81) that others may have 'copied, but Mr de Lolme has thought'. Quite certainly De Lolme displays many penetrating insights – infra, n.81 & n.83, and 217, n.93, n.104 & n.107 – often indeed coinciding with those of Williams!

[69] D. Williams, *Letters on Political Liberty*, 16–20.

[70] Catharine Macaulay, *Observations on a Pamphlet, Entitled, Thoughts on the Cause of the Present Discontents*, 1770, 10.

[71] Obadiah Hulme, *Historical Essay on the English Constitution*, 1771, 140–2, 151–2. His contention that the abandonment of the Saxon practice of annual parliaments and the introduction of a landed qualification for membership had produced 'a down right rank aristocracy, of the rich in land' (125–6), is in accord with a modern assessment that after the legislation of 1711 'there was a sharp decline in the proportion of people who had even a formal share in the political life of the nation' (J. Cannon, *Parliamentary Reform 1640–1832*, 36). James Burgh's *Political Disquisitions*, 1774, expressed similar views (I, v).

[72] Richard Watson, in his sermon *The Principles of the Revolution Vindicated*, 1776 (p. 7).

[73] J. L. De Lolme, *The Constitution of England*, 60, 297.

[74] D. Williams, *Letters on Political Liberty*, 9, 48.

[75] Ibid., 8.

[76] See the detailed analysis of these themes in W. B. Gwyn, *The Meaning of the Separation of Powers*; J. W. Gough, *Fundamental Law in English Constitutional History*; and M. J. C. Vile, *Constitutionalism and the Separation of Powers*.

[77] See W. B. Gwyn, 91–5, and M. J. C. Vile, 72–5.

[78] Henry St John, Viscount Bolingbroke, *Remarks on the History of England*, second edition (1747), 82–4.

[79] Obadiah Hulme, op.cit., 112.

[80] D. Williams, *Letters on Political Liberty*, 7, particularly on Montesquieu.

[81] Ibid., 7–8, 10, 48–9. Priestley's *Essay on the First Principles of Government; and on the nature of Political, Civil, and Religious Liberty*, in 1768, itself a fairly impressive attempt at definition (12–13) concurs that *political* is the chief safeguard of *civil* liberty (54ff.). De Lolme observed, perceptively, that 'to give one's suffrage is not liberty itself, but only a means of procuring it . . . which may degenerate into mere form' in face of 'the silent, powerful, and ever active conspiracy of those who govern' (196–203).

[82] Watson (op.cit. 11) expressed a Ponet-like right of the people 'to lop off the rotten gangrened members, and to purge the corruptions of the body politic'.

[83] Again cf. De Lolme, 'reciprocal actions and re-actions produce the freedom of the Constitution' (150).

[84] *Letters on Political Liberty*, 9–10.

[85] Ibid., 73–6, 81–2.

[86] Ibid., 20–23. Thus 'the reluctant revolutionaries of 1689 became the complacent conservatives of 1750' (G. H. Guttridge, *English Whiggism and the American Revolution*, 10–11).

[87] *Letters*, 24–7, 29. On the whole vexed question of the intentions of George III and the 'myth of the double cabinet' see I. R. Christie, *Myth and Reality in Late-Eighteenth-Century British Politics*, 17, 27–54; and H. Butterfield, *George III and the Historians*, 193–299.

[88] *Letters*, 13, 29–30.

[89] Ibid., 32–3. In the same year, in his *Scheme for the Coalition of Parties*, Soame Jenyns (whose drily humorous realism is often reminiscent of Williams although his ultimate conclusions are very different) wrote that 'parties I see many, but I cannot discern one principle amongst them . . . They have all been ready to support government, whenever they have enjoyed the administration of it.' He suggests not annual parliaments but an annual administrative lottery! (7–8).

[90] Coming close to the cynical view that, in terms of public opinion, the only mistake of George III was to lose the war!

[91] D. Williams, *Letters on Political Liberty*, 43–6.

[92] Ibid., 34–5.

[93] Much of this again resembles De Lolme's contention that the search for liberty in face of the 'conspiracy of those who govern requires a degree of knowledge, and a spirit of perseverance, which are not to be expected from the multitude' (op.cit., 203–4, see also 208–9).

[94] As in Cartwright's hope for a '*grand national association*'.

[95] D. Williams, *Letters on Political Liberty*, 35–8.

[96] William Jones, *Speech on the Nomination of Candidates to represent the County of Middlesex*, 1780, 55.

[97] Horace Walpole, *Last Journals*, II, 332.

[98] D. Williams, *Letters*, 38–9.

[99] See Dame Lucy Sutherland. 'The City of London in Eighteenth-Century Politics', and 'The City of London and the Opposition to Government, 1768–74'; also John Stevenson, Introduction to *London in the Age of Reform*. For the general justice of Williams's analysis see I. R. Christie, *Wilkes, Wyvill and Reform*, 72–115, and E. C. Black, *The Association*, 32–82.

[100] D. Williams, *Letters on Political Liberty*, 24–5.

[101] Ibid., 47, 73, 76.

[102] James Mackintosh, in his *Vindiciae Gallicae*, 1791, was to make a fairly obvious allusion: 'it has been well remarked, that a multitude, if it was composed of *Newtons*, must be a mob' (222–3).

[103] D. Williams, *Letters*, 49–52, 69–70.

[104] Even the radical Catharine Macaulay had conceded that 'democratical power can never be preserved from anarchy without representation' (*Observations on a Pamphlet*, 20). De Lolme observed shrewdly that 'a *representative* Constitution places the remedy in the hands of those who feel the disorder; but a *popular* Constitution places the remedy in the hands of those who cause it' (op.cit., 226, see also 204).

[105] In his *Disquisitions on Several Subjects*, which also appeared in 1782, Soame Jenyns derides 'a form of government, which we have heard sometimes recommended as the most perfect, in which all are governed by all' as meaning in effect 'no government at all' (147–8).

[106] D. Williams, *Letters on Political Liberty*, 53–7.

[107] Yet again, one cannot escape the striking resemblance to De Lolme: 'How then shall the People … resist the phalanx of those who have engrossed to themselves all the power, in the State? … By using the same weapons as they do, the same order, the same kind of discipline' (op.cit., 211).

[108] D. Williams, *Letters*, 64–9.

[109] Cf. Jebb: 'A people is free, when such constitutional checks exist, as render it impracticable for ministers to betray the public cause', *Works*, II, 460.

[110] D. Williams, *Letters on Political Liberty*, 60–1, 69–71.

[111] Ibid., 61–3, 66–7; much of this is reminiscent of the 'kite-flying' noticed above, 73–4.

[112] Ibid., 58–60; James Burgh had suggested that the introduction of annual parliaments (with subsequent exclusion of two-thirds of membership for three years by rotation) would ensure contests to avoid rather than bribery to secure election (*Political Disquisitions*, I, 129–30); John Jebb, *Address to the Freeholders of Middlesex*, 1779, had declared the representative the proxy of the known will of his electors (*Works*, II, 463n.). By a supreme irony, James Martin, to whom the *Letters* were dedicated, was to vote *against* the repeal of the Test and Corporation Acts in March, 1790, in accordance with the supposed wishes of his constituents.

[113] Cartwright deemed all evils 'light and trivial in comparison of *the one great evil of a long parliament*' (*Take Your Choice!*, xxii), while Macaulay considered septennial parliaments a violation of constitutional principles (*Observations on a Pamphlet …*, 11).

[114] D. Williams, *Letters on Political Liberty*, 77–8.

[115] Supra, 54; infra, 127, 150–1.

[116] See J. G. A. Pocock, *Politics, Language and Time*, 113. Burgh's *Political Disquisitions* cited 'the commonly received doctrine, that servants and those who receive alms, have no right to vote for members of parliament', while William Jones, in *The Principles of Government: A Dialogue between a Scholar and a Peasant*, 1782, made the latter ready to enfranchise 'all who were not upon the parish' (6). Carl B. Cone (*The English Jacobins*, 8–14) has pointed to social discrimination in Richard Price's own Newington Green congregation, where the members' domestic servants 'sat in the back pews. They were the governed; they had no voice in the business affairs of the meeting.' J. Jean Hecht, in *The Domestic Servant Class in Eighteenth-Century England* (1, 77–80, 178) concurs that this, one of the largest occupational groups, was considered valueless to the community – an attitude that was hardened by a persistent tendency for 'servants to assert themselves … in an aggressive fashion'. W. A. Speck

[117] (*Stability and Strife, England 1714–1760*, 57) suggests that in parts of London they made up over twenty per cent of the population. The potential for what one can only term class-mischief envisaged by their betters was to receive extreme expression in a later work of Williams himself: infra, 150–1.

[117] D. Williams, *Letters on Political Liberty*, 79–84.

[118] Granville Sharp, in *The Claims of the People of England*, also published in 1782, observed that 'the representation of many Boroughs is now commonly esteemed a mere pecuniary property' (13).

[119] D. Williams, *Letters* 85.

[120] Second edition (1784), 100 ff.

[121] J. W. Osborne, *John Cartwright*, 23.

[122] See P. A. Brown, *The French Revolution in English History*, 13.

[123] P.R.O., T.S. 11/1133 (7392), 'Resolutions and Orders ...', I, 81, 85, 88.

[124] Op.cit., Vol. 53, (1782), 389.

[125] Op.cit., LXVI, Jan–June 1782, 551–5; B. C. Nangle, *The Monthly Review. First Series, 1749–1789*, 22, 146.

[126] M. Dawes, *The Nature and Extent of Supreme Power*, 1783 (10–11); addressed to Williams and also to the S.C.I. – whose members' 'more laudable employ is to provide for their subsistence', Nature having 'bestowed only on a few an understanding fit for complicated researches' in government! (i–iii).

[127] *Journal Encyclopédique ou Universel*, Bouillon, VIII, i, 27–35; Gabriel Bonno (*La Constitution Britannique devant l'opinion française ...*, 150) cites the review in the context of allegedly diminished prestige of the British Constitution in French eyes – which now perceived a transatlantic emigration of earlier liberties.

[128] D. Williams, 'Incidents', 17–18; for a less complimentary portrait of Brissot see R. C. Darnton, in *Journal of Modern History*, No. 3 (1968), 301–27.

[129] *Journal du Licée de Londres*, Février 1784, 313–14.

[130] See below, 96–100.

[131] J.-P. Brissot, *Mémoires (1754–1793)*, ed. Cl. Perroud, I, 367–8; see also *Journal*, 317-18.

[132] *Mémoires*, I, 389–90.

[133] *Journal*, 334.

[134] J.-P. Brissot, *Correspondence et Papiers*, ed. Cl. Perroud, 77.

[135] Infra, 114.

[136] Dated as at Liège, 1783–89.

[137] *Journal*, 318–333.

[138] *Mémoires*, II, 7–8; see also *The Life of J. P. Brissot* 'Written by Himself', English transln., London, 1794, 40–44.

[139] Thus the Preface likens Ministers of the Crown to 'a band of rogues known as *sleepers*, who give travellers a narcotic powder in order to rob them more easily'! Or again, 'In France government is not an art, still less a science: no one thinks about it' (6). Page three of the second edition, envisaging an awakening of the people in order to reclaim their rights, remarks in note (b) that 'we are promised this event for the year 1789'.

[140] *The Life of J.-P. Brissot*, 44–5; oddly, Brissot had spent a few days in an English debtors' prison prior to return to France (*Mémoires*, I, 391–2).

[141] D. Williams, *Lessons to a Young Prince*, 1790/1, 78. No independent confirmation has been found, but French sources (infra, 122) place Williams in the salon of the Marquise de Condorcet several years before his visit of 1792–93.

[142] See also above, 20 and 205, n.138, 71.

Chapter Five

[1] J.-P. Brissot, *Correspondance et Papiers*, 140–1; the same letter thanks Williams for his translation of the prospectus of a 'Société Gallo-Americaine' in which Brissot was involved.

[2] A literal translation would be *dragging* gait, which raises questions in the context of some remarks of Williams himself about his health at this time – infra, 89.

[3] See Frontispiece.

[4] F. A. Wendeborn, *Der Zustand des Staats, der Religion, der Gelehrsamkeit und der Kunst in Grosbritanien gegen das Ende des achtzehnten Jahrhunderts*, Berlin, 1785, Vol. 3, 367–9, 372–3; translation by courtesy of Robert James.

[5] Perhaps an allusion to his participation in the translation of Voltaire?

[6] D. Williams, *Lectures on Education*, II, 137, 154; III, 19, 306; *Lectures on Political Principles*, 247; a private letter in February 1789 refers to 'a series of engagements which have distressed me, quite laid me up' (J. Nichols, *Illustrations of the Literary History of the Eighteenth Century*, IV, 847).

[7] The Park Street address (or addresses) variously described as 'Grosvenor Square' and 'Upper Grosvenor Street corner'.

[8] N. L. W. MS 10337E, 37–9; infra, 160.

[9] *The Town and Country Magazine or Universal Repository*, Supplement for 1778, 675–8.

[10] See W. Phelps, *History of Somerset*, Vol. 2, 137–8; *D.N.B.*, I, 1382; Venn, *Alumni Cantabrigiensis*, 2. 1752–1900, Vol. I, A–C, 199; S. H. Cassan, *Lives of the Bishops of Bath and Wells*, 179.

[11] P.R.O., Exch. Decrees, E. 126.34 (Trinity Term, 1793), 1096; the entry in J. Foster, *Alumni Oxoniensis*, 1715–1886, III, 922, relating to Thomas Martyn of Awliscombe, Devon, seems to fit. The web of personal and career relationships is woven closer by the fact that Frances's great-grandfather, Samuel Squire (whose *Enquiry into the Foundation of the English Constitution*, 1753, was commended by Williams) had been an earlier incumbent of St Anne's. Infra, Appendix III.

[12] Infra, 159.

[13] N.L.W. MS 10337E, 37–9.

[14] N.L.W. MS 10336E (11). Perhaps significantly, a French source (*Lettres de Madame Roland*, II, 204) mentions Williams in 1790 as 'publicly advocating divorce'.

[15] Supra, Chapter Two.

[16] D. Williams, *Lectures on Education*, III, 286–91, 297, 311, 314, 316, 319–20.

[17] Ibid., III, 320–5.

[18] Ibid., 339. The statement that 'the apprehensions of men in religion are so low, that they conceive their duty in religion to consist in atonements ... by which they may be skreened from the displeasure of God' (340) is uneasily reminiscent of the Calvinist injunction that 'the Christian man should aspire to a loftier goal than the salvation of his soul'!

[19] Thomas Paine was to express a similar token of respect for this particular adversary: *Rights of Man*, Part II, 1792, 253.

[20] D. Williams, *Apology*, 1–6.

[21] Ibid., 8, 92, 156.

[22] Ibid., 89–91, 101.

[23] Ibid., 115.

[24] Ibid., 143–4.

[25] Ibid., 145–7.

[26] Ibid., 153–5.

[27] See W. R. D. Jones, *The Tudor Commonwealth 1529–1559*, 67–71, 220–1.

[28] D. Williams, *Apology*, 158–9.

[29] Supra, 29; see also C. Vereker, *Eighteenth-Century Optimism*, 53–4, 60, 64, 67.

[30] D. Williams, *Apology*, 160–6.

[31] Cf. the cynical remark of Frederick the Great that religion attached to Heaven an idea of equality which prevented the rich man from being massacred by the poor.

[32] D. Williams, *Apology*, 171–3.

[33] Ibid., 177, 179–81.

[34] Ibid., 182–5, 195.

[35] Ibid., 186–7.

[36] Ibid., 196–7.

[37] A thought-provoking phrase!

[38] D. Williams, *Apology*, 200–2. The presence among his papers of recipes, some herbal, for curatives of sundry ailments suggests a literal interpretation of this remark! (N.L.W., MS 10338E (7, 23, 51, *et al.*))

[39] *Lectures on Education*, III, 321.

[40] See D. O. Thomas, *The Honest Mind* ..., 25.

[41] *Monthly Review*, III, Sept.–Dec., 1790, 353; *Critical Review*, Vol. 67(1789), 477.

[42] Anon. ('Vericolus'), op.cit., 1, 11, 24, 84, 133.

[43] By Peter France (ed. *Incidents ...*), who observes that very little now seems to separate Williams from such atheists as Holbach (113).

[44] See T. Morris, *A General View ...*, 18, and Brissot, supra, 85.

[45] Edward Smith's *Life of Sir Joseph Banks* (recipient of one of the many side-thrusts directed at erstwhile acquaintances of Williams) stretches a comment by Thomas Morris into a 'flat confession' of this charge (180).

[46] Morris's *General View ...* (18) discerns a deliberate technique.

[47] As perusal of John Wardroper's *Kings, Lords and Wicked Libellers* will amply confirm!

[48] D. Williams, *Royal Recollections*, 3, 27–8, 39–40, 53, 63–4, 103. I. Macalpine and R. Hunter, *George III and the Mad-Business*, 11, and J. Brooke, *King George III*, 285, confirm this picture of familiar talks with common people. The *Morning Post* for 25 April 1780 had parodied Dunning's Motion: 'Resolved – That the Royal Family has increased, is increasing, and ought to be diminished'.

[49] In view of the Prince's all too well known characteristics it is difficult not to suspect a tongue in cheek beneath this obsequious tugging of the forelock!

[50] D. Williams, *Royal Recollections*, 15–16, 24, 26, 102. See J. Wardroper, op.cit., 117.

[51] *Royal Recollections*, 5, 11, 92.

[52] See J. Ehrman, *The Younger Pitt. The Years of Acclaim*, 616–7.

[53] *Royal Recollections*, 10, 37–8.

[54] Ibid., 67–9.

[55] The assertion is true: see N. Sykes, *Church and State in England in the XVIIIth Century*, 375–6.

[56] A notion which surfaced again in very different circumstances when Williams acted as 'consultant' to the Girondins: infra, 130–1.

[57] *Royal Recollections*, 14, 25–7, 29–31, 68.

[58] Ibid., 29–30.

[59] The recurrent phrase (50, 100, 106) alludes to a remark of Martin himself, wittily turned against him (for he combined eccentricity with boring delivery) by Lord North in a debate in December 1783: see Namier and Brooke, *The History of Parliament. The House of Commons 1754–1790*, III, 113–4.

[60] D. Williams, *Royal Recollections*, 107.

[61] Ibid., 7, 55.

[62] Ibid., 88–9; both the choice of targets and the nature of very many of these 'hits' are uneasily reminiscent of *Orpheus*!

[63] *Royal Recollections*, 54–6, 89.

[64] Ibid., 76–8, 91; infra, 155–6.

[65] See J. Ehrman, op.cit., 671, n.1; Loren Reid, *Charles James Fox*, Chapter 15; John Cannon, *The Fox-North Coalition*, 208–19. After an epic poll of forty days Fox had taken second place in a double-seat constituency – expenditure of over £9,000 having failed to keep him out.

[66] *Royal Recollections*, 38, 47–8, 78–80.

[67] *Georgiana*, ed. the Earl of Bessborough, 4, 249. John Wardroper gives a highly entertaining picture of both 1784 and 1788 elections as seen in contemporary caricature and verse: cartoonists depicted how 'a fox ousts the Duchess of Devonshire's baby' and 'The Devonshire Minuet, danced to Ancient British Music' (with near-explicit slogans); other prints, now lost, portrayed Georgiana in 'a variety of canvassing positions' (Wardroper, op.cit., prints 15, 16; pp. 102–3; see also, anon., *History of the Westminster Election, 1784*, 254).

[68] See Loren Reid, loc.cit.; J. Wardroper, 22 (prints 15,16), 100–7, 118 (print 22); J. Ehrman, 217–8.

[69] Hood was an Admiral!

[70] D. Williams, *Royal Recollections*, 62, 96–7.

[71] Wardroper, 100, 118–22; Reid, 200; Ehrman, 218.

[72] Bessborough, 4; Wardroper, 102–3, 118; Reid, 202–3; Ehrman, 218.

[73] *Royal Recollections*, 49, 93–4.

[74] *Critical Review*, Vol. 66 (1788), 343; *Monthly Review*, LXXIX, Jly–Dec., 1788, 468.

[75] *Analytical Review*, II, Sept–Dec., 1788, 354.

[76] See I. Macalpine and R. Hunter, *George III and the Mad-Business*, vii, xii, xv, 3–7, 45; J. Brooke, *King George III*, 322–3. For a very full analysis of the Regency Crisis see John W. Derry, *The Regency Crisis and the Whigs 1788–9.*

[77] Its author was J. L. de Lolme.

[78] Peter France, ed. *Incidents . . .*, 111.

[79] Arguably, imperfect in a double sense: that which was usual with Williams (its unrepresentative nature), but now also in that a fully competent Parliament includes a participant *King*.

[80] D. Williams, *Constitutional Doubts*, title-page, 1–2.

[81] Ibid., 29–30.

[82] Fox was abroad when the crisis broke, was late in hearing the news, and did not get back to London until 24 November. Thereafter his overstatement of his case was such as to cause the Duchess of Devonshire later to look back to 'that beginning of all negligence and want of *ensemble* which together with the indulgence of imprudent language has destroy'd the importance of the opposition' (W. Sichel, *Sheridan*, II, Appendix III, 'Georgiana, Duchess of Devonshire's Diary', 400). See also J. W. Derry, op.cit., passim; J. Ehrman, op.cit., Chapter XX; L. Reid, op.cit., Chapter 18.

[83] Which he describes as having first exposed the absurdity of petitioning an imperfect body to reform

itself, and for the French translation of which he claims considerable circulation and influence: *Constitutional Doubts*, 2.

84 *Constitutional Doubts*, 2–3, 14–15.

85 Ibid., 3–5.

86 An ingenious distinction, by which much depended on both diagnosis and prognosis of the royal illness. Thus the anonymous author (De Lolme) of *The Present National Embarrassment Considered* deplored any inference that 'the weighty national concern is, in short, to be decided by *the oaths* of Medical Gentlemen' and the government of the nation, already removed from St James's to Westminster, to be finally located in the College of Physicians! (65). (Re-issued as *Observations upon the late National Embarrassment.*)

87 D. Williams, *Constitutional Doubts*, 5–6.

88 A phrase reminiscent of John Almon's *Address to the Interior Cabinet*, 1782.

89 A gibe so common among Pitt's detractors that Wardroper (op.cit.) devotes a chapter (96–110) to 'The Virgin Minister'. Even Paine's *Rights of Man* (III, 241) refers to 'what may be called a maiden character in politics'.

90 *Constitutional Doubts*, 11–13.

91 Ibid., 17–21.

92 Ibid., 23–6. The Prince had already told the Duchess of Devonshire that he would refuse any *limited* Regency (W. Sichel, *Sheridan*, II, Appdx III, 'Diary', 411).

93 An anonymous *Dialogue on the Regency*, 1788, deplored an attempt 'to appoint a phantom, a new unheard-of puppet', suspected Pitt of wanting to be Regent himself, and pointed to the constitutional danger of legislative usurpation of executive power (11–15). De Lolme's *Observations upon the late National Embarrassment*, 1789, stated roundly that ministerial efforts 'to assume the authorities of the Crown to themselves' were unconstitutional (76–7).

94 D. Williams, *Constitutional Doubts*, 27–30.

95 De Lolme, 70–77; *Monthly Review*, LXXIX, Jly–Dec., 1788, 552 – though it also saw what underlay 'the moderate shew of political scepticism'!

96 T. Paine, *Rights of Man*, I, 99–100.

97 A title which internal evidence suggests is accurate: a footnote explains a reference to 'civil war' by that lecture's first having been delivered during the American hostilities (113, n.), while several references to France are clearly much closer in composition to the Preface dated 30 May 1789 (a7).

98 D. Williams, *Political Principles*, a5.

99 Ibid., a5-a6 dorse.

100 Ibid., 21, 23, 38, 94, 101, 108, 264–8.

101 Ibid., 31, 144.

102 Ibid., 12–14, 96.

103 Ibid., 203–5.

104 Ibid., 7, 14.

105 Ibid., 10–11, 20, 25, 31.

106 Ibid., 42, 142–5, 227.

107 Ibid., 40–6. This passage may go some way to explain an absence of enthusiasm for any project of general public education which is disappointing to those who would see him as a radical socio-political reformer. To David Williams education as a reforming principle derives from the gradual and spontaneous development of natural forces of self- and mutual-improvement within society; superimposed from above by any governmental agency, it represents an inhibiting rather than a liberating force.

108 Ibid., 96–7.

109 Ibid., 134, 169–70.

110 Ibid., 146–7, 164–6, 173–5; yet occasionally the concept of the reforming monarch surfaces, as in the question: 'Is not the peasantry of France less oppressed, better fed, and happier, as the power of the nobility yields to that of the crown?'

111 Ibid., 164, 172, 275.

112 Ibid., 141.

113 Ibid., 149, 168–9, 181, 191–3, 202: in particular, he points to the gross absurdity of submitting the legislature to executive direction, as in the royal power of dissolution; modern commentators concur as to the increase in the later decades of the century of the weapon of timing the dissolution of Parliament to ministerial advantage.

114 Ibid., 36, 81–2, 131.

115 Ibid., 133–5.

116 Ibid., 135–9. Williams later suggests a possible substitution of *constitutional* for political liberty, and

also urges the danger to the 'judicious foundations' of civil, political/constitutional liberty of any governmental exercise of a 'dispensing power' (234–6). Cartwright endorsed these distinctions made by a 'very able writer . . . whose work I earnestly recommend' (*Letter . . . to a Friend at Boston . . .* (1793), 25–30), but was later (in *An Appeal, Civil and Military . . .* (1799), 16 & n.) to prefer the term '*legal protection*' to '*civil liberty*'.

[117] The assertion that 'political bodies, to have one soul, one spirit, one interest; should have their members and parts united vitally; and not by such feeble bondages as contracts and treaties' precedes a prophetic forecast that 'this truth will be exemplified in the consequences of political accommodations with Ireland': *Political Principles*, 114.

[118] Ibid., 156–8; oddly, Rousseau's name does not occur in this context.

[119] Ibid., 132, 147, 170–1, 226. This argument, a commonplace in such contemporaries as Price or Watson, goes right back to Ponet's assertion in his *Short Treatise of politike power*, 1556, that 'all laws do agree, that men may revoke their proxies and letters of Attorney' (D.vi and G.i.b–G.vi.b).

[120] *Political Principles*, 228.

[121] Ibid., 148–153.

[122] Ibid., 117–8, 153; Montesquieu's exclusion of 'such as are in so mean a situation, as to be deemed to have no will of their own' is dismissed with savage contempt – unless pertaining to servile courtiers or priesthood!

[123] Ibid., 154–5.

[124] Ibid., 158–9 & n.; supra, 83–4.

[125] Ibid., 36–7, 95, 140; supra, 81 for the army analogy.

[126] Ibid., 189, 195, 213, 216.

[127] Ibid., 221–5. Paine, in 1791, was to observe that 'there is in all European countries a large class of people of that description, which in England is called the "*mob*". Of this class were those who committed the burnings and devastations in London in 1780, and of this class were those who carried the heads upon spikes in Paris' (*Rights of Man*, I, 22).

[128] A.S.P. Woodhouse, ed., *Puritanism and Liberty*, 71.

[129] W. Ogilvie's *Essay on the Right of Property in Land*, in 1781, had commended 'a progressive Agrarian Law' to correct abuses in land-holding and asserted that no individual had a right 'to any more than an equal share of the soil of his country' (12–13, 141–3). This 'wild imagination' was that of a university professor! The 'loi agraire' was to be a recurrent bugaboo during the French Revolution.

[130] *Political Principles*, 60–3.

[131] Ibid., 64–8.

[132] Ibid., 84–5.

[133] Ibid., 250. In fact, this general idea was current among several thinkers – including Godwin and Condorcet (infra, 147) – well before the first draft of Malthus' *Essay on the Principle of Population* appeared in 1798. T. H. Hollingsworth points out that its distinctive contribution rests in the addition of the principle of 'geometric and arithmetic progressions' (see his 1973 edition of the *full* version which first appeared in 1803, Preface, ix–x, xviii–xix; I, 1, 8, 10; III, 4.17).

[134] Infra, 232, n.108.

[135] *Political Principles*, 246, 254–5, 258.

[136] *Analytical Review*, V, Sept.–Dec., 1789, 310–3; *Critical Review*, Vol. 70, 1790, 360–4; *Monthly Review*, II, May–Aug., 1790, 394–8 – all a very far cry from the encomium of Thomas Morris, *General View*, 17–18.

[137] Peter France (ed., '*Incidents*', 117) suggests some similarities between the work and Godwin's *Political Justice*, and indeed Godwin's diary records that during the genesis of that book, in 1792, he met David Williams, Mackintosh, and others in 'occasional meetings, in which the principles of my work were discussed' (C. Kegan Paul, *William Godwin: His Friends and Contemporaries*, I, 71).

[138] *Political Principles*, 274–5; infra, 115.

[139] An allusion to Necker's recall in August of 1788. Indeed, Williams goes on to ask: 'in what essential quality of a real statesmen, has Mr. Necker the advantage of Dr. Adam Smith?' (277).

[140] *Political Principles*, 277.

[141] *Lessons to a Young Prince*, title-page.

[142] Ibid., iv; a little later he cannot resist the gibe that 'I know your Royal Highness is not remarkable for long or patient attention' (10).

[143] The Sinking Fund Act of 1786 and the calculations and advice of Richard Price therewith associated were stock targets for Williams.

[144] *Lessons to a Young Prince*, 3–5.

[145] Ibid.; his attribution of the actual notions of the coalition and the India Bill to Burke, and of the hereditary regency to Wedderburn are in part confirmed by recent research – see J. W. Derry, *The Regency Crisis*, 52, 76–7.

[146] *Lessons to a Young Prince*, 9, 11, 13.

[147] *Thraliana*, ed. K. C. Balderstone, 724–5; the Prologue to Greatheed's play was written by one identified, tantalisingly, as 'the Rev Mr Williams'.

[148] *Lessons to a Young Prince*, 17–21.

[149] Ibid., 22: Rousseau's *Social Contract* propounds an association 'in which each, while uniting himself with all, may still obey himself alone, and remain as free as before' (14).

[150] *Lessons to a Young Prince*, 22–4. Again, see Rousseau (as yet not mentioned in this work), *Social Contract*, 22, 25–8, 94.

[151] *Lessons to a Young Prince*, 25–34. If this last reference was to Pitt's reforms of 1787 it was unkind, for the measures won almost universal approval even from the minister's opponents – see J. Ehrman, op.cit., 271–3.

[152] *Lessons to a Young Prince*, 34–5. On the extent of press subsidies, by government and opposition, in the late eighteenth century, see A. Aspinall, *Politics and the Press c. 1780–1850*, especially Chapter III. David Williams was later to conquer his own aversion to such subsidies: infra, 141.

[153] *Lessons to a Young Prince*, 37.

[154] Ibid., 42–3 and Plate I. Such euphoria does not blind Williams to the two endemic diseases in Alfred's society: 'the superstitious dominion of ecclesiastics, and the slavery of the peasants' who are shown by a dotted circle outside the body politic proper (43–4, Plate I).

[155] Ibid., 45.

[156] Ibid., Plates II and III.

[157] A late-medievalist may well cavil at the attribution of any will to the feet of the body politic – yet as early as 1556 Ponet had contended that 'common wealths . . . may live, when the head is cut off, and may put on a new head' (*Short Treatise of politike power*, G.i.b-G.vi.b).

[158] *Lessons to a Young Prince*, 47–8.

[159] Anon., *A Defence of the Constitution of England against the Libels that have been lately published on it . . .*, 1–7, 59.

[160] Anon., *The Civil and the Ecclesiastical Systems of England defended and fortified*, 6–7 (note).

[161] The *Critical Review*, Vol. 70, 1790, 455, commended the freedom, impartiality, and independent principles of an author recognized from a previous publication. But the *Monthly*, IV (Jan.–Apr., 1791), 63–7, derided the '*copper-plates*', deplored such obtrusive taking to task of the Heir-Apparent, and combined grudging recognition of the author's apparent lack of bias with the stinging comment on his air of political misanthropy that 'while he appears to espouse no sect or party, it seems pretty clear that no sect or party will espouse him'. (Infra, 224 n.39, for reviews of the later, 1791, edition.)

Chapter Six

[1] Supra, 85–6.

[2] Reading of the article on 'Jean Pierre Brissot' in Vol. II of *Biographical Anecdotes of the Founders of the French Republic . . .*, 1798, leaves no doubt in my mind as to authorship. The internal evidence in regard to content and ideas, style and phraseology (even including the long-familiar device of third-person reference to 'David Williams . . . occupied by peculiar plans or experiments in the education of youth'!), is surely confirmed by the anonymous editor's allusion to its author as 'an English Gentleman whose name has long been deservedly respected in the republic of letters, and who for many years was the intimate friend and correspondent of that great man' (II, iii–iv).

[3] The term is that of Williams (ibid., II, 10), but is matched in implication by a modern biographer's reference (Jean Francois-Primo, *La Jeunesse de J.-P. Brissot*, 167) to 'le conseiller, le Maître fraternel'.

[4] On the accuracy of this assessment see A. Cobban, *A History of Modern France*, I, 124, 129–30, and A. Goodwin, *The French Revolution*, 30, 32.

[5] D. Williams, 'Incidents', 18–19; *Biographical Anecdotes*, II, 10–11.

[6] D. Williams, *Biographical Anecdotes*, II, 11–12.

[7] J.-P. Brissot, *Correspondance et Papiers*, ed. Cl. Perroud, No. XCIX (230), is a letter from Brissot to Williams, dated 25 April 1789, which gives an account of his experiences in 'the electioneering fire'.

[8] Jérôme Pétion (incidentally, a boyhood friend of Brissot), op.cit., 76–80: a full quotation, in French translation, of the passage on Civil and Political Liberty (as found, incidentally, supra, p. 77 of this work), followed by lengthy development and discussion of the points therein, exectly as embodied in Brissot's *Journal du Licée de Londres* (I, 318ff.), which makes Pétion's expression of homage to the 'unknown author of this excellent passage' rather surprising!

[9] A phrase reminiscent of R. R. Palmer's thesis.

[10] See D. Jarrett, *The begetters of Revolution. England's involvement with France, 1759–1789*, 250, and Philip A. Brown, *The French Revolution in English History*, 29.

[11] Mackintosh, op.cit., 17, 162, 370; Romilly, op.cit., 1, 3.

[12] Mary Wollstonecraft, op.cit., 151.

[13] While only the second and subsequent editions of *Lessons to a Young Prince* contained the additional Tenth Lesson devoted to Burke, these first allusions to Burke and Price are in Lesson Eight.

[14] See Burke's *Reflections on the Revolution in France*, 14.

[15] D. Williams, *Lessons to a Young Prince*, 71–3, 122–3. Even Mary Wollstonecraft was ready to allow that Price's zeal 'may have carried him further than sound reason can justify', and discerned the Utopian reveries of a benevolent mind 'tottering on the verge of the grave' (op.cit., 33–4).

[16] D. Williams, *Lessons to a Young Prince*, 71–3.

[17] Supra, 81.

[18] That is, as combining reason and experience.

[19] *Lessons to a Young Prince*, 51–6.

[20] Infra, 128–9.

[21] *Lessons to a Young Prince*, 64–5.

[22] Whose constituent parts he himself, in an earlier work (supra, 97), had described as dissimilar *nations*.

[23] A simplistic interpretation of John Adams's *A Defence of the Constitutions of Government of the United States of America* (Philadelphia, 1787). For Adams was particularly concerned to answer a charge of Turgot that the Americans, instead of concentrating all authority at one centre were endeavouring to balance powers. Adams not only rejects Turgot's idea of a single assembly, endowed with all authority, legislative, executive, and judicial. He goes on not only to express sentiments largely coincidental with those of Williams himself, but also to sound a note of prophecy of peculiar relevance to future French experience. Thus: 'what is to hinder this assembly from transgressing the bounds which they have prescribed to themselves, or which the convention has ordained for them? ... All nations, under all governments, must have parties; the great secret is to control them: there are but two ways, either by a monarchy and standing army, or by a balance in the constitution. Where the people have a voice, and there is no balance, there will be everlasting fluctuations, revolutions, and horrors, until a standing army, with a general at its head, commands the peace, or the necessity of an equilibrium is made appear to all ...' (3–4, 372, 378, 382).

[24] D. Williams, *Lessons to a Young Prince*, 66–70.

[25] Ibid., 72–3, 77–9.

[26] Ibid., 80–2. On the distinction between 'active' citizens (with voting rights in primary assemblies based on age and taxation paid) and 'passive' citizens with civil liberties, and the further limitations on eligibility for election to various functions see: A. Goodwin, *The French Revolution*, 91–2; F.-A. Hélie, *Les Constitutions de la France*, 273–4; and P. Campbell, *French Electoral Systems and Elections 1789–1957*, 46–50.

[27] *Lessons to a Young Prince*, 82–3.

[28] Not easily identified. Incidentally, Mackintosh, whilst scathing about such preposterous disenfranchisement, urged the adoption of a *hierarchy* of elections as the only alternative to 'tumultuous electoral Assemblies, or a tumultuous Legislature' (*Vindiciae Gallicae*, 224–8, 247).

[29] *Lessons to a Young Prince*, 86–9.

[30] See A. Goodwin, op.cit., 107.

[31] See M. J. C. Vile, op.cit., 176–7, 189; M. Duverger, *Les Constitutions de la France*, 51–5; D. Jarrett, op.cit., 282; A. Goodwin, *The Friends of Liberty*, 101–6.

[32] D. Williams, *Lessons to a Young Prince*, 90–1; supra, n.23.

[33] Local authorities were given powers of police and local justice.

[34] *Lessons to a Young Prince*, 92–5.

[35] Ibid., 117–8.

[36] Ibid., 118–9 and Plate 1. The House of Lords, he observes, is a remnant of that body and its power of judicial appeal a derivative.

[37] Ibid., 119–20.

[38] Burke's ambitious self-interest is an obvious target (135, 179), while the reception accorded an emissary of the Literary Fund (infra, 168, for a detailed account) produced an impression of personal insanity (140). The content of his *Reflections* combines 'bombast, substituted for philosophy' and 'indelicate allusions, to assist the sale of the work' (154–5). As to interpretation of events, those involved in such violence as the March to Versailles were no more Economists, Patriots, and Atheists than the Gordon Rioters of 1780 (127–8), while the claim that the Assignats were the issue not of ignorance but of necessity (152) coincides with modern opinion. But a plea that 'the Jacobins are Patriots, inclined to constitutional democracy' (152–3) may later have been embarrassing!

[39] D. Williams, *Lessons to a Young Prince*, 168, 179, 181–2. This new edition evoked additional reviews: the *Critical Review* (New. Ser., Vol. 1, 1791, 230–1) had no doubt as to the identity of the '*Old* Statesman'

and was complimentary on style and quality of analysis, but found the perceptive attack on Burke marred by too much personal allusion. In general, the *Monthly* (New Ser., IV, Jan.–Apr. 1791, 364) and *Analytical Review* (IX, Jan.–Apr., 1791, 452–4) shared these judgements.

[40] D. Williams, *Lessons to a Young Prince*, end-page.

[41] *Leçons* ..., 85–6.

[42] 'Incidents', 19–20.

[43] *Biographical Anecdotes*, II, 12.

[44] J.-P. Brissot, *Correspondance et Papiers*, No. CXXIV, 257–9.

[45] *Biographical Anecdotes*, 14; Bentham's Memoirs and Correspondence, *Works*, X, 226, 268–70, confirm the contact.

[46] Infra, 119–20, for John Hurford Stone.

[47] Supra, 114.

[48] J. Pétion, 'Le voyage de Pétion à Londres', ed. and introd. Marcel Reinhard, *Revue d'Histoire Diplomatique*, Paris (1970), 53.

[49] D. Williams, *Biographical Anecdotes*, II, 14.

[50] M. Reinhard, op.cit., 20–22.

[51] This must cast doubt on Waring's assertion (*Recollections and Anecdotes of Edward Williams*, 48) that Talleyrand visited the home of David Williams.

[52] Archives Nationales, F.7.4774.70: the 'Dossier Pétion' consists of papers seized as evidence against 'Pétion ex député, emigré'. The same letter mentioned inclusion of 'the Prospectus for a continuation of the History of England to let my friends see how I am employed'.

[53] D. Williams, 'Incidents', 19–20. The *Lettres de Madame Roland* (II, 204, 744) mention a visit by Bancal when in England.

[54] Cardiff Public Library, MS.5.36.

[55] *Gazette Nationale ou Le Moniteur Universel*, No. 319, 14 Novembre 1792, in *Réimpression de l'Ancien Moniteur*, Paris, 1847, tom 14, 464.

[56] Others so recognized include Paine, Bentham, Mackintosh, and Priestley.

[57] See J. G. Alger, *Englishmen in the French Revolution*, 63–76, and *Paris in 1789–94*, 325–8, 356–7; Lionel-D. Woodward, *Hélène-Maria Williams et ses amis*, 11, 69–70. Helen-Maria Williams was no relation of David, but the fact that her father was indeed Welsh may have contributed to some confusion. Oddly enough, it was to 'Mrs Helena Williams' that Brissot's family handed on some of his papers: M. Tourneux, *Bibliographie* ..., IV, 205 (21995).

[58] *A Complete Collection of State Trials*, ed T. B. Howell and T. J. Howell, Vol. XXV, Cols. 1297–99.

[59] Library of the Royal Botanic Gardens, Kew: Banks Correspondence, Vol. 2, 85–6.

[60] D. Williams, 'Incidents', 20.

[61] Certainly this interpretation won some contemporary acceptance: thus the notice in *The New Monthly Magazine*, VI (Jly–Dec, 1816), 73–4, credits him with 'the courage to oppose the ferocious designs of the Jacobins'.

[62] D. Williams, 'Jean Pierre Brissot', *Biographical Anecdotes*, II, 16–17.

[63] 'Incidents', loc.cit. Despite some very divergent estimates among modern historians as to the genuinely representative nature of elections to the Convention (ranging between ten and twenty percent of adult males as having cast their votes, in an atmosphere variously described as free from overt intimidation or as one in which the moderates were terrified by the September Massacres) the membership was homogeneously middle-class: see A. Patrick, *Men of the First French Republic*, 33–4, 152, 298; M. J. Sydenham, *The Girondins*, 117, 182; J. H. Stewart, *Documentary Survey*, 370.

[64] D. Williams, 'Incidents', 20–1.

[65] J.-P. Brissot, *Correspondance et Papiers*, No. CLIX, 305–6.

[66] D. Williams, loc.cit.

[67] N. L. W., MS 15269 C (1); *La Topographie de Paris (et) Nomenclature Générale des Rues* ..., A. Franklin, publ. Maire, 1808, Planche 7. A.

[68] E. Bernardin, *Jean-Marie Roland et le Ministère de l'Intérieur*, 15; I. M. Tarbell, *Madame Roland*, 179.

[69] *La Marquise de Condorcet* ..., A. Guillois, 77; J. Michelet, *Les Femmes de la Révolution*, 86.

[70] All contemporaries concur as to the punctilious attire of David Williams. It was perhaps symbolic that many of the attacks made on the 'English connection' both in the Jacobins Club and the Convention itself were led by Marat and by his ally known to the English as '*shabby Chabot*' (see anon., *Biographical Anecdotes*, I, 102).

[71] Date, in 1793, of the crucial petition for the arrest of the Girondins.

[72] Mme Roland, *An Appeal to Impartial Posterity*, I, 43–4.

[73] Ibid., II, 46.

[74] Moreover, only one Girondin was elected to the Convention from Paris.

[75] Mme. Roland, *An Appeal to Impartial Posterity*, I, 103.

[76] J. G. Alger, *Paris in 1789–94*, 325–8; *Englishmen in the French Revolution*, 117. The exact date of arrival of Williams in Paris is not certain; but if he was indeed there at this time then Bowyer's information that he had gone to Bath (supra, 120) was incorrect!

[77] *Journal des Débats et de la Correspondance de la Société des Jacobins*, notably the sessions of 6, 16, 20, 21, 23, 28 November, and 3, 7, 8, 12, 19, 23, and 24 December (by this last date Condorcet is added to the list denounced).

[78] *Réimpression de l'Ancien Moniteur*, tom 14, 683–6.

[79] Dated 13 December 1792 and addressed to him as 'Anglois, convention Nationale … Paris' before amendment as cited above, 122.

[80] Whose attitude may well have reflected his bizarre misadventures in England – where he published *The Chains of Slavery*, 1774.

[81] A recollection in J. G. Millingen, *Recollection of Republican France, From 1790 to 1801*, 283; one would like to know Williams's reaction to being dubbed a creature of Pitt!

[82] *A Journal during a residence in France …*, II, 496.

[83] *J. P. Brissot … to his Constituents*, trans., London, 1794, 99–100; *Memoirs of Bertrand Barère*, trans., London, 1896, II, 55.

[84] J.-P. Brissot, *Mémoires*, II, 244–5, 305.

[85] See J. Francois-Primo, *La Jeunesse de J.-P. Brissot*, 169.

[86] A phrase from *Letters on Political Liberty* which Brissot cites with approval in his *Journal du Licée de Londres*, I, 332.

[87] D. Williams, *Biographical Anecdotes*, II, 17–18.

[88] Paine, aged 56, and Condorcet, 50, were the doyens; Sieyès was 45 and the others under 40 – Pétion, Vergniaud, Gensonne, Barère, Danton, and Barbaroux (replacing Brissot). See Alengry, *Condorcet*, 175, 192–3, and Marc Frayssinet, *La Republique des Girondins*, Toulouse, 1903, 49–67.

[89] A Mathiez, *Girondins et Montagnards*, 83–4.

[90] Usually accorded fuller recognition by French than by English-speaking historians.

[91] F. Aulard, *Histoire Politique de la Révolution Française*, 110, n.1; 280 & n.2.

[92] F. Alengry, op.cit., 5, n.1.

[93] See Frayssinet, op.cit., Chapter III.

[94] F. Alengry, op.cit., 197–215; confirmed by Mme Roland (above, 173) and by Antoine Guillois, op.cit., 77.

[95] C.P.L., MS.2.192, ii.

[96] Which is dated at '*3 janvier*'.

[97] Typical but perhaps not original: this realist/utilitarian point had been made in Bentham's *Fragment on Government*, 1776, 42, and was to be repeated in his *Anarchical Fallacies* (*c.* 1796, his own critique of French Declarations of Rights), *Works*, ed. J. Bowring, 1843, II, 498.

[98] D. Williams, 'Observations', 1–2; his friend Brissot, in his address … *to his Constituents*, 1794, 7, was to deplore 'the preachers up of an Agrarian law' (infra, 148).

[99] 'Observations', 3.

[100] Sub-title in their record of Debates.

[101] 'Observations', loc.cit.

[102] Written in 1573 against the background of Huguenot dissidence and near-endemic civil war, Hotman's historical approach and appeal to Nature and History as twin guides (printed in *Constitutionalism and Resistance in the Sixteenth Century*, ed. J. H. Franklin, 68, 70) would have appealed to Williams.

[103] D. Williams, 'Observations', 5. Condorcet's other adviser, Paine, had contributed to the much-admired Pennsylvania Constitution.

[104] 'Observations', 7–8.

[105] Peter Campbell, *French Electoral Systems and Elections 1789–1957*, 46–50, pointing to the element of electoral conservatism almost throughout the revolutionary changes, observes the comparative *generosity* of the franchise for elections to the States General.

[106] Female suffrage was suggested in several projects submitted, but was usually dismissed on the ground of educational deficiencies.

[107] Quite literally, an Anglo-Saxon categorisation!

[108] Specific exclusion of domestic servants from the franchise of 1791 (see J. H. Stewart, *Documentary Survey*, 236, and F.-A. Hélie, *Les Constitutions de la France*, 274) had displeased Mackintosh who observed (*Vindiciae Gallicae*, 224–8) that they 'subsist as evidently on the produce of their own labour as any other class', and that *all* contribute through *indirect* taxation. The decree of 11 August 1792 confirmed this exclusion in elections to the Convention (Hélie, 329–30). Brissot's views (*Mémoires*, II,

199) are of interest: 'A free Constitution, doubtless could not establish universal equality ... there would have to be, as before, rich and poor; and the latter ... would still depend, for their subsistence, on the employment which the rich have given them. Domestic service is one of these employments. But domestic service should not be considered base under a. free Constitution ...' One English contribution to the debate, that of J. Smith, *Remarques Sur la Constitution de 1791* derided the unjust exclusion of domestics on the ground of excessive exposure to their masters' influence, observing that, being in general celibate, they are more independent than those with families such as workers in industry or agriculture! (op.cit., 14). Most English submissions (of about 300 received in toto) commended a fiscal qualification. Indeed H. T. Dickinson, in *Liberty and Property* (250–2) points out that most radicals, including at one stage Paine, tended to categorize women, children, and domestics as entirely dependent on their masters and hence incapable of exercising independent rights. One suspects that what David Williams really feared was irresponsible obduracy rather than excessively docile tractability – at least as far as servants were concerned!

[109] D. Williams, 'Observations', 10–12.

[110] Ibid., 12–16; one notes the incongruous combination of a perceptive analysis of the earthy realities of the present with an idealised notion of the 'Anglo-Saxon' past.

[111] Supra, 19.

[112] Directly contrary to his own contentions in *The Philosopher*, supra, 19.

[113] D. Williams, 'Observations', 17–18.

[114] Ibid., 18–21.

[115] Ibid., 21–2. Indeed, as part of this policy, a cheap and extensively circulating press, duty-free, should be nurtured. In this context one is not surprised by the suggestion that 'useful writers should be considered as the children of the public & their old age & families preserved from want'! (22–3).

[116] Ibid., 23–4.

[117] Phrases underlined in the manuscript.

[118] Ibid., 24–6.

[119] Again, underlined in the original – but note the slightly different choice of term.

[120] There is little doubt what Williams would have thought about the riots which later destroyed Girondin printing presses, including that of Brissot's *Patriote française*; nor would the spectacle of some 43 deputies remaining in the Convention through the night, expecting to die at their post of duty, have failed to remind him of the Gordon Riots (see M. J. Sydenham, op.cit., 153–4; A. Patrick, op.cit., 301).

[121] D. Williams, 'Observations', 26–7.

[122] Ibid., 27–8.

[123] A reference which, in turn gives added credence to Bowyer's information – supra, 120.

[124] D. Williams, 'Observations', 29–32.

[125] F. Alengry, *Condorcet*, I, 224–5.

[126] Ibid., 227–9, 239. Frayssinet, *La Republique des Girondins* (63), and Baker, *Condorcet. From Natural Philosophy to Social Mathematics* (320), concur in making Condorcet the principal architect of the Girondine.

[127] As in his *Essai sur la Constitution et les Fonctions des Assemblées Provinciales*, 1788, his translation and annotation of Livingston's *Examen du Gouvernement d'Angleterre comparé aux Constitutions des États-Unis*, 1789, and his *Réflexions sur la Révolution de 1688, et sur celle du 10 Août 1792*, n.d.

[128] See 'The Calculus of Consent', in K. M. Baker, op.cit., 225–44.

[129] Duncan Black, *The Theory of Committees and Elections*, Cambridge Univ., 1958, 57–9, 64–6, 77–9, 159–80, 183–4, 212.

[130] For Condorcet spoke English.

[131] In regard to specific political tenets, while Williams is not named in Baker's analysis of Condorcet, the reader familiar with his thought finds remarkable (though not complete) coincidence: the dread of large assemblies and of the populace (especially urban); the reservations as to the exercise of democracy by the unenlightened, fear of anarchical misrepresentation of the meaning of popular sovereignty, and striving to reconcile scientific elitism with the principle of consent; the advocacy of a hierarchy of electoral assemblies which shall truly transmit the public will while inculcating a spirit of citizenship; the suspicion of any corporate spirit *within* an assembly which would then become a vested interest tempted to make rather than to reflect decisions; the determination to institutionalize a right of protest and also, whilst repudiating any notion of balancing powers, to secure the maximum dispersal of power which is consistent with national sovereignty (Baker, 225–44, 253, 256–63, 269–71, 322–5).

[132] The Girondins' vague Deism and dislike of dogma and of clericalism would have been congenial to Williams, but, ironically it was to be Robespierre who introduced the cult of the Supreme Being!

[133] 'La Constitution Girondine', L. Duguit et H. Monnier, *Les Constitutions et les principales Lois politiques de la France depuis 1789*, 36–8.

[134] Duguit et Monnier, 57–8.

[135] Ibid., 54–7.

[136] Ibid., 46–7.

[137] Ibid., 48–50.

[138] Bastid indeed places the whole project within the evolution of the concept of *Le Gouvernement d'Assemblée* (309), comparing the Convention with the Long Parliament (128) and pointing first to the fact that the proposed single-chamber assembly was not solely legislative in nature, and second to the recourse to annual elections in order to prevent its becoming tyrannical (308–10). He sees the reaction against the English tradition of balanced powers, reinforced by the failure of the 1791 Constitution, as leading to an obsession with enforcing maximum accountability in all governmental functions. M. J. C. Vile, in an equally stimulating discussion (*Constitutionalism and the Separation of Powers*, 191–4) does not go all the way with Bastid in attributing to Condorcet an explicit advocacy of gouvernement d'assemblée, and emphasizes the in-built safeguards against that body's abuse of its powers. In the present writer's opinion, Williams would have been horrified by such a concept. Michel Troper's *La séparation des pouvoirs et l'histoire constitutionelle française* (179–87) totally rejects Bastid's contention and stresses the absolute separation of powers.

[139] Supra, 128–9.

[140] Duguit et Monnier, 58–63.

[141] Aulard's stress on its guarantees of freedom and quest for maximum participation (op.cit., 283–6) contrasts with Mathiez's strictures (op.cit., 87–92) on the potentially contentious separation of powers – Sydenham (op.cit., 149) concurs with the view that a complex electoral process would restrict effective participation to the well-to-do. Gasnier-Duparc, in *La Constitution Girondine* ... (240, 258), concluded that its abstract ideas and ingenious theories ignored realities. But more recently Deslandres (*Histoire Constitutionelle de la France* ..., I, 257–73), discerning a work at once extremely democratic and maladroitly conceived, was surely near the mark in sensing also its reflection of circumstances and of current fears and passions – and the inevitable alienation of Paris.

[142] In which Aulard (op.cit., 286) and Mathiez (op.cit., 84) for once concur.

[143] Alengry, op.cit., I, 240, 246.

[144] *Memoirs of Bertrand Barère*, trans., London, 1896, II, 93, 243; IV, 137.

[145] K. M. Baker, *Condorcet*, 325.

[146] Bastid (op.cit., 307) describes it as the most detailed text ever submitted to a French constituent body.

[147] M. Duverger, *Les Constitutions de la France*, 56–7.

[148] F. Alengry, op.cit., IV, 308.

[149] Ibid., II, 453; M. J. Sydenham, op.cit., 150–1, 192–8; A. Aulard, op.cit., 286, 296.

[150] D. Williams, 'Incidents', 21.

[151] Moreover, at the time of writing, he would not have wished to overstate his involvement in revolutionary activities!

[152] 'Incidents', loc.cit.

[153] A. Goodwin, *The Friends of Liberty* (26 and Chapter 7) refers to the persistent delusion that revolution in Britain would accompany hostilities.

[154] D. Williams, 'Jean Pierre Brissot', in *Biographical Anecdotes*, II, 18–19.

[155] 'Incidents', 21–2. On 17 December the British Ambassador had described Roland and Brissot as struggling to save the King in order to humiliate Robespierre (J. M. Thompson, *Robespierre*, I, 303); the attempt rebounded. Infra, 139, for evidence of a belief that Williams was involved in one last desperate attempt to save Louis – which may well have accelerated his departure.

[156] 'Incidents', 22.

[157] Ibid., 23–5.

[158] Printed in full by J. Holland Rose, 'Documents relating to the Rupture with France in 1793', Part II, *E.H.R.*, XXVII, 1912, 324–30.

[159] 'Incidents', loc.cit.

[160] Infra, 229, n.14; 147 & 231, n.83.

[161] 'Incidents', 25–6.

Chapter Seven

[1] See E. P. Thompson, in *Power & Consciousness*, ed C. C. O'Brien and W. D. Vanech, 152.

[2] Ironically, Andrew Kippis, in *An Address* ... at his interment, spoke of good news from France as giving

pleasure in his last painful illness (16). Certainly the September Massacres and the Terror would have appalled him.

3 See D. O. Thomas, *The Honest Mind* ..., 206, 332.

4 R. Price, *Observations on the Nature of Civil Liberty*, 1776, 13. His *Observations on the Importance of the American Revolution*, 1785, makes the interesting comment that 'it has been often justly observed, that a legislative body very numerous is little better than a mob' (65, n.).

5 Supra, 82–4, 106–7, 127–30.

6 See Gwyn A. Williams, *The Search for Beulah Land*, also *W.H.R.*, Vol. 3, 1967, 441–72; J. T. Griffith, *Rev. Morgan John Rhys* ..., prints much valuable source-material. Born but a few miles away from Waenwaelod, Rhys was taught by the same dissenting clergyman as Williams, many of whose political and religious attitudes he shared while his record in the field of practical *popular* education is far superior. Rhys had indeed preceded Williams in a visit to revolutionary France (for rather different, indeed religious, motives) in 1791–92.

7 See David Davies, *The Influence of the French Revolution on Welsh Life and Literature*, 33–4, and J. T. Griffith, op.cit., 230–3.

8 J. T. Griffith, 233; Gwyn A. Williams, *The Search for Beulah Land*, 53, 74.

9 See F. Rosen, 'Progress and Democracy: William Godwin's Contribution to Political Philosophy', London Ph.D. thesis, 200, 205–6.

10 Thomas Holcroft, *A Letter to the Right Honourable William Windham* ..., 7, 23, 39, 47–8.

11 J. Cartwright, *The Commonwealth in Danger*, 1795, xvi, and A. Young, *The Constitution Safe without Reform*, 1795, an explicit rebuttal, 4.

12 Supra, 97. Thomas Erskine's *Causes and Consequences of the present War with France*, 1797, 4–6, has a perceptive analysis of these issues. Professor Christie's recent *Stress and Stability in Late Eighteenth-Century Britain* identifies patriotic revulsion against the French example as a very considerable anti-revolutionary force (217–18).

13 Infra, 147.

14 Infra, 231, n.83. William Belsham's *Memoirs of the Reign of George III*, 1795, Vol. IV, 421–31, ascribes to the Girondins, including Le Brun, a real wish to keep the peace, and to Grenville a provocative arrogance.

15 Gwyn A. Williams, *Artisans and Sansculottes*, 102.

16 Infra, 162.

17 A note directs the reader to his *Letters on Political Liberty*, 1782.

18 D. Williams, 'Incidents', 26–7.

19 Though the number of gaps caused by destruction of many documents makes this far from conclusive!

20 P.R.O., T.S.11. 3510A.; 'Mr Reeves's Report on Sedition &c 29 April 1794'. For a recent treatment of the whole background of repression in 1793–94 see Chapter 8 of A. Goodwin, *The Friends of Liberty*. One notorious spy and infiltrator, William Metcalfe, sometimes chaired a meeting!

21 P.R.O., T.S.11. 3501 and 3510A. The same is true of *A Convention, the Only Means of Saving Us from Ruin*, 1793, by Joseph Gerrald, who fell foul of the law. His appeal to Saxon precedent cites 'that truly enlightened man David Williams' (even in the *1796* edition, 36n.*), while both phraseology and content of the 'Plan of Convention' (especially 43–45) are strikingly reminiscent of *Letters on Political Liberty*.

22 P.R.O., T.S.11, 4053; infra, 159.

23 David Williams, 'Incidents', 27–30. Professor David Williams published a detailed account of this bizarre story in 'The Missions of David Williams and James Tilly Matthews to England (1793)', *E.H.R.*, LIII, 1938, 651–68. Whether Matthews was in fact insane is very doubtful.

24 C.P.L., MS 5.36 (9); infra, 162.

25 Ibid.

26 *Convention Nationale*, Janvier 1793: *Discours de Marat* ..., 14–15, 22, 32. Brissot was to be accused (*Procès* ..., 35–6, 172) of being an agent of Pitt and of seeking to frighten France with the spectre of English armies.

27 *Rapport* ..., 11, 28.

28 *Appel au Peuple*, 3–4.

29 (Perhaps losing something in translation: 'rebel; they have preached to you so often and so successfully the holy duty of insurrection') *Appel au Peuple*, 6–7.

30 'Incidents', 30. The tone and phraseology of this declaration echo those of a small broadsheet of 1795: *Citizen Thelwall: Fraternity and Unanimity to the Friends of Freedom*: 'I therefore quitted the societies, not from any desertion of the cause, not from any change of principle ...' (op.cit., 3). Indeed, the reader familiar with the hand and mind of Williams will look long and hard at the notes for a Thelwall lecture (in T.S.11. 3501) on 'Political & Moral Importance of ... Liberty of Speech'.

[31] See Carl B. Cone, *The English Jacobins*, 212.

[32] B.L. has a bound collection of its proceedings and publications. Robert Hall, *Apology for the Freedom of the Press* ..., 1793, wrote scathingly of an assembly of court-sycophants, led by a placeman (15–16). Carl Cone (op.cit., 145–7) is doubtful as to the reality of any meeting but not as to that of influential support.

[33] Thus 'an Englishman is more *jealous* of Power, than ambitious to partake of it'(5); 'Men must be trained to Liberty; and a whole Nation cannot so easily practice it as a Committee of conceited Academicians can lay down definitions' (19).

[34] Explicitly-stated on the title-page and page 7 of the first edition.

[35] Supra, 72–4.

[36] *Monthly Review*, XXII (enlarged ser.,), Jan.–Apr. 1797, 463–4; see also XVII, Sept.–Dec. 1803, 441–2.

[37] R. Watson, op.cit., 16–20. Wakefield wrote as from 'the ground-floor of this grand and stable edifice, where myself, and my mess-mates of the *swinish multitude*, were regaling ourselves ... on our *cheese-parings* and *candles' ends* [to provide] a more firm foundation for our aristocratical and prelatical superiors, who are frisking and feasting in the upper rooms' (16). His declaration that a large-scale invasion would succeed, that the former social fabric was crumbling, and that great revolutions were afoot (9,35,44) led to prompt imprisonment. A letter from prison, asserting that his jailers would have been ready to persecute Christ and his apostles for subversion, and that 'if you stop short, but a single step, of unrestrained liberty in the investigation of truth, it is impossible to fix any limit to every excess of the most despotical inhumanity' (T.S.11. 3510A), is reminiscent of a David Williams of other days.

[38] Supra, 223, n.2.

[39] N.L.W., MS. 10332D: coverage was to range from foreign policy, arts, science and industry, to literature, religion and morality, and 'the Entertainment of the Fair Sex'!

[40] D. Williams, *Egeria*, 3–4.

[41] See A. Aspinall, *Politics and the Press c.1780–1850*, especially Chapters III, VI, and VII – though Williams is not mentioned.

[42] S. Morison, *The History of The Times, "The Thunderer" in the Making 1785–1841*, 68 and n.1, 72.

[43] B.L., MSS Addl. 33124, Pelham Papers, Miscellaneous Papers, 1770–1816, 78 (1–8). S. Morison's ascription is incorrect; the hand is that of Williams.

[44] C.P.L., MS 3. 160, and *two* further copies in 'Pelham Papers ... Relating to France, 1782–1803': B.L., MSS Addl. 33121 (88–121 and 122–47).

[45] P.R.O. (Kew), F.O. 27/67 (No 10); see also N.L.W., MS.15269C (5).

[46] P.R.O. (Kew), F.O. 27/67 (No 5) and F.O. 323/4.

[47] An obituary in the *Gentleman's Magazine* (1816, 89) attests an accepted oral tradition of a confidential mission; its assertion that Williams had been observed visiting the homes of important members of the then French administration receives considerable extra credence from his own allusions ('Private Paper', 12–13, 16, 21–3) which demonstrate considerable knowledge of personalities and intrigue in Bonapartist France.

[48] Peter France, edition of *Incidents*, 125–7.

[49] The *Monthly Review* (Enlarged Ser., LXII, May–Aug., 1810, 210–1) met confusion and obscurity, and a painful impression of learning misapplied. Peter France (op.cit., 127–8) finds it a melancholy performance by one apparently already enfeebled in body and mind.

[50] Op.cit., 3rd Ser., XX, May 1810, 1–23. Infra, 191 for its perceptive comment.

[51] N.L.W., MS. 10338E (4&5), 'France. Conspiracy of Despots'.

[52] D. Williams, *Parochial Police*, 2nd. edn., 1797, 5.

[53] Supra, 223, n.2.

[54] 'Jean Pierre Brissot', *Biographical Anecdotes*, II, 15.

[55] 'Incidents', 31.

[56] Ibid., 31–3. Helen Maria Williams alike deplored the seating of 'a vulgar and sanguinary despot on the ruins of a throne', regretted Girondin failure to put down the first sign of Jacobin 'rebellion against the sovereignty of the people', and was content to leave to history the judgement between Robespierre and Brissot, between the Mountain and the Gironde (*Sketch of the Politics of France* ..., 1795, I, 6, 71; II, 77–9).

[57] D. Williams, 'Incidents', 33–4.

[58] *Egeria*, Preface, 5.

[59] Peter France (op.cit., 126) suggests the parallel with Burke.

[60] *Parochial Police*, 12–13, 15–16, 19, 22, 25; in 1793 Arthur Young had published a book entitled: *The Example of France, a Warning to Britain*.

[61] D. Williams, *Egeria*, 6, 9.

[62] Ibid., 66–8, 78–9, 149.

[63] D. Williams, *Egeria*, 233; a footnote identifies this favourite phrase of Brissot.

[64] Ibid., 279, 284.

[65] D. Williams, *Preparatory Studies for Political Reformers*, 23–4, 81–6.

[66] Ibid., 131.

[67] Thus 'the parent of the French revolution was not philosophy, but ministerial profligacy, producing pecuniary disorder' (Ibid., 214).

[68] *Egeria*, 161–3. An undated note (N.L.W., MS. 10338E (66)) also develops the American relationship between political equality and equality of condition. Williams was not alone in appraising the unique American potentialities: see R. Price, *Observations on the Importance of the American Revolution*, 9, 68.

[69] 'Private Paper', 17–20, 33.

[70] Infra, 167–78.

[71] *Réclamations de la Littérature ... suivi du Prospectus ... d'un pareil établissement*, traduit ... par le cit. Blondet ... An XI, 6, 13, 132–3, 135.

[72] *Egeria*, 305–6, 311, 319.

[73] Infra, 159–61.

[74] *Parochial Police*, 2.

[75] Ibid., 3–4.

[76] Supra, 44.

[77] D. Williams, *Egeria*, 123.

[78] Ibid., 184. It may be fair to relate such utterances to contemporary fears not only of foreign invasion but of domestic insurrection symbolised by the so-called 'Despard Conspiracy' (see Marianne Elliot, *Past & Present* No 75, 46–61). Williams's books include a tract on *British Liberty* by 'Amicus Patriae' (when he identifies as Wm. Losack in a note dating its appearance as immediately following Despard's execution).

[79] *Egeria*, 126, 129, 146; see also 127, 134, 143.

[80] *Preparatory Studies ...*, 189–90. A more personal tragedy of missed opportunity is that of Fox, whose weak compromise in a coalition ruined his political repute, threw suspicion over his subsequent pretensions, and vitiated his later conduct of opposition: ibid., 192–3, 239–40.

[81] Ibid., 194–5.

[82] J. E. Cookson's *The Friends of Peace*, a study of 'Anti-war liberalism in England, 1793–1815', in part as 'a "symbolic" protest against a ruling class and the social system on which it depended' (118), does not mention David Williams. Yet he exemplifies much of the evolution and cross-currents of the thought explored therein.

[83] Thomas Erskine, *Causes and Consequences of the present War with France*, ran through 41 editions. Williams cannot be *identified* with this school of thought. He would have echoed Belsham's picture of Pitt as immortalised in history as having added more to the burdens and subtracted more from the liberties of the subject than any other statesman since 1688 (110–1, 132–3), and the similarly acid comments of Towers (15, 18, 22, 40), but Erskine's allusion (4, 6, 43, 49) to policies calculated as 'an inducement to the lower orders to revolt' would have worried him!

[84] Published in 1810.

[85] D. Williams, *Preparatory Studies*, 227–37.

[86] See J. W. Osborne, *John Cartwright*, 46–7.

[87] See J. E. Cookson, *The Friends of Peace*, 169–84.

[88] *Preparatory Studies*, 252–3.

[89] Ibid., 239.

[90] 'Private Paper', 5.

[91] *Egeria*, 36–7.

[92] Supra, 108 & 219, n.133.

[93] T. R. Malthus, *An Essay on the Principle of Population*, ed T. H. Hollingsworth, Book III, 4, 17.

[94] D. Williams, *Egeria*, 37, 41.

[95] Ibid., 51–3.

[96] Infra, 155–6.

[97] *Egeria*, 55–6, in the Study on 'Political Passions'.

[98] Supra, 222, n.129.

[99] *J. P. Brissot ... to his Constituents*, 7.

[100] T. Spence, *The Rights of Man*, 1793, 3.

[101] Supra, 31–2, 107–8.

[102] Supra, 108, 116.

[103] D. Williams, *Egeria*, 38–40.

[104] Ibid., 40.

[105] D. Williams, *Egeria*, 62.

[106] Ibid., 174, 179–80, 198, 206.

[107] Ibid., 214–5, 218–9, 220–3. Predictably, Price had 'obtained a little temporary popularity, by ringing alarms on this confusion of ideas', and by Sinking Fund calculations which would amuse 'every school-boy of fourteen'.

[108] In *Preparatory Studies*, 241–2, and several lengthy documents, including a draft letter to the Chancellor of the Exchequer headed 'Income Tax': N.L.W. MS 10337E (46–9), 10338E (13–14). In general, indirect taxation is least offensive and direct the lightest, if imposed with judgement. Yet Williams is among those who regard Income Tax (introduced 1798) as 'the Harbinger of Peril', possibly of levelling principles; for doubtless Court parasites obtain immunity and the burden falls on the industrious and professional classes with limited incomes 'who are confounded with the Dregs of the People'.

[109] N.L.W. MS 10338E (54) condemns 'all restraints on productive Labour' and 'the verbose nonsense of your Boards of Agriculture & Trade . . . Leave Labor & mechanic Industry to their natural competitions'. Ibid., (63) deplores 'insidious restraints' on capital, while (85) asks 'What right have you . . . by sending down Troops – to tie down that labor to any definite price, when it might naturally, & by the general advance of national Wealth, raise higher'.

[110] *Preparatory Studies*, 111–2. J. A. W. Gunn (see *Beyond Liberty and Property*, 225–6) sees Williams as 'a conventional economic individualist'.

[111] *Preparatory Studies*, 127.

[112] By now a long-handled tar-brush, extending from self-seeking political factions first to their demagogic appeal to the lower orders and now to any irresponsible or disorderly action by those orders as such.

[113] A good round figure, but a very valid point.

[114] D. Williams, *Parochial Police*, 19–25. The spectre depicted looks back to the 'hydra-headed monster' of the Tudors and Stuarts, but also forward to Jack London's *The Iron Heel*.

[115] D. Williams, *Parochial Police*, 26–9.

[116] Ibid., 31–4.

[117] Ibid., 38–41.

[118] Supra, 72–4.

[119] See J. R. Western, 'The Volunteer Movement as an Anti-Revolutionary Force, 1793–1801', *E.H.R.*, LXXI, 1956, 607–10. Incidentally, the first few pages (602–5) of this article suggest that much of Williams's analysis may well have been more cogent in contemporary eyes than in the judgement of hindsight.

[120] Supra, 140.

[121] D. Williams, *Egeria*, 155–8.

[122] Ibid., 159.

[123] *Preparatory Studies*, 92, 179, 196. Godwin's *Political Justice* was equally sceptical about the fitness for power of 'the grovelling views of the great mass of mankind' (114) and equally elitist: 'Infuse just views into a certain number of the liberally educated and reflecting members; give to the people guides and instructors; and the business is done . . . but in a gradual manner' (152–3).

[124] Infra, 155.

[125] D. Williams, *Preparatory Studies*, 140–3.

[126] This is one of the few occasions on which he takes cognizance of Richard Price as a political philosopher.

[127] D. Williams, *Egeria*, 6, 10–11, 13–14, 17–18, 58, 92.

[128] Ibid., 74, 77–8.

[129] Ibid., 154.

[130] *Preparatory Studies*, 3–4.

[131] Ibid., 4, 18, 29–30, 33.

[132] Ibid., 67. A fascinating aspect of the use, through history, of the analogy of disease in the body politic is the alternating appeal (according to circumstance) by conservatives and by radicals, to surgery or to a combination of philosophic acceptance with reliance on 'natural' remedies.

[133] Ibid., 69. Williams even trots out the stock reply to those who identify parliamentary corruption with saleable boroughs, that several of the most independent-minded Members have purchased their seats (56).

[134] Ibid., 91–3, 102–3, 108–9.

[135] Supra, 120.

[136] *Preparatory Studies*, 109.

[137] Ibid., 116–21.

[138] D. Williams, *Preparatory Studies*, 128.

[139] Ibid., 130–1, 136–41. The recurrence of the terminology of the once-derided French Constitution of 1791 is all too indicative.

[140] Ibid., 167–72.

[141] Ibid., 201–3, 245.

[142] Infra, 173.

[143] Supra, 97, 102, 109–10.

[144] Supra, 73–4, 80–4, 127–30.

[145] D. Williams, *Claims of Literature*, 64–73.

[146] B. Mandeville, *Essay on Charity, and Charity Schools*, in Vol. I, *The Fable of the Bees*, 267, 286: 'Charity, where it is too extensive, seldom fails of promoting Sloth and Idleness ... The more Colleges and Alms-houses you build the more you may.' 'Multitudes of People [must] inure their Bodies to work for others and themselves besides.'

[147] W. Godwin, *Enquiry Concerning Political Justice*, 612–8.

[148] T. Bentley, *The Rights of the Poor*.

[149] G. Dyer, op.cit., 11, 25.

[150] T. Cooper, op.cit., ,66–7.

[151] *Claims of Literature*, 73–4, 94.

[152] J. B. Florian's *Analytical Course of Studies*, 1796, 1–8, projects an approach similar to Williams's to be undertaken in an Academy at Bath (76).

[153] D. Williams, *Claims of Literature*, 94–8.

[154] *Memoirs, Correspondence and Private Papers of Thomas Jefferson*, ed. T. J. Randolph, 1829, IV, 8–10.

[155] *Monthly Review*, Enlgd Ser., XL, Jan.–Apr., 1803, 33–4.

[156] *Anti-Jacobin Review and Magazine*, XI, Jan.–Apr., 1802, 165.

[157] Ibid., I, (July to December 1798), 1799, facing page 115, has a large print (*c*.30 by 12 inches) in black and white from the original cartoon; the *Anti-Jacobin; or Weekly Examiner*, July 9, 1798, prints the verses in full – the B.L. copy is annotated in Canning's own hand – pages 282–7.

[158] Indeed the *Anti-Jacobin Review* again (II, Jan.–Apr., 1799, 57, 60–1), in identifying as chief authors of the anonymously-published *Public Characters*, 'Dyer and Wakefield, both so well known in the democratic literature of the times', decries their favourable sketch of such an abettor of democracy and irreligion. More than half a century later a glowing tribute to Williams (*The Book of Days ...*, ed. R. Chambers, 1863, I, 826–7) deplores such denigration of 'an originator whom all the upper classes of that day must have regarded as himself a social pest ...'

Chapter Eight

[1] The first communication addressed to Williams, headed 'Martyn agt Beadon', was in fact dated from the Exchequer Office as early as 7 January 1793: N.L.W., MS 10337E (9–12).

[2] P.R.O., PROB 11. 1097 (375 dorse to 378 dorse).

[3] N.L.W., MS 10337E (5–8); for Richard Beadon see supra, 127.

[4] P.R.O., Exch. Decrees, Vol. 29, IND 16864 (57). E.126.34, pp. 1096–99.

[5] An executor's account lists a total paid of over £800 for 1783–94; a further payment dated 1797 came to over £146 (N.L.W., MS 10333E (33, 53)). Other entries, in a small booklet (C.P..L., MS 1.153, pp. 1–2 at end of book) record receipts of money from the Beadons in 1808.

[6] The American Bank, chartered by Hamilton in 1791 as a copy of the Bank of England, had not been interfered with by Jefferson after his election in 1801 – Williams, who had welcomed his success, could thus be Jeffersonian in political and Hamiltonian in financial attitudes.

[7] N.L.W., MS 10333E (61, 65, 67, 69, 75).

[8] N.L.W., MS 10337E (21–2) and C.P.L. MS 1.153 (p. 5 at end of booklet).

[9] N.L.W., MS 10333E (77).

[10] N.L.W., loc.cit. (103–4).

[11] Supra, 141–2.

[12] N.L.W., MS 15269 (12, 13).

[13] Supra, 141–2; infra, 171, 173–4, 175.

[14] B.L., MS Addl., 33120 (117–22).

[15] The consideration given was quite serious, including a Commission and an abortive attempt at the use of 'catamarans' against French ships near Boulogne in September/October 1804: see H. F. B. Wheatley and A. M. Broadley, *Napoleon and the Invasion of England*, I, 302–11.

[16] B.L., MS Addl. 33120 (208–11) and also N.L.W., MS 10336E (31–5) for a duplicate copy, also in Williams's own hand.

[17] N.L.W., MS 10338E (1) – the habit referred to by Wendeborn (supra, 88) persisted, apparently for reasons of health.

[18] *Reports from Committees of the House of Commons*, X (1803), 651–728. Thomas Williams, himself a Member of the Commons, had perhaps pre-emptively sought appointment of this Enquiry into the Copper trade, to which he gave repeated and copious evidence. See J. R. Harris, *The Copper King*, and John Rowlands, *Copper Mountain*.

[19] The inventor Watt described the magnate as 'a perfect tyrant and not over tenacious of his word and will screw damned hard': Harris, xvii.

[20] C.P.L., MS 5.36 (1): undated notes by David Williams.

[21] His authorship, whose inherent probability is suggested by a note in his papers (*ut supra*) describing the Bishop's 'alternate Offers & Menaces' and claiming the Archbishop of Canterbury's approval of his efforts at mediation, is confirmed by a contemporary manuscript note on a copy of the *Letter*: see Harris, 162, n.6, and *Y Traethodydd*, Jan., 1947, 42.

[22] *Letter to the Bishop of Bangor*, 4, 6–8, 10–11.

[23] Ibid., 14–15; see also 26–7.

[24] Ibid., 28–30.

[25] See J. Rowland, *Copper Mountain*, 133–4, for this long and bitter dispute.

[26] D. Williams, *Letter to the Bishop of Bangor*, 32–6.

[27] Ibid., 36–9.

[28] Ibid., 93; T. B. Howell and T. J. Howell, *Complete Collection of State Trials*, XXVI, 1819, 463–528.

[29] C.P.L., 'Proposal for Publishing ...' (David Williams, Pantscallog Colln.).

[30] *Public Characters for 1798–9*, 513.

[31] Supra, 119–20.

[32] Vol. LXII, Part I, 166:

> 'The Attic Hume – whose spirit, as it flew,
> To kindred genius gave the honour due –
> For Williams caught the mantle which it threw.
>   Cloath'd with this garment, may the favour'd man
> Complete the learned work the Sage began;
> Old England's annals all their light assume,
> And the *new* David shine a *second Hume*.'

[33] C.P.L., MS. 5.36 (9), supra, 195; C.P.L., D.W.7, is a 'Release and Indemnity' dated 23 January 1795, in which Bowyer concedes a verbal contract and Williams accepts the payment offered; the *Cambrian Register*, Vol. 3, 532–3, takes seriously the threat of withdrawal of the Crown's acceptance of dedication but also credits the contention that Williams 'had removed from Russell-street to Brompton, for the purpose of executing' the task!

[34] Supra, 140–1; infra, 169.

[35] D. Williams, *History of Monmouthshire*, i–ii.

[36] C.P.L., MS 5.36 (2, 3).

[37] D. Williams, op.cit., ix–xi.

[38] Ibid., iii–iv.

[39] Ibid., 71–2, 150–1.

[40] Ibid., 78, 83.

[41] Ibid., 99–100.

[42] Ibid., 53–4, 348–9.

[43] Ibid., 122–3.

[44] Ibid., 133, 136, 153–4.

[45] Ibid., 180–7, 204, 213

[46] Ibid., 248, 254; the recognition that Gwent became English in regard to administration of justice, but remained part of Llandaff diocese, followed (344) by the statement that 'in the Hearth-Books, at the Tax-Office, Monmouthshire is considered' Welsh, confirm that the ground was well prepared for what was to become a correspondence-column perennial!

[47] Ibid., 313, 316–7.

[48] Ibid., 319–24.

[49] Interest in canals recurs in the private papers of David Williams (N.L.W., MS 10338E (116–21); 10337E (40); 10336E (1–6); C.P.L. MS 5.36 (7)), but with no evidence of actual involvement.

[50] *History of Monmouthshire*, 324–9.

[51] Underlining the contrast with the direction of his *political* thought.

[52] Williams expresses his thanks to its owners, the Salusbury family.

[53] Ibid., 331.

[54] D. Williams, *History of Monmouthshire*, 350–1.

[55] Ibid., 353–9. The Appendix (198–9) cites grants by Monmouthshire Agriculture Society, in 1793, to those with long service in husbandry of 'Certificates of their servitude and behaviour', and also two-guinea prizes for 'Labourers having reared the largest family without parochial assistance'.

[56] *Cambrian Review*, II, 455–69. The last comment is fully justified – indeed Williams himself attempted to forestall such criticism by offering the Appendix as 'a collateral narrative' (Appdx., 1). Therein Iolo addresses the author as 'ci-devant Reverend' and proffers the challenging assertion that 'the North Walian idiom is far more corrupt than the Silurian' (17, 85–6).

[57] *British Critic.*, VIII, 1796, 296–75.

[58] *Monthly Review*, New Ser., XX, May–Aug., 1796, 127–9; *Analytical Review*, XXIV, Jly–Dec., 1795, 124–30.

[59] Infra, 181.

[60] On Vaughan, who kept a large store in Caerphilly, see H. Simons, 'Ty Vaughan and Evan Evans', *Caerphilly* (Caerphilly Local History Society), October 1970, 46–52. On Pryce, of Watford Fawr, see H. P. Richards, *David Williams*, 34.

[61] N.L.W., MS 10333E (27, 29, 47, 51, 55, 85).

[62] Who was on close enough terms with Williams to indulge in badinage on the servant problem: 'it was well on the late occasion wch you describe that you were truly a Philosopher, or your Welsh patience would have been exhausted . . . if [only] it were possible to live without servants . . .' (C.P.L. loc.cit.).

[63] C.P.L., MS 5.36 (5).

[64] Presumably the man still occupying Waunwaelod at the Tithe Commutation.

[65] C.P.L., MS 5.36 (11, 15).

[66] E. V. Lucas, *David Williams. Founder of the Royal Literary Fund*. A very recent treatment, with the penetrating insight of one close to the fullest source-material, is that of Nigel Cross contained in *The Common Writer: Life in Nineteenth Century Grub-Street.*

[67] D. Williams, 'Incidents', 34: such a college 'might rank General Literature with Medicine'. The notion of some sort of 'college' was to persist.

[68] One has no difficulty in recalling such cases! Supra, 9, 162.

[69] 'Incidents', 34–6. 36 dorse has a note, deleted, 'See Claims of Literature p. 103', which dates the manuscript at after 1802.

[70] 'Incidents', 37–43.

[71] Ibid., 37–43.

[72] Ibid., 44–7.

[73] Ibid., 47–8; *Claims of Literature*, 102–4.

[74] 'Incidents', 48; *Claims of Literature*, 103–6.

[75] Martin's link with the Fund survived the gibes in *Royal Recollections*.

[76] 'Incidents', 50.

[77] R.L.F., 'Papers & Letters relating to the Foundation of the Society', K.

[78] R.L.F., 'Minutes', Vol. I, 1790–1817, 1–3; 'Incidents', 50.

[79] *An Account of the Institution of . . . A Literary Fund*, 3–4.

[80] It ran through twelve editions between 1796 and 1812.

[81] *Pursuits of Literature*, Part IV, 12–13 n.h. Attacks upon the Fund's allegedly patronizing distribution of a pittance continued well into the next century, and the great authors of the day for long remained aloof (see Nigel Cross, op.cit.).

[82] Vol. LXVIII, 1798, 23–4 (Jan) and 379–83 (May).

[83] R.L.F., Minutes of General Committee, I, 15, 20, 27, 35.

[84] Ibid., 110–11.

[85] N.L.W., MS 10331E (36–9).

[86] It is indeed one of several abortive efforts to undertake periodical or newspaper publication: we have noted (supra, 140–1) the 'Imperial Gazette', while an 'Indenture betw. Joseph Downes of Fleet Street and the Reverend David Williams', dated 1 June 1789 records the transfer of a quarter share in the *General Advertiser* ('shortly to assúme the title . . . of the Patriot and General Advertiser') to Williams for £600. It was never signed (C.P.L., D.W.7).

[87] R.L.F., Minutes of General Committee, I, 126.

[88] The work, as published, is dated 1802; but both 'Incidents', 51, and R.L.F. File 'Mr Williams's Claims of Literature' refer to 1801.

[89] 'Incidents', 51–2; Minutes, loc.cit.; *Claims of Literature*, ii, 5–6.

[90] 'Incidents', 52–3; expressions of relief are interspersed with waspish comments on Burges' literary efforts – Peter France ('*Incidents———*', 7) suggests that the over-lengthy treatment of the incident may be a clue to the date of composition of the manuscript.

91 'Incidents', 55–7. The terminology suggests a premonition of death, but Williams was writing of a disorder which had 'led me to the Verge of the Grave, & which has not yet wholly left me' as early as 1805: Minutes, I, 218.

92 Supra, 156, for its comments on Williams's views on Charity Schools.

93 Anti-Jacobin Review, XI, Jan–April, 1802, 162–70. The praise for the conduct, and compositions, of Boscawen, Fitzgerald, Pye, and D'Israeli is unstinted – but quite clearly David Williams had not served a long enough apprenticeship in respectability!

94 R.L.F., Minutes of General Committee, I, passim.

95 Claims of Literature, 139.

96 An Account of the Institution of . . . a Literary Fund, 5–10, 28.

97 Ibid., 1801, 2. It has justly been observed (by Nigel Cross in The Common Writer) that this sensitive decision forfeited much publicity which would have served to attract subscribers and deter applicants.

98 Claims of Literature, 117–18, 145–6; Minutes of General Committee, 5, 240. A scathing notice of D'Israeli's Calamities of Authors, in the Quarterly Review in 1812 (VIII), was to deride bestowal of a miserable pittance by a 'joint-stock-patronage-company' whose members 'write verses in praise of their own benevolence, and recite them themselves' (112–14).

99 Minutes, I, 9 (4 Feb 1791), which established the principle of an expected letter of acknowledgement; De Lolme was helped again in 1792 (25): I. D'Israel's Calamities of Authors, 1812, records that 'the walls of the Fleet too often enclosed the English Montesquieu' (II, 261–3).

100 Minutes, 22–3 (4 May 1792); N.L.W., MS 10333E (49) is an order drawn on (and accepted by) Williams for Oswald, dated at Paris, 19 April 1792.

101 Minutes, I, 61, 66, 139, 144, 221, 269, 330.

102 The Times, 15 May 1890; Minutes, I, 109; the work was in two long vols.

103 Iolo MS at N.L.W. contain a fair number of letters from David Williams, but the latter's papers yield only a booklet in C.P.L. from Iolo.

104 N.L.W., Iolo MS 21283E (542); Minutes, I, 45

105 Iolo MS 21283E (543)

106 Ibid., (544).

107 Ibid., (545), 28 July, 1794 (which asks Iolo to reply to 'Dr Hooper's Pantygotre' during the next three weeks); (546), 1 October 1795; (547), 29 December 1795. One would hope that Iolo's draft review of the History, with its comment 'I wish you had been in possession of more ample documents . . . at the time' never reached Williams (MS 21286E (1032)).

108 R.L.F., Minutes, I, 137; Iolo MS 21283E (548), 20 March 1801; Ibid. (549).

109 Minutes, I, 179. What would Reeves (or Burges) have made of Iolo's Newgate Stanzas:

'No jails I dread, no venal court,
And where belorded fools resort,
   I scare them with a frown;
John Reeves and all his gang defeat,
And if a tyrant king I meet,
   Clench fist and knock him down.'

110 Presumably, the small booklet in C.P.L. David Williams Collection.

111 N.L.W., Iolo MS 21283E (552).

112 R.L.F., Minutes, I, 215.

113 Ibid., 240.

114 Ibid., 326, 371.

115 Iolo MS 21285E (886); failure to acknowledge the previous benefaction is attributed to postal delays!

116 N.L.W., MS 10331E (5) is an undated draft of the Rùles of the Literary Fund Club, with limited membership & a black-ball exclusion proviso.

117 R.L.F., Minutes, I, 28, 34; N.L.W., MS 10331E (9–12).

118 Ibid., (15).

119 Ibid., (9–12, 13–16, 17–20). Such toasts are perhaps the convivial equivalent of I. R. Christie's 'Intellectual Repulse of Revolution' by the elite of the political nation (Stress and Stability . . ., Chapter VI).

120 Times, 22 June 1807.

121 Account of the Institution of . . . a Literary Fund, 1799, 86–9. The contributors' poetic pretensions were derided; but presumably the consumption of (as in 1800) a basic bottle of port per head, plus sherry, beer, and punch, ensured a not-over-critical reception of 'their appalling verses' – see N. Cross, op.cit.

122 As is clearly inferred by Williams himself: Account for 1809, 5.

123 R.L.F. File: 'Message from the Prince of Wales respecting a House' (E).

124 Minutes, I, 426.

[125] R.L.F. Minutes, I, 188.

[126] R.L.F. File, 'Message from the Prince of Wales ...' (F).

[127] Minutes, I, 200–3.

[128] Ibid., I, 206–10.

[129] R.L.F. File, 'House: 36 Gerrard Street, Soho', (A,C); Minutes, I, 213.

[130] N.L.W., MS 10333E (77), 10336E (9).

[131] A fair allusion to a minuted decision of 5 May: Minutes, I, 204.

[132] Minutes, I, 216–8.

[133] R.L.F. File, 'Message from the Prince of Wales' (M); the apprehension of over-ambitious plans derives from an 'Expose' which, writes Fitzgerald, Williams 'would have acted more prudently never to have read'.

[134] Minutes, I, 230–4; R.L.F. File, 'House: 36 Gerrard Street, Soho' (B).

[135] R.L.F. File, 'House: 36 Gerrard Street, Soho' (D).

[136] Appendix I.

[137] N.L.W. Iolo MS 21283E (572, 578, 583).

[138] Ibid., (586), and MS 21285E (886).

[139] N.L.W. MS 10331E (60–1).

[140] R.L.F., Registered Case File No. 335; Minutes, I, 411–2.

[141] Registered Case File 335 (3); this was done – a note in a later hand pointing out that payment of £50 is not entered in the Minutes for 14 February 1816 (416), is readily explained by Williams's presence.

[142] Registered Case File 335 (6).

[143] *Cambrian Register*, Vol. 3, 534.

[144] Registered Case File 335 (9); Minutes, I, 426–7. Miss Watkins was asked to apply the grant to funeral expenses 'if it should be more agreeable to her feelings'.

[145] *Cambrian Register*, Vol 3, 534–5.

[146] *D.W.N.B.*, 1031 (R. T. Jenkins).

[147] N.L.W., MS 10337E (35–6).

[148] Westminster City Library: St Anne's Soho, Burials 1813–1817, 246.

[149] P.R.O., PROB 11.1582/411; Miss Watkins's Will (PROB 11/2015/258(13)) expressed a wish 'to be buried in the same vault' as her uncle.

[150] R.L.F. File: 'Portrait of the Rev. David Williams, the Founder' (A), Extract from Minutes. By a letter reported to the General Committee on 11 March 1802 'A Subscriber' had set in train private contributions for such a portrait (Minutes, I, 310; 'Portrait' File (B)).

[151] R.L.F. File: 'Portrait of the Rev David Williams ...', Letter (B).

[152] Thus the account for 1801 (16–34) includes in the names of various classes of subscribers or poetical contributors such figures as Thomas Hooper of Pantygoitre, the Marquis of Bute, R. B. Sheridan, Sir Robert Peel, and I. D'Israeli.

[153] Op.cit., 127.

Chapter Nine

[1] As in the magisterial treatment of Richard Price by D. O. Thomas.

[2] Supra, xvii.

[3] Peter France, ed. *Incidents ...*, 6, 113, 125, 127; *Critical Review*, 3rd Ser., XX, May 1810, 1.

[4] J. A. W. Gunn describes Williams as 'already sensitized to social complexity before Burke raised the insight into dogma' (*Beyond Liberty and Property*, 228 – see also 208, 222), and concurs with Alengry in finding that 'the resemblances between Williams's writings and those of Comte are remarkable' (222, n.72).

[5] Julia Wedgwood, *Personal Life of Wedgwood the Potter*, 34.

[6] The number 13 and device of blackballing were typically masonic.

[7] C. J. Phillips, op. cit., 80.

[8] T. W. Thomas, in *Pebyll Seion*, 113.

[9] D. H. Munro's assertion (in 'Self-interest and Benevolence Reconciled through Associationism', *A Guide to the British Moralists*, Fontana/Collins 1972, p. 122) that 'the basic physical pleasures which man shares with the other animals become transformed in (Hartley), through the mechanism of association, into other types of pleasure ... a hierarchy which is headed by the pleasures of the moral sense' might have been written of Williams also.

[10] See Charles Vereker, *Eighteenth-Century Optimism*, Parts One and Two.

[11] J. W. Yolton, *John Locke and Education*, 10, 27.

[12] F. Alengry, *Condorcet ...*, 216.

[13] Sir Ernest Barker, *Political Thought in England 1848–1914*, 70–1, 79–80, 88. Spencer, apparently, knew nothing of Comte until after 1850; one wonders whether either ever knew of David Williams.

[14] Supra, 156.

[15] Supra, 54.

[16] Supra, 65, 155–6.

[17] John Taylor, *Records of My Life*, II, 400.

[18] N.L.W., MS 10336E (43–5).

[19] N.L.W., MS 10338E (38).

[20] If one may schematize as to background: Williams wrote toward the end of an era in which the struggle for 'liberty' had been concerned to free the individual from religious and political absolutism and to establish Commonwealth conceptions of civil and political rights. Some common ground between his religious and his political philosophy may partly lie in the determination fully to define and establish those freedoms. As early as the Putney Debates of the mid-seventeenth century the question had been raised as to whether man's full political and social potential could be realized within a society still blatantly inegalitarian. But most political thinkers still envisaged almost unconditional property rights as a virtually sacrosanct component of individual civil liberties. In retrospect, it is easy to see that as society and the economy became increasingly complex then from several sources (not least, humanitarian) the conviction emerged of a need for a socio-economic Leviathan which would protect the weaker individual from the jungle law of market forces and guarantee his basic social rights, much as Hobbes's Leviathan had done for civil liberties. In time, this would be seen by many as both preconditional for and correlative of the full and genuine exercise of democratic political rights. It could indeed be argued that this combines a residual Tudor Commonwealth or paternalist ideal (which had reflected a conviction that the post-Reformation State had taken over the socio-economic and moral functions and sanctions of the Catholic Church) with a more recently emergent belief in political democracy. But this debatable synthesis was one that Williams most certainly was not prepared to make. For his strain of collectivism looked backward rather than forward. The notion that *corporate* democratic political power might legitimately determine individual economic and social liberties in any redistributive sense would not have appealed to him!

[21] Williams, while one of the relatively few political theorists from Britain to see it at first hand, was not alone in his disillusion when events in France proved this difficult to achieve. Romilly moved from admiration to disgust, while Priestley, who at first professed himself republican in Paris but royalist in London, deemed 'A Fabian Retreat' to be prudent after war broke out: see E. Halévy, *Growth of Philosophic Radicalism*, 171–3; Mary P. Mack, *Jeremy Bentham*, 440–1.

[22] John Ehrman's very recent analysis (in *The Younger Pitt: The Reluctant Transition*) of the climate of opinion in England in 1792–93 observes that a *French* enemy made it easier to 'identify patriotism with the preservation of the existing structure' (158).

[23] For close parallels with his position among French philosophes see H. C. Payne, *The Philosophes and the People*, especially 82–4, 110, 130–1, 171; also C. Vereker, op. cit., 217.

[24] J. A. W. Gunn ascribes to him not only important and original insights and emphases, especially regarding organicism and the identification and significance of public opinion (supra, 152–3 for the 'Public Mind'), but also a major influence upon the notions of liberty held by other contemporary reformers, notably Cartwright (*Beyond Liberty and Property*, 206, 215, 221, 223–4, 250, 254–5).

[25] D. Williams, 'Incidents', 57–8, 47a/59.

[26] What was first numbered 59, and reads as a continuation of 58, has been re-numbered, transposed, and bound in as 47a.

[27] Supra, 4, 35–6, 40, 44.

[28] Thomas Morris, *General View*, 19–20. This striking example of wisdom *before* the impact of his visit to France is slightly puzzling in the light of the provenance of Morris's biography which was written for Condorcet's *Chronique du mois*.

[29] Ibid., 20–4.

[30] *Critical Review*, VI, Dec., 1792, 457–9.

[31] Ibid., 3rd Ser., XX, May 1810, 1, 4, 5–7, 11.

[32] Supra, 92, 176.

[33] Supra, 142.

Appendix I

[1] Dr T. W. Thomas, in *Pebyll Seion*, 113.

[2] D. Williams, in *N.L.W. Journal*, VII (1951), 116; T. W. Thomas, op. cit., 122; A. Gordon, *D.N.B.*, 393; and T. Rees and J. Thomas, *Hanes Eglwysi Annibynnol Cymru*, II, 414.

[3] Personal knowledge; a list of those contributing to the publication of *Pebyll Seion* in 1904 included 'Mr Edward Hedges, Caerphilly'.

[4] 'Incidents', 2.

[5] Note again his daughter's dropping of the 'Abraam'.

[6] Eglwysilan Parish Registers, Vol. IV, p. 10, No. 33.

[7] Ibid., Vol. IV, p. 65, No. 225; p. 47, No. 152.

[8] Ibid., Vol. II, p. 27.

[9] C.P.L., MS 5.36 (5).

[10] P.R.O., PROB 11, 1582/411.

[11] P.R.O., PROB 11, 2015/258 (13) – see Appendix II.

Appendix II

[1] *N.L.W. Journal*, VII (1951), 116–9; X (1957), 412–14.

[2] P.R.O., PROB 11 1582/411.

[3] P.R.O., PROB 11/2015/258(13).

[4] *Western Mail*, letter dated 3 May, 1980, from Rev Walter Evans, Holywell.

[5] Rev Walter Evans, loc. cit.; D. Williams, *N.L.W. Journal*, VII, 116–17.

[6] C.P.L., MS 5.36(7).

[7] Dated 14 November 1803: almost certainly that cited supra, 156.

[8] *Papers of Benjamin Franklin*, Vol. 21, 213.

[9] Supra, 8–10.

[10] Victoria & Albert Museum, Forster Collection: 213.48.F.11.

[11] *N.L.W. Journal*, X, (1957), 121–36 – plus, possibly, the *Appel au Peuple*.

[12] C.P.L., MS 3.221; undated press cuttings.

[13] P.R.O., PROB 11/2015/258(13).

Appendix III

[1] E. F. Rimbault, *Soho and its Associations* ..., 153.

[2] Supra, 90, 159.

[3] Supra, 219, n.11.

[4] J. H. Cardwell, *et al.*, *Two Centuries of Soho*, 147, and *Men and Women of Soho, Famous and Infamous*, 132–40. Thomas Martyn, *An address to the Inhabitants of the Parish of St. Anne, Westminster*, 1777, 7, n*.

[5] The original cartoon-print is extant among a large collection of source-material bound in (at 112A) with *Soho in the Olden Time* by the Rev Charles Bull, in Westminster City Library.

[6] T. Martyn, op. cit.; J. H. Cardwell *et al.*, *Men and Women of Soho* ..., 132–40; St Anne Soho Parish Records, Vol. 44. Burials 1775–1812.

[7] Supra, 90, 159.

[8] Supra, 159.

[9] St Anne Soho Parish Records, Vol. 44. Burials 1775–1812, 8; Vol. 45. Burials 1813–1817, 246.

Bibliography

PRIMARY SOURCES

A. MANUSCRIPT

Archives Nationales, Paris
F7. 4774.70: 'Dossier Petion'

British Library: Manuscripts Department
B.L.MSS. Addl. 33110, 33120, 33124 (Pelham Papers)

Cardiff Public Library
MS. 1.153 (Booklet)
MS. 2.191 ('Incidents in my own Life which have been thought of some Importance')
MS. 2.192 ('Observations On the late Constitution of France with a View to the formation of a new Constitution')
MS. 3.160 ('Private Paper. December 1802')
MS. 3.161 (Biography by 'B.D.')
MS. 3.221 (Miscellanea)
MS. 5.36 (Correspondence)
MS. 7 (Indenture between Joseph Downes and David Williams; Release and Indemnity, Robert Bowyer to David Williams)

Dr Williams's Library
MS. RNC. 38.5, 6 ('State of the Dissenting Interest ... 1773' J. Thompson)
MS. RNC. 38.15 (Catalogue of Books. Presbyterian College, Carmarthen)
MS. RNC. 38.106 (Minute Books of the Body of Protestant Dissenting Ministers of the Three Denominations in ... London and Westminster, Vol. 2)
Microfilm 83, 2 (Presbyterian Fund Minute Book, 1749–1826)

Glamorgan County Record Office
Eglwysilan Parish Registers, Vols. I to IV
Tithe Apportionment, 1841: P/1/4, Eglwysilan

Greater London Record Office
P.74/LUK/164: Micro, X26/12 (St Luke's, Chelsea, Parish Records)

Keele University Library
Wedgwood MSS

National Library of Wales
MS. 10329B (W. J. Evans)
MS. 10331E, 10332D, 10333E, 10336E, 10337E, 10338E (Dr T. W. Thomas)
MS. 13146 (Llanover)
MS. 15268C (Martin Donation: Includes Evan Evans copies), 15269C (Misc. Letters)

MS. 21283E, 21285E, 21286E (Iolo Morganwg)
MS. 5452D, 5453C (Henllan: Thomas Morgan)
MS. Addl. 244D (Cymreigyddion)
Professor David Williams MSS

Public Record Office (Chancery Lane)
Exch. Decrees IND 16864(57) Trinity Term 1793: E. 126.34 (pp. 1096–9)
Non-Parochial Registers RG. 4.336 (Mint Meeting, Exeter)
PROB. 11.1097 (Edward Beadon); 11. 1582/411 (David Williams); 11.2015/258(13) (Mary Watkins)
T.S. 11/956/3501; 11/961/3507; 11/962/3508; 11/965/3510A; 11/1133/7392 (Treasury Solicitors Papers)

Public Record Office (Kew)
F.O. 323/4; 27/67 (Correspondence and Papers re. Lord Whitworth's Mission to Paris, 1802–03)

Royal Botanic Gardens Library, Kew
Banks Correspondence. Vol. 2 (85–7)

Royal Literary Fund
Minutes of General Committee. Vol. I, 1790–1817
Files: Class: Corporation
              Papers and Letters relating to the Formation of the Society
              Mr Williams's Claims of Literature
              Message from the Prince of Wales respecting a House
Files: Class: House
              36 Gerrard Street, Soho
              Portrait of the Rev. David Williams, the Founder
Registered Case No. 335: Revd. David Williams, Founder of the Society, and Miss Mary Watkins, his Niece
'Letters from a Lady to a modern Moral Reformer ...', 1777 (bound in with a volume of pamphlets, etc.)

Victoria and Albert Museum Library
Forster Collection. 213.48.F.11 (Letters of Garrick and David Williams 1772–1775. Includes also the 'pirate' quarto edition of the *Letter to David Garrick*)

Westminster City Library
Parish Records, St Anne's Soho: Baptisms, Vol. 3; Burials, Vol. 43, 44, 45

B. PRINTED

Anonymous
    Appel au Peuple (Paris, 1793–? David Williams).
    Biographical Anecdotes of the Founders of the French Republic (2 vols., London, 1797, 1798).
    The Civil and the Ecclesiastical Systems of England defended ... (London, 1791).
    A Defence of the Constitution of England ... (London, 1791).
    A Dialogue on the Regency (London, 1788).
    Examen du Gouvernement d'Angleterre, comparé aux Constitutions des États Unis (M. Livingston, trans. with notes by M. J. A. Caritat, marquis de Condorcet, London, 1789).
    A Genuine Collection of the Several Pieces of Political Intelligence ... (London, 1766).
    History of the Westminster Election (London, 1784).
    Letters addressed to the Apologist for the Religion of Nature (London, 1790).

The Letters of Junius, ed. J. Cannon (Oxford, 1978).

Orpheus. Priest of Nature and Prophet of Infidelity, or the Eleusinian Mysteries Revived. A Poem in Three Cantos (London, 1781).

A Petition ... concerning Freedom in Religion (London, 1781).

A Plan for Rendering the Militia of London Useful and Respectable (London, 1782).

The Present National Embarrassment Considered (London, 1789).

Public Characters of 1798–9 (London, 1799).

Sentiments for Free Devotion (London, c. 1771).

A Sketch of the History and Proceedings of the Deputies appointed to Protect the Civil Rights of the Protestant Dissenters (London, 1813).

Tyranipocrit (Rotterdam, 1649).

Adams, John, *A Defence of the Constitutions of Government of the United States of America* (Philadelphia, 1787).

Almon, John, *The Honest Elector's Proposal* (London, 1767).

—— *An Address to the Interior Cabinet* (London, 1782).

Analytical Review, The

Annual Biography

Anti-Jacobin: or, Weekly Examiner, The

Anti-Jacobin Review and Magazine, The

d'Archenholz, J. W. von, *A Picture of England* (English translation, London, 1789).

Archives Parlementaires (Prem. Sér., Paris, 1898–1900).

Association for Preserving Liberty and Property, *Publications* (London, 1793).

Bacon, Francis, *Essays*, (introdn., M. J. Hawkins, London, 1972).

Badcock, S., *A Slight Sketch of the Controversy between Dr. Priestley and his Opponents* (n.d., 1782?, London).

Barère, Bertrand, *Memoirs*, trans. De V. Payen-Payne (London, 1896).

Belsham, William, *Memoirs of the Reign of George III*, Vol. IV (London, 1795).

—— *Remarks on a Late Publication* (London, 1800).

Bentham, Jeremy, *A Fragment on Government* (1776) and *An Introduction to the Principles of Morals and Legislation* (1789), in *A Fragment on Government*, ed. W. Harrison (Oxford, 1948).

—— *Anarchical Fallacies; being An Examination of The Declarations of Rights issued during The French Revolution* (c. 1797), in *Works*, ed. J. Bowring, Vol. II (Edinburgh, 1843).

—— *Memoirs ... including Autobiographical Conversations and Correspondence*, in *Works*, ed. J. Bowring, Vol. X (Edinburgh, 1843).

Bentley, Thomas, *Bentleyana; or, A Memoir of Thomas Bentley*, ed. J. Boardman (Liverpool, 1851).

—— *Journal of a Visit to Paris 1776*, ed. Peter France (University of Sussex Library, 1977).

Bentley, Thomas, *The Rights of the Poor*, (London, 1791).

Bisset, Robert, *The History of the Reign of George III*, Vol. V (London, 1803).

Bogue, David, *An Essay on the Divine Authority of the New Testament* (Portsea, 1801).

—— and Bennett, James, *The History of Dissenters, from the Revolution to the Year 1808* (London, 1833).

Bolingbroke, Henry St. John, Viscount, *Remarks on the History of England* (London, 1747).

Bowles, John, *The Real Grounds of the Present War with France* (London, 1793).

Brissot de Warville, J.-P., *Journal du Licée de Londres* (Paris and London, 1784).

—— *Rapport fait au nom du Comité de Défense Générale* (Paris, 1793).

—— *J. P. Brissot to his Constituents ...*, (English translation, London, 1794).

—— *The Life of J.-P. Brissot* (English translation, London, 1794).

—— *Mémoires*, ed. Cl. Perroud (2 vols, Paris, 1910).

—— *Correspondance et Papiers*, ed. Cl. Perroud (Paris, 1912).

Burgh, James, *Political Disquisitions; or, An Enquiry into public Errors, Defects, and Abuses* (London, 1774).

Burke, Edmund, *Edmund Burke on Government, Politics and Society*, ed. B. W. Hill (London, 1975).

—— *Reflections on the Revolution in France*, ed. F. G. Selby (London, 1924).

—— *Thoughts on the Cause of the Present Discontents* (London, 1770).

Callender, J. T., *The Political Progress of Britain* (Edinburgh, 1792).

Cambrian Register, The

Cartwright, John, *American Independence the Interest and Glory of Great Britain* (London, 1774).

—— *Take Your Choice!* (London, 1776) —— *A Letter to a Friend at Boston* (London, 1793).

—— *The Commonwealth in Danger* (London, 1795).

—— *An Appeal, Civil and Military, on the English Constitution* (London, 1799).

Clayton, N., *A Sermon preached ... at the Octagon Chapel, Liverpool* (1776).

Clarke, Samuel, MS alterations to *The Book of Common Prayer* (1724) presented by his son to British Museum in 1768.

Collection of several papers relating to the application made to Parliament in 1772 and 1773 (B.L.).

Collot-d'Herbois, J. M., *Rapport fait ... contre l'ex ministre Roland* (Paris, An II).

Comenius, John Amos, *Orbis Pictus*, facsimile of 1695 edn, ed. J. E. Sadler (Oxford/London, 1968).

—— *The Great Didactic*, introd. and trans. M. W. Keatinge (London, 1896).

—— *Selections*, ed. J. Piaget (Paris/Lausanne, 1957).

Condorcet, M. J. A. Caritat, marquis de, *Essai sur la Constitution et les Fonctions des Assemblées Provinciales* (Paris, 1788).

—— *et al.*, *La Chronique du Mois, ou Les Cahiers Patriotiques* (1791–3).

Cooper, Thomas, *A Reply to Mr Burke's Invective* (London, 1792).

Cornish, Jos., *A Blow at the Root of all Priestly Claims* (London, 1775).

Critical Review, The

Dawes, Manasseh, *An Essay on Intellectual Liberty Addressed to the Rev. Mr David Williams*, (London, 1780).

—— *Philosophical Considerations ... on Matter and Spirit and Philosophical Necessity* (London, 1780).

—— *An Essay on Crimes and Punishments ...*, (London, 1782).

—— *The Nature and Extent of Supreme Power, in a Letter to the Rev. David Williams*, (*Author of Letters on Political Liberty*) (London, 1783).

Day, Thomas, *The Dying Negro, A Poem* (London, 1775).

—— *The Desolation of America: A Poem* (London, 1777).

—— *Two Speeches of Thomas Day* (S.C.I., London, 1780).

—— *Reflections upon the Present State of England, and the Independence of America* (London, 1783).

De Lolme, John Lewis, *The Constitution of England* (English translation, London, 1777).

—— *Observations upon the late National Embarrassment* (London, 1789).

D'Israeli, Isaac, *Calamities of Authors* (2 vols, London, 1812).

Dyer, George, *The Complaints of the Poor People of England* (London, 1793).

Erskine, Thomas, *A View of the Causes and Consequences of the Present War with France* (London, 1797).

Evans, John, *A Sketch of the Denominations into which the Christian World is Divided ...* (London, 1796).

Fell, John, *Genuine Protestantism; or, the Unalienable Rights of Conscience Defended ...* (London, 1773).

Ferry de St Constant, J. L., *Londres et les Anglais* (Paris, 1804).

Fitzgerald, Percy, *The Life of David Garrick* (London, 1899 edn.).

Florian, J. B., *An Essay on an Analytical Course of Studies* (London, 1796).

Franklin, Benjamin, *The Papers of Benjamin Franklin*, ed. W. B. Willcox *et al.*, Vols. 21, 22 (New Haven and London, 1978, 1982).

—— *Calendar of the Papers of Benjamin Franklin in the Library of the American Philosophical Society*, ed. Isaac Minnis Hays: Vols II–IV of *Franklin Bi-Centennial Celebration* (Philadelphia, 1906–8).

Fownes, Joseph, *An Enquiry into the Principles of Toleration* (London, 1772).

Garrick, David, *The Private Correspondence of David Garrick*, ed. James Boaden (2 vols., London, 1831, 1832).

General Advertiser, and Morning Intelligencer, The

General Evening Post, The

Gentleman's Magazine, The

Georgiana, Duchess of Devonshire, 'Diary', printed in Walter Sichel, *Sheridan*, Vol. II, Appendix III (London, 1909).

—— *Georgiana* (Extracts from correspondence), ed. The Earl of Bessborough (London, 1955).

Gerrald, Joseph, *A Convention, the Only Means of Saving Us from Ruin* (London, 1793, 1796).

Godwin, William, *Enquiry Concerning Political Justice* (1793, ed. I. Kramnick, London 1976).

Grégoire, Abbé, H.-B., *Histoire des Sectes Religieuses*, I (Paris, 1828).

Hall, Robert, *An Apology for the Freedom of the Press, and for General Liberty* (London, 1793).

Hamilton, Alexander, *et al.*, *The Federalist* (1787–8), ed. W. J. Ashley (London and New York, 1922).

Hanway, Jonas, *The Citizen's Monitor: Shewing the Necessity of a salutary Police*, (London, 1780).

Hartley, David, *Observations on Man* ... (2 vols., London, 1749).

Harrington, James, *Oceana*, ed. S. B. Liljegren (Heidelberg, 1924).

Helvetius, C. A., *A Treatise on Man, his Intellectual Faculties and his Education*, trans. W. Hooper (2 vols., London, 1777).

Heywood, Samuel, *The Right of the Protestant Dissenters to a Complete Toleration asserted* (London, 1789).

Hitchin, Edward, *Free Thoughts on the Late Application of some Dissenting Ministers to Parliament* (London, 1772).

Hobbes, Thomas, *Leviathan*, ed. M. Oakeshott (Oxford, 1946).

Holcroft, Thomas, *Memoirs of the Late Thomas Holcroft*, ed. William Hazlitt, Vol. III (London, 1816).

—— *A Letter to the Right Honourable William Windham* (London, 1795).

Holbach, Paul H. D., Baron d', *Système de la Nature* (2 vols, London, 1770).

Hollis, John, *Essays meant as an Offering in support of Rational Religion* (London, 1790).

Hotman, Francois, *Francogallia*, in *Constitutionalism and Resistance in the Sixteenth Century*, ed. and trans. J. H. Franklin (New York, 1969).

Hulme, Obadiah, *An Historical Essay on the English Constitution* (London, 1771).

Hume, David, *Dialogues Concerning Natural Religion* (1779), ed. and introd. Norman K. Smith (Indianapolis/New York, 1947).

—— *Hume: Theory of Politics*, ed. F. Watkins (London, 1951).

Hutchinson, Benjamin, *A Sermon, preached On Friday, February 27, 1778* (London, 1778).

Jacobins, *Journal des Débats et de la Correspondance de la Société des Jacobins*, November 1792 to February 1793.

Jebb, John, *An Address to the Freeholders of Middlesex* (1779) in *Works*, ed. John Disney, Vol. II (London, 1787).

Jefferson, Thomas, *Memoirs, Correspondence and Private Papers of Thomas Jefferson*, ed. T. J. Randolph, Vol. IV (London, 1829).

Jenyns, Soame, *The Objections to the Taxation of our American Colonies* (London, 1765).

—— *A Scheme for the Coalition of Parties, Humbly Submitted to the Publick* (London, 1772).

—— *Disquisitions on Several Subjects* (London, 1822 reprint of 1782 edn.).

—— *Thoughts on a Parliamentary Reform* (London, 1784).

Johnson, Samuel, *The False Alarm* (London, 1770).

—— *Taxation no Tyranny* (London, 1775).

Jones, William, *A Speech on the Nomination of Candidates to represent the County of Middlesex* (1780), in

—— *An Inquiry into the Legal Mode of Suppressing Riots with a Constitutional Plan of Future Defence* (1780, 2nd. edn., London, 1782).

—— *The Principles of Government. In a Dialogue between a Scholar and a Peasant* (London, 1782).

Journal Encyclopédique ou Universel, Nov., 1782.

Keir, James, *An Account of the Life and Writings of Thomas Day, Esq.* (London, 1791).

Kippis, Andrew, *A Vindication of the Protestant Dissenting Ministers* (London, 1773).

—— *An Address, delivered at the Interment of the late Dr Richard Price* (London, 1791).

Lanjuinais, J. D., *Rapport Lu le lundi 9 avril 1793, a la Convention nationale, au nom du comité des Six, établi pour analyser les projets de Constitution* (Paris, 1793).

Lanthenas, F., *De la Liberté Indéfinie de la Presse ...* (Paris, 1791).

Lindsey, Theophilus, *Sermon preached at ... Essex Street* (London, 1774).

—— *Discourse addressed to the Congregation in Essex Street* (London, 1793).

Locke, John, *Two Treatises of Civil Government,* ed. W. S. Carpenter (London and New York, 1955).

—— *Some Thoughts Concerning Education,* abrgd. edn., F. W. Garforth (London, 1964).

—— *John Locke on Education,* ed. P. Gay (New York, 1964).

Lofft, Capel, *Three Letters on the Question of Regency* (Bury and London, 1788).

—— *On a Revival of Reform* (London, 1809–10).

London Magazine, The

Losack, William, ('Amicus Patriae') *British Liberty ...* (London, c. 1803).

Macaulay, Catharine, *Observations on a Pamphlet, Entitled, Thoughts on the Cause of the Present Discontents* (London, 1770).

—— *An Address to the People ...* (London, 1775).

Mackintosh, James, *Vindiciae Gallicae* (London, 1791).

Mandeville, Bernard, *The Fable of the Bees: or, Private Vices, Publick Benefits,* ed. F. B. Kaye (2 vols., Oxford, 1924).

Marat, J. P., *The Chains of Slavery* (London, 1774).

—— *Discours de Marat ... sur la défense de Louis XVI* (Paris, 1793).

Martyn, Thomas, *An Address to the Inhabitants of ... St. Anne ...* (London, 1777).

Mathias, T. J., *The Pursuits of Literature,* Part IV (London, 1797).

Mauduit, Israel, *The Case of the Dissenting Ministers* (London, 1772).

Miles, William A., *The Correspondence of William Augustus Miles on the French Revolution 1789–1817,* ed. C. P. Miles (2 vols., London, 1890).

—— *The Conduct of France towards Great Britain examined* (London, 1793).

Millingen, J. G., *Recollections of Republican France, From 1790 to 1801* (London, 1848).

Milton, John, *Of Education. To Master Samuel Hartlib,* in *Complete Prose Works,* Vol. II, ed. E. Sirluck (New Haven and London, 1959).

Montesquieu, Charles Louis de Secondat, Baron de la Brede et de, *The Spirit of the Laws,* trans. Nugent (London, 1858).

Monthly Repository, The

Monthly Review, The

Moore, John, *Journal during a Residence in France ...* (2 vols., London, 1793).

Morning Chronicle, and London Advertiser, The

Morning Post, and Daily Advertiser, The

Morris, Thomas, *A General View of the Life and Writings of the Rev. David Williams* (London, 1792).

'*Octagon Liturgy*' (Liverpool, 1763).

Ogilvie, William, *An Essay on the Right of Property in Land* (London, 1781).

Oldfield, T. H. B., *History of the Original Constitution of Parliaments, From the Time of the Britons to the present Day* (London, 1797).

Oswald, John, *Review of the Constitution of Great-Britain* (London, c. 1793).

—— *Le Gouvernement du Peuple ...,* French Transln. (Paris, 1793).

Paine, Thomas, *Rights of Man,* ed. H. B. Bonner (London, 1946).

Palmer, John, *Free Thoughts on the inconsistency of conforming to a Religious Test ... with the True Principles of Protestant Dissent* (London, 1779).

Parliamentary History of England, Vols. XVI, XVIII (London, 1813).

Pétion, Jérôme, *Avis aux François sur le Salut de la Patrie* (Paris, 1789).

—— 'Le voyage de Pétion à Londres', 1791, ed. M. Reinhard, Revue d'Histoire Diplomatique (Paris, 1970).

Political Register, The, (John Almon).

Ponet, John, A Short Treatise of politike power, and of the true Obedience which subiectes owe to kynges and other ciuile Gouernours (1556).

Price, Richard, Observations on the Nature of Civil Liberty, The Principles of Government, and the Justice and Policy of the War with America (London, 1776).

—— Observations on the Importance of the American Revolution (London, 1785).

—— A Discourse on the Love of Our Country (London, 1789).

Priestley, Joseph, An Essay on the First Principles of Government; and on the nature of Political, Civil, and Religious Liberty (London, 1768).

—— A View of the Principles and Conduct of the Protestant Dissenters, with respect to the Civil and Ecclesiastical Constitution of England (London, 1769).

—— An Address to Protestant Dissenters of All Denominations, On the Approaching Election (London, 1774).

—— Miscellaneous Observations relating to Education (Bath, 1778).

—— The Doctrine of Philosophical Necessity Illustrated (London, 1777).

—— Disquisitions relating to Matter and Spirit (London, 1777).

—— A Free Discussion of the Doctrines of Materialism, and Philosophical Necessity (London, 1778).

—— A Letter to the Right Honourable William Pitt (London, 1787).

Quarterly Review, The

Rees, Abraham, The Cyclopaedia; or Universal Directory, Vol. XXXIX (London, 1819).

Rees, Thomas, A Sketch of the History of The Regium Donum (London, 1834).

Reeves, John, Thoughts on the English Government (London, 1795).

Reid, William Hamilton, The Rise and Dissolution of the Infidel Societies in this Metropolis (London, 1800).

Réimpression de l'Ancien Moniteur. Gazette Nationale ou Le Moniteur Universel (Paris, 1847).

Revolution Society, An Abstract of the History and Proceedings of the Revolution Society in London (London, 1789).

—— The Correspondence of the ... (London, 1792).

Richmond, Charles Lennox, Duke of, A Letter ... to Lieutenant Colonel Sharman (London, 1792 reprint).

Roland (de la Platière), Madame M.-J. P., An Appeal to Impartial Posterity, English Transln. (2 vols., London, 1796).

—— Lettres de Madame Roland, ed. Cl. Perroud, II (Paris, 1902).

Romilly, Samuel, Thoughts on the Probable Influence of the French Revolution on Great Britain (London, 1790).

—— Memoirs of the Life of Sir Samuel Romilly (3 vols., London, 1840).

Rous, George, Thoughts on Government: occasioned by Mr. Burke's Reflections (London, 1790).

—— A Letter to the Right Honourable Edmund Burke (London, 1791).

Rousseau, Jean-Jacques, The Social Contract, ed. G. D. H. Cole (London and New York, 1941).

—— Émile, ed. P. D. Jimack (London and New York, 1977).

Sharp, Granville, The Claims of the People of England (London, 1782).

Smith, J., Remarques Sur la Constitution de 1791, trans. Citoyen Maudru (Paris, c. 1792).

Society for Constitutional Information, Miscellaneous Collection of Printed Resolutions, Published Extracts (London, 1780–2).

Society for the Establishment of a Literary Fund, An Account of the Institution of the ... (London, 1799).

—— Ibid., 1801.

—— Ibid., 1809.

Somerville, Thomas, My Own Life and Times 1741–1814 (Edinburgh, 1861).

Spence, Thomas, The Rights of Man (London, 1793).

—— One Pennyworth of Pig's Meat; or, Lessons for the Swinish Multitude (London, 1793–5).

—— *The Important Trial of Thomas Spence* (London, 1801).

Squire, Samuel, *An Enquiry into the Foundation of the English Constitution* (London, 1753).

St James's Chronicle

State Trials, A Complete Collection of State Trials, ed. T. B. Howell and T. J. Howell, Vol. XXV (London, 1818), XXVI (1819).

Taylor, John, *Records of My Life* (2 vols., London, 1832).

Thelwall, John, *The Natural and Constitutional Rights of Britons* (London, 1795).

—— *Citizen Thelwall. Fraternity and Unanimity To the Friends of Freedom* (London, n.d.).

Thomas, Benjamin, *A Letter to the ... Lord Bishop of Landaff* (Marlborough, 1774).

—— *The Political and Religious Conduct of the Dissenters Vindicated* (London, 1777).

Times, The

Towers, Joseph, *Thoughts on National Insanity* (London, 1797).

Town and Country Magazine or Universal Repository, The

Wakefield, Gilbert, *A Reply to some parts of the Bishop of Llandaff's Address ...* (London, 1798).

Walker, John, translation of *Manual of the Theophilanthropes, or Adorers of God, and Friends of Men* (London, 1797).

Walpole, Horace, *Last Journals*, ed. A. Francis Steuart, Vol. II (London and New York, 1910).

Waring, Elijah, *Recollections and Anecdotes of Edward Williams* (London, 1850).

Watson, Richard, *The Principles of the Revolution vindicated in a Sermon* (Cambridge, 1776).

—— *An Address to the People of Great Britain* (London, 1798).

Wedgwood, Josiah, *Letters of Josiah Wedgewood to Thomas Bentley, 1772 to 1780*, ed. Katherine E. Farrer (London, 1903).

—— *Selected Letters*, ed. Ann Finer and George Savage (London, 1965).

Wendeborn, Friedr. Aug., *Der Zustand des Staats, der Religion, der Gelehrsamkeit und der Kunst in Grosbritannien gegen das Ende des achtzehnten Jahrhunderts*, Vol. 3 (Berlin, 1785).

Westminster Magazine

Wilkes, John, *To the Gentlemen, Clergy, and Freeholders of the County of Middlesex* (London, 1790).

Williams, David, *The Philosopher: in Three Conversations* (London, 1771, in three Parts).

—— *A Letter to David Garrick, Esq., on his conduct as Principal Manager and Actor at Drury-Lane* (London, 1772).

—— Ibid., Second, 'Pirate', Quarto edition, printed and published by J. Williams and G. Corrall (London, n.d. (1778)).

—— *Essays on Public Worship, Patriotism, and Projects of Reformation* (Second edition, London, 1774; first edition, 1773).

—— *A Treatise on Education ...* (London, 1774).

—— *Sermons, chiefly upon Religious Hypocrisy ...* (2 vols., London, 1774).

—— *A Liturgy on the Principles of the Christian Religion ...* (London, 1774).

—— *The Morality of a Citizen; in a Visitation Sermon ...* (London, 1776).

—— *A Liturgy on the Universal Principles of Religion and Morality* (London, 1776).

—— *A Sermon preached at the Opening of a Chapel in Margaret-Street, Cavendish-Square ... On Sunday, April 7th, 1776* (London, 1776).

—— *A Letter to the Body of Protestant Dissenters; and to Protestant Dissenting Ministers, of all Denominations* (London, 1777).

—— *Unanimity in all the parts of the British Commonwealth, necessary to its Preservation, Interest, and Happiness ...* (London, 1778).

—— *The Nature and Extent of Intellectual Liberty, in a letter to Sir George Savile, Bart. ...* London, 1779).

—— *Lectures on the Universal Principles and Duties of Religion and Morality, as they have been read in Margaret-Street, Cavendish-Square, in the Years 1776 and 1777* (London, 1779).

—— *A Treatise on Toleration; the Ignorant Philosopher; and a Commentary on the Marquis of Becaria's Treatise on Crimes and Punishments*, trans. from Voltaire (London, 1779).

—— *A Plan of Association, on Constitutional Principles, for the parishes, tithings, hundreds, and counties of Great Britain; by which the outrages of mobs, and the necessity of a Military Government will be prevented, and the English Constitution in a great measure restored* (London, 1780).

—— *Constitutions of a Philosophical Society* (London, *c*. 1780–1).

—— *The Dramatic Works of Voltaire*, Vol. II, trans. D. Williams (London, 1781).

—— *Letters on Political Liberty* (London, 1782; second edition, 1784).

—— *Lettres sur La Liberté Politique*, French transln. of above (first edition, Liège, 1783; second edition, Liège, 1783–89).

—— *Royal Recollections on a Tour to Cheltenham, Gloucester, Worcester and Places Adjacent, in the year 1788* (London, eleventh edn., 1788).

—— *Constitutions of a Society to Support Men of Genius and Learning in Distress* (London, 1788).

—— *Constitutional Doubts, humbly submitted to his Royal Highness The Prince of Wales; on the pretensions of the Two Houses of Parliament to appoint a Third Estate* (London, 1788–9).

—— *Lectures on Education, Read to a Society for Promoting Reasonable and Humane Improvements in the Discipline and Instruction of Youth* (London, 1789, 3 vols.).

—— *Lectures on Political Principles; the subjects of eighteen books, in Montesquieu's Spirit of Laws: read to students under the author's direction* (London, 1789).

—— *An Apology for professing the Religion of Nature in the Eighteenth Century of the Christian Aera … Also a Liturgy on The Principles of Theism* (London, fourth edition, 1789; first edition, 1788).

—— *Lessons to a Young Prince, by an Old Statesman, on the Present Disposition in Europe to a General Revolution.* The Fifth Edition, *With the Addition of a Lesson on the Mode of Studying and Profiting By Reflections on the French Revolution by the Right Honourable Edmund Burke* (London, 1790).

—— Ibid., Seventh Edition, with Appendix (London, 1791).

—— *Leçons à Un Jeune Prince …*, French translation of first edition of above (Paris, 1790).

—— *Proposal for Publishing a complete History of England* (London, 1792).

—— *Observations Sur La Dernière Constitution de la France, Avec des vues pour la formation de la nouvelle constitution*, traduit de l'anglois par le Citoyen Maudru (Paris, 1793).

—— *The History of Monmouthshire* (London, 1796).

—— *A Letter to the Right Rev. Dr. Warren, on His Conduct as Bishop of Bangor* (1796).

—— *Regulations of Parochial Police; combined with the Military and Naval Armaments to produce the Energy and Security of The Whole Nation* (London, first and second editions, 1797, fourth edition, 1803).

—— *'Jean Pierre Brissot'*, in *Biographical Anecdotes of the Founders of the French Republic*, Vol. II (London, anon., 1798).

—— *Claims of Literature: the Origins, Motives, Objects, and Transactions, of the Society for the Establishment of A Literary Fund* (London, 1802).

—— *Réclamations de la Littérature …*, trad. cit. Blondet (Nantes & Paris, An. XI).

—— *Egeria, or Elementary Studies on the Progress of Nations in Political Oeconomy, Legislation, and Government* (London, 1803).

—— *Preparatory Studies for Political Reformers* (London, 1810).

Williams, Helen Maria, *Letters containing A Sketch of the Politics of France…*, 3 vols., (London, 1795).

Wollaston, William, *The Religion of Nature delineated* (London, 1726).

Wollstonecraft, Mary, *A Vindication of the Rights of Men* (London, 1790).

Wraxall, N. W., *Historical Memoirs of My Own Time* (2 Vols., London, 1815).

Wyvill, Christopher, *A Defence of Dr. Price, and the Reformers of England* (London, 1792).

Young, Arthur, *The Example of France, a Warning to Britain* (London, 1793).

—— *The Constitution Safe without Reform* (London, 1795).

SECONDARY AUTHORITIES

Alengry, F., *Condorcet, Guide de la Révolution Française* (Paris, 1904; Slatkine Reprint, Geneva, 1971).

Alger, J. G., *Englishmen in the French Revolution* (London, 1889).

—— *Paris in 1789–94* (London, 1902).

—— 'British Visitors to Paris, 1802–1803', *E.H.R.*, XIV (1899), 739–41.

Aspinall, A., *Politics and the Press c.1780–1850* (London, 1949).

Athenaeum, The

Aulard, F.-A., *La Révolution française* . . ., XVIII (Jan.–Juin, 1890), 142–3.

—— *Le Culte de la Raison et Le Culte de l'Être Suprême* (Paris, 1892).

—— *La Révolution française* . . ., XXXIV (Jan.–Juin, 1898), 502–54.

—— *Études et Leçons sur la Révolution française*, 2nd. Ser., IV, *La Séparation de l'Église et de l'État* (Paris, 1898).

—— *Histoire Politique de la Révolution Française* (Paris, 1926).

'R.B.', *Thomas Bentley 1730–1780, Of Liverpool, Etruria, and London* (Guildford, 1927).

Bailyn, B., *The Ideological Origins of the American Revolution* (Cambridge, Mass., 1967/77).

Baker, K. M., *Condorcet. From Natural Philosophy to Social Mathematics* (Chicago and London, 1975).

Baker, N., 'Changing Attitudes towards Government in Eighteenth-century Britain', in *Statesmen, Scholars and Merchants*, ed. A. Whiteman *et al.* (Oxford, 1973), 202–19.

Barker, Sir E., *Political Thought in England 1848 to 1914* (Oxford, 1947).

Bastid, P., *Le Gouvernement d'Assemblée* (Paris, 1956).

Baumer, F. L., *Modern European Thought. Continuity and Change in Ideas, 1600–1950* (New York and London, 1977).

Beloff, M., ed., *The Debate on the American Revolution 1761–1783* (London, 1949).

Bernardin, E., *Jean-Marie Roland et le Ministère de l'Intérieur* (Paris, 1964).

Black, D., *The Theory of Committees and Elections* (Cambridge, 1958).

Black, E. C., *The Association. British Extraparliamentary Organization 1769–1793* (Cambridge, Mass., 1963).

Bonno, G., *La Constitution Britannique devant l'opinion française de Montesquieu à Bonaparte* (Paris, 1932).

Bonwick, C., *English Radicals and the American Revolution* (N. Carolina, 1977).

Boulton, J. T., *The Language of Politics in the Age of Wilkes and Burke* (London and Toronto, 1963).

Bourne, H. R. Fox, *English Newspapers* (London, 1887).

Boyd, W., *Emile for Today* (London, 1956).

Brewer, J., *Party ideology and popular politics at the accession of George III* (Cambridge, 1976).

Brockett, A., *Nonconformity in Exeter 1650–1875* (Manchester and Exeter, 1962).

Brooke, J., *The History of Parliament. The House of Commons 1754–1790: Introductory Survey* (Oxford, 1968). See also Namier, Sir L.

—— *King George III* (London, 1972).

Brown, L. M., and Christie, I. R., eds., *Bibliography of British History, 1789–1851* (Oxford, 1977).

Brown, P., *The Chathamites* (London and New York, 1967).

Brown, P. A., *The French Revolution in English History* (London, 1918).

Bull, C., *Soho in the Olden Time* (Westminster, 1849).

Butterfield, H., *George III, Lord North and the People 1779–80* (London, 1949).

—— *George III and the Historians* (London, 1957).

Campbell, P., *French Electoral Systems and Elections* (London, 1958).

Cannon, J., *The Fox-North Coalition* (Cambridge, 1969).

—— *Lord North* (London, 1970).

—— *Parliamentary Reform 1640–1832* (Cambridge, 1973).

—— ed., *The Whig Ascendancy* (London, 1981).

Cardwell, J. H., *et al.*, *Two Centuries of Soho* (London, 1898).

—— *Men and Women of Soho* (London, n.d. (1903)).

Chambers, R., ed., *The Book of Days* (London, 1863).

Chancellor, E. B., *Knightsbridge and Belgravia* (London, 1909).

—— *The Romance of Soho* (London, 1931).

Chappell, E. L., *Historic Melingriffith* (Cardiff, 1940).

Christie, I. R., *Wilkes, Wyvill and Reform* (London and New York, 1962).

—— *Crisis of Empire: Great Britain and the American Colonies, 1754–1783* (London, 1966).

—— *Myth and Reality in Late-Eighteenth-Century British Politics* (Berkeley and Los Angeles, 1970).

—— *British History since 1760. A Select Bibliography* (London, 1970).

—— 'The Historians' Quest for the American Revolution', in *Statesmen, Scholars and Merchants*, ed. A. Whiteman *et al.* (Oxford, 1973).

—— *Stress and Stability in Late Eighteenth-Century Britain* (Oxford, 1984).

City of Cardiff Public Libraries, Forty-fifth Annual Report (Cardiff, 1907).

Cobban, A., *A History of Modern France. Vol. I: 1715–1799* (London, 1961).

—— *Aspects of the French Revolution* (London, 1971).

Cone, C. B., *The English Jacobins* (New York, 1968).

Cragg, G. R., *The Church and the Age of Reason 1648–1789* (London, 1966).

—— 'The Churchman', in *Man Versus Society in Eighteenth-Century Britain*, ed. J. L. Clifford (Cambridge, 1968).

Cross, N., *The Common Writer: Life in Nineteenth Century Grub-Street* (Cambridge, 1985).

Cumming, I., *Helvetius. His Life and Place in the History of Educational Thought* (London, 1955).

Darnton, R. C., 'The Grub Street Style of Revolution: J.-P. Brissot, Police Spy', *Journal of Modern History*, No. 3 (1968), 301–27.

Davies, A., 'La Révolution Française et le Pays de Galles', *Annales Historiques de la Révolution Française*, XXVII (1955), 202–12.

Davies, D., *The Influence of the French Revolution on Welsh Life and Literature* (Carmarthen, 1926).

Davies, E., ed., *Theophilus Jones, Historian: His Life, Letters and Literary Remains* (Brecon, 1905).

Derry, J. W., *The Regency Crisis and the Whigs 1788–9* (Cambridge, 1963).

—— *English Politics and the American Revolution* (London, 1976).

Deslandres, M., *Histoire Constitutionelle de la France ...*, I (Paris, 1932)

Dickinson, H. T., *Liberty and Property. Political Ideology in Eighteenth-Century Britain* (London, 1977).

—— 'The Eighteenth-century Debate on the "Glorious Revolution"', *History*, 61 (1976), 28–45.

Dictionary of National Biography

Dictionary of Welsh Biography down to 1940

Duguit, L., et Monnier, H., *Les Constitutions et les principales Lois politiques de la France depuis 1789* (Paris, 1915).

Duverger, M., *Institutions Politiques et Droit Constitutionnel* (Paris, 1963).

Dybikowski, J., 'David Williams and ... civil and political liberty', *Enlightenment and Dissent*, 3 (1984), 15–39.

Ehrman, J., *The Younger Pitt. The Years of Acclaim.* (London, 1969).

—— *The Younger Pitt. The Reluctant Transition* (London, 1983).

Ellery, E., *Brissot de Warville* (Boston and New York, 1915).

Elliott, M., 'The "Despard conspiracy" reconsidered', *Past and Present*, 75 (1977), 46–61.

Fäy, B., *La Franc-Maçonnerie et la Révolution Intellectuelle du XVIIIe Siècle* (Paris, 1961 edn.).

Feiling, K. G., *The Second Tory Party 1714–1832* (London and New York, 1959).

Fisher, S. G., *The True Benjamin Franklin* (Philadelphia, 1899).

Fitzpatrick, M., 'Toleration and Truth', *Enlightenment and Dissent*, I (1982), 3–31.

Fletcher, F. T. H., *Montesquieu and English Politics (1750–1800)* (London, 1939, and Philadelphia, 1980).

Foord, A. S., 'The Waning of the "Influence of the Crown"', *E.H.R.*, LXII (1947), 484–507.

—— *His Majesty's Opposition 1714–1830* (Oxford, 1964).

Forbes, D., *Hume's Philosophical Politics* (Cambridge, 1978).

Foster, J., *Alumni Oxoniensis, 1715–1886*, III (Oxford, Kraus Repr., 1968).

France, P., 'David Williams, Prêtre de la Nature. Lecteur de Voltaire et de Rousseau', *Dix-huitième Siècle* (Paris, 1979), 381–91.

—— ed., 'Incidents in my own life . . .' by David Williams (University of Sussex Library, 1980).

François-Primo, J., La Jeunesse de J.-P. Brissot (Paris, 1932).

Frayssinet, M., La République des Girondins (Toulouse, 1932).

Gasnier-Duparc, A., La Constitution Girondine de 1793 (Rennes, 1903).

George, M. D., London Life in the Eighteenth Century (London, 1925).

—— Catalogue of Political and Personal Satires, VII (1793–1800), (London, Br. Mus., 1978 edn.).

Ginter, D. E., 'The Loyalist Association Movement of 1792–93 and British Public Opinion', Historical Journal, IX (1966), 179–90.

Goodwin, A., The French Revolution (London, 1959).

—— ed., The American and French Revolutions, 1763–1793. New Cambridge Modern History, VIII (Cambridge, 1965).

—— The Friends of Liberty: The English Democratic Movement in the Age of the French Revolution (London, 1979).

Gough, J. W., Fundamental Law in English Constitutional History (Oxford, 1971).

Griffith, J. T., Rev. Morgan John Rhys: the Welsh Baptist hero of civil and religious liberty of the eighteenth century (Lansford, Pa., and Carmarthen, 1899 and 1910).

Guillois, A., La Marquise de Condorcet . . . (Paris, 1897).

Gunn, J. A. W., Beyond Liberty and Property (Kingston and Montreal, 1983).

Guttridge, G. H., English Whiggism and the American Revolution (Berkeley and Los Angeles, 1963).

Gwyn, W. B., The Meaning of the Separation of Powers (New Orleans, 1965).

Halévy, É., A History of the English People in the Nineteenth Century: I. England in 1815 (London, 1937).

—— The Growth of Philosophic Radicalism (trans. M. Morris, London, 1934 edn.).

Halkett, S., and Laing, J., Dictionary of Anonymous and Pseudonymous English Literature, Vol. 7 (Edinburgh and London, 1934).

Hans, N., New Trends in Education in the Eighteenth Century (London, 1951).

—— 'Franklin, Jefferson, and the English Radicals at the End of the Eighteenth Century', Proceedings of the American Philosophical Society, 98 (Philadelphia, 1954), 406–26.

Harris, J. R., The Copper King (Liverpool, 1964).

Harris, R. W., Political Ideas 1760–1792 (London, 1963).

Hay, D., 'Property, Authority and the Criminal Law', in Albion's Fatal Tree, D. Hay et al. (London, 1975), 17–63.

Hecht, J. J., The Domestic Servant Class in Eighteenth-century England (London, 1956).

Hélie, F.-A., Les Constitutions de la France (Paris, 1880).

Henriques, U. R. Q., Religious Toleration in England 1787–1833 (London, 1961).

Hill, B. and C., 'Catherine Macaulay and the Seventeenth Century', W.H.R. 3 (1967), 381–402.

Hill, B. W., 'Executive Monarchy and the Challenge of Parties, 1689–1832', Historical Journal, XIII (1970), 379–401.

Hill, J. E. C., 'The Norman Yoke', in Puritanism and Revolution (London, 1965), 50–122.

Holt, A., Walking Together. A Study in Liverpool Nonconformity 1688–1938 (London, 1938).

Holt, R. V., The Unitarian Contribution to Social Progress in England (London, 1952).

Hone, J. A., 'Radicalism in London, 1796–1802', in London in the Age of Reform, ed. J. Stevenson (Oxford, 1977), 79–101.

Jarrett, D., The Begetters of Revolution. England's involvement with France 1759–89 (London, 1973).

Jenkins, B., 'The aims and work of Richard Price, 1723–1791' (University of Wales M.A. thesis, 1927).

Jeremy, W. D., The Presbyterian Fund (London, 1885).

Jones, J. M., 'Calvinistic Methodists and Groeswen . . .', Western Mail, 18 and 19 November 1897.

Judges, A. V., 'Educational Ideas, Practice and Institutions', in New C. M. H., VIII,. 143–73.

Kemp, Betty, King and Commons 1660–1832 (London and New York, 1957).

Langford, P., 'London and the American Revolution', in *London in the Age of Reform*, ed. J. Stevenson (Oxford, 1977), 55–78.

Laski, H. J., *Political Thought in England: From Locke to Bentham* (Oxford, 1950).

Lefebvre, G., *The Coming of the French Revolution* (Princeton, 1949).

—— *The French Revolution: From its Origins to 1973* (London, 1972).

Lillywhite, B., *London Coffee Houses* (London, 1963).

Lincoln, A., *Some Political and Social Ideas of English Dissent 1763–1800* (Cambridge, 1938).

Lloyd, J. H., *The History, Topography, and Antiquities of Highgate* (Highgate, London, 1888).

Lucas, E. V., *David Williams. Founder of the Royal Literary Fund* (London, 1920).

Macalpine, I., and Hunter, R., *George III and the Mad-Business* (London, 1969).

Maccoby, S., *English Radicalism, 1786–1832. From Paine to Cobbett* (London, 1955).

Mack, M. P., *Jeremy Bentham. An Odyssey of Ideas 1748–1792* (London, Melbourne, Toronto, 1962).

Manning, B. L., *The Protestant Dissenting Deputies* (Cambridge, 1952).

Marshall, D., *English People in the Eighteenth Century* (London, 1956).

—— *Eighteenth-Century England* (London, 1962).

—— *Dr. Johnson's London* (New York and London, 1968).

Masters, B., *Georgiana* (London, 1981).

Mathiez, A., *La Théophilanthropie et le Culte Décadaire* (Paris, 1904).

—— *The French Revolution* (trans. C. A. Phillips, New York, 1928).

—— *Girondins et Montagnards* (Paris, 1930).

McLachlan, H., *English Education under the Test Acts. Being the History of the Nonconformist Academies 1662–1820* (Manchester, 1931).

Meteyard, E., *The Life and Works of Josiah Wedgwood* (2 vols., London, 1865–6).

Michelet, J., *Les Femmes de la Révolution* (Paris, 1854).

Mitchell, A., 'The Association Movement of 1792–3', *Historical Journal*, IV (1961), 56–77.

'Morien', 'The Founder of the Literary Fund', *Western Mail*, 22 and 27 May 1890.

Morison, S., *The History of the Times. "The Thunderer" in the Making 1785–1841* (London, 1935).

Murch, J., *History of the Presbyterian and General Baptist Churches in the West of England* (London, 1835).

Namier, L., *The Structure of Politics at the Accession of George III* (London, 1965).

—— *England in the Age of the American Revolution* (London, 1961).

—— and Brooke, J., *The History of Parliament. The House of Commons 1754–1790* (London, 1964).

Nangle, B. C., *The Monthly Review: First Series 1749–1789* (Oxford, 1934).

—— *The Monthly Review: Second Series 1790–1815* (Oxford, 1955).

Notes and Queries

Ogden, H. V. S., 'The State of Nature and the Decline of Lockeian Political Theory in England, 1760–1800', *American Historical Review*, XLVI (1940), 21–44.

O'Gorman, F., *The Whig Party and the French Revolution* (London and New York, 1967).

—— *The Rise of Party in England. The Rockingham Whigs 1760–82* (London, 1975).

Osborne, J. W., *John Cartwright* (Cambridge, 1972).

Owen, J. B., *The Pattern of Politics in Eighteenth Century England* (London, 1962).

Palmer, R. R., *The Age of the Democratic Revolution* (2 vols., Princeton, New Jersey, 1959, 1964).

Pares, R., *King George III and the Politicians* (Oxford, 1953).

—— *Limited Monarchy in Great Britain in the Eighteenth Century* (London, 1960).

Parssinen, T. M., 'Association, convention and anti-parliament in British radical politics, 1771–1848', *E.H.R.*, LXXXVIII (1973), 504–33.

Patrick, A., *The Men of the First French Republic* (Baltimore and London, 1972).

Paul, C. K., *William Godwin: His Friends and Contemporaries* (London, 1876).

Payne, H. C., *The Philosophes and the People* (Yale, New Haven and London, 1976).

Peaston, A. E., *The Prayer Book Reform Movement in the XVIIIth Century* (Oxford, 1940).

Peters, M., 'The "Monitor" on the constitution, 1755–1765; new light on the ideological origins of English radicalism', *E.H.R.*, LXXXVI (1971), 706–27.

Phillips, C. J., 'The Life and Work of David Williams', (University of London Ph.D. thesis, 1951).

Plumb, J. H., *England in the Eighteenth Century (1714–1815)* (London, 1953).

—— *The First Four Georges* (London, 1961).

—— 'Political Man', in *Man versus Society in Eighteenth–Century Britain*, ed. J. L. Clifford (Cambridge, 1968), 1–21.

—— 'British Attitudes to the American Revolution', in *In the Light of History* (London, 1972), 70–87.

Pocock, J. G. A., *Politics, Language and Time* (London, 1972).

—— *Three British Revolutions: 1641, 1688, 1776* (Princeton, New Jersey, 1980).

Pole, J. R., *Political Representation in England and the Origins of the American Republic* (London, 1966).

Pons, J., *L'Éducation en Angleterre entre 1750 et 1800* (Paris, 1919).

Porritt, E. and A. G., *The Unreformed House of Commons. Vol. I. England and Wales* (Cambridge, 1909).

Prosser, H., 'David Williams', *Wales*, II (1912), 564–9, 619–24, 667–74.

Radzinowicz, L., *A History of the English Criminal Law and its Administration from 1750. Vol. I. The Movement for Reform* (London, 1974).

Rees, T., *History of Protestant Nonconformity in Wales* (London, 1883).

Reid, L., *Charles James Fox: A Man for the People* (London, 1969).

Reinhard, M., *Nouvelle Histoire de Paris: La Révolution 1789–1799* (Paris, 1971).

Reith, C., *The Police Idea. Its History and Evolution in the Eighteenth Century and After* (London, New York, Toronto, 1938).

Richards, H. P., *David Williams (1738–1816)* (Cowbridge, n.d. (1980)).

—— 'Rev. David Williams, Pwllypant and Cwm', *Caerphilly* (Journal of the Caerphilly Local History Society), 4 (1977), 25–33.

Rimbault, E. F., *Soho and its Associations, Historical, Literary, and Artistic* (London, 1895).

Robbins, C., *The Eighteenth-Century Commonwealthman* (Cambridge, Mass., 1961).

Roberts, H. P., 'The History of the Presbyterian Academy Brynllywarch-Carmarthen', *Trans. Unitarian Historical Society*, Vol. IV, Part 4 (Oct., 1930), 333–64.

Roberts, J. M., *The French Revolution* (Oxford, 1978).

Robertson, J. M., *A History of Freethought*, II (London, 1936).

Robinson, E., 'R. E. Raspe, Franklin's "Club of Thirteen", and the Lunar Society', *Annals of Science*, II (1955), 142–4.

Roddier, H., *J.-J. Rousseau en Angleterre au XVIIIe siecle* (Paris, 1950).

Rose, J. H., 'Documents relating to the Rupture with France in 1793', *E.H.R.*, XXVII (1912), 117–23, 324–30.

Rose, R. B., 'The Priestley Riots of 1791', *Past and Present*, 18 (1960), 68–88.

Rosen, F., 'Progress and Democracy: William Godwin's Contribution to Political Philosophy' (University of London Ph.D. thesis, 1965).

Rudé, G., *Wilkes and Liberty* (Oxford, 1962).

—— *Revolutionary Europe, 1783–1815* (London, 1964).

—— *The Crowd in History* (New York and London, 1964).

—— *Hanoverian London* (London, 1971).

—— 'The London "Mob" of the Eighteenth Century', *Historical Journal*, II (1959), 1–18.

Sabine, G. H., *A History of Political Theory* (London, 1966).

Sadler, J. E., *J. A. Comenius and the Concept of Universal Education* (London, 1966).

St Anne's Soho Magazine, New Ser., III (1872).

Schofield, R. E., *The Lunar Society of Birmingham* (Oxford, 1963).

Schwoerer, L. G., *"No Standing Armies!"* (Baltimore and London, 1974).

Sheppard, F. H. W., ed., *Survey of London*: XXXIII and XXXIV, *The Parish of St. Anne Soho* (London, 1966); XXXIX, *The Grosvenor Estate in Mayfair. Part I, General History* (London, 1977); XLI, *Southern Kensington, Brompton* (London, 1983).

Simons, H., 'Ty Vaughan and Evan Evans', *Caerphilly* (Journal of the Caerphilly Local History Society) (1970), 46–52.

Smith, E., *The Life of Sir Joseph Banks* (London, 1911).

Speck, W. A., *Stability and Strife in England 1714–1760* (London, 1977).

Stephens, J., 'The London Ministers and Subscription 1772–1779', in *Enlightenment and Dissent*, 1 (1982), 43–71.

Stevenson, J., ed., *London in the Age of Reform* (Oxford, 1977), 'Introduction', xiii–xxvi.

—— *Popular Disturbances in England 1700–1870* (London and New York, 1979).

Stewart, J. H., *A Documentary Survey of the French Revolution* (New York, 1965).

Stewart, W. A. C., *Progressives and Radicals in English Education 1750–1970* (London, 1972).

—— and McCann, W. P., *The Educational Innovators. Vol. I: 1750–1880* (London, 1970).

Stromberg, R. N., *Religious Liberalism in Eighteenth-Century England* (Oxford, 1954).

Sutherland, Dame L., 'The City of London in Eighteenth-Century Politics', in *Essays presented to Sir Lewis Namier*, ed. R. Pares and A. J. P. Taylor (London and New York, 1956), 49–74.

—— 'The City of London and the Opposition to Government, 1768–74', in *London in the Age of Reform*, ed. J. Stevenson (Oxford, 1977), 30–54.

Sydenham, M. J., *The Girondins* (London, 1961).

—— *The French Revolution* (London, 1965).

Sykes, N., *Church and State in England in the XVIIIth Century* (Cambridge, 1934).

Tarbell, I. M., *Madame Roland. A Biographical Study* (London, 1896).

Thomas, D. O., *The Honest Mind. The Thought and Work of Richard Price* (Oxford, 1977).

Thomas, G. W., 'Principles and Practice of Modern Education … in the Dissenting Academies in England' (University of London M.A. thesis, 1949).

Thomas, P. D. G., *Lord North* (London, 1976).

Thomas, T. W., 'The Rev. David Williams (Waenwaelod), Founder of The Royal Literary Fund', in *Pebyll Seion*, ed. C. T. Thomas and E. Bush (Cardiff, 1904), 113–22.

Thomas, W. P., 'Nonconformist Academies in Wales in the Eighteenth Century', (University of Wales M.A. thesis, 1928).

Thompson, E. P., *The Making of the English Working Class* (London, 1968).

—— 'The Moral Economy of the English Crowd in the Eighteenth Century', *Past and Present*, 50 (1971), 76–136.

—— 'Disenchantment or Default?', in *Power and Consciousness*, ed. C. C. O'Brien and W. D. Vanech (London and New York, 1969), 149–81.

Thompson, J. M., ed., *English Witnesses of the French Revolution* (Oxford, 1938).

Toohey, R. E., *Liberty and Empire: British Radical Solutions to the American Problem, 1774–1776* (Lexington, Kentucky, 1978).

Tourneux, M., *Bibliographie de l'Histoire de Paris pendant la Révolution Française*, I, III, IV (Paris, 1890).

Troper, M., *La séparation des pouvoirs et l'histoire constitutionelle française* (Paris, 1973).

Tuetey, A., *Répertoire Général des Sources Manuscrites de l'Histoire de Paris pendant la Révolution Française*, VIII (Paris, 1908).

Veitch, G. S., *The Genesis of Parliamentary Reform* (London, 1965 reprint).

—— 'A View of English Nonconformity in 1773', *Congregational Historical Society Transactions*, 5 (1911–12), 205–22, 261–77, 372–85.

Vereker, C., *Eighteenth-Century Optimism* (Liverpool, 1967).

Vile, M.J. C., *Constitutionalism and the Separation of Powers* (Oxford, 1967).

Viner, J., 'Man's Economic Status', in *Man versus Society in Eighteenth-Century Britain*, ed. J. L. Clifford (Cambridge, 1968), 22–53.

Wardroper, J., *Kings, Lords and Wicked Libellers. Satire and Protest 1760–1837* (London, 1973).

Watson, J. S., *The Reign of George III, 1760–1815* (Oxford, 1960).

Watts, M. R., *The Dissenters: from the Reformation to the French Revolution* (Oxford, 1978).

Watts, R., 'Joseph Priestley and Education', in *Enlightenment and Dissent*, 2 (1983), 83–100.

Wedgwood, J., *The Personal Life of Josiah Wedgwood the Potter* (London, 1915).

Werkmeister, L., *The London Daily Press, 1772–92* (Lincoln, Nebraska, 1963).

Wheeler, H. F. B., and Broadley, A. M., *Napoleon and the Invasion of England* (2 vols., London and New York, 1908).

Western, J. R., 'The Volunteer Movement as an Anti-Revolutionary Force, 1793–1801', *E.H.R.*, LXXI (1971), 603–14.

White, J. R., *Radicalism and its Results, 1760–1837* (London, 1967).

Willey, B., *The Eighteenth-Century Background* (London, 1965).

Williams, D., 'The Missions of David Williams and James Tilly Matthews to England (1793)', *E.H.R.*, LIII (1938), 651–68.

—— 'Documents. More Light on Franklin's Religious Ideas', *American Historical Review*, LXIII (1938), 802–13.

—— 'Un document inédit sur la Gironde', *Annales Historiques de la Révolution Française*, LXXXIX (1938), 411–31.

—— 'French Opinion Concerning the English Constitution in the Eighteenth Century', *Economica*, X, No. 30, 295–308.

—— 'A Priest of Nature'. *Welsh Review*, V (1946), 36–41.

—— 'The David Williams Manuscripts', *N.L.W. Journal*, VII (1951), 116–19.

—— 'A Bibliography of the Printed Works of David Williams (1738–1816)', *N.L.W. Journal*, X (1957), 121–36.

—— 'A Further Note on the Manuscripts and Printed Books of David Williams (1738–1816)', *N.L.W. Journal*, X (1957), 412–14.

Williams, E. N., *The Eighteenth Century Constitution* (Cambridge, 1960).

Williams, G. A., *Artisans and Sans-Culottes* (London, 1968).

—— *The Search for Beulah Land* (London, 1980).

—— 'Morgan John Rhees and his Beula', *W.H.R.*, 3 (1967), 441–72.

Williams, W. P., 'David Williams ', *Welsh Outlook* (Cardiff, 1926), 90–2.

Woodhouse, A. S. P., *Puritanism and Liberty* (London, 1938).

Woodward, L.-D., *Hélène-Maria Williams et ses amis* (Paris, 1930).

Yolton, J. W., *John Locke and Education* (New York, 1971).

Index